Organisation & Management and Business Communication

Organisation & Management and Business Communication

[For C.A. Course (P.E. I - Paper : 4)]

Sampat Mukherjee
Sanjib Kumar Basu

NEW AGE INTERNATIONAL (P) LIMITED, PUBLISHERS
New Delhi • Bangalore • Chennai • Cochin • Guwahati • Hyderabad
Jalandhar • Kolkata • Lucknow • Mumbai • Ranchi

First Edition : 2005

NEW AGE INTERNATIONAL (P) LIMITED, PUBLISHERS
4835/24, Ansari Road, Daryaganj,
New Delhi - 110 002
Visit us at : www.newagepublishers.com

Offices at :
Bangalore, Chennai, Cochin, Guwahati, Hyderabad, Jalandhar,
Kolkata, Lucknow, Mumbai and Ranchi

Rs. 140.00

ISBN : 81-224-1644-6

Published by New Age International (P) Ltd.,
4835/24, Ansari Road, Daryaganj, New Delhi-110 002 and
typeset by Power Composer, Delhi
printed in India at Ajit Printers, Delhi

PREFACE

The principles of management are universally applicable irrespective of the size and nature of the organisation. These principles are widely practised throughout the world, especially in business organisations these principles get popularity due to their effectiveness and success. Over the years, the concept of management has undergone many changes. Now it is recognised as a profession.

Communication is very important in our day to day life. We can express our feelings, give directions, share our views through communication. Communication skill development is a key to success in life. Not only in individual level, the ways and techniques used in communication play an important role in group level, particularly when an individual is working in a group.

Recognising the importance of principles of management and role of communication in business world and other fields of life, not only diferent universities in India have prescribed these two subjects at their under-graduate level, a number of professional institutions like the Institute of Chartered Accountants of India has also included these two related subjects in a paper in their syllabus for the foundation course (known as professional examination - 1).

This book is a sincere attempt to explain the operating functions of management and tools of communications in a simple and lucid language. The primary object of writing this book is to meet the requirements of C.A. (Professional Examination - One) students. However, this book will also be very useful for the students doing B.Com., M.Com., M.B.A and other professional courses. Even a layman who is interested in knowing basics of management principles and communication skill will find this book extremely useful.

We are very happy to place this book in the hands of our esteemed readers, especially the students. We are confident that they will find the book very useful, as it has been presented strictly according to the syllabus. We request our readers to kindly send us their valuable suggestions and comments for further and continuous improvement of the book.

We are thankful to Mr. Palas Lahiri and Mr. Bapi Das for collaborating in our endeavour.

Sampat Mukherjee

Sanjib Kumar Basu

CONTENTS

PART A
Organisation and Management

PART B
Business Communication

PART A

Organisation & Management

Chapter 1

Nature of Organisation and Management

1.1 ORGANISATION

At different phases of our lives, each of us is associated with some kind of organisation – a college, a football club, a musical group, a hospital or a business. These organisations do differ from one another in more ways than one. Some, like a giant corporation like General Motors, or the army, may be organised very formally. Others, like local football team in a particular locality, may be less formally organised. But irrespective of their differences, all the organisations of which each of us is a member have some basic common features.

The most common element of an organisation seems to be a goal or a purpose. The goals do differ – to win trophy, to entertain an audience or to sell a product profitably. But without a goal an organisation will cease to exist. An organisation must be endowed with leaders, managers responsible for helping organisations achieve their goals. In some organizations, it is very easy to identify the leader(s). In others, who the leaders actually are probably will not be that obvious. But an organisation without a manager is like a ship without a rudder. It will have no clear direction.

Any modern society is influenced by managers and their organisations. The term 'organisation' is defined as a group of two or more people working together in predetermined fashion to attain a set of goals such as profits, the discovery of knowledge, national defence, or social welfare (managing a charitable trust or dispensary). Different types of organisation pervade our society.

1.2 TYPES OF ORGANISATION

We live and work in a world of organisations. The family into which we are born, the school or college in which we do our education, the religious place where we go for worship and retail shop from which we buy our daily requirements are all organisations. Examples of other organisations are: hospitals, clubs, charitable societies, co-operatives, government and its agencies, business and industrial undertakings and professional firms and so on. Thus there are several types of organisations engaged in varied activities.

Broadly, organisations could be categorized as economic, educational, administrative, cultural, social, religious, political, professional and military organisations. There may be other categorizations too.

Organisations could be distinguished in terms of primary and secondary organisations. A family, a small group and a small community are primary organisations. Their size is comparatively limited. Members are emotionally and personally involved in a primary organisation. Such involvement is almost total. Relations are natural and spontaneous and not contractual. Satisfactions are dominantly psychological. Face-to-face interactions are intense. There are no precisely defined obligations. These are usually informal organisations. A secondary organisation exhibits opposite characteristics. Involvement of members is more rational, calculated and contractual. Interactions tend to be impersonal and formal. Task assignments and roles of members are generally prescribed. A business enterprise, a government department and a college are examples of secondary organisations. They differ in size, nature of goals, degree of permanence, formality, complexity, range of services, functions, prestige and status, resource use patterns, structure, processes and so on. These organisations are basically known as formal organisation.

1.3 WHY ORGANISATIONS ARE NEEDED

Organisations are effective tools for serving human needs. This is why organisations in one form or another will always be with us. Organisations are needed because they perform three vitally important functions:

1. They enable us to accomplish certain things which we could not do so well–or do at all–as individuals.
2. They add to our stock of knowledge on a continuing basis.
3. They serve as an important source of careers for professional people.

The Effectiveness of Organisations

Organisations are the major social unit people have deliberately devised for getting things done or to achieve some specific goal or goals.

The most distinguishing feature of an organisation which distinguishes it from other social units such as groups or committees is a deliberate design and specific goals. Thus an organisation is a human instrument created for some specific purpose. By overcoming our limitations as individuals, organisations enable us to reach goals that would otherwise be very difficult or even impossible to attain.

Organisations are distinguished from other social units, such as families, classes, races, tribes, etc, by their design and objectives. Certain characteristics of organisations promote the achievement of their objectives, viz., the division of labour, systems for co-ordinating and controlling the activities of members and the ability to change membership. As H. J. Reitz has put it: "The division of labour has permitted organisations to produce goods or services on a large scale, with increasing sophistication. At the same time, requirements for systems to control or coordinate these activities have increased."

By providing important knowledge that has been gathered and recorded over the years organisations act as a continuous bridge between the past, present and future generations. Furthermore, organisations themselves do add to our stock of knowledge by developing new and more efficient ways of doing things.

Organisations as a Source of Careers

Needless to say, in our country more than 90% of the people work in some organisations. The various organisations provide their employees with a source of livelihood. They also provide personal satisfaction and self-fulfilment to their employees.

1.4 MEANING AND NATURE OF MANAGEMENT

What do managers have in common? They get things done through their organisations. One management scholar, Mary Parker Follett, described management as "the art of getting things done through people." Peter Drucker, a noted management theorist, explains that managers give direction to their organisations, provide leadership, and decide how to use organisational resources to accomplish goals. Getting things done through people and other resources and providing direction and leadership are what managers do. These activities apply not only to top executives but also to a leader of a cleaning crew, a supervisor in a bottling plant, or a director of marketing. Moreover, management often is considered universal because it uses organisational resources to accomplish goals and attain high performance in all types of profit and not-for-profit organisations. Thus the definition of management is as follows:

Management is the attainment of organisational goals in an effective and efficient manner through planning, organizing, leading and controlling organisational resources.

There are two important ideas in this definition: (1) the four functions of planning, organising, leading and controlling and (2) the attainment of organisational goals in an effective and efficient manner. Managers use a multitude of skills to perform these functions. Figure 1.1 illustrates the process of how managers use resources to attain organisational goals.

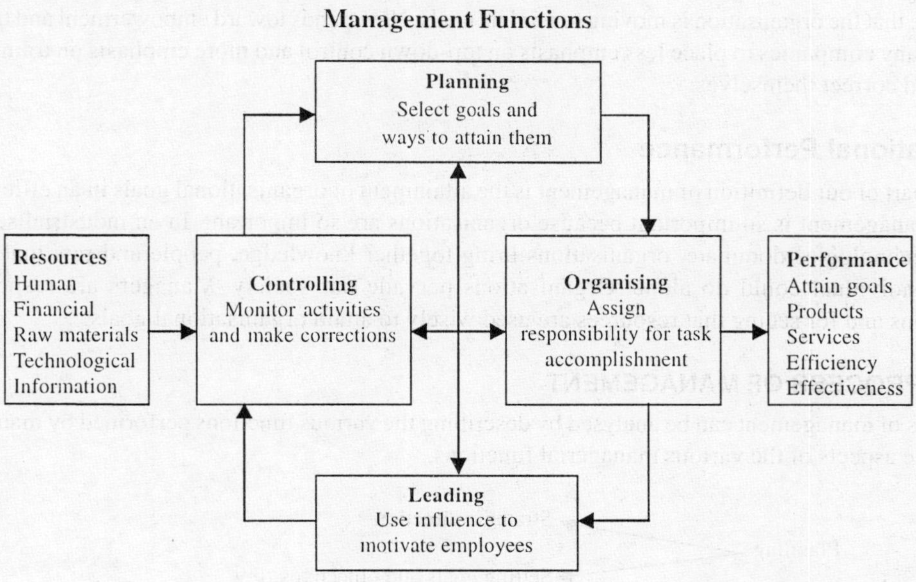

Fig. 1.1 : The Process of Management

The Four Management Functions

Planning

Planning defines where the organisation wants to be in the future and how to go there. Planning means defining goals for future organisational performance and deciding on the tasks and use of resources needed to attain them. A lack of planning – or poor planning – can hurt an organisation's performance, however.

Organising

Organizing typically follows planning and reflects how the organisation tries to accomplish the plan. Organising involves the assignment of tasks, the grouping of tasks into departments, and the allocation of resources to departments. Employees set their own work schedules, organising themselves to accomplish their tasks.

Leading

Providing leadership is becoming an increasingly important management function. Leading is the use of influence to motivate employees to achieve organisational goals. Leading means creating a shared culture and values, communicating goals to employees throughout the organisation and infusing employees with the desire to perform at a high level. Leading involves motivating entire departments and divisions as those individuals working immediately with the manager. In an era of uncertainty, international competition and a growing diversity of the workforce, the ability to shape culture, communicate goals and motivate employees is critical to business success.

Controlling

Controlling is the fourth function in the management process. Controlling means monitoring employee's activities, determining whether the organisation is on target toward its goals, and making corrections as necessary. Managers must ensure that the organisation is moving toward its goals. New trends toward empowerment and trust of employees have led many companies to place less emphasis on top-down control and more emphasis on training employees to monitor and correct themselves.

Organisational Performance

The other part of our definition of management is the attainment of organisational goals in an efficient and effective manner. Management is so important because organisations are so important. In an industrialised society, where complex technologies dominate, organisations bring together knowledge, people and raw materials to perform tasks, no individual could do alone. Organisations pervade our society. Managers are responsible for these organisations and for seeing that resources are used wisely to attain organisational goals.

1.5 THE PROCESS OF MANAGEMENT

The process of management can be analysed by describing the various functions performed by management. Fig.1.2 shows some aspects of the various managerial functions.

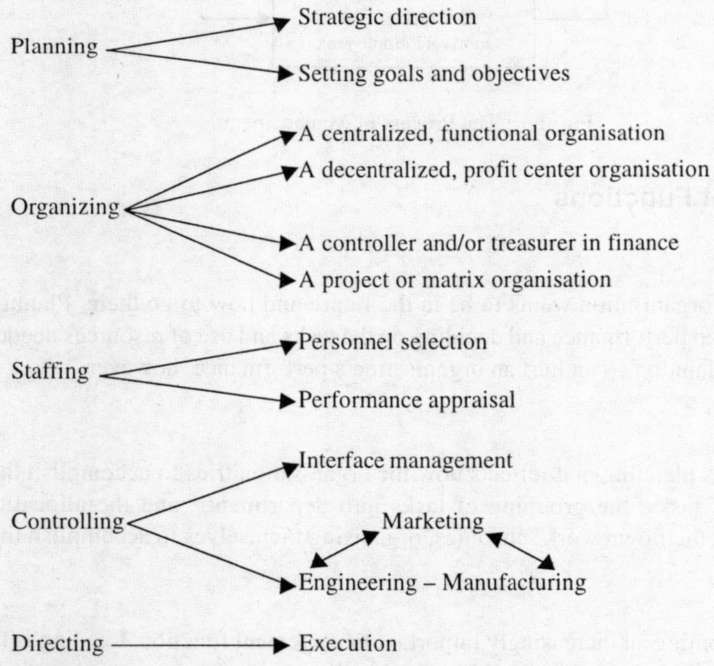

Fig.1.2 : The management process

POSDCORB: Luther Gulick, however, has provided a useful breakdown of managerial functions by coining the word POSDCORB for the initial letters of management functions: planning, organising, staffing, directing, coordinating, reporting and budgeting.

The chart portrays the initial management process or cycle. Three other functions may also be included to complete the picture: decision-making, controlling and communicating.

1.6 CO-ORDINATION

Coordinating is one of the managerial functions alongside planning, organising, motivating and controlling. Co-ordination is the last important function of a manager. It involves the development of unity of purpose and harmonious implementation of plans for achieving common organisational goals.

Ralph C. Davis defined it as "the function of relating activities with respect to time and order of performance". Co-ordination deals with the task of blending effort in order to ensure successful attainment of organisational objectives. Lack of coordinated efforts leads to disorder or even total chaos.

In short, the coordinator of an enterprise also directs the activities of the group in such a manner that it brings harmony within the organisation with a view to achieving common purpose. As a coordinator, a manager has to perform the function of securing and maintaining unified action within the organisation.

Basic Features

There are five basic features of coordination. These are listed below:

1. Coordination is a continuous process.
2. It is the function of an executive, and not of a supervisor.
3. It is an orderly arrangement of group effort.
4. Its objective is to secure unity of action and purpose.
5. It is also directed toward achieving a common organisational goal.

FOUR PRINCIPLES OF COORDINATION

There are four broad principles (or rules) which guide the executives in achieving coordination within an enterprise. These are the following:

1. The principle of direct contact

The first and foremost principle of coordination is that it should be exercised through direct contact of the people who have been given different responsibilities. Coordination can be secured easily by direct contacts and communication.

2. Early action

The second important principle is that coordination should be achieved in the early stages of planning and policy formulation. It would be quite easy to secure the willing and enthusiastic adherence of all concerned to a new principle and policy if they have participated from the very beginning of the process.

3. Reciprocal relation of various factors

The third principle of coordination is that all the factors in a particular situation have reciprocal relationship to one another. When X works for Y, for instance, each finds himself (or herself) influenced by the other and both are influenced by all the persons in the total situation.

4. Continuous process

The fourth and final principle of coordination is that it should be a continuous process. It must go on all the time. It should not be left to chance. In fact, it is duty of the coordinator to constantly ensure that the efforts of the group are directed toward achieving the common goal.

NEED FOR COORDINATION

Whether coordination is or is not a separate function of management, it is of considerable importance. The importance of coordination was highlighted by Chester I. Bernard when he stated that, "The quality of coordination is the crucial factor in the survival of an organisation". L. Urwick went on to say that, "The purpose of the organisation itself is coordination". Peter Drucker also considers coordination as the essence of the organisation. In recent years, coordination has assumed added significance largely due to the growing complexity of business and specialisation of functions within the organisation.

When a number of people are working together to carry out a task, coordination is the only method of synchronization of their activities or sub-tasks. It is an important method by which a manager can avoid potential sources of conflicts among members of a group performing different sub-tasks. Through coordinator duplication of effort and work at cross purposes can be avoided. Various problems of co-ordination are faced by empire builders who always expect cooperation from others but are not prepared to maintain balanced relation with others. It is the task of the manager to cope with such disruptive influences. The need for coordination also arises due to line and staff conflict. The specialist might follow his own principle and may not give weightage to the views of others.

According to Harold Koontz, the need for coordination arises from the diversity of tasks to be undertaken and of persons to carry them out. It emerges as soon as operations begin to multiply or become more and more complex due to the fact that more than one person is concerned with it.

The need for and importance of coordination arises due to the following reasons:

1. ***Conflict resolution*:** In general, each individual in an organisation seeks to achieve its goals and objectives in his own way without being bothered about the impact of his actions on others. Moreover, there is always difference of opinion among individuals regarding the methods to be used for achieving these goals and objectives. Coordination becomes absolutely essential for harmonising such conflicts.
2. ***Synergic effect:*** Through coordination it is possible to achieve total result which will be far in excess of the sum of the individual parts. Experience has shown that total accomplishment of 10 employees of a department whose efforts are properly coordinated will be far greater than that the sum of the individual achievements. This is known as the synergic effect.
3. ***Key to other functions:*** The importance of coordination lies largely in the fact that it is the key to other managerial functions, viz., decision making, planning, directing and controlling. The different elements of a plan, parts of an organisation and phases of a controlling operation must all be coordinated.
4. ***Emphasizing human relations*:** Coordination lays considerable emphasis on the human aspects of an organisation. The stress is on human relations. The general level of morale in an organisation is considerably affected by coordination. In the absence of proper coordination among group members, there would exist considerable uncertainty in any work situation.
5. ***Retention of efficient personnel:*** Sound coordination has a significant effect on the development and retention of efficient people in an organisation. If executives get job satisfaction they will tend to stay longer with company. They will develop a sense of involvement and belonging, i.e., they will feel that they have their rightful position in the organisation which they themselves have secured.

1.7 MANAGERIAL ACTIVITIES

One of the most interesting finding about managerial activities is how busy managers are and how hectic the average workday can be. The manager's involvements are so widespread and voluminous that there is little time for quite reflection. Managers shift gears quickly. Significant crises are interspersed with trivial events in no predictable sequence.

Manager's work is fast paced and requires great energy. As soon as a manager's daily calendar is set, unexpected disturbances erupt. New meetings are required. During time away from the office, executives catch up on work related reading and paperwork.

Manager Roles

Mintzberg's observations and subsequent research indicate that diverse manager activities can be organised into ten roles. A role is a set of expectations for a manager's behavior. These roles are divided into three conceptual categories: informational (managing by information); interpersonal (managing through people); and decisional (managing through action). Each role represents activities that managers undertake to ultimately accomplish the functions of planning, organising, leading and controlling. Although it is necessary to separate the components of the manager's job to understand the different roles and activities of a manger, it is important to remember that the real job of management cannot be practiced as a set of independent parts; all the roles interact in the real world of management. As Mintzberg says, "The manager who only communicates or only conceives never gets anything done, while the manager who only 'does' ends up doing it all alone".

***Informational Roles*:** Informational roles describe the activities used to maintain and develop an information network. General managers spend about 75 percent of their time talking to other people. The monitor role involves seeking current information from many sources. The manager acquires information from others and scans written materials to stay well informed. The disseminator and spokesperson roles are just the opposite: The manager transmits current information to others both inside and outside the organisation, who can use it. With the trend toward empowerment of lower-level employees, many managers are sharing as much information as possible.

***Interpersonal Roles*:** Interpersonal roles pertain to relationships with others and are related to the human skills. The figurehead role involves handling ceremonial and symbolic activities for the department or organisation. The manager represents the organisation in his or her formal managerial capacity as the head of the unit. The leader role encompasses relationship with subordinates, including motivation, communication and influence. The liaison role pertains to the development of information sources both inside and outside the organisation. An example is a face-to-face discussion between a controller and plan supervisor to resolve a misunderstanding about the budget.

***Decisional Roles*:** Decisional roles pertain to those events about which the manager must make a choice and take action. These roles often require conceptual as well as human skill. The entrepreneur role involves the initiation of change. Managers are constantly thinking about the future and how to get there. Managers become aware of problems and search for improvement projects that will correct them. The disturbance handler role involves conflicts among subordinates or between the manager's department and other departments. For example, the division manager for a large furniture manufacturer got involved in a personal dispute between two section heads. One section head was let go because he did not fit the team. The resource allocator role pertains to decisions about how to allocate people, time, equipment, budget and other resources to attain desired outcomes. The manager must decide which projects receive budget allocations, which of several customer complaints receive priority and even how to spend his or her own time. The negotiator role involves formal negotiations and bargaining to attain outcomes for the manger's unit of responsibility. For example, the manager meets and formally negotiates with others–a supplier about a late delivery, the controller about the need for additional budget resources or the union about a worker grievance during the normal workday.

1.8 MANAGEMENT AND ADMINISTRATION

The two terms 'management' and 'administration' are often used synonymously. In this title we shall focus on management but most of what is said also applicable to administration.

The distinction between management and administration is also related to the level of organisation. As Dalton E. Mc Farland put it: "In business firms, administration refers to higher, policy-determining level. One seldom regards the first-line supervisor as an administrator; he is a manager. In the health care fields and in many service organisations, problems (such as flu vaccine distribution) are administered.

Administration may be defined as "the guidance, leadership and control of the efforts of a group of individuals towards some common goals". Others often prefer the synthetic term 'administrative management' (which is concerned with problem-solving and decision-making aspects of the organisation), to distinguish it from 'operative management' which, as the name implies, is concerned with the operational aspects of the business. Some experts like Oliver Sheldon draw a distinction of their own.

Definition

The former is defined as that function in the industry which is concerned with policy-determination, the co-ordination of finance, production, distribution as also the establishment of organisation and ultimate control of the executives. Contrarily, the latter is that process concerned with execution of the policies within certain limits set by the administration and employment of the organisation for the purpose of accomplishing objectives laid down by the former.

Essence of Administration

Administration is more important at higher levels whereas management is more important at lower levels in the firm's organisational pyramid. Thus administration is a top-level function while management is a bottom-level one. The fundamental point of distinction between these two aspects is that whereas the former is the process of laying down broad policies and goals of the organisation, the latter directs and guides the operational or functional aspects of the organisation towards realising the objectives set forth by the former.

A closer look reveals that the scope of management is broader than that of administration. In so far as management comprises both the process of planning and policy-making as also their execution, management embraces both administrative management and operative management.

However, the cardinal point is that the distinction drawn above between the two aspects of organisation serves no real purpose. In fact, the process of management is the same in all enterprises and at all levels in the organisation. In truth, management is as much responsible for planning as administration is. It is in fact, a common experience that the same sets of personnel are supposed to discharge both the above functions.

1.9 IS MANAGEMENT AN ART OR A SCIENCE

Discussions about management often raise the question whether it should be considered as an art or science. The emphasis on any activity classed as an art is "on applying skills and knowledge and accomplishing an end through deliberate efforts". From this point of view, management is clearly an art. As we know, management principles are being applied not for the sake of gaining knowledge but for their application in concrete situations. And so long as the art of applying basic management, principles in practice is important to the job of manager, management is surely an art. Contrarily, science involves "seeking new knowledge through the use of a rigorous method of collecting data, classifying and measuring it, setting up hypotheses and testing those hypotheses". In fact, in the 19th century, management has given increased attention to its scientific aspect. In any case, art and science are basically complementary concepts. Or, in other words, theory and practice of management are mutually helpful inasmuch as art is totally practical and science is theoretical in character to some extent.

It was M.P. Fellott, who first defined management as an art, but there was no universal agreement with her point of view. For instance, Luther Gulick defined management as a 'field of knowledge' that "seeks to systematically understand why and how men work together systematically to accomplish objectives and to make these co-operative systems more useful to mankind". According to Gullick, "management already meets the requirements for a field of knowledge, because it has been studied for some time and has been organised into a series of theories". These theories, to be discussed in the next chapter, "are still to general and subjective". However, Gullick is quite optimistic that "management is on its way to becoming a science, because it is being studied systematically and because the management theories that exist are being tested against experience. Once management attains the status of science, its field will reliably inform or instruct managers what to do in a particular situation and enable them to predict the consequences of their actions".

Management can well be described as a science. But, at best, like Economics and Political Science, it is a social science and inexact at that. This is because management is now a theory possessing a number of principles relating to coordination, organisation, decision-making and so on. And we cannot conduct the same kind of experiments in management as we can in natural sciences like Physics or Chemistry. But inasmuch as the theory of management improves our understanding and practice of management and substitutes rationality for confusion, it is scientific in character.

Still Gullick would admit that "for the foreseeable future and perhaps, even beyond, the practice of management will remain in many ways an art". True enough, we are hearing about management almost everyday and in various situations we can safely recommend a specific course of action. Moreover, the development of computers has vastly improved the manager's ability to judge the outcome of an individual decision such as the decision to produce an optimum mix of various products with limited resources. But our growth has been grossly inadequate in any branch of science and in management, which basically involves working with people, we have to learn many things in the years to come. But it seems that one day our understanding of human behaviour will be complete. Till then managers will have no other option than to rely on their fallible judgement and on insufficient information most of the time. So the conclusion is that while some aspects of management are becoming more scientific, much of management will remain an art.

1.10 IS MANAGEMENT A PROFESSION?

We have noted that management is partly an art and partly a science. Now the question is: It is a profession? For answering this question it is essential to define the characteristics of professionals.

According to E.H. Schein: "Professionals make decisions based on general principles. The existence of management courses and training programmes indicates that there are certain dependable management principles. Professionals also attain their status by meeting certain objective standards of performance".

Definition of Profession

A profession may be defined as a field where training is intellectual in nature, a field in which one enters for the service of others and in which financial reward is not considered as a measure of success. Another definition may be preferred: Profession is a field which is supposed to possess a well-defined body of knowledge, "one which is learned, intellectual and organised; one with entry restricted by examination or education; and one which is concerned primarily with service to others.

How far management is a profession. Now the question is whether management is a profession or not, or, more precisely, whether it meets the above criteria. In fact, management meets the first criterion – the body of knowledge requirement. "This is true from the vocational understanding of the functions of business, the general core disciplines found in typical schools of business, the graduate programmes where function organisations, social institutions, social responsibilities and policy are emphasized". In fact, various disciplines lie behind these approaches: mathematics, economics, statistics, sociology, anthropology and psychology. These disciplines and various aspects thereof provide for managerial decision-making. In other words, they help develop a body of knowledge useful for managerial applications.

However, management fails the test of professionalism on another criterion. Anybody can label himself as a manager and apply it to the operations of business.

However, it should be borne in mind that managers are never "self-made"; instead they are products of the classroom and research. Education and training are regarded by society as vital to managerial progression and success, and typically the educated managers are the ones to whom portions of power and real responsibility are given. Thus the market-place tends to eliminate the so-called self-made manager. So, management is not an outright profession but it is making giant strides in that direction. And the benefits of the development are indeed innumerable. Every enterprise presents possibilities for the application of the art and science of management and virtually every business is a potential source of employment of professional managers. The field of management, therefore, offers abundant opportunities for self-expression and financial remuneration to those who can and do qualify.

1.11 UNIVERSALITY OF MANAGEMENT

We have already defined management as a process. A closer scrutiny reveals that there are three aspects to a such a definition:

1. Firstly, there is the need for co-ordination of resources.
2. Secondly, there is need to give consideration to performance of the managerial functions.
3. Finally, since management is purposeful in nature, it is necessary to include the purpose of the management process.

The manager of an enterprise coordinates the resources of an organisation, especially financial resources, physical resources and personnel to enable the organisation to reach its stated goals or objectives. The co-ordination of resources is achieved through the primary functions of the management process. In the final analysis management is nothing but "the co-ordination of all resources through the processes of planning, organisation, leading and controlling in order to attain stated objectives.

The above definition of management as a purposive, co-ordinative process is universal in its application to all forms of group behaviour. The term 'management' is not restricted (confined) to business enterprises alone. It is applicable whenever prople attempt to reach a stated goal through group efforts.

Secondly, the concept of universality of management is also applicable to all levels of managers within an organisation who participates in the coordination of resources and the exercise of one or all of the managerial functions. "All work to achieve the stated objectives". Since management lies at the heart of all human activity it is universally applicable. It is applicable to business organisations, hospitals, universities, churches or governmental agencies, as well as in our personal live. As Trewatha and Newport argue: "In fact, before any organisation can achieve its goals effectively and efficiently, management is required to co-ordinate the physical factors of money, materials, information, marketing, machines and people. Thus it is referred to as a process in which individuals utilise human and material resources in seeking to accomplish predetermined objectives".

The concept of universality implies that management and activities are transferable from one organisation to another. This mainly happens in the case of military people who often join industry after retirement. There are, of course, instances where such transfers have not been successful.

Thirdly, there is need for flexibility. Managers must have sufficient flexibility when they adjust to new organisational environment. Each organisation has a different environment and for a manager, to be effective in moving from one organisation to another, he or she must be capable of adapting to change.

Chapter 2

The Evolution of Management Thought

2.1 INTRODUCTION

Working for a global company with plants scattered throughout the world is getting to be commonplace. In the past ten years or so, companies with complex systems, IBM, Colgate Palmolive have challenged their employees to manage on a global scale. Managers now lead employees whom they seldom, if ever, see and who may know more about solving a problem than they do. Although new methods of managing employees are needed to keep pace with changes in today's organisations and technology, let's not discard what happened in management before the arrival of the information superhighway. The reason is that management today reflects the evolution of concepts, viewpoints and experiences gained over many decades.

During the thirty years following the Civil War, the United States emerged as a leading industrial nation. The shift from an agrarian to an urban society was abrupt and, for many Americans, meant drastic adjustment. Never before in the nation's history had so many individuals made so much money so quickly. By the end of the century a new corporate capitalism ruled by a prosperous professional class had arisen. Captains of industry freely wielded mergers and acquisitions and engaged in cutthroat competition as they create huge monopolies in the oil, meat, steel, sugar and tobacco industries. The federal government did nothing to interfere with these monopolies. On the one hand, new technology born of the war effort offered the promise of progress and growth. On the other hand, rapid social change and a growing disparity between rich and poor caused increasing conflict and instability.

The year 1886 marked several important turning points in business and management history. Henry R. Towne (1844 -1924), an engineer and cofounder of the Yale Lock Company, present a paper titled "The Engineer as an Economist" to the American Society of Mechanical Engineers. In that paper Towne proposed that the American Society of Mechanical Engineers create an economic section to act as a clearinghouse and forum for "shop management" and "shop accounting". Shop management would deal with the subjects of organisation, responsibility, report and the "executive management" of industrial works, mills and factories. Shop accounting would treat the nuts and bolts of time and wage systems, cost determination and allocation, book-keeping methods and manufacturing accounting. Thus 1886 marked the origins of several well-known, large-scale enterprise; modern management thought and practice.

The emergence of large-scale business enterprise in Canada, the United States and Western Europe raise issues and created challenge that previously had applied only to governments. Businesses needed the equivalent of government leaders managers – to hire and train employees and then to lead and motivate them. Managers also were needed to develop plans and design and work units and, while doing so, make a profit, never a requirement for government.

During the nineteenth century, theorists have developed numerous responses to the same basic management question: What is the best way to manage an organisation? In following sections we discuss the five most widely accepted viewpoints of management that have evolved since about 1886: traditional (or classical), behavioural, systems, contingency and quality. These viewpoints are based on different assumptions about the behaviour of people in organisations, the key goals of an organisation, the types of problems faced, and the methods that should be used to solve those problems.

2.2 TRADITIONAL VIEWPOINT

The oldest and perhaps most widely accepted view of management is the traditional (or classical) viewpoint. It is split into three main branches: bureaucratic management, scientific management and administrative management. All three emerged during roughly the same time period, the late 1890s through the early 1990s, when engineers were trying to make organisation run like well-oiled machines.

2.2.1 Bureaucratic Management

Bureaucratic management relies on rules, a set hierarchy, a clear division of labour and detailed procedures. Max Weber (1864 – 1920), a German social historian, is most closely associated with bureaucratic management. Although Weber was one of the first theorists to deal with the problems of organisations, he wasn't widely recognized by managers and scholars in the United States until his work was translated into English in 1947. He was concerned primarily with the broad social and economic issues facing society; his writings on bureaucracy represent only part of his total contribution to social theory.

Bureaucratic management provides a blueprint of how an entire organisation should operate. It prescribes seven characteristics: a formal system of rules, impersonality, division of labour, hierarchical structure, a detailed authority structure, lifelong career commitment and rationality. Together these characteristics represent a format, somewhat rigid method of managing.

Benefits of Bureaucracy: The expected benefits of bureaucratic management are efficiency and consistency. A bureaucracy functions best when many routine tasks need to be done. Then lower level employees can handle the bulk of the work by simply following rules and procedures. The fruits of their labour should be of standard (high) quality and produced at the rate necessary to meet organisational goals.

Cost of Bureaucracy: The same aspects of bureaucratic management that can increase one organisation's efficiency can lead to great inefficiency in another. The following are five, often unanticipated, drawbacks of bureaucratic management.

1. **Rigid rules and red tape.** Rigid adherence to rules and routines for their own sake is a frequent complaint of employees and customers of many organisations. Such a system leaves little room for individual freedom and creativity.
2. **Protection of authority.** Managers in a bureaucratic organisation may ignore issues of employee productivity while protecting and expanding their own authority.
3. **Slow decision making.** Large, complex organisations depend heavily on timely decision. In a highly bureaucratic organisation, however, adherence to rules and procedures may take precedence over effective, timely decision making. When that happens, rules take on a life of their own. Formally and ritual delay decisions at every level until all the red tape has been cleared, petty insistence on power and status privileges has been satisfied and any chance of blame for errors in judgment has been minimised.
4. **Incompatibility with changing technology.** Advancing technology may make bureaucratic management inappropriate. If the technology changes rapidly, the employees must be able to go directly to the person who has the information they need to do their jobs.
5. **Incompatibility with professional values.** More and more professionals are being hired by bureaucratic organisations to fill important decision-making positions. Professional values include advancing knowledge, serving clients and customers, and finding innovative solutions to problems. These values often are incompatible with the bureaucratic need for efficiency, order, and consistency.

Assessing Bureaucratic Management: Not all bureaucratic organisations are inefficient and unprofitable. In fact, bureaucratic management is still widely and successfully used. This approach is most effective when (1) large amounts of standard information have to be processed and an efficient processing method has been found;

(2) the needs of the customer are known and aren't likely to change; (3) the technology is routine and stable, so employees can be easily and quickly taught how to operate machine; and (4) the organisation has to coordinate the activities of numerous employees in order to deliver a standardised service or product to the customer.

2.2.2 Scientific Management

As manufacturing firms became larger and more complex in the late 1800s, not all managers could continue to be directly involved with production. Many began to spend more of their time administratively in planning, scheduling and staffing activities. Also, managers were hard-pressed to keep up with advances in the new, machine-oriented production technology. The distancing of management from the physical production of goods created a need for operations specialists who could solve the personnel and productivity problems that accompanied rapid industrialisation and threatened operating efficiency.

Frederick W. Taylor. Thus the stage was set for Frederick Winslow Taylor (1856-1915) to do his pioneering work in scientific management. Whereas bureaucratic management looks at broad organisational structures and work systems, ***Scientific management*** focuses on individuals and their machines or tools. Its philosophy is that management practices should be based on proven fact and observation, not on hearsay or guesswork.

Taylor, an American mechanical engineer, started out as a foreman at Midvale Steel Company in Philadelphia. He believed that increased productivity ultimately depended on finding ways to make workers more efficient by using objective, entific techniques.

Taylor used time-and-motion studies to analyse work flows, supervisory techniques, and worker fatigue. A ***time-and-motion study*** involves identifying and measuring a worker's physical movements when performing a task and then analysing the results. Movements that slow production are dropped. One goal of a time-and –motion study is to make a job highly routine and efficient. Eliminating wasted physical effort and specifying an exact sequence of activities reduce the amount of time, money and effort needed to make a product.

What motivates employees to work to their capacity? Taylor believed that money was the answer. He supported the individual piecework system as the basis for pay. If workers met a certain production standard, they were to be paid at a standard wage rate. Workers who produced more than the standard were to be paid at a higher rate for all the pieces they produced, not just for those exceeding the standard. Taylor assumed that workers would be economically rational; that is, they would follow management's orders to produce more in response to financial incentives that allowed them to earn more money. Taylor argued that managers should use financial incentives if they were convinced that increases in productivity would more than offset higher employee earnings.

The Gilbreths. Frank (1868-1924) and Lillian (1878-1972) Gilbreth formed an unusual husband-and-wife engineering team who made significant contributions to scientific management. Frank used a revolutionary new too – motion pictures – to study worker's motions. For instance, he identified eighteen individual motions that a bricklayer uses to lay bricks. By changing the bricklaying process, he reduced the eighteen motions to five, increasing a worker's overall productivity by more than 200 percent.

Henry Gantt. Taylor's associate, Henry Gantt (1861-1919), focused on "control" systems for production scheduling. His Gantt charts are still widely used to plan project timeliness and have been adapted for computer scheduling applications. The ***Gantt chart*** is a visual plan and progress report. It identifies various stages of work that must be carried out to complete a project, sets a deadline for each stage, and documents accomplishments. Gantt also established quota systems and bonuses for workers who exceeded their quotas.

Assessing Scientific Management. Taylor and other early proponents of scientific management would applaud the efforts of KFC, Honda, Canon, Intel and other organisations that have successfully applied their concepts. These firms make finished products faster and cheaper than Taylor could ever have dreamed. Organisations are increasingly taking for granted his idea that managers can't expect employees to do their jobs properly without adequate skills and training. Taylor's work has led today's managers to improve their employee selection and training process and to seek the one best way to perform each task.

Unfortunately, most proponents of scientific management misread the human side of work. When Frederick Taylor and Frank Gilbreth formulated their principles and methods, they thought that workers were motivated primarily by a desire to earn money to satisfy their economic and physical needs. They failed to recognize that workers also have social needs and that working conditions and job satisfaction often are more important than money. Managers today can't assume that workers are interested only in higher wages. Dividing jobs into their simplest tasks and setting clear rules for accomplishing those tasks won't always lead to a quality product, high morale and an effective organisation. Today's employees often want to participate in decisions that affect their performance; many want to be independent and hold jobs that give them self-fulfillment.

2.2.3 Administrative Management

Administrative management focuses on the manager and basic managerial functions. It evolved early in the twentieth century and is most closely identified with Henri Fayol (1841-1925), a French industrialist. However, his most important writings on management weren't translated into English until 1930. Fayol credited his success as a manager to the methods he used, rather than to his personal qualities. He felt strongly that, to be successful, managers had only to understand the basic managerial functions – planning, organising, leading and controlling – and apply certain management principles to them. He was the first person to group manager's functions in this way.

Like the other traditionalists, Fayol emphasized formal structure and processes, believing that they are necessary for the adequate performance of all important tasks. In other words, if people are to work well together, they need a clear definition of what they're trying to accomplish and how their tasks help meet organisational goals.

Fayol developed the following fourteen management principles and suggested that managers receive formal training in their application.

1. **Division of labour.** The more people specialize, the more efficiently they can perform their work.
2. **Authority.** Managers have the right, the authority, to give orders to get things done.
3. **Discipline.** Members of an organisation need to respect the rules and agreements that govern it.
4. **Unity of command.** Each employee must receive instructions about a particular operation from only one person to avoid conflicting instructions and confusion.
5. **Unity of direction.** Managers should coordinate the efforts of employees working on projects, but only one should be responsible for an employee's behaviour.
6. **Subordination of individual interest to the common good.** The interests of individual employees should not take precedence over the interests of the entire organisation.
7. **Remuneration.** Pay for work done should be fair to both the employee and the employer.
8. **Centralisation.** Managers should retain final responsibility but should also give their subordinates enough authority to do their jobs properly.
9. **Scalar chain.** A single uninterrupted line of authority should run rank to rank from top management to the lowest level position in the company.
10. **Order.** Materials and people should be in the right place at the right time. In particular, people should be in the jobs or positions best suited to them.
11. **Equity.** Managers should be both friendly and fair to their subordinates.
12. **Stability and tenure of staff.** A high rate of employee turnover is not efficient.
13. **Initiative.** Subordinates should be given the freedom to formulate and carry out their own plans.
14. **Esprit de corps.** Promoting team spirit gives the organisation a sense of unity.

Managers still use many of Fayol's principles of administrative management, but different managers seldom apply them in exactly the same way. Situations vary and so, too, does the application of these principles.

ASSESSING TRADITIONAL MANAGEMENT

Traditional management's three branches – bureaucratic, scientific and administrative — still have proponents, are often written about and continue to be applied effectively.

All three branches of traditional management emphasize the formal aspects of organisation. Traditionalists are concerned with the formal relations among an organisation's departments, tasks and processes. Weber, Taylor, the Gilbreths, Gantt, and Fayol replace seat-of-the-pants management practices with sound theoretical and scientific principles. Managers began to stress the division of labour, hierarchical authority, rules and decisions that would maximise economic rewards.

Traditional management stresses the manager's role in a hierarchy. In bureaucratic management the relationship between expertise and organisational level is strong. Because of their higher position and presumed greater expertise, superiors are to be obeyed by subordinates. Administrative and scientific management's emphasis on logical processes and strict division of labour are based on similar reasoning.

Although traditionalists may recognize that people have feelings and are influenced by their friends at work, their overriding focus is on efficient and effective job performance. Taylor considered the human side of work in terms of eliminating bad feelings between workers and management and providing employees with financial incentives to increase productivity. Job security, career progression and protection of workers from employer's whims are considered important by traditionalists. However, they do not recognize informal or social relationship among employees at work. Taylor and Frank Gilbreth focused on well-defined rules intended to ensure efficient performance, the primary standard against which employees were to be judged.

2.3 BEHAVIOURAL VIEWPOINT

During the 1920s and 1930s, the United States and other industrialised nations experienced radical social and cultural changes. Mass production triggered a second industrial revolution. Assembly line released flood of inexpensive goods – cars, appliances and clothing – into an increasingly consumer-oriented society. The overall standard of living rose and working conditions in many industries improved.

In one of the era's most dramatic changes, unskilled workers increased their ability to influence management decisions by forming powerful labour unions. Eventually professionals and skilled workers, as well as unskilled labourers, formed unions to bargain for better pay, increased benefits and improved working conditions.

Against this backdrop of change and reform managers were forced to recognize that people have needs, cherish values and want respect. They were now leading workers who did not appear to exhibit what the early traditional management. That is, workers weren't always performing up to their physiological capabilities, as Taylor had predicted rational people would do. Nor were effective managers consistently following Fayol's fourteen principles. By exploring these inconsistencies, those who favoured a behavioural viewpoint of management gained recognition. The ***behavioural*** (human relations) ***viewpoint*** focuses on dealing effectively with the human aspects of organisations. Its proponents look at how managers do what they do, how managers lead subordinates and communicate with them and why managers need to change their assumptions about people if they want to lead high-performance teams and organisations.

FOLLETT'S CONTRIBUTIONS

In the early decades of the last century, Mary Parker Follett (1868-1933) made important contributions to the behavioural viewpoint of management. She believed that management is a flowing, continuous process, not a static one and that if a problem has been solved, the method used to solve it probably generated new problems. She stressed (1) involvement of workers in solving problems and (2) the dynamics of management, rather than static principles. Both ideas contrasted sharply with the views of Weber, Taylor and Fayol.

Follett studied how managers did their jobs by observing them at work. Based of these observations, she concluded that coordination is vital to effective management. She developed four principles of coordination for managers to apply.

1. Coordination is best achieved when the people responsible for making a decision are in direct contact.
2. Coordination during the early stages of planning and project implementation is essential.
3. Coordination must be worked at continuously.
4. Coordination should address all the factors in a situation .

Follett believed that the people closest to the action could make the best decisions. For example, she was convinced that first-line managers are in the best position to coordinate production tasks. And by increasing communication among themselves and with workers, these managers can make better decisions regarding such tasks than managers up the hierarchy can.

Follett also believed that managers should find ways to help resolve interdepartmental conflict. Properly handled, conflict can stimulate and integrate managerial and production efforts. As part of the conflict resolution process, every one involved should try to understand the other's views and the situations they face.

BARNARD'S CONTRIBUTIONS

Chester Barnard (1886-1961) studied economics at Harvard but failed to graduate because he didn't finish a laboratory course in science. He was hired by AT&T, and in 1927 he became president of New Jersey Bell. Barnard made two significant contributions to management, which are detailed in his book, *The Functions of the Executive.*

Barnard viewed organisations as social systems that require employee cooperation if they are to be effective. According to Barnard, manager's main roles are to communicate with employees and motivate them to work hard to help achieve the organisation's goals. In this view, successful management also depends on maintaining good relations with people outside the organisation with whom managers deal regularly. He stressed the idea that managers have to examine the organisation's external environment and adjust its internal structure to balance the two.

Another of Barnard's significant contributions is the *acceptance theory of authority*. This theory holds that employees have free wills and thus will choose whether to follow management's orders. That is, employees will follow orders if they (1) understand what is required, (2) believe that the orders are consistent with organisational goals, and (3) see positive benefits to themselves in carrying out the orders.

THE HAWTHORNE CONTRIBUTIONS

The strongest support of the behavioural viewpoint emerged from studies carried out between 1924 and 1933 at Western Electric Company's Hawthorne plant in Chicago. The Hawthorne Illumination Tests, begun in November 1924 and conducted in three departments of the plant initially were developed and directed by Hawthorne's engineers. They divided employees into two groups: a test group, whom they subjected to deliberate changes in lighting, and a control group, for whom lighting remained constant throughout the experiment. When lighting conditions for the test group were improved the group's productivity increased, as expected. The engineers were mystified, through, by a similar jump in productivity upon reducing the test group's lighting to the point of twilight. To compound the mystery, the control group's output kept rising, even though its lighting condition didn't change. Western Electric called in Harvard professor Elton Mayo to investigate these peculiar and puzzling results.

Mayo and Harvard colleagues Fritz Roethlisberger and William Dickson devised a new experiment. They placed two groups of six women each in separate rooms. They changed various conditions for the test group and left conditions unchanged for the control group. The changes included shortening the test group's coffee breaks, allowing it to choose its own rest periods, and letting it have a say in other suggested changes. Once again, output of both the test group and the control group increased. The researchers decided that they could rule out financial incentives as a factor because they hadn't changed the payment schedule for either group.

The researchers concluded that the increases in productivity weren't caused by a physical event but by a complex emotional chain reaction. Because employees in both groups had been singled out for special attention, they had developed a group pride that motivated them to improve their performance. The sympathetic supervision they received further reinforced that motivation. These experimental results led to Mayo's first important discovery: When employees are given special attention, productivity is likely to change regardless of whether working conditions change. This phenomenon became known as the *Hawthorne effect.*

However, an important question remained unanswered: Why should a little special attention and the formation of group bonds produce such strong reactions? To find the answer Mayo interviewed employees. These interviews yielded a highly significant discovery: Informal work groups, the social environment of employees greatly influence productivity.

The writings of Mayo, Roethlisberger and Dickson interpreted the basic conclusions that emerged from the Hawthorne studies and helped outline the behavioural viewpoint of management. They suggested that awareness of employee feelings and encouragement of employee participation in decision making can reduce resistance to change.

ASSESSING THE BEHAVIOURAL VIEWPOINT

The behavioural viewpoint of management goes beyond the traditionalist's mechanical view of work by stressing the importance of group dynamics, complex human motivations, and the manager's leadership style. It emphasizes the employee's social and economic needs and the influence of the organisation's social setting on the quality and quantity of work produced. The following are the basic assumptions of the behavioural viewpoint.

- Employees are motivated by social needs and get a sense of identity through their associations with one another.
- Employees are more responsive to the social forces exerted by their peers than to management's financial incentives and rules.
- Employees are most likely to respond to managers who can help them satisfy their needs.
- Managers need to coordinate work with the participation of their subordinates to improve efficiency.

These assumptions don't always hold in practice, of course. Improving working conditions and manager's human relations skills won't increase productivity. Economic aspects of work are still important to the employee, as Taylor believed. The major union contracts negotiated in recent years, for instance, focus on job security and wage incentives. And, although employees enjoy working with co-workers who are friendly, low salaries tend to lead absenteeism and turnover. The negative effects of clumsy organisational structure, poor communication and routine or boring tasks won't be overcome by the presence of pleasant co-workers.

2.4 SYSTEM VIEWPOINT

During World War II the British assembled a team of mathematicians, physicists and others to solve various wartime problems. These professionals formed the first operations research (OR) group. Initially, they were responsible for analysing the makeup, routes and speeds of convoys and probable locations of German submarines. The team developed ingenious ways to analyse complex problems that couldn't be handled solely by intuition, straightforward mathematics, or experience. The British and Americans further developed this approach (called systems analysis) throughout the war and applied it to many problems of war production and military logistics. Later, systems analysis became an accepted tool in the Department of Defense (DoD) and the space program, as well as throughout private industry.

SYSTEMS CONCEPTS

A ***system*** is an association of interrelated and interdependent parts. The human body is a system with organs, muscles, bones, nerves and a consciousness that links all its parts. An organisation is an internal system with many employees, teams, departments and levels that are linked to achieve its goals. An organisation also is linked externally to suppliers, customers, shareholders and regulatory agencies. A competent systems-oriented manager makes decisions only after identifying and analysing how other managers, departments, customers or others might be affected by the decisions.

The ***systems viewpoint*** of management represents an approach to solving problems by diagnosing them within a framework of inputs, transformation process, outputs and feedback, as shown in Figure 2.1. The system involved may be an individual, a work group, a department, or an entire organisation.

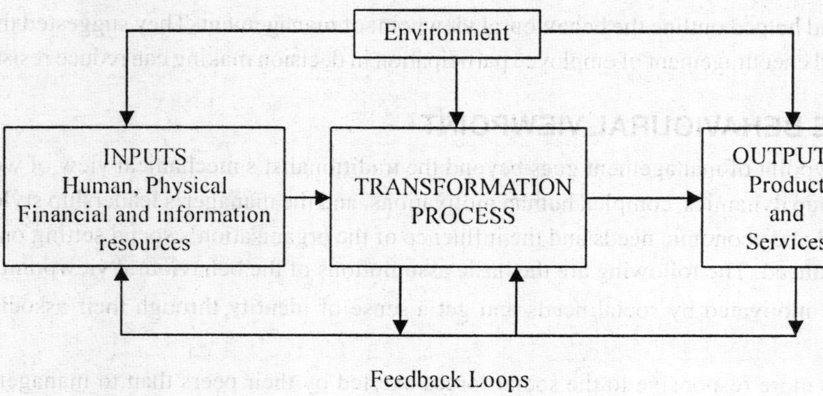

Figure : 2.1

Inputs are the physical, human, material, financial and information resources that enter a transformation process. At a university, for example, inputs include students, faculty, money and buildings. **Transformation process** comprises the technologies used to convert inputs into outputs. Transformation processes at a university include lectures, reading assignments, lab experiments, term papers and tests. **Outputs** are the original inputs (human, physical, material, information and financial resources) as changed by a transformation process. Outputs at a university include the graduating students. For a system to operate effectively, it must also provide for feedback. **Feedback** is information about a system's status and performance. One form of feedback at a university is the ability of its graduates to get jobs. In an organisation, feedback may take the form of marketing surveys, financial reports, production records, performance appraisals and like. In the systems viewpoint, management's role is to facilitate transformation processes by planning, organising, leading and controlling.

QUANTITATIVE TECHNIQUES

While some advocates of systems analysis were suggesting that managers look at inputs, transformation processes, and outputs before making a decision, other systems advocates were developing quantitative techniques to aid in managerial decision making. Quantitative techniques have four basic characteristics:

1. **The primary focus is on decision making.** The solution identifies direct actions that managers can take, such as JIT to reduce inventory costs.

2. **Alternatives are based on economic criteria.** Alternative actions are presented in terms of measurable criteria, such as costs, revenues and dealer returns.
3. **Mathematical models are used.** Situations are simulated and problems are analysed by means of mathematical models.
4. **Computers are essential.** Computers are used to solve complex mathematical models that would be too costly and time-consuming to process manually, such as statistical process controls.

The range of quantitative decision-making tools available to management has expanded greatly during the past two decades. Today's managers have inventory decision models, statistical decision theory, linear programming and many other aids for solving complex problems.

ASSESSING THE SYSTEMS VIEWPOINT

System analysis and quantitative techniques have been used primarily to manage transformation processes and in the technical planning and decision-making aspects of management. These techniques haven't yet reached the stage where they can be used effectively to deal with the human aspects of management. Variables representing behavioural considerations and human values are difficult, if not impossible, to build into a mathematical model. Because these subjective variables must still be taken into account, judgments about people will continue to be a vital part of managerial decision making.

Organisations no doubt will continue to develop more sophisticated systems in order to increase productivity. Such systems will require changes in many aspects of day-to-day operations. These changes will not come without struggle and pain. Yet for organisations to survive they must install and utilise increasingly sophisticated systems to help managers make decisions.

2.5 CONTINGENCY VIEWPOINT

The essence of the **contingency viewpoint** (sometimes called the contingency or situational approach) is that management practices should be consistent with the requirements of the external environment, technology, and capabilities of the people involved. These relationships are summarized in Figure 2.2. It was developed in the mid-1960s by managers and others who had tried unsuccessfully to apply traditional and systems concepts to actual managerial problems. Proponents of the contingency viewpoint contend that different situations require different practices. As one manager put it, the contingency viewpoint really means that "it all depends".

Proponents of the contingency viewpoint advocate using the other three management viewpoints independently or in combination, as necessary, to deal with various situations. However, this viewpoint doesn't give managers free rein to indulge their personal biases and whims. Rather, managers are expected to determine which methods are likely to be more effective than others in a given situation. Applying the contingency viewpoint requires the development and use of all six managerial competencies. Managers must be able to diagnose and understand a situation thoroughly – to determine which approach is most likely to succeed – before making a decision. The manager's communications competency then is essential in actually implementing the decision.

CONTINGENCY VARIABLES

The essence of the contingency viewpoint is that management practices should be consistent with the requirements of the external environment, the technology used to make a product or deliver a service and the people who work for the organisation.

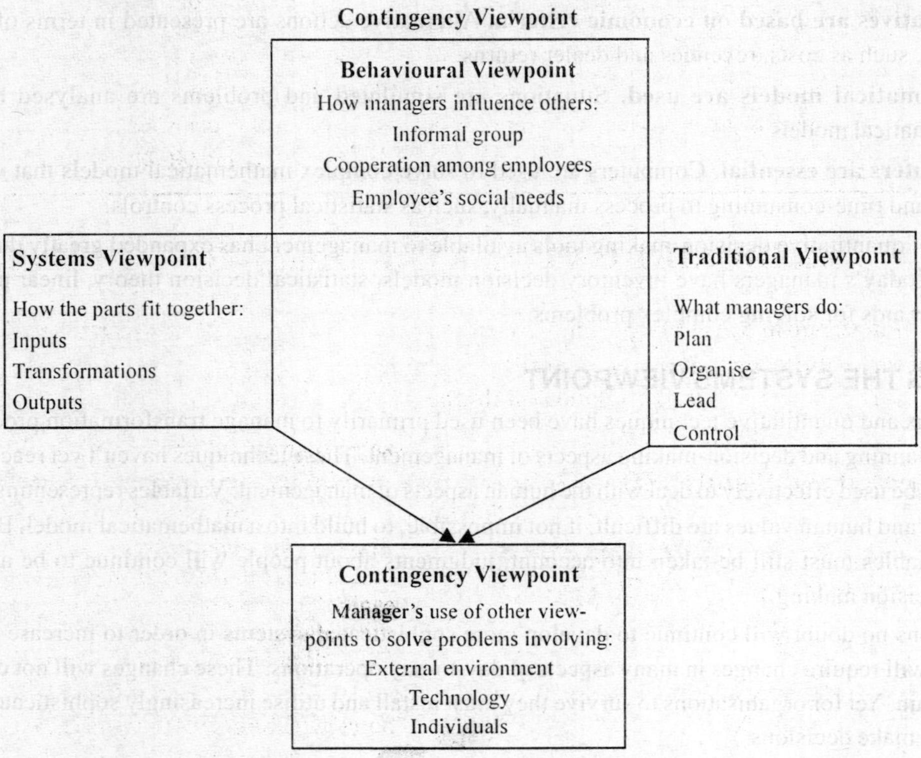

Figure : 2.2

The relative importance of each contingency variable depends on the type of managerial problem being considered. For example, in designing an organisation's structure a manger should consider the nature of the company's external environment and the corresponding information processing requirements.

ASSESSING THE CONTINGENCY VIEWPOINT

The contingency viewpoint of management is useful because of its diagnostic approach, which clearly departs from the one-best-way approach of the traditionalists. The contingency viewpoint encourages managers to analyse and understand situational differences and to choose the solution best suited to the organisation, the process and the people involved in each situation.

Critics argue that the contingency viewpoint really is nothing new. They say that it is merely a meshing of techniques from the other viewpoints of management. The contingency viewpoint does draw heavily from the other approaches. However, it is flexible, allowing managers to apply the principles and tools from those approaches selectively and where most appropriate. It holds that a manager should rely on absolute principles from the traditional, behavioural and systems viewpoints only after properly diagnosing the realities of the situation. Such a diagnosis looks at the nature of a situation and the means by which the manager can influence it.

2.6 QUALITY VIEWPOINT

In the present century are new management viewpoints – beyond the contingency viewpoint — likely to emerge? The answer is yes. Today's organisations are dynamic and whether large or small, local or global, face formidable new management challenges. Organisations feel pressure from customers and competitors to deliver high – quality products and/or services on time, reward ethical behaviour of employees and develop plans to manage highly diverse workforces effectively. Customer demand for high – quality products and services may be the dominant theme for the foreseeable future. Quality is defined as how well a product does what it is supposed to do – how closely and reliably it satisfies the specifications to which it is built. Managers in successful organisations are quality conscious and understand the link between high – quality goods and/or services, and competitive advantage.

Total quality management (TQM) is the continuous process of ensuring that every aspect of production builds in product quality. Quality must be stressed repeatedly so that it becomes second nature to everyone in an organisation and its suppliers. Moreover, training, strategic planning, product design, management information systems, marketing and other key activities all play a role in meeting quality goals.

The godfather of the quality movement was W. Edwards Deming (1900-1993). Initially, U.S. managers rejected his ideas and not until his ideas had helped rebuild Japan's industrial might after World War II were his ideas accepted in the United States. He taught eager Japanese managers how to use statistics to assess and improve quality. In 1951, Japan established the Deming Prize for corporate quality in his honour.

Deming stressed the need for all employees to use statistics to improve quality and productivity, build trust, and work closely with customers. Deming believed that poor quality is 85 percent a management problem and 15 percent a worker problem. His ideas and methods include the following:

- Poor quality is unacceptable. Defective workmanship, products and services are not to be tolerated.
- Gather statistical evidence of quality during the process, not at the end of the process. The earlier an error is caught, the less the cost to correct it.
- Rely on a few suppliers that have historically provided quality, not on sampling inspections to determine the quality of each delivery.
- Depend on training and retraining employees to use statistical methods in doing their jobs, not on slogans, to improve quality.
- Employees should feel free to report any conditions that detract from quality.

2.7 INTEGRATION OF MANAGEMENT VIEWPOINTS AND COMPETENCIES

In this Chapter, we identified five management competencies that are essential for future success as a manager. Each of the five managerial viewpoints stresses at least one of these competencies more than others.

The traditional viewpoint sought to identify management competencies that efficiently organised the work of employees. Each level of management was assigned specific goals and tasks to accomplish in an allotted time period. The structure of the organisation governed relations between manager and manager and employee. It was the manager's job to plan, organise and lay out the task for the employee; it was the employee's job to follow the manager's instructions. Employees were thought of as "rational" people who were motivated primarily by money.

The behavioural viewpoint focused on developing two competencies: communication and teamwork. It was the manager's job to acknowledge the social and emotional needs of employees and to develop harmonious relationships in the workplace. This viewpoint stressed that employee behaviours are greatly affected by their interactions with peers. If managers communicated with employees and satisfied their workplace needs, the organisation would be more effective.

The systems viewpoint stressed that managers should focus on how various inputs, transformation processes and outputs are related to the organisation's goals. The organisation was viewed as a "whole," rather than simply the sum of its various departments or divisions. This wholeness requires managers to develop their communication, strategic thinking and action and global awareness competencies. To develop these competencies, managers use quantitative models to help them understand complex organisational relationships.

The contingency viewpoint draws from each of the other viewpoints and involves a somewhat different set of competencies. Deciding whether to draw on one set of skills in a competency or on several skills across competencies is the job of the manager. How an organisation is designed depends on its external environment, the skills of its employees, and the technology used to transform raw materials into finished products.

The quality viewpoint stresses meeting customer's expectations in terms of the value (performance and quality) of goods and services. Top management is responsible for putting the systems into place to achieve quality. One way for top management to gain the support of employees in such an effort is to design TQM practices that reward employees for meeting quality goals. The TQM philosophy requires a high level of coordination throughout the organisation. One way for achieving that coordination is through teamwork. In quality conscious organisations, teamwork means sharing both responsibility and decision making. Managers delegate decision-making authority to employees, permitting them to manage themselves – but only after they have received the necessary training. Deming's philosophy of statistical quality control not only provides a method for analysing deviations from standards, but it also provides a way to increase communication between employees.

Chapter 3

Business Environment

3.1 INTRODUCTION

The world as we know it is undergoing tremendous and far-reaching change. This change can be understood by defining and examining components of the external environment.

The external organisational environment includes all elements existing outside the boundary of the organisation that have the potential to affect the organisation. The environment includes competitors, resources, technology and economic conditions that influence the organisation. It does not include those events so far removed from the organisation that their impact is not perceived.

The organisation's external environment can be further conceptualised as having two layers: general and task environments.

The general environment is the outer layer that is widely dispersed and affects organisations indirectly. It includes social, demographic and economic factors that influence all organisations about equally. Increases in the inflation rate are the part of the organisation's general environment. These events do not directly change day-to-day operations, but they do affect all organisations eventually. The task environment is closer to the organisation and includes the sectors that conduct day-to-day transactions with the organisation and directly influence its basic operations and performance. It is generally considered to include competitors, suppliers and customers.

The organisation also has an internal environment, which includes the elements within the organisation's boundaries. The internal environment is composed of current employees, management and especially corporate culture, which defines employee behaviour in the internal environment and how well the organisation will adapt to the external environment.

Location of the Organisation's General, Tasks and Internal Environments

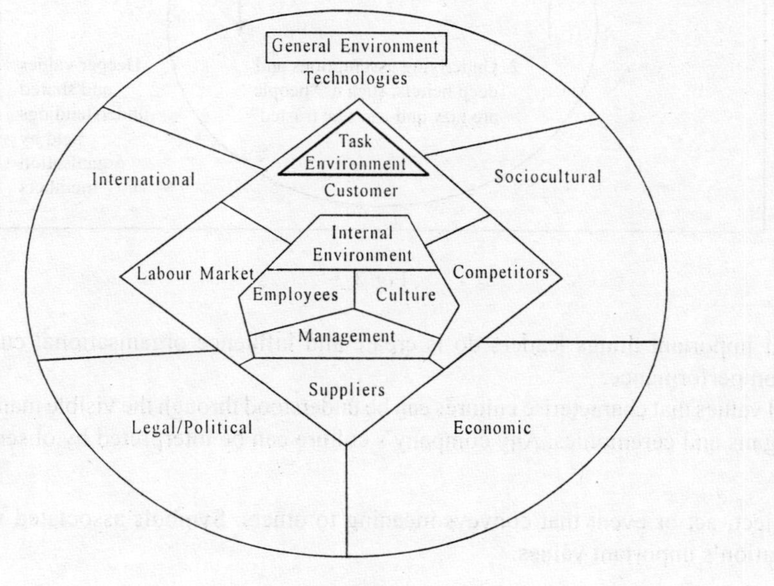

Fig. 3.1

Fig 3.1 illustrates the relationship among the general, task and internal environments. As an open system, the organisation draws resources from the external environment and releases goods and services back to it.

3.2 THE INTERNAL ENVIRONMENT: CORPORATE CULTURE

The internal environment within which managers work includes corporate culture, production technology, organisation structure and physical facilities. Of these, corporate culture has surfaced as extremely important to competitive advantage.

3.2.1 Culture

Culture can be defined as the set of key values, beliefs, understandings and norms shared by members of an organisation. The concept of culture helps managers understand the hidden, complex aspects of organisational life. Culture is a pattern of shared values and assumptions about how things are done within the organisation. This pattern is learned by members as they cope with external and internal problems and taught to new members as the correct way to perceive, think and feel. Culture can be analysed at three levels. As the surface level are visible artifacts, which include such things as manner of dress, patterns of behaviour, physical symbols, organisational ceremonies and office layout. Visible artifacts are all the things one can see, hear and observe by watching members of the organisation. At a deeper level are the expressed values and beliefs, which are not observable but can be discerned from how people explain and justify what they do. These are values that members of the organisation hold at a conscious level. They can be interpreted from the stories, language and symbols organisation members use to represent them.

Levels of Corporate Culture

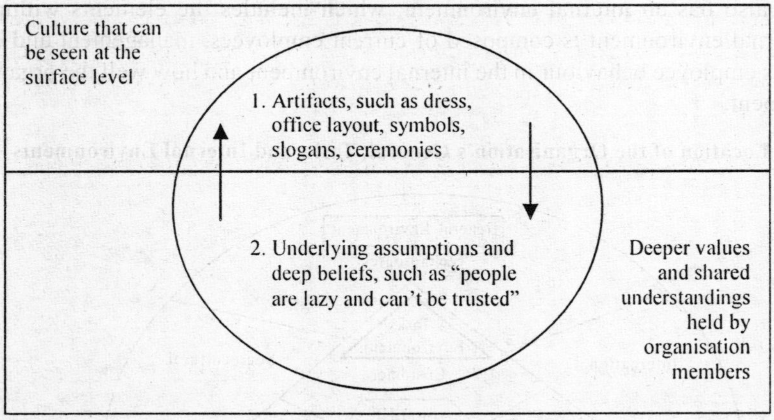

Fig. 3.2

One of the most important things leaders do is create and influence organisational culture because it has a significant impact on performance.

The fundamental values that characterise cultures can be understood through the visible manifestations of symbols, stories, heroes, slogans and ceremonies. Any company's culture can be interpreted by observing these factors.

Symbols

A symbol is an object, act or event that conveys meaning to others. Symbols associated with corporate culture convey the organisation's important values.

Stories

A story is a narrative description based on true events that is repeated frequently and shared among organisational employees. Stories are told to new employees to keep the organisation's primary values alive.

Heroes

A hero is a figure who exemplifies the deeds, character and attributes of a strong culture. Heroes are role models for employees to follow. Heroes show how to do the right thing in the organisation. Companies with string cultures take advantage of achievements to define heroes who uphold key values.

Slogans

A slogan is a phrase or sentence that succinctly expresses a key corporate value. Many companies use a slogan or saying to convey special meaning to employees. Cultural values can be discerned in written public statements, such as corporate mission statements or other formal statements that express the core values of the organisation.

Ceremonies

A ceremony is a planned activity that makes up a special event and is conducted for the benefit of an audience. Managers hold ceremonies to provide dramatic examples of company values. Ceremonies are special occasions that reinforce valued accomplishments, create a bond among people by allowing them to share an important event and celebrate heroes.

In summary, organisational culture represents the values, understandings and basic assumptions that employees share and these values are signified by symbols, stories, heroes, slogans and ceremonies. Managers help define important symbols, stories and heroes to shape the culture.

3.2.2 Board of directors

Board of directors is there in companies formed under the Companies Act, 1956 looking after general management of the firm to ensure that it is being operated in a way that best serves the shareholder's interests.

3.2.3 Employees

Employees are the people who actually do the work in an organisation. Employees are the major force within an organisation. It is important for an organisation that employees embrace the same values and goals as the organization. However, they differ in beliefs, education, attitudes and capabilities. When managers and employees work toward different goals everyone suffers.

3.3 GENERAL ENVIRONMENT

The general environment represents the outer layer of the environment. These dimensions influence the organisation over time but often are not involved in day-to-day transactions with it. The dimensions of the general environment include international, technological, sociocultural, economic and legal-political.

International. The international dimension of the external environment represents events originating in foreign countries as well as opportunities for domestic companies in other countries. The international environment provides new competitors, customers and suppliers and shapes social, technological and economic trends, as well.

Today, every company must think internationally. Managers who are used to thinking only about the domestic environment must learn new rules to cope with goods, services and ideas circulating around the globe. For example, products and services exist in a one-world market. Moreover, competitors in a global village come from all over. A company that does not export still will run into competitors in its own marketplace, including some from developing nations.

The global environment represents an everchanging and uneven playing field compared with the domestic environment. Changes in the international domain can abruptly turn the domestic environment upside down.

Technological. The technological dimension includes scientific and technological advancements in a specific industry as well as in society at large. In recent years, the most striking advances have been in the computer industry. A greeting card that plays "Happy Birthday" holds more computing power than existed in the entire world before 1950. The emerging "life sciences" industry, which brings together agriculture, biotechnology and pharmaceuticals, may soon produce grains that taste like meat and cotton that can produce its own colour. These and other technological advances can change the rules of the game; thus, every organisation must be ready to respond.

Sociocultural. The sociocultural dimension of the general environment represents the demographic characteristics as well as the norms, customs and values of the general population. Important sociocultural characteristics are geographical distribution and population density, age and education levels. Today's demographic profiles are the foundation of tomorrow's workforce and consumers.

Demography also shapes society's norms and values. Recent sociocultural trends that are affecting many companies include the trend toward no smoking, the anticholesterol and reduced fat fervor, the greater purchasing power of young children and the increased diversity of consumers, with specialized markets for groups.

Economic. The economic dimension represents the general economic health of the country or region in which the organisation operates. Consumer's purchasing power, the unemployment rate and interest rates are part of an organisation's economic environment. Because organisations today are operating in a global environment, the economic dimension has become exceedingly complex and creates even more uncertainty for mangers. The economies of countries are more closely tied together than ever before.

One significant recent trend in the economic environment is the frequency of mergers and acquisitions. The corporate economic landscape is being altered. The impact of these deals on employees can be overwhelming, creating uncertainty about future job security. The merger is just the beginning of employee uncertainty, because about half of the acquired companies are resold.

Legal-Political. The legal-political dimension includes government regulations at the local, state, central levels as well as political activities designed to influence company behaviour.

Managers must recognize a variety of pressure groups that work within the legal-political framework to influence companies to behave in socially responsible ways.

3.4 TASK ENVIRONMENT

The task environment includes those sectors that have a direct working relationship with the organisation, among them customers, competitors, suppliers and the labour market are important.

Customers. Those people and organisations in the environment who acquire goods or services from the organisation are customers. As recipients of the organisation's output, customers are important because they determine the organisation's success. Patients are the customers of hospitals, students the customers of schools and travellers the customers of airlines.

Competitors. Other organisations in the same industry or type of business that provide goods or services to the same set of customers are referred to as competitors. Each industry is characterised by specific competitive issues. The recording industry differs from the steel industry and the pharmaceutical industry. Despite the competitive wars being waged worldwide, competitors in some industries are finding that they can cooperate to achieve common goals.

Suppliers. The raw materials the organisation uses to produce its output are provided by suppliers. A steel mill requires iron ore, machines and financial resources. The relationship between manufactures and suppliers has traditionally been an adversarial one, but many companies are finding that cooperation is the key to saving money, maintaining quality and speeding products to market. Cooperation with suppliers is becoming the rule rather than the exception.

Labour Market. The labour market represents people in the environment who can be hired to work for the organisation. Every organisation needs a supply of trained, qualified personnel. Unions, employee associations and the availability of certain classes of employees can influence the organisation's labour market. Two labour market factors having an impact on organisations right now are (1) the necessary for continuous investment in human resources through recruitment, education and training to meet the competitive demands of the borderless world and (2) the effects of international trading blocks, automation and shifting plant location upon labour dislocations, creating unused labour pools in some areas and labour shortages in others.

3.5 THE ORGANISATION-ENVIRONMENT RELATIONSHIP

Why do organisations care so much about factors in the external environment? The reason is that the environment creates uncertainty for organisation managers and they must respond by designing the organisation to adapt to the environment or to influence the environment.

Environmental Uncertainty

Organisations must manage environment uncertainty to be effective. *Uncertainty* means that managers do not have sufficient information about environmental factors to understand and predict environmental needs and changes. As indicated in Figure 3.3, environmental characteristics that influence uncertainty are the number of factors that affect the organisation and the extent to which those factors change. A large multinational has thousands of factors in the external environment creating uncertainty for managers. When external factors change rapidly, the organisation experiences very high uncertainty; Firms must make efforts to adapt to these changes. When an organisation deals with only a few external factors and these factors are relatively stable, managers experience low uncertainty and can devote less attention to external issues.

Two basic strategies for coping with high environmental uncertainty are to adapt the organisation to changes in the environment and to influence the environment to make it more compatible with organisational needs.

Adapting to the Environment

If the organisation faces increased uncertainty with respect to competition, customers, suppliers or government regulation, managers can use several strategies to adapt to these changes, including increased planning and forecasting, a flexible structure and mergers or joint ventures.

The External Environment and Uncertainty

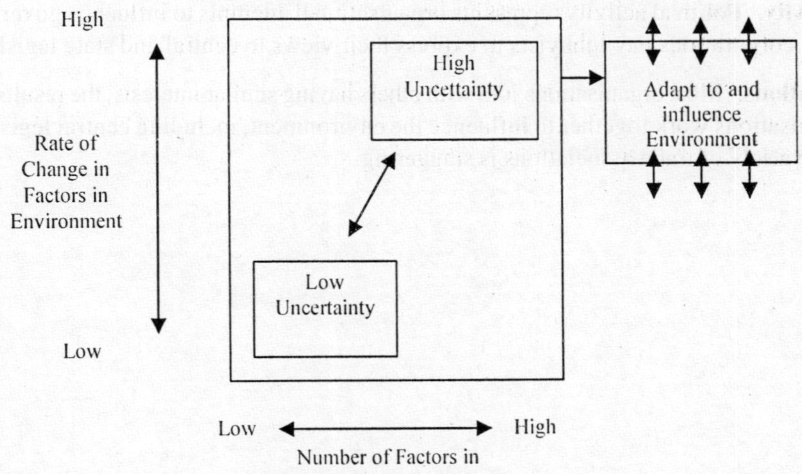

Fig. 3.3

Forecasting and Planning. Forecasting and planning for environmental changes are major activities in many corporations. Planning departments often are created when uncertainty is high. Forecasting is an effort to spot trends that enable managers to predict future events. Forecasting techniques range from quantitative economic models of environmental business activity to newspaper clipping services. Planning can soften the adverse effect of rapid shifts in the environment.

Flexible Structure. An organisation's structure should enable it to effectively respond to shifts in the environment. Research has found that a loose, flexible structure works best when organisations experience uncertainty created by shifts in the external environment or by innovation within the organisation, while a tight structure is most effective in a certain environment.

Mergers and Joint Ventures. Mergers are a major factor in a company's external environment. A merger is also a way to reduce uncertainty. A merger occurs when two or more organisations combine to become one.

A joint venture involves a strategic alliance or program by two or more organisations. This typically occurs when the project is too complex, expensive or uncertain for one firm to do alone. Today, keeping pace with rapid technological change and competing in the global environment have stretched the resources of even the richest companies. Joint ventures are on the rise. Many small businesses are turning to joint ventures with large firms or with international partners. A larger partner can provide sales staff, distribution channels, financial resources or a research staff. Small businesses seldom have the expertise to deal internationally, so a small company joins with overseas experts who are familiar with the local rules.

Influencing the Environment

The other major strategy for handling environmental uncertainty is to reach out and change those elements causing problems. Widely used techniques for changing the environment include advertising and public relations, political activity and trade association.

Advertising and Public Relations. Adverting has become a highly successful way to manage demand for a company's products. Companies spend large amounts of money to influence consumer tastes. Advertising is an important way to reduce uncertainty about customer.

Public relations is similar to advertising, except that its goal is to influence public opinion about the company itself. Most companies care a great deal about their public image.

Political Activity. Political activity represents organisational attempts to influence government legislation and regulation. Many corporations pay lobbyists to express their views to central and state legislators.

Trade Associations. Most organisations join with others having similar interests; the results is a trade association. In this way, organisations work together to influence the environment, including central legislation and regulation. The number and variety of trade associations is staggering.

Chapter 4

Social Responsibility

4.1 INTRODUCTION

Business organisations are vital organs of society catering to its ever–growing and changing needs. As business has certain expectation on society, society also has a right to expect business to behave in a responsible manner and to discharge certain social duties. The social responsibility of business is rooted in its economic role.

4.2 WHAT IS SOCIAL RESPONSIBILITY?

The concept of corporate social responsibility, is easy to understand: it means distinguishing right from wrong and doing right. It means being a good corporate citizen .The formal definition of social responsibility is management's obligation to make choices and take actions that will contribute to the welfare and interests of society as well as the organisation.

As straightforward as this definition seem, social responsibility can be a difficult concept to grasp, because different people have different beliefs as to which actions improve society's welfare. To make matters worse, social responsibility covers a range of issues, many of which are ambiguous with respect to right or wrong. For example, if a bank deposits the money from a trust fund into a low – interest account for 90 days, from which it makes a substantial profit, has it been unethical? How about two company's engaging in intense competition. Is it socially responsible for the stronger corporation to drive the weaker one into bankruptcy? These examples contain moral, legal and economic considerations that make socially responsible behaviour hard to define. A company's environmental impact must also be taken into consideration.

4.3 RESPONSIBILITY TO WHOM?

Organisational Stakeholders

One reason for the difficulty understanding social responsibility is that managers must confront the question "responsibility to whom?" Recall from Chapter 3 that the organisation's environment consists of several sectors in both the task and general environment. From a social responsibility perspective, enlightened organisations view the internal and external environment as a variety of stakeholders.

A stakeholder is any group within or outside the organisation that has a stake in the organisation's performance. Each stakeholder has a different criterion of responsiveness, because it has a different interest in the organisation.

Fig. 4.1 illustrates important stakeholders for an auto manufacturer. Investor and shareholders, employees, customers and suppliers are considered primary stakeholders, without whom the organisation cannot survive. Investors, shareholders and supplier's interests are served by managerial efficiency – that is, use of resources to achieve profits. Employees expect work satisfaction, pay and good supervision. Customers are concerned with decisions about the quality, safety and availability of goods and services. When any primary stakeholder group becomes seriously dissatisfied, the organisation's viability is threatened.

Stakeholders Relevant to an Auto Manufacture

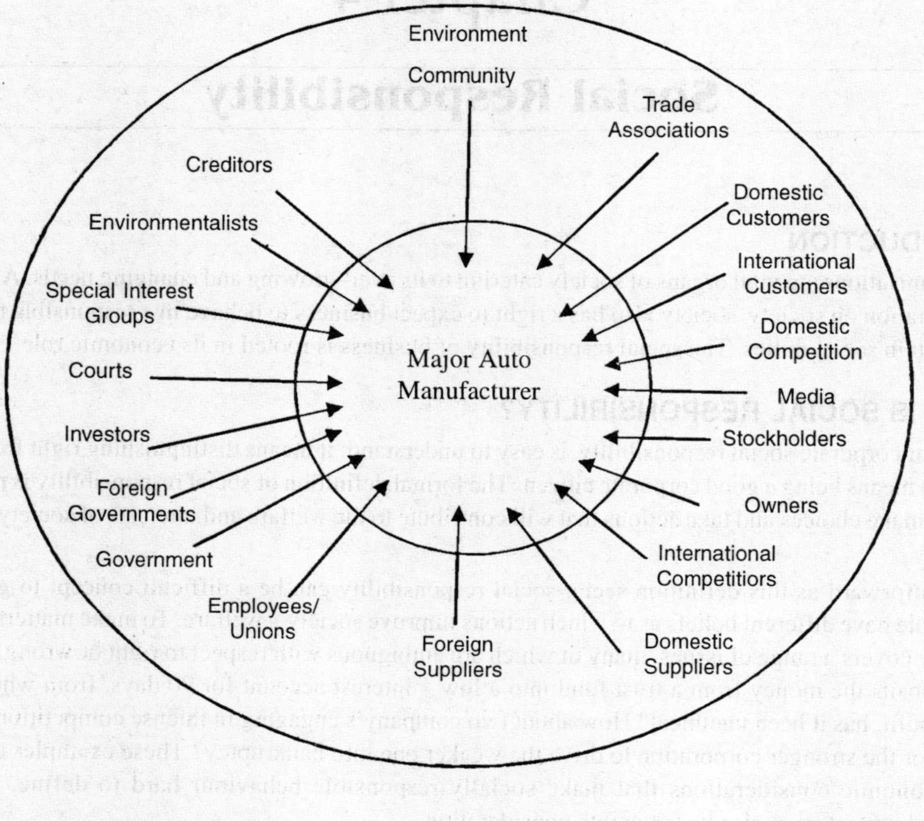

Fig. 4.1

Other important stakeholders are the government and the community. Most corporations exist only under the proper charter and licenses and operate within the limits of safety laws, environment protection requirements and other laws and regulations in the government sector. The community includes local government, the natural and physical environments and the quality of life provided for residents. Special interest groups, still another stakeholder, may include trade associations, political action committees, professional associations and consumerists. Socially responsible organisations consider the effects of their actions upon all stakeholders.

Today, special interest groups continue to be one of the largest stakeholder concerns that companies face. Environmental responsibility has become a primary issue as both business and public acknowledge the damage that has been done to our natural environment.

4.4 Evaluating Corporate Social Performance

One model for evaluating corporate social performance is presented in Fig. 4.2. The model indicates that total corporate social responsibility can be subdivided into four criteria – economic, legal, ethical and discretionary responsibilities. The responsibilities are ordered from bottom to top based on their relative magnitude and the frequency with which manager's deal with each issue.

Criteria of Corporate Social Performance

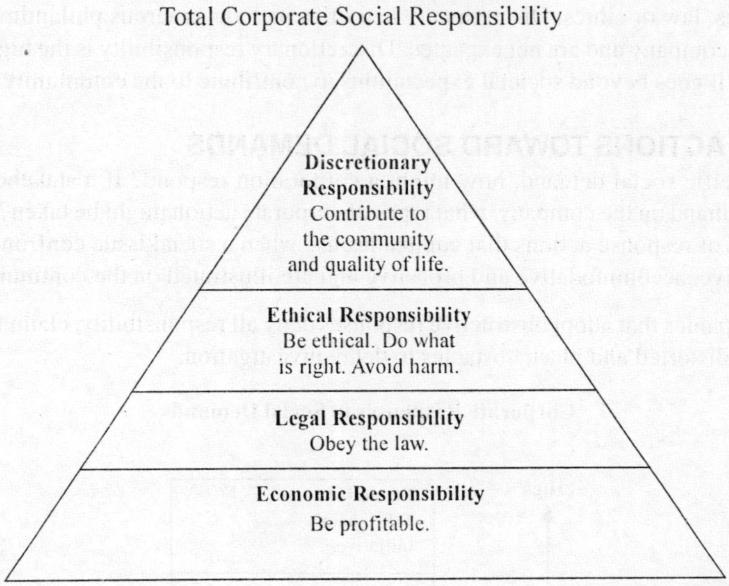

Fig. 4.2

Economic Responsibilities

The first criterion of social responsibility is economic responsibility. The business institution is, above all, the basic economic unit of society. Its responsibility is to produce the goods and services that society wants and to maximise profits for its owners and shareholders. Economic responsibility, carried to the extreme, is called the profit – maximising view, advocated by Nobel economist Milton Friedman. This view argues that the corporation should be operated on a profit – oriented basis, with its sole mission to increase its profits so long as it stays within the rules of the game.

The purely profit – maximising view is no longer considered an adequate criterion of performance. This approach means that economic gain is the only social responsibility and can lead companies into trouble.

Legal Responsibilities

All modern societies lay down ground rules, laws and regulations that businesses are expected to follow. *Legal responsibility* defines what society deems as important with respect to appropriate corporate behaviour. Businesses are expected to fulfill their economic goals within the legal framework. Legal requirements are imposed by local town councils, state legislators and central regulatory agencies.

Organisations that knowingly break the law are poor performers in this category. Intentionally manufacturing defective goods or billing a client for work not done is illegal.

Ethical Responsibilities

Ethical responsibility includes behaviours that are not necessarily codified into law and may not serve the corporation's direct economic interests. Organisation decision makers should act with equity, fairness and impartiality, respect the rights of individuals, and provide different treatment of individuals only when relevant to the organisation's goals and tasks. *Unethical* behaviour occurs when decisions enable an individual or company to gain at the expense of society.

Discretionary Responsibilities

Discretionary responsibility is purely voluntary and guided by a company's desire to make social contributions not mandated by economics, law or ethics. Discretionary activities include generous philanthropic contributions that offer no payback to the company and are not expected. Discretionary responsibility is the highest criterion of social responsibility, because it goes beyond societal expectations to contribute to the community's welfare.

4.5 CORPORATE ACTIONS TOWARD SOCIAL DEMANDS

Confronted with a specific social demand, how might a corporation respond? If a stakeholder such as the local government places a demand on the company, what types of corporate action might be taken? Management scholars have developed a scale of response actions that companies use when a social issue confronts them. These actions are obstructive, defensive, accommodative and proactive and are illustrated on the continuum in Exhibit 4.3.

Obstructive. Companies that adopt obstructive responses deny all responsibility, claim that evidence of wrong doing is misleading or distorted and place obstacles to delay investigation.

Corporate Responses to Social Demands

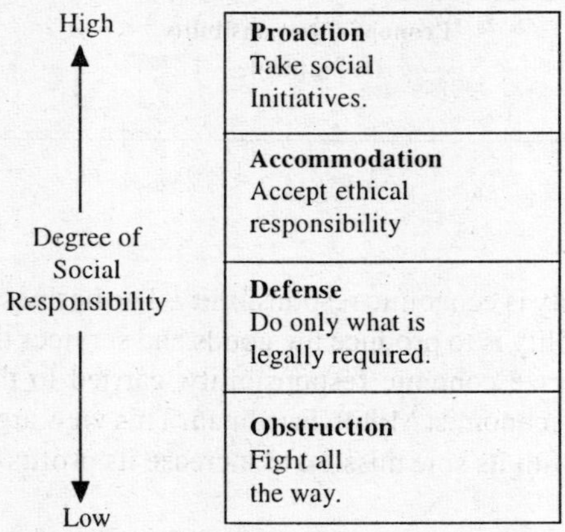

Fig. 4.3

Defensive. The defensive response means that the company admits to some errors of omission or commission. The company cuts its losses by defending itself but is not obstructive. Defensive managers generally believe that "these things happen, but they are nobody's fault".

Accommodative. An accommodative response means that the company accepts social responsibility for its actions, although it may do so in response to external pressure. Firms that adopt this action try to meet economic, legal and ethical responsibilities. If outside forces apply pressure, managers agree to curtail ethically questionable activities. Companies often will hire an ethics consultant to help them clean up their act and improve their public image.

Proactive. The proactive response means that firms take the lead in social issues. They seek to learn what is in the public interest and respond without coaxing or pressure from stakeholders. Many companies, make generous donations to universities, other charitable groups as a way of reaching out and improving society.

Obstructiveness tends to occur in firms whose actions are based solely on economic considerations. Defensive organisations are willing to work within the letter of the law. Accommodative organisations respond to ethical pressures. Proactive organisations use discretionary responsibilities to enhance community welfare.

Chapter 5

Planning

5.1 INTRODUCTION

In designing an environment for the effective performance of individual working together in groups a manager's most essential task is to see that everyone understands the group's purposes and its method of attaining them. If group effort is to be effective, people must know what they are expected to accomplish. This is the function of planning.

Planning involves selecting missions and objectives and the actions to achieve them. It requires decision making, that is, choosing from among alternative future courses of action. Plans thus provide a rational approach to pre-selected objectives. It brings the gap from where we are to where we want to go.

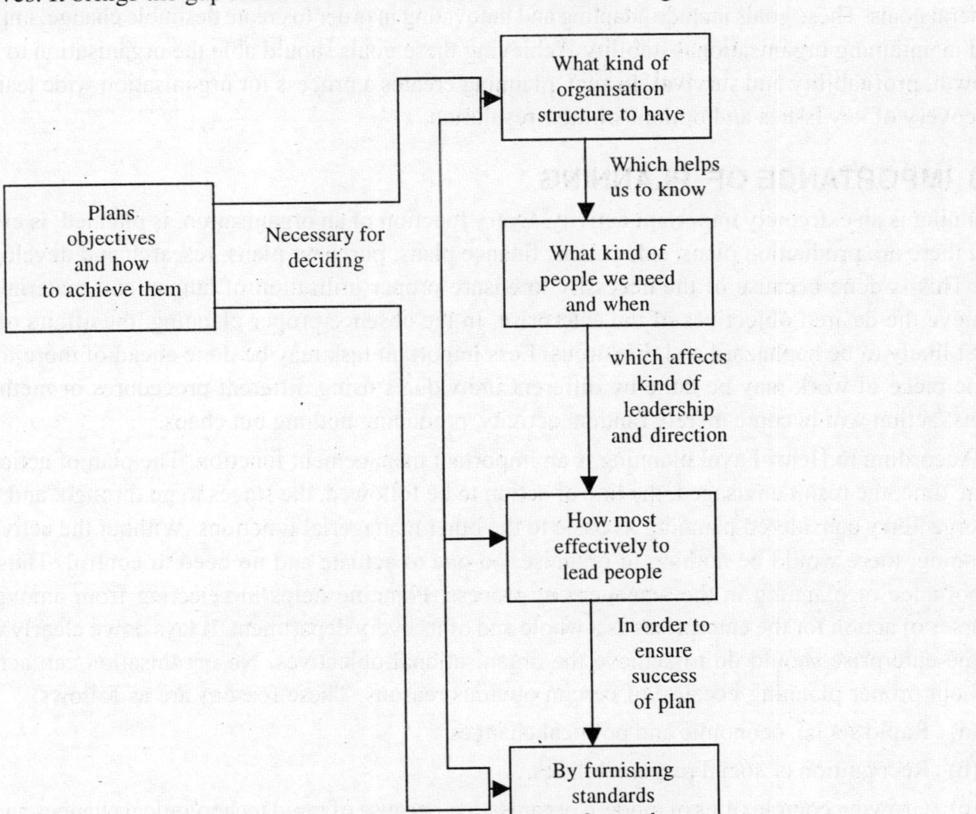

Plans As The Foundation Of Management

Fig. 5.1

5.2 DEFINITION AND NATURE OF PLANNING

Planning is the most basic managerial function. When done properly, it sets the direction for the organising, leading and controlling functions. Planning is the formal process of (1) choosing the organization's vision, missions and overall goals for both the short run and long run; (2) devising divisional, departmental and even individual goals based on organisational goals; (3) choosing strategies and tactics to achieve those goals; and (4) allocating resources (people, money, equipment and facilities) to achieve the various goals, strategies and tactics.

"Planning is the process of deciding in advance what is to be done, who is to do it, how it is to be done and when it is to be done".

Kenneth H. Killen –

"Planning is the selecting and relating of facts and the making and using of assumptions regarding the future in the visualisation and formulation of proposed activities believed necessary to achieve desired results".

G. R. Terry –

If undertaken properly, planning should assist in (1) identifying future opportunities, (2) anticipating and avoiding future problems, (3) developing courses of action (strategies and tactics) and (4) understanding the risk and uncertainties associated with various options. Thus the organisation will have a better chance of achieving its general goals. These goals include adapting and innovating in order to create desirable change, improving productivity and maintaining organisational stability. Achieving these goals should able the organisation to achieve long –term growth, profitability and survival. In sum, planning creates a process for organisation wide learning, including the discovery of key issues and options of their resolution.

5.3 IMPORTANCE OF PLANNING

Planning is an extremely important activity. Every function of an organisation, is planned, is evident from the fact that there are production plans, sales plans, finance plans, purchase plans, research and development plans and so on. This is done because of the necessity to ensure proper utilisation of human and material resources so as to achieve the desired objectives of the enterprise. In the absence proper planning, the affairs of any enterprise are most likely to be haphazard and disastrous. Less important task may be done ahead of more important one or the same piece of work may be done by different individuals using different procedures or methods. Thus, without plans, action will become merely random activity, producing nothing but chaos.

According to Henri Fayol planning is an important management function. The plan of action is, at one and the same time, the result envisaged, the line of action to be followed, the stages to go through, and the methods to use. George Terry considered planning as basic to the other managerial functions. Without the activities determined by planning, there would be nothing to organise, no one to actuate and no need to control. Thus, it emphasises the importance of planning in the management process. Planning helps in selecting from among alternative future courses of action for the enterprises as a whole and of its every department. It lays down clearly what every segment of the enterprise should do to achieve the organisational objectives. No organisation can achieve its objectives without proper planning because of certain obvious reasons. These reasons are as follows:

(a) Rapid social, economic and political changes.

(b) Recognition of social responsibilities.

(c) Growing complexities of modern organisation because of rapid technological changes and keen competition.

(d) Uncertainties caused by trade cycles.

(e) Growth of trade unionism.

(f) Lack of certain resources.

(g) Need for research and development activities.

(h) Increasing government control over business.

(i) Globalization.

These are the challenges before the mangers of modern era which can be dealt with effectively only through proper planning. Good planning is the foundation of efficient management.

5.4 PERVASIVENESS OF PLANNING

Planning is the first function of managers. It is a function which initiates subsequent functions of orgnising, staffing, directing and controlling. In fact, the other management functions may be regarded as the 'follow-up' functions to implement organisational plans. Without planning, there is little to organise, direct, control and co-ordinate. Thus the planning function and the plans of the organisation provide the nucleus around which all other functions are determined and carried out.

Another aspect of pervasiveness of planning is that, planning is a basic function of all managers, from the chief executive at the top down to the level of supervisor. The complexity and intensity of planning function differs from level to level. Even so, no manager can ignore the planning function. Highly successful organisations owe their success to a large extent to the soundness of their planning function and the importance they attach to the function. An organisation which plans well is likely to be more successful.

5.5 PHILOSOPHIES OF PLANNING

Planning in organisations is based on certain alternative philosophies or conceptual values, whether they are explicit or implicit. Russel Ackoff in his book 'Concept of Corporate Planning' identified three philosophies of planning which are outlined below:

(a) Satisficing philosophy: This is a conservative-cautions philosophy and believes in relative status quo, stability, continuity and slow change. It seeks paths of least resistance and is content with using known, tried and tested methods for planning. The approach finds virtue in setting reasonable goals which are feasible and attainable with ordinary efforts, available resources, knowledge and information. Emphasis is placed on simple, tangible and quantifiable goals so that the possibility of their being interpreted and understood in diverse ways is minimal. The satisficing approach seeks comfort in an environment which is mostly devoid of complexity and uncertainty, so that problems of adaptation are easy to tackle. Even if the environment is complex, attempts are made to make simplifying assumptions or to avoid a direct confrontation with it.

(b) Optimising philosophy: This is a philosophy wedded to logical, scientific and rational thinking for planning purpose. It is directed towards achieving the one best way of doing things so as to maximise the results. A high premium is placed on precise and perfect plans and decisions based on systematic, prior investigation, analysis and evaluation of alternative courses. Variables are sought to be quantified in this approach also, as in satisficing approach, but quantification is meant for the purpose of applying quantitative techniques to arrive at optimal solutions to problems.

(c) Adaptivising philosophy: This is a dynamic philosophy which seeks to blend rationality and reality in practice. It aims at making organisations as dynamic and adaptive entities which adjust with the changes in the environment. It recognises the complexity of the environment and the need to understand it, to cope with it and even to gain command over it. A high degree of flexibility is sought to be built into organisational planning. Organisational action is designed not merely to make adjustments but also to partly influence the environmental behaviour, through innovative and creative approaches.

5.6 APPROACHES TO PLANNING

The process of planning is changing. Traditionally, strategy and planning has been the domain of top managers. However, top managers no longer control the planning process; everyone becomes involved. In some companies, planning is being taken out of the executive boardroom an central planning department to become a part of everyday work throughout the organisation. We will first discuss traditional, top-down approaches to planning and then examine some of the newer approaches that emphasize bottom-up planning and employee involvement.

Traditional Approaches to Planning

Traditionally, corporate planning has been done entirely by top executives, by consulting firms or most commonly, by central planning departments. Central planning departments are groups of planning specialists who report directly to the CEO or president. The approach was popular during the1970s. Planning specialists were hired to gather data and develop detailed strategic plans for the corporation as a whole. This planning approach was top down because goals and plans were assigned to major divisions and departments from the planning department after approval by the president.

Although traditional approaches to planning still are popular with many companies, formal planning increasingly is being criticised as inappropriate for today's fast-paced environment. There are a number of problems with traditional, formal planning:

- Planners may be out of touch with day-to-day realities. Central planning departments often are out of touch with the constantly changing realities faced by line managers and front-line workers, who are tuned to the needs of customers.
- Formal plans may inhibit flexibility. When plans and goals are set by top executives or a central planning department, managers and workers throughout the organisation may be stuck trying to follow a plan that no longer works due to changes in the environment or other factors.
- Formal plans may limit creativity and learning. When managers and workers follow a set of strict goals and plans outlined by someone else, they have less incentive to think for themselves and come up with creative new business ideas. Motivation and enthusiasm may also suffer.

Modern Approaches to Planning

To overcome some of the problems of traditional planning, managers are trying new approaches. A more recent approach to planning is the decentralised planning staff, which evolved when planning experts were assigned to major departments and divisions to help managers develop their own strategic plans. This change helped resolve some of the conflicts between planners and staff because corporate planners were no longer writing their own strategic plans and handing them down to line managers.

Today, some companies are taking decentralised planning even farther and involving workers at every level of the organisation in the planning process. In this new paradigm, middle managers and planning staff work with line managers and front-line workers to develop dynamic plans that meet the organisation's needs. In a complex and competitive business environment, traditional planning done by a select few no longer works. Strategic thinking and execution become the exception of every employee. Planning comes alive when employees are involved in setting goals and determining the means to reach them.

5.7 STEPS IN THE PROCESS OF PLANNING

It is often difficult to specify the steps in the planning process for all organisations because of their differences in size and complexity. Never the less, it is possible to suggest some important steps for effective planning. The following steps are applicable in most types of plans –

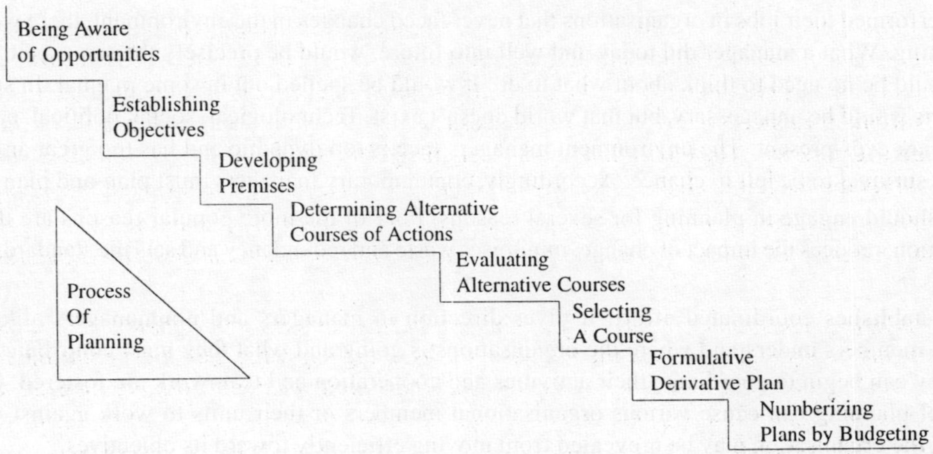

Fig. : 5.2

1. *Being Aware of Opportunities:* An awareness of opportunities in the external environment as well as within the organisation is the real starting point of planning. We should take a preliminary look at possible future opportunities and see them clearly and completely know where we should in the light of our strengths and weaknesses, understand what problems we wish to solve and why and know that we except to gain.
2. *Establishing Objectives:* In planning a major programme, the second step is to establish objectives for the entire enterprise and then for each subordinate work unit, for the long term as well as for the short range. Objectives specify the expected results and indicate the end points of what is to be done, where the primary emphasis is to be placed and what is to be accomplished by the network of strategies, policies, procedures, rules, budgets and programmes.
3. *Developing Premises:* A third logical step in planning is to establish, circulate and obtain agreement to utilise critical planning premises such as forecast, applicable basic policies and existing company plans. They are assumptions about the environment in which the plan is to be carried out.
4. *Determining Alternative Courses:* The fourth step in planning is to search for and examine alternative courses of action, especially those not immediately apparent. There is seldom a plan for which reasonable alternatives do not exist and quite often an alternative that is not obvious proves to be the best.
5. *Evaluating Alternative Courses:* Having sought out alternative courses and examined their strong and weak points, we must next evaluate them by weighing them in the light of premises and goals. Because there are so many alternative courses in most situations and there are numerous variables and limitations to be considered, evaluation can be exceedingly difficult.
6. *Selecting a Course:* This is the point at which the plan is adopted - the real point of decision making. Occasionally, an analysis and evaluation of alternative courses will disclose that two or more are advisable and the manager may decide to follow several courses rather than the one best course.
7. *Formulating Derivative Plans:* At the point, when a decision is made, planning is seldom complete and a seventh step is indicated. Derivative plans are almost invariably required to support the basic plan.
8. *Numberising plans by Budgeting:* After decisions are made and plans are set, the final step to give them meaning, is to numberise them by converting them to budgets. The overall budget of an enterprise represents the sum total of income and expenses, with resultant profit or surplus and budgets of major balance sheet items.

5.8 PLANNING IN UNCERTAIN ENVIRONMENT

If managers performed their jobs in organisations that never faced changes in the environment, there would be little need for planning. What a manager did today and well into future, would be precisely the same as it was decades ago. There would be no need to think about what to do. It would be spelled out in some manual. In such a world, planning efforts would be unnecessary, but that world doesn't exist. Technological, social, political, economic and legal changes are ever-present. The environment managers face is too dynamic and has too great an effect on an organisation's survival to be left to chance. Accordingly, contemporary managers must plan-and plan effectively.

Managers should engage in planning for several reasons. Four of the more popular reasons are that planning provides direction, reduces the impact of change, minimises waste and redundancy and sets the standards to facilitate control.

Planning establishes coordinated effort. It gives direction to managers and nonmanagers alike. When all organisational members understand where the organisations is going and what they must contribute to reach the objectives, they can begin to coordinate their activities and cooperation and teamwork are fostered. On the other hand, a lack of planning can cause various organisational members or their units to work against one another. Consequently, the organisation may be prevented from moving efficiently toward its objectives.

By forcing managers to look ahead, anticipate change, consider the impact of change and develop appropriate responses, planning reduces uncertainty. It also clarifies the consequences of the actions managers might take in response to change. Planning, then, is precisely what managers need in a chaotic environment.

Planning also reduces overlapping and wasteful activities. Coordination before the fact is likely to uncover waste and redundancy. Furthermore, when means and ends are clear, inefficiencies become obvious.

Finally, planning establishes objectives or standards that facilitate control. If organisational members are unsure of what they are attempting to achieve, how can they determine whether they have achieved it? In planning, objectives are developed. In the controlling function of management, performance is compared against the established objectives. If and when significant deviations are identified, corrective action can be taken. Without planning, then, there truly cannot be effective control.

5.9 FLEXIBILITY OF PLANS

One of the desirable characteristics of organisational plans is their flexibility. Plans should be designed in such a manner that there is built-in scope for adjusting them to meet the emerging requirements of the future, which could not have been anticipated. Flexible plans are a partial safeguard against the danger of possible losses posed by unexpected future events and changes in the behaviour of internal and external variables which have a bearing on the organisation's activities. Flexible plans remain largely relevant even in the face of unexpected future changes within certain limits. The enterprises can still maintain its broad directions and make adjustments within the basic framework of objectives, strategies and plans.

The greatest virtue of flexible plans is that they permit the enterprise to move towards its goals in the midst of environment changes. In other words, they help the enterprise to achieve a sort of dynamic equilibrium in relation to its environment. This is very much valued by many enterprises especially when they have to function in an uncertain and turbulent environment.

There are however some limit to flexibility in planning. The first limitation is that management cannot keep its options open for a long time. It has to make up its mind on a range of enterprise issues which arise in the course of implementation of plans. Though the environmental behaviour is not always conducive for such firm resolves and commitments and though the management could not be sure of correctness of such commitments, there is no escape from the obligation.

The second limitation arises out of costs of flexibility. Inflexible, firm plans are least expensive. Building flexibility in plans is akin an insurance policy to cover risk and paying premium on it regularly. If everything is normal, the premium appears to be an avoidable cost.

A third limitation is that flexibility cannot always be built into some types of plans and projects. The enterprise has no way but to make firm commitments and reconcile with the possibility of its plans going off the track.

5.10 FORECASTING

Forecasting has assumed great importance in the modern business world which is characterised by growing competition, rapidity of change in environment, fast technological changes and increased government control. For successful business operation, it is essential that all decisions are based on the careful analysis of data concerning the future course of events rather than guesses, intuition or hunches of the owner of the business. Forecasting aim at reducing the area of uncertainty that surrounds management decision-making with respect to costs, production, sales, profit, pricing etc. . If the future were known with certainty, there would have been no need of forecasting. But the future is highly uncertain and so there is a general need to have an organised system of forecasting in the organisation.

Forecasting is an essential ingredient of planning process. It was Henry Fayol, who first of all, emphasized the significance of forecasting the future for effective management.

According to Allen, " Forecasting is a systematic attempt to probe the future by influence from unknown factors."

According to John G. Glover, " Forecasting is the research procedure to discover those economic, social and financial influences governing activity so as to predict or estimate current and future trends, which may have a bearing on company policies or future financial, production and marketing operation."

5.10.1 Importance of Forecasting as an Element of Planning

The importance of forecasting is apparent from the role it plays in planning. Forecasting is an important part of effective planning. A manager who is planning is also supposed to make some forecasts about the future. A systematic attempt to probe the future by inference from known facts helps integrate all management planning so that unified overall plans can be developed into which division and departmental plans can be meshed. Forecasting helps in taking sound policy decisions which are necessary for the achievement of organisational objectives. By focusing attention on the future, forecasting assists in bringing unity of purpose in planning.

Forecasting has assumed great importance in the modern business world which is characterised by growing competition, rapidity of change in environment, fast technological changes and increased government control. For successful business operation, it is essential that all decisions are based on the careful analysis of data concerning the future course of events rather than on guesses, intuition or hunches of the owners of the business. Forecasting aims at reducing the area of uncertainty that surrounds management decision-making with respect to costs, production, sales, profits, pricing etc. If the future were known with certainty, there would have been no need of forecasting. But the future is highly uncertain and so there is a great need to have an organised system of forecasting in the organisation.

Forecasting is also necessary for efficient managerial control as it can disclose the areas where control is lacking. Forecast of sales is a must in order to control the costs of production and the productivity of personnel. Forecasting will help in anticipating the areas where there is a great need to be attentive to control the costs.

5.11 PLANNING PREMISES

While planning, a manager has to consider certain factors or assumptions just as a navigator tries to get information about the weather before sailing. The assumptions about the future are known as planning premises. In other words, premises are planning assumptions about the future setting in which planning takes place. These premises are varied and important in different degrees for different organisations under different situations. In order to make effective plans, it is essential that the planning premises are based on systematic forecasting.

Planning premises are those things or factors which materially bear on plans. Some of these factors are external to the organisation, while others are internal to it. A brief discussion of the external and internal premises is given below-

External Premises

The premises are derived from the external environment of the business. They are generally beyond the control of an organisation. The important external premises are as follows:

(a) General Business Environment – It includes the various economic, political, social and technological factors of the environment in which business operates. Government policies and controls are a part of the environment. A change in any of these factors has an important influence on the business planning. For instance, political instability, strict government controls, tough fiscal measures, etc, make it difficult to achieve the targets set at the planning stage.

(b) Product Market – The purpose of developing premises in respect of product market is determination of the kind of market available for the products and services of the organisation. It encompasses all those items which influence the demand for a product or service such as testes of consumers, increase in their standard of living, elasticity of demand, nature of competition etc.

(c) Factor Market – Every business organisation makes use of various factors of production, namely, men, materials, money, machinery etc. It is necessary to make forecasts in respect of the availability of these factors. Some of these factors are external to the organisations which are affected by its decisions. For instance, availability of materials is external to the enterprise. But the promoters of a business can provide capital to the business from their own resources.

Internal Premises

The internal premises are the factors that are internal to an organisation such as sales forecast, existing policies and programmes of the organisation, investment policies, philosophy of management etc. The other internal premises include attitudes of key executives and commitment and loyalty of the subordinates. Internal premises are generally controllable. If there is a systematic forecasting about these, the management can achieve effective planning.

5.12 USING MANAGEMENT BY OBJECTIVES TO IMPLEMENT PLANS

Management by objectives (MBO) is a method whereby managers and employees define goals for every department, project and person and use them to monitor subsequent performance. A model of the essential steps of the MBO process is presented in the next page. Four major activities must occur in order for MBO to be successful:

1. *Set goals:* This is the most difficult step in MBO. Setting goals involves employees at all levels and looks beyond day-to-day activities to answer the question "What are we trying to accomplish?" A good goal should be concrete and realistic, provide a specific target and time frame and assign responsibility. Goals may be quantitative or qualitative, depending on whether outcomes are measurable.
2. *Develop action plans:* An action plan defines the course of action needed to achieve the stated goals. Action plans are made for both individuals and departments.
3. *Review progress:* A periodic progress review is important to ensure that action plans are working. Periodic checkup allows managers and employees to see whether they are on target or whether corrective action is necessary. MBO is to achieve goals. The action plan can be changed whenever goals are not being met.

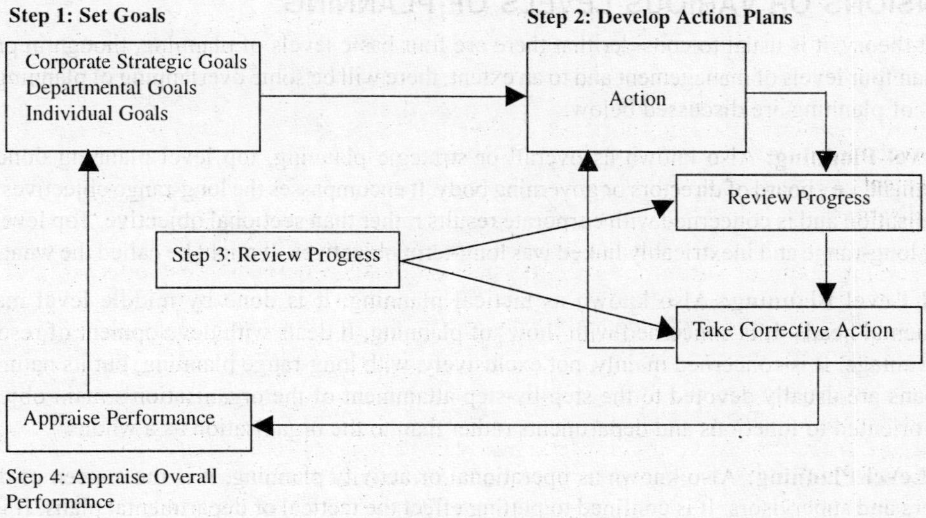

Model of the MBO Process

4. *Appraise overall performance:* The final step in MBO is to carefully evaluate whether annual goals have been achieved for both individuals and departments. Success or failure to achieve goals can become part of the performance appraisal system and the designation of salary increases and other rewards. The appraisal of departmental and overall corporate performance shapes goals for the next year. The MBO cycle repeats itself on an annual basis.

Benefits and Problems with MBO

Many companies, have adopted MBO and most managers believe the MBO is an effective management tool. Managers believe they are better oriented toward goal achievement when MBO is used. Like any system, MBO achieves benefits when used properly but results in problems when used improperly.

The benefits of the MBO process can be many. Corporate goals are more likely to be achieved when they focus manager and employee efforts. Performance is improved because employees are committed to attaining the goal, are motivated because they help decide what is expected and are free to be resourceful. Goals at lower levels are aligned with and enable the attainment of goals at top management levels.

Problems with MBO occur when the company faces rapid change. The environment and internal activities must have some stability for performance to be measured and compared against goals. When new goals must be set every few months, there is no time for action plans and appraisal to take effect. Also, poor employer-employee relations reduce effectiveness because there is an element of distrust between managers and workers. Sometimes goal "displacement" occurs if employees focus exclusively on their operational goals to the detriment of other teams or departments. Overemphasis on operational goals can harm the attainment of overall goals. Another problem arises in mechanistic organisations characterised by rigidly defined tasks and rules that may not be compatible with MBO's emphasis on mutual determination of goals by employee and supervisor. In addition, when participation is discouraged, employees will lack the training and values to jointly set goals with employers. Finally, if MBO becomes a process of filling out annual paperwork rather than energising employees to achieve goals, it becomes an empty exercise. Once the paperwork is completed, employees forget about the goals, perhaps even resenting the paperwork in the first place.

5.13 DIMENSIONS OR VARIOUS LEVELS OF PLANNING

In management theory, it is usual to consider that there are four basic levels of planning, though in practice there may be more than four levels of management and to an extent, there will be some overlapping of planning operations. The four levels of planning are discussed below:

(i) **Top Level Planning:** Also known as overall or strategic planning, top level planning done by the top management, i.e., board of directors or governing body. It encompasses the long-range objectives and policies of organisation and is concerned with corporate results rather than sectional objective. Top level planning is entirely long-range and inextricably linked was long-term objectives. It might be called the what of planning.

(ii) **Second Level Planning:** Also known as tactical planning, it is done by middle level managers and departmental heads. It is concerned with 'how' of planning. It deals with development of resources to the best advantage. It is concerned mainly, not exclusively, with long-range planning, but its nature is that the time spans are usually devoted to the step-by-step attainment of the organisation's main objectives. It is, in fact, oriented to functions and departments rather than to the organisation as a whole.

(iii) **Third Level Planning:** Also known as operational or activity planning, it is the concen of departmental managers and supervisors. It is confined to putting effect the tactical or departmental plans. It is usually for short-term and may be revised quite often to be in tune with the tactical planning.

(iv) **Corporate Planning:** Corporate planning is a recent concept which has gained popularity these days. It may be defined as a systematic and comprehensive process of long-range planning taking into account of the resources and capability of the organisation and the environment within which it has to operate and viewing the organisation as a total corporate unit.

Corporate planning is specifically strategic in nature as it takes the overall view of the organisation. Its time span is normally over a minimum period of five years and frequently extends very much longer than this. A corporate plan must be frequently updated. Most organisations review performance at least once a year, so that modifications may be made in the light of experience.

5.14 TYPES OF PLANS

Keeping in mind that a plan encompasses any course of future action, we can see that plans are varied. They are classified as – 1) Purposes or missions, 2) Objectives, 3) Strategies, 4) Policies, 5) Procedures, 6) Rules, 7) Programmes and 8) Budgets.

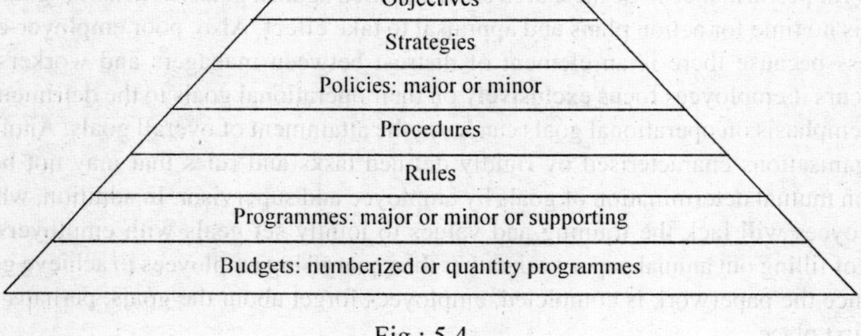

Fig.: 5.4

Purposes or Missions

Every kind of organised operation has – or at least should have, if it is to be meaningful – purposes or missions. In every social system, enterprises have a basic function or task which is assigned to them by society. The purpose of a business generally is the production and distribution of goods and services.

Objectives

Objectives or goals are the ends towards which activity is aimed. They represent not only the end point of planning but the end toward which organising, staffing, leading and controlling are aimed. The objective of a business might be to make a certain profit by providing a given line of home entertainment.

Strategies

The word 'strategies' means –

1. General programmes of action and deployment of resources to attain comprehensive objectives.
2. The determination of the basic long-term objectives of an enterprise and the adoption of courses of action and allocation of resources necessary to achieve these goals.

Thus, a strategy might include such major policies as to market directly rather than through distributors.

Policies

Policies define an area within which a decision is to be made and ensure that the decision will be consistent with and contribute to an objective.

There are many types of policies. Examples include policies to hire only university – trained engineers or to encourage employee suggestion for improved cooperation, to conform strictly to a high standard of business ethics, to set competitive prices rather than cost plus pricing.

Procedures

Procedures are plans that establish a required method of handling future activities. They are guides to achieve to action rather than to thinking and they detail the exact manner in which certain activities must be accomplished.

Let us look at an example of the relationship between procedures and policies. Company policy may grant employees vacation, procedures established to implement this policy will provide for scheduling vacations to avoid disruption of work, setting methods and rates of vacations pay, maintaining records to assure each employee of a vacation and spelling out the means for applying for a vacation.

Rules

Rules spell out specific required action or nonaction, allowing no discretion. They are usually the simplest type of plan.

A procedure might be looked upon as a sequence of rules. A rule, however, may or may not be part of a procedure. For example, 'No smoking' is a rule quite unrelated to any procedure, but a procedure governing the handling of orders may incorporate the rule that all orders must be confirmed the day they are received.

Programmes

Programmes are a complex of goals, policies, procedures, rules, task assignments, steps to be taken, resources to be employed and other elements necessary to carry out a given course of action. Programmes are ordinarily supported by budgets.

Budgets

A budget is a statement of expected results in numerical terms. It may be referred to as a 'numberised programme'. In fact, the financial operating budget is often called a "Profit Plan". It may be expressed either in financial terms or in terms of labour-hours, units of product, machine-hours, or any other numerically measurable term.

5.15 CLASSIFICATION OF PLANNING

Planning can be classified on different bases which can be shown in the following chart.

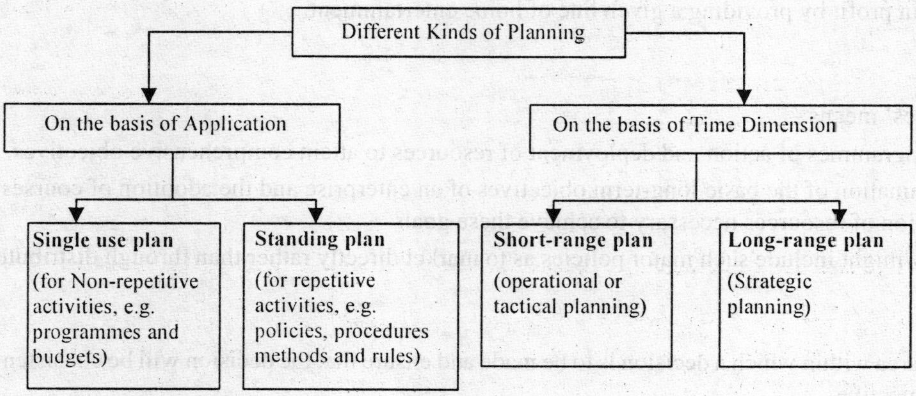

Fig. 5.5

A. On the basis of Application

(a) Single use plans: As the name suggests, single use plans are developed to achieve a specific end. When that end is reached, the plan is dissolved. The major types of single use plans are programmes and budgets.

(b) Standing plans: Standing plans are designed for situations that add often enough to justify a standardised approach.

Example: It would be inefficient for a bank to develop a single plan for processing a loan application of each new client. Instead, it uses one standing plan that anticipates in advances whether to approve or turn-down any request based on the information furnished, credit rating and the like.

The major types of standing plans are policies, procedures, methods and rules.

B. On the basis of time dimension

(a) Long range planning: Long range planning sets long-term goals for the enterprise and then proceeds to formulate specific plans for attaining these goals. It involves an attempt to anticipate, analyse and make decisions about basic problems and issues which have significance reaching well beyond the present operating horizon of the enterprise. Long-term plans are also called strategic plans.

(b) Short range planning: Short range planning is concerned with the determination of short-term activities to accomplish long-term objectives. Short-range planning relates to a relatively short period and has to be consistent with the long-range plans. Operational or tactical plans are generally related to short period.

5.16 ADVANTAGES OF PLANNING

Good and scientific planning can result in the following advantages:

1. *Focuses attention on objectives*: As planning is directed towards achieving enterprise objectives, the very act of planning focuses attention on those objectives. Writing down i.e., identification of objectives is the first step in planning.
2. *Reduces uncertainty*: Planning helps in minimising the uncertainties of future, because it involves anticipation of future events. Effective planning is the result of deliberate thinking based on facts and figures. Sufficient provision is made in the plans to offset these uncertainties.
3. *Ensure economical operation:* Planning involves a lot of mental exercises which is directed towards achieving efficient operation in the enterprises. This helps in better utilisation of resources and thus minimising costs.
4. *Improves motivation:* The effective planning system ensures participation of all managers which improves their motivation. It improves the motivation of workers also, because they know clearly what is expected of them.
5. *Improves competitive strength:* Effective planning gives a competitive edge to the enterprise over other enterprises that do not have planning or have ineffective planning. This is because planning may involve expansion of capacity, changes in the work methods, , technological changes etc.
6. *Facilitates control:* Planning facilitates the managers in performing their functions of control . Planning and control are inseparable in the sense that unplanned action cannot be controlled because control involves keeping activities on the predetermined course by rectifying deviations from plans.
7. *Encourages innovation and creativity:* Planning helps innovative and creative thinking among the managers, because many new ideas come to the mind of a manager when he is planning.
8. *Achieve better coordination:* Planning secures unity of direction towards the organisational objectives. There is an integrated effort throughout the enterprise. Thus, there will be better coordination in the organisation.

5.17 LIMITATIONS OF PLANNING

Often, planning fails to achieve the expected results. There are many reasons of failure of planning in practice. These include –

1. Due to lack of reliable facts and figures, planning loses its values. In order to make planning successful, the planner must determine the reliability of facts and figures.
2. Planning is a time consuming and costly process. They may delay action in certain cases. Again, planning involves costs of gathering and analysing information. If the management is not willing to spend on planning, the result may not be good.
3. Planning is a forward looking process. The planer must possess the required initiative. The planner should take adequate follow up measures to see that plans are understood and implemented properly.
4. Resistance to change is another important factor which puts limits on planning. Sometimes, planners themselves do not like change and on other occasions, they do not think it desirable to bring change, as it will create resistance on the part of the workers.
5. Internal inflexibility in the organisation may compel the planners to make rigid plans. This may deter the managers from taking initiative and doing innovative thinking.
6. Psychological factors also limit the scope of planning. Some people consider present as more important than future because present is less uncertain. Such persons are psychologically opposed to planning.

7. The effectiveness of planning is sometimes limited, because of external factors which are beyond the control of the planners. External stringencies are very difficult to predict. Sudden break out of war, government controls, natural hazards and many other factors are beyond the control of management.

5.18 STRATEGIES TO OVERCOME LIMITATIONS OF PLANNING

The strategies to overcome the limitations of planning are briefly discussed below:

1. Careful Premising – The planning premises constitute the frame -work within which planning is done. They are the assumptions of what is likely to happen in future. Planning always requires some assumptions to be made regarding future events. The planning premises should be set up very carefully. Due weightage be given to the relevant factors at the time of premising.
2. Management Information System – An efficient management information system should be installed so that all relevant facts and figures are made available to the managers before they perform the planning function. Availability of right type of information will help in overcoming the problems of incomplete understanding of the objectives and resistance to change on the part of the subordinates.
3. Setting Clear-cut Objectives – The statement of clear-cut objectives is necessary for efficient planning. Objectives should not only be understandable but rational also. The overall objectives of the enterprise must be the guiding pillars for determining the objectives of various departments. This would help in having coordinated planning in the enterprise.
4. Dynamic Managers – The persons concerned with the task of planning should be dynamic in outlook. They must take the required initiative to make business forecasts and develop planning premises. A manager should always keep in mind that planning is looking ahead and he is making plans for future which is highly uncertain.
5. Availability of Resources – Determination and evaluation of alternatives should be done in the light of resources available to the management. Alternatives are always present in any decision problem, but their relative plus and minus values are to be evaluated in the light of the resources available. The alternative which is chosen should not only be concerned with the objectives of the enterprise, but also capable of being accomplished with the help of the given resources.
6. Flexibility – Some element of flexibility must be introduced in the planning process, because modern business operates in an environment which keeps on changing. For achieving effective results, there should always be a scope to make necessary addition, deletion or alteration in the plans as is demanded by the circumstances.
7. Cost–benefit Analysis – The planners must undertake cost-benefit analysis, to ensure that the benefits of planning are more than the costs involved in it. This necessarily calls for establishing measurable goals, clear insight to the alternative courses of action available, premising reasonably and formulation of derivative plan, keeping in view that environment is fast changing.

5.19 PRINCIPLES OF PLANNING

The important principles of planning are discussed below:

1. *Principle of contribution to objectives* – The purpose of plans and their components is to develop and facilitate the realisation of organisational aims and objectives. Long-range plans should be interwoven with medium-range plans which, in turn, should be meshed with short-range ones in order to accomplish organisational objectives more effectively and economically.

2. *Principle of limiting factors* – Planning must take the limiting factors (manpower, money, machines, materials and management) into account by concentrating on them when developing alternative plans, strategies, policies, procedures and standards.
3. *Principle of pervasiveness of planning* – Planning is found at all levels of management. Strategic planning or long-range planning is related to top management, while intermediate and short-range planning are the concern of middle and operative management respectively.
4. *Principle of navigational change* – This principle requires that managers should periodically check on events and redraw plans to maintain a course towards a desired goal. A manager should check his plans to ensure that these are progressing as required. He should change the direction of his plans if he faces unexpected events.
5. *Principle of flexibility* – Flexibility should be built into organisational plans. Possibility of error in forecasting and decision-making and future uncertainties are the two common factors which call for flexibility in managerial planning. The principle of flexibility states the management should be able to change an existing plan because of changes in environment, without undue cost or delay, so that activities keep moving towards established goals.

5.20 ESSENTIAL REQUISITES OF AN EFFECTIVE PLAN

An effective plan is one which helps in the better management of the enterprise. In order to be effective, a plan should possess the following characteristics:

1. *A plan should be specific:* The more specific it is, the less chance there is for it to be misinterpreted. Objectives should be clearly defined. The means of carrying out the plan should also be indicated in unambiguous terms.
2. *A plan should be logical:* The more facts it is based on, the better it is. If facts are not available, reasonable assumptions must be made about the future.
3. *A plan should be complete and integrated:* A plan is said to be complete, when it is comprehensive enough to cover all actions expected from the individuals and sections of the undertaking as a whole.

   It is said to be an integrated one, when various administrative plans are so welded into one another that the whole undertaking operates at the peak of its efficiency.
4. *A plan should be flexible:* No plan is infallible nor can it cover all possible contingencies. Conditions under which a plan will be most effective change as do the variables and factors on which the plan is formulated. Therefore, it is essential to introduce some flexibility in every plan.
5. *A plan should be capable of being controlled:* Effective planning of business activities depends upon the ability to foresee with almost accuracy the nature and requirements of future events relating to industry in general and the business undertaking in particular. Therefore, the plan must distinguish between controllable and uncontrollable future environment for better administrative control.

5.21 PLANNING AND CONTROLLING

Planning and controlling are inseparable – the siamese twins of management. Any attempt to control without plans is meaningless, since there is no way for people to tell whether they are going where they want to go unless they first know where they want to go. Plans thus furnish the standards of control.

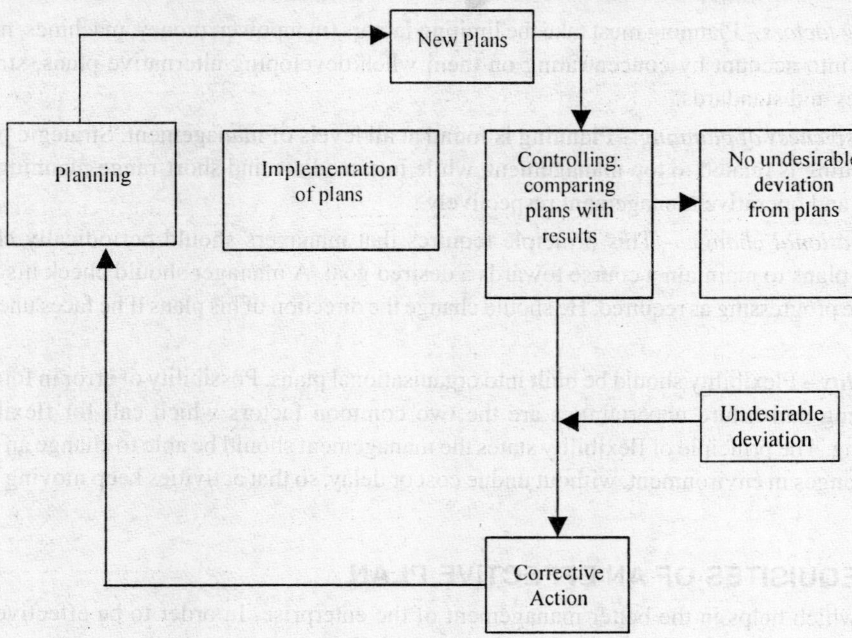

Close Relationship of Planning And Controlling

Fig. 5.6

Chapter 6

Business Policy and Strategy

6.1 DEFINITION AND IMPORTANCE OF STRATEGY

The concept of corporate strategy is analogous to that of the war. Strategy in an area of management is concerned with the general direction and long-time policy of the business as distinct from short-time policy of the business and may be defined as its long term objectives and the general means by which it intends to achieve them.

Strategic decisions are, by definition, of such importance they affect the future of the organisation as a whole. Yet they may be primarily concerned with particular dimensions or aspects of the business. For example, the post-war decision of U.K.'s Marks and Spencer to enter food retailing was concerned with their product range. Their second major initiative-opening a store in Paris-was concerned with their geographical market. Such decisions about products and markets are of paramount importance to business firms.

In business firms, strategic decisions are concerned with such critical issues as breadth of product line, geographical scope, industry position, extent of vertical integration and orientation towards growth. Strategic writers, treats strategy as almost exclusively concerned with the relationship between the firm and its environment and hence, with the selection of the products it produces and the market in which it sells those products. Thus by strategic decision making, top management determines the position of the firm relative to its environment.

In a competitive industry, a particular firm formulates its basic strategy to position itself relative to the market and competitors. The importance of strategic choices is clear. Good strategy will provide an opportunity for survival and growth. Poor strategy will doom a firm to decline, deterioration and eventual death.

So, strategy is the pattern of decisions in an organisation that determines and reveals its objectives, purposes or goals, products and principal policies and plans for achieving those goals and defines the range of business the company is to pursue, the kind of economic and human organisation it is, or intends to be, and the nature of the economic and non-economic contribution it intends to make to its shareholders, employees, customers and communities.

6.2 PURPOSE OF STRATEGY

Within the overall strategy of an organisation, executives define an explicit strategy, which is the plan of action that describes resource allocation and activities for dealing with the environment and attaining the organisation's goals. The essence of strategy is choosing to perform different activities or to execute activities differently than competitors do. Strategy necessarily changes over time to fit environment conditions, but to remain competitive. Companies develop strategies that focus on core competencies, develop synergy and create value for customers.

Core Competence. A company's core competence is something the organisation does especially well in comparison to its competitors. A core competence represents a competitive advantage because the company acquires expertise that competitors do not have. A core competence may be in the area of superior research and development, mastery of a technology, manufacturing efficiency or customer service.

Synergy. When organisational parts interact to produce a joint effect that is greater than the sum of the parts acting alone, synergy occurs. The organisation may attain a special advantage with respect to cost, market power, technology or management skill. When properly managed, synergy can create additional value with existing resources, providing a big boost to the bottom line.

Value Creation. Exploiting core competencies and attaining synergy help companies create value for their customers. Value can be defined as the combination of benefits received and costs paid by the customer. A product that is low in cost but does not provide benefits is not a good value. Delivering value to the customer should be at the heart of strategy. Managers need to understand which parts of the company's operation create value and which do not. A company can be profitable only when the value it creates is greater than the cost of resources. When a company does not accurately appraise its value-creating potential, it may become complacent.

6.3 LEVELS OF STRATEGY

Another aspect of strategic management concerns the organisational level to which strategic issues apply. Strategic managers normally think in terms of three levels of strategy-corporate, business and functional-as illustrated in Fig 6.1.

Corporate-Level Strategy. The question *What business are we in?* concerns corporate-level strategy. Corporate-level strategy pertains to the organisation as a whole and the combination of business units and product lines that make up the corporate entity. Strategic actions at this level usually relate to the acquisition of new business; additions or divestments of business units, plants or product line; and joint ventures with other corporations in new areas. An example of corporate-level strategy was when the Netherlands-based Philips Electronics sold more than 20 business units, ranging from cable operations to car navigation systems, in order to focus on the core businesses of consumer electronics and semiconductors. Selling off other business units was part of new chairman and president Cor Boonstra's strategy to cut costs, refocus the company and engineer a turnaround at Europe's largest consumer electronics manufacturer.

Business-Level Strategy. The question *How do we compete?* concerns business-level strategy. Business-level strategy pertains to each business unit or product line. It focuses on how the business unit competes within its industry for customers. Strategy decisions at the business level concern amount of advertising, direction and extent of research and development, product changes, new-product development, equipment and facilities and expansion or contraction of product lines.

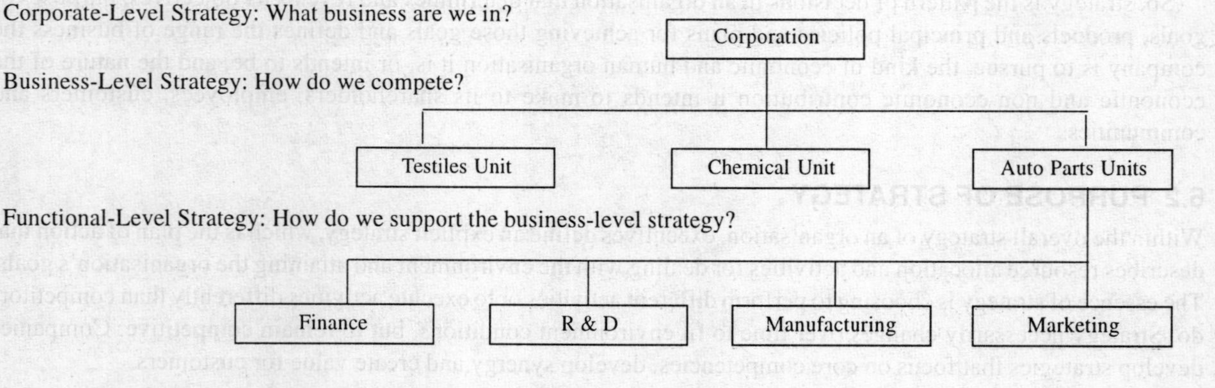

Fig. 6.1: Three Levels of Strategy in Organisations

Functional-Level Strategy. The question *How do we support the business-level competitive strategy?* concerns functional-level strategy. It pertains to the major functional departments within the business unit. Functional strategies involve all of the major functions, including finance, research and development, marketing and manufacturing.

6.4 STRATEGY FORMULATION VERSUS IMPLEMENTATION

The final aspect of strategic management involves the stages of formulation and implementation. Strategy formulation includes the planning and decision making that lead to the establishment of the firm's goals and the development of a specific strategic plan. Strategy formulation may include assessing the external environment and internal problems and integrating the results into goals and strategy. This is in contrast to strategy implementation, which is the use of managerial and organisational tools to direct resources toward accomplishing strategic results. Strategy implementation is the administration and execution of the strategic plan. Managers may use persuasion, new equipment, changes in organisation structure or a reward system to ensure that employees and resources are used to make formulated strategy a reality.

Strategy Formulation

According to R.W. Griffin, strategy formulation is the set of processes involved in creating or determining an organisation's strategy. This set of processes consists of the following four steps:

1. **Strategic goals:** The first step in formulating strategy is to set strategic goals for the organisation. Such goals are broadest goals established at the organisational level and serve to guide the overall fortunes of the organisation. The organisation may also have various strategic goals and these goals might change over time.
2. **Environmental analysis:** In the next stage, the organisation conducts what Michael E. Porter calls an environmental analysis. This analysis involves looking very closely and carefully at the task environment in order to ascertain the primary opportunities available to the organisation as well as its major threats. Porter's approach to environment analysis or his framework of analysis identifies the following five competitive forces:
   - (i) **Threat of New Entrants:** This refers to the extent to which new competitors can easily enter a particular market or market segment. For example, it is fairly easy to enter the fast food market. But it is very costly and at the same time, extremely difficult to join the automobile industry, due to huge capital requirement in plant, equipment, materials and distribution systems.
   - (ii) **Jockeying among Contestants:** This new term is used to refer to the competitive relationship between dominant firms in the industry. In oligopolistic industries like fast food or soft drinks firms often engage in intensive price wars, competitive advertising and new product introduction.
   - (iii) **Threat of Substitute Products:** This refers to the extent to which alternative products or services may supplement or reduce the need for existing or even well-established products or services. Microcomputers, for examples, eliminate the need for typewriters, large mainframe computers and even calculators.
   - (iv) **Power of Buyers:** This refers to the extent to which buyers of the products or services in an industry have the ability to influence the suppliers. In case of high value items like aircraft, such as American Airlines, United Airlines or KLM or JAL have considerable influence over the price they are willing to pay, the delivery date of the order and so forth.
   - (v) **Power of Suppliers:** This indicates the extent to which suppliers have the ability to influence potential buyers. Large oligopolistic firms can exert some influence over their buyers.
3. **Organisational Analysis:** This phase of strategy formulation involves a detailed diagnosis of the strengths and weaknesses of the organisation. According to H.W. Henry, this analysis has to be as detailed and thorough as possible and should include at least the following six areas of an organisation:
   - (i) Human resources (quality and quantity of appropriate managerial personnel, etc.)
   - (ii) Physical resources (plant and equipment, office space, etc.)
   - (iii) Financial resources (cash, assets, lines of credit, debt, etc.)

(iv) Information resources (quality and quantity of available information about competitors, etc.)

(v) Market position (market share, strength of product line, etc.)

(vi) Research and development efforts (quality and quantity breakthrough expected form R&D efforts, etc.)

While a major portion of such information is readily available from an organisation management information system as a matter of routine, other types of information can be obtained specifically for the strategy-formulation process. No doubt, efforts needed to gather the necessary data will be a good investment.

4. **Matching Organisations and Environment:** After establishing strategic goals and completing environmental and organisational analysis, the organisation moves to the final stage of strategy formulation. In this step, it has to match the strengths and weaknesses of the organisation with the corresponding opportunities presented and threats posed by the external environment. Fig 6.2 shows how an organisation matches itself with its environment opportunities and threats.

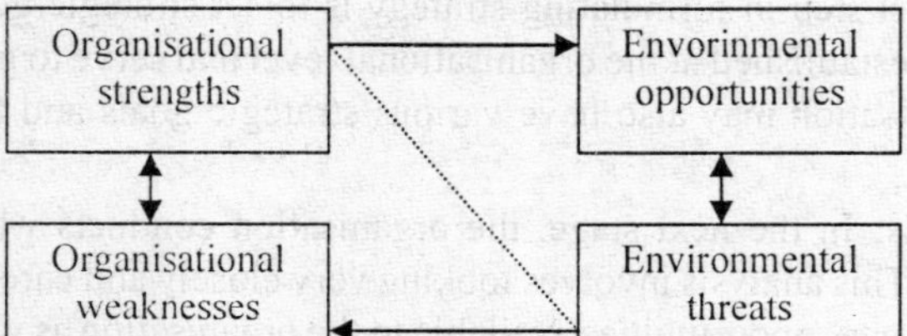

Fig 6.2 : Matching Organisations and Environment

The framework presented in Fig 6.2 suggests several specific relationships of considerable interest to managers and strategists. Prima facie, organisational strengths and weaknesses and environmental opportunities and threats are usually interrelated.

Secondly, organisational strengths should generally be targeted toward environmental opportunities.

Thirdly, the organisation should recognise that its weaknesses are particularly valuable to environmental threats.

Finally, to the extent possible, the firm might also use its strengths to offset environmental threats, at least partly. This action uses an organisational strength (say, surplus funds) to constrain an environmental threat (strong power of suppliers).

Strategy Implementation

After strategy is formulated, it must be implemented. These two processes are no doubt different but interrelated because both are inherent (and distinct) parts of strategic planning. There are four major components of strategy implementation, which are summarised in Fig 6.3.

(i) **Understanding the place of planning in the organisation:** First there is the need on the part of the organisation to recognise the importance of planning both an on-going activity and an organisational subsystem. It has to be borne in mind that planning is not a stable, cross-sectional process, but a dynamic, continuous activity that pervades all part of the organisation.

(ii) **Action Planning:** In the next stage, there is need for action planning. It is the commitment to strategic planning. It represents short-term, day-to-day plans necessary to execute the strategic plans of the organisation. Tactical plans, single-use plans and standing plans are all examples of action plans.

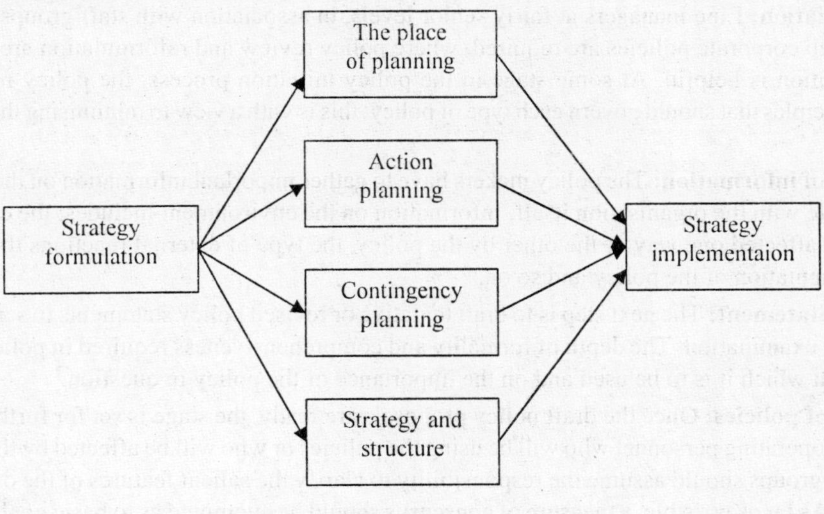

Fig 6.3 : Strategy Implementation

(iii) **Contingency Planning:** In reality, plans do not always work out as intended. Contingency planning is necessary to overcome any disruptions that occur to planning premises due to external (environmental) changes. Since planning premises guide the original strategy in case of unexpected changes there is need for a change in the current strategy or the adoption of a completely new strategy. The essence of contingency planning is anticipating possible changes and developing responses to them.

(iv) **Strategy and Structure:** The last element of strategy implementation is the recognition of the link that exists between that strategy and the structure of the organisation. This is a major aspect of the discussion of organisational design process in a later chapter.

6.5 CORPORATE POLICIES

Corporate policies are official statements of corporate intents and aims over a broad front of its activities. They are specific and practical guidelines formulated at the top management level to serve as criteria, constraints and directions for managerial decision-making and action. Policies are regarded as operative or real goals which the true character of the organization.

Policies may be classified as major or minor. In relative terms, major policy decisions include those which have a direct and substantial bearing on the survival and growth of the enterprise. In formulating corporate policy, the Board of Directors has to take into account the approach and philosophy that would guide their thinking and the realities of the environment in which the enterprise has to function. The process of formulating major policies is the process of matching the business philosophy of the enterprise with the realities of the social, economic, legal and cultural environment.

Within the framework of corporate policy, the functional departments have to formulate policies in relation to their respective functions. These policies have to be based on the premises provided by the overall corporate policies. The purpose of these minor policies is to guide the lower levels of management and the operative levels in making decisions.

Policy formulation: The approach to over-all policy formulation and control involves the following major steps:

Step 1. Policy initiation: Line managers at fairly senior levels, in association with staff groups determine the areas corporate and sub corporate policies are required, where policy review and reformulation are called for and where policy clarification is helpful. At some stage in the policy initiation process, the policy makers have to establish the basic principles that should govern each type of policy; this is with a view to minimising the opportunistic nature of policies.

Step 2. Collection of information: The policy makers have to gather important information on the environment. This might be available with the organisation itself. Information on the environment includes: the external groups which are likely to be affected one way or the other by the policy, the type of external reactions that are likely to arise from the implementation of the policy and so on.

Step 3. Tentative Statement: The next step is to draft tentative or revised policy statements to serve as basic for further discussion and examination. The depth of formality and comprehensiveness required in policy formulation depends on the level at which it is to be used and on the importance of the policy in question.

Step 4. Approval of policies: Once the draft policy proposals are ready, the stage is set for further meaningful deliberations with the operating personnel who will be using the policies or who will be affected by them. Managers at senior level or staff groups should assume the responsibility to clarify the salient features of the drafts proposals and clear any doubts. As far as possible, a measure of consensus should be attempted as to basic goals and premises of the policies. It may sometimes be necessary to combine elements from the alternative sets of policy proposals to design a new alternative.

Step 5. Releasing and interpreting policies: The proper mode of releasing the policies and the timing of their release should be determined by the policy makers. Written policies could be circulated formally and explained informally to all the concerned people. Interpretation of policies is to be done against the backdrop of enterprise goals, objectives and strategies, so as to enable the executives who use them to develop a systems perspective.

6.6 DIFFERENCE BETWEEN POLICY AND STRATEGY

Policies are general statements or understandings which guide our thinking in decision making. They ensure that decisions fall within certain boundaries. They usually do not require action but are intended to guide managers in their commitment to the decisions they ultimately make.

The essence of policy is discretion. Strategy, on the other hand, concerns the direction in which human and material resources will be applied in order to increase the chance of achieving selected objectives.

Certain major policies and strategies may be essentially the same. A policy to develop only those new products that fit into a company's marketing plan, or one to distribute only through retailers, may be an essential element of a company's strategy for new product development or marketing. One company may have a policy of growth through acquisition of other companies, while another may have a policy of growing only by expanding present markets and products. While these are policies, they are also essential elements of major strategies. Perhaps one way to draw a meaningful distinction is to say that policies will guide our thinking in decision making-if a decision is to be made-while strategies imply that an enterprise has made the decision to commit resources in a given direction.

6.7 MAJOR KINDS OF STRATEGIES AND POLICIES

For a business enterprise (and with some modification, for other kinds of organisations as well), the major strategies and policies that give an overall direction to operations are likely to be in the following areas:

Growth

Growth strategies give answers to such questions as how much growth should occur and how fast, where and how it should occur.

Finance

Every business enterprise and for that matter, any nonbusiness enterprises must have a clear strategy for financing its operations. There are various ways of doing this and usually many serious limitations.

Organisation

Organisational strategy has to do with the type of organisational pattern an enterprise will use. It answers such practical questions as how centralised or decentralised decision-making authority should be, what kinds of departmental patterns are most suitable and how to design staff positions. Naturally, organisation structures furnish the system of roles and role relationships that help people to accomplish objectives.

Personnel

There can be many major strategies in the area of human resources and relationships. They deal with such topics as union relations, compensation, selection, hiring, training and appraisal, as well as with special areas such as job enrichment.

Public Relations

Strategies in this area can hardly be independent but must support other major strategies and efforts. They must also be designed in the light of the company's type of business, its closeness to the public and its susceptibility to regulation by government agencies. To develop strategies in any area, we must ask the right questions. While no set of strategies can be formulated that will fit all organisations and situations, certain key questions will help any company to discover what its strategies should be.

Products or Services

A business exists to furnish products or services. In a very real sense, profits are merely a measure-although an important one-of how well a company serves its customers.New products or services, more than any other single factor, determine what an enterprise is or will be.

Marketing

Marketing strategies are designed to guide managers in getting products or services to customers and encouraging customers to buy. Marketing strategies are closely related to product strategies; they must be interrelated and mutually supportive. As a matter of fact, Peter Drucker regards the two basic business functions as innovation (for example, the creation of new goods or services) and marketing. A business can scarcely survive without at least one of these functions and preferably both.

6.8 EFFECTIVE IMPLEMENTATION OF STRATEGIES

It is one thing to develop clear and meaningful strategies. It is another matter and one of very great practical importance, to implement strategies effectively. If strategic planning is to be successful, we must take certain steps to implement it. Following are eight recommendations that should be considered by managers who wish to put their strategies to work.

1. ***Communication of strategies to all key decision-making managers.*** It does little good to formulate meaningful strategies unless we communicate them to all those managers who are in a position to make decisions on programs and plans designed to implement them. Nothing has been communicated unless it is clear to the receiver.
2. ***Developing and communicating planning premises.*** Managers must develop premises critical to plans and decisions, explain them to all those in the decision-making chain and give instructions to develop programs and make decisions in line with them.

3. ***Action plans contributing to and reflecting major objectives and strategies.*** Action plans are tactical or operational programs and decisions, major or minor that takes place in various parts to an organisation. If they do not reflect desired objectives and strategies, the result will be vague hopes or useless intentions. If care is not taken in this area, strategic planning is not likely to have a bottom-line impact, that is, to have an important effect on company profits.
4. ***Regular review of strategies.*** Even carefully developed strategies may cease to be suitable if conditions change. Therefore, they should be reviewed from time to time, certainly not less than once a year for major strategies and perhaps more often.
5. ***Development of contingency strategies and programes.*** Where considerable change in competitive factors or other elements in the environment may occur, strategies for such contingencies should be formulated. No one, of course, can wait to make plans until a future is certain. But even then, one need not be totally unprepared if certain possible contingencies do occur. Contingency plans can give us this degree of preparation.
6. ***Making organisation structure fit planning needs.*** The organisation structure with its system of delegations should be designed to help managers accomplish goals and make the decisions necessary to put plans into effect. If possible, one person should be responsible for the accomplishment of each goal and for implementing strategies to achieve this goal.
7. ***Continuing emphasis on planning and implementing strategy.*** Even where may have a workable system of objectives and strategies and their implementation, it can easily fail unless responsible managers continue to stress the nature and importance of these elements. This process may seem tedious and unnecessarily repetitious, but it is the best way to make sure that members of an organisation learn about them.
8. ***Creating a company climate that forces planning.*** People tend to allow problems and crises that arise today to interfere with effective planning for tomorrow. The only way to ensure that planning of all kinds will be done is to develop strategies carefully and to take pains to implement them.

6.9 STRATEGIC PLANNING

Meaning of Strategic Planning

Strategic planning is defined as "the process of determining the major objectives of an organisation and then adopting the courses of action and allocating the resources necessary to achieve those objectives". It is the process that includes "a set of interactive and overlapping decisions leading to the development of an effective strategy for a firm. According to W.F. Glueck and N.L. Sunder, the process includes the following:

i. The determination of the firm's mission.
ii. The selection of goals or objectives the firm wishes to pursue;
iii. The formulation of opportunities and threats arising out of the firm's external environment;
iv. An assessment of the internal strengths and weaknesses of the firm;
v. The identification of feasible strategic alternatives available to the firm;
vi. The choice of an alternative (s) the firm wishes to pursue;
vii. The development of an operational plan to facilitate achievement of the firm's objectives;
viii. The design of a control or feedback system to monitor the firm's performance while the strategic plan is being implemented.

Advantages Of Strategic Planning:

Managers undertake strategic planning for a number of reasons:

(i) First, there is a feeling among most managers that strategic planning will increase organisational effectiveness.

(ii) Secondly, the strategic planning process itself promotes feelings of accomplishment and satisfaction. As managers and planners work together to formulate strategy and implementation plan, they develop confidence in their situation. This may be a source of gratification and satisfaction for managers.

(iii) Thirdly, strategic planning facilitates adaptation to change.

(iv) Fourthly, strategic planning is a process through which the efforts of divisions, functions and individuals can be co-ordinated.

(v) Fifthly, when there is a major change or reorganisation in top management strategic planning can help to educate the new top management team about the internal and external opportunities and constraints the team members face.

(vi) Finally, when the performance of an organisation is not quite satisfactory, strategic planning may be undertaken to identify the problems and solutions.

Strategic Planning vs. Tactical Planning

The end result of strategic planning is "to provide the organisation with an overall context for the development of more specific plans, policies, forecasts and budgets." Strategic planning focuses upon what the organisation will achieve if all key managerial functions be carried out with a view to accomplishing organisational goals. But, tactical planning is concerned with current and future activities, focusing upon the effective allocation of resources to assure their implementation. Just as wars in general are guided by strategic planning, a single battle may be won (or lost) due to tactical planning.

Although the two types of planning are different, there is need to integrate the two into one over-all system with a view to accomplishing organisational objectives. The development of tactics is largely based on strategic plans. Recent studies have revealed that by reviewing and adjusting plans annually, decision makers can keep both strategic and tactical plans sufficiently flexible, thus permitting their adjustment to changing environmental factors while maintaining their focus upon organisational objectives.

Steps in the Strategic Planning Process

Strategic planning involves not only the development of organisational objectives but also specifications for how they will be accomplished. The development of strategic plans forces managers to broaden their concern from an exclusive focus on short-range matters to a detailed examination of various broad organisational issues. Various steps are involved in the strategic planning process. The process of strategic planning is presented as a sequence of eight core tasks, which are summarised as below:

Task 1: Develop Mission And Goals

As indicated previously, organisational mission and goals are developed by answering questions such as: What business are we in? What are we committed to? and What results do we want to achieve? General goals provide broad direction for decision making and may not change from year to year. The mission and goals are not developed in isolation. They are influenced by diagnosis of environmental threats and opportunities and diagnosis of the organisation's strengths and weaknesses.

Task 2: Assess Threats And Opportunities

Strategic planning helps managers identify the threats and opportunities and to take them into account in developing the organisation's mission, goals, plans and strategies. Political forces and stakeholders within and outside the organisation play a key role in determining the organisation's mission and goals, as well as exerting pressures for changing them. Top managers negotiate with powerful stakeholders (boards of directors, banks, governments, major customers and suppliers) in an attempt to influence those forces. To be effective, strategic planning must include a careful diagnosis of these forces.

Task 3: Assess Strengths And Weaknesses

The assessment of internal strengths and weaknesses enables managers to identify an organisation's core competencies and to determine which need to be improved. This assessment covers factors such as the organisation's relative competitive position, ability to adapt and innovate, human resources skills, technological capabilities, financial resources, managerial depth and the values and background of its key employees. Core organisational competencies represent strengths, as do the individual's managerial competencies. Most individuals find that assessing their strengths is easier than assessing their weaknesses. The same is true for organisations when assessing their strengths and weaknesses.

Task 4: Formulate Strategies

The assessment process and development of organisational goals are closely linked to formulating organisational strategies. Potential strategies, in turn, must be evaluated in terms of (1) environmental forces, (2) the organisation's strengths and weaknesses and (3) the likelihood that the strategies will help the organisation achieve its mission and goals.

Task 5: Develop A Strategic Plan

After formulating alternative strategies and selecting among them, management is ready to develop a strategic plan. The plan should contain (1) a statement of organisational mission and goals; (2) strategies for obtaining and utilising the necessary technological, marketing, financial and human resources to achieve those goals; (3) strategies for manufacturing processes and conducting R&D; and (4) strategies for developing and utilising organisational and employee competencies. The strategic plan may also include a summary of the diagnosis of external opportunities and threats and internal strengths and weaknesses.

Task 6: Develop Tactical Plans

The purpose of tactical plans is to help implement strategic plans. Middle and first-line managers and employee teams normally base tactical plans on the organization's strategic plan.

Task 7: Control And Assess Results

Strategic and tactical planning must be accompanied by controls to ensure implementation of the plans and evaluation of their results. If the plans haven't produced the desired results, managers and teams may need to change the controls, mission, goals or strategies or the plans themselves. The lack of planning can lead to extinction by instinct and poor, drawn-out planning can lead to paralysis by analysis. A thorough assessment of the results of planning should reveal whether either of these conditions exists.

Task 8: Repeat The Planning Process

The forces that affect organisations are constantly changing. Sometimes these changes are gradual and foreseeable. At other times they are abrupt and unpredictable. Whatever the nature of change, managers and other employees need to be ready to adapt or innovate by repeating the planning process. Hence planning is an ongoing process – it is always a means, never an end in itself.

6.10 STRATEGIC MANAGEMENT

Strategic management is the set of decisions and actions used to formulate and implement strategies that will provide a competitively superior fit between the organisation and its environment so as to achieve organisational goals. Managers ask questions such as "What changes and trends are occurring in the competitive environment? Who are our customers? What products or services should we offer? How can we offer those products and services most efficiently?" Answers to these questions help managers make choices about how to position their organisation in the environment with respect to rival companies. Superior organisational performance is not a matter of luck. It is determined by the choices managers make. Top executives use strategic management to define an overall direction for the organisation, which is the firm's grand strategy.

Grand Strategy

Grand strategy is the general plan of major action by which a firm intends to achieve its long-term goals. Grand strategies fall into three general categories: growth, stability and retrenchment. A separate grand strategy can also be defined for global operations.

Growth: Growth can be promoted internally by investing in expansion or externally by acquiring additional business divisions. Internal growth can include development of new or changed products or expansion of current products into new markets. External growth typically involves diversification, which means the acquisition of businesses that are related to current product lines or that take the corporation into new areas.

Stability: Stability, sometimes called a pause strategy, means that the organisation wants to remain the same size or grow slowly and in a controlled fashion. After organisations have undergone a turbulent period of rapid growth, executives often focus on a stability strategy to integrate strategic business units and ensure that the organisation is working efficiently.

Retrenchment: Retrenchment means that the organisation goes through a period of forced decline by either shrinking current business units or selling off or liquidating entire businesses. The organisation may have experienced a precipitous drop in demand for its products or services, prompting managers to order across-the-board cuts in personnel and expenditures.

Global Strategy

In addition to the three preceding alternatives – growth, stability and retrenchment – companies may pursue a separate grand strategy as the focus of global business. In today's global corporations, senior executives try to formulate coherent strategies to provide synergy among worldwide operations for the purpose of fulfilling common goals. A systematic strategic planning process for deciding on the appropriate strategic alternative should be used. The grand strategy of growth is a major motivation for both small and large businesses going international.

In the international arena, companies face a strategic dilemma between global integration and national responsiveness. Organisations must decide whether they want each global affiliate to act autonomously or whether activities should be standardised and centralised across countries. This choice leads manager to select a basic grand strategy alternative such as globalisation versus multidomestic strategy. Some corporations may seek to achieve both global integration and national responsiveness by using a transnational strategy.

Globalisation: When an organisation chooses a strategy of globalization, it means that its product design and advertising strategies are standardised throughout the world. This approach is based on the assumption that a single global market exists for most consumer and industrial products. The theory is that people everywhere want to buy the same products and live the same way. People everywhere want to drink Coca-Cola and wear Levi blue jeans.

Globalisation enables marketing department alone to save cost. For example, Colgate-Palmolive Company sells Colgate toothpaste in more than 40 countries. For every country where the same commercial runs, it saves $1 million to $2 million in production costs alone. More millions have been saved by standardising the look and packaging of brands.

Multidomestic Strategy: When an organisation chooses a multidomestic strategy, it means that competition in each country is handled independently of industry competition in other countries. Thus, a multinational company is present in many countries, but it encourages marketing, advertising and product design to be modified and adapted to the specific needs of each country. Many companies reject the idea of a single global market. Parker Pen launched a single international ad campaign and reduced pen styles from 500 to 100, causing a strategic disaster. New pens and advertising campaigns have now been developed for each market.

Transnational Strategy: A transnational strategy seeks to achieve both global integration and national responsiveness. A true transnational strategy is difficult to achieve, because one goal requires close global coordination while the other goal requires local flexibility. However, many industries are finding that, although increased competition means they must achieve global efficiency, growing pressure to meet local needs demands national responsiveness.

Although most multinational companies want to achieve some degree of global integration to hold costs down, even global products may require some customisation to meet government regulations in various countries or some tailoring to fit consumer preferences. In addition, some products are better suited for standardisation than others. Most large multinational corporations with diverse products will attempt to use a partial multidomestic strategy for some product lines and global strategies for others.

6.11 DIFFERENCE BETWEEN STRATEGIC MANAGEMENT AND PLANNING

Strategic management differs from strategic planning. All strategic planning approaches attempt to find an optimal match between the resources and capabilities available within the firm (strengths and weaknesses) and the external market conditions and environmental trends (opportunities and threats). This match or coalignment (often called a SWOT analysis) results in a strategy, whose efficiency translates into should level of corporate performance. The basic dimensions of this simple approach are illustrated in the basic strategy model shown in Fig 6.4.

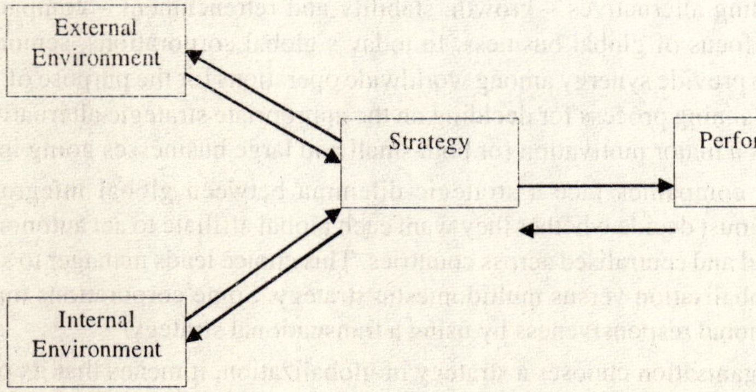

Fig 6.4 : The Basic Strategy Model

A key element in the basic strategy model is the reciprocal influence of all of the variables. The degree of success of an organisation would be manifested in some level of performance (arrow from strategy to performance) and in turn, the performance level would serve as feedback, indicating that further adaptations of strategy might be in order (arrow from performance to strategy).

However, the model presented in Fig 6.5 has to be modified and amplified to consider the implementation of strategy. Management needs to include the 'soft' sides of strategy, political feasibility and organisational acceptability.

Thus, a complete model would include explicit consideration of management values and prevailing corporate culture, as shown in Fig 6.5.

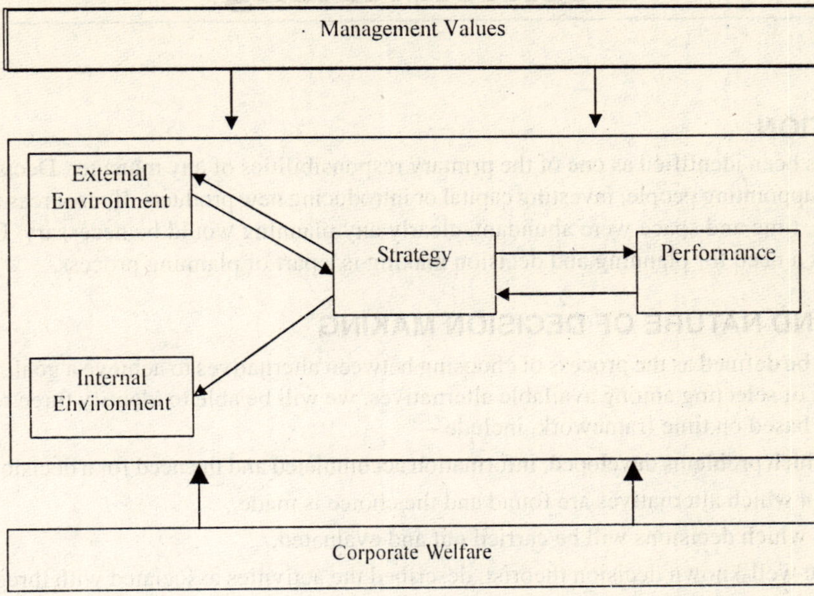

Fig 6.5: The Corporate Strategy Model

Fig 6.5 suggests a sequence of activities in the strategy management process. The activities constitute the fundamental components of strategic management:

1. Environmental trends analysis and scenario building.
2. Industry and competitive analysis.
3. Identification of past and current strategy.
4. Strategy evaluation.
5. Identification of competitive advantages.
6. Strategic choice.
7. Cultural analysis.
8. Strategic change.

Chapter 7

Decision Making

7.1 INTRODUCTION

Making decisions has been identified as one of the primary responsibilities of any manager. Decision may involve allocating resources, appointing people, investing capital or introducing new products. If resources like men, money, machinery, materials, time and space were abundant, clearly any planning would be necessary. But resources are scarce and so there is a need for planning and decision making is a part of planning process.

7.2 MEANING AND NATURE OF DECISION MAKING

Decision making can be defined as the process of choosing between alternatives to achieve a goal. But if we closely look into this process of selecting among available alternatives, we will be able to identify three relatively distinct stages. These stages, based on time framework, include –

1. The past, in which problems developed, information accumulated and the need for a decision was perceived.
2. The present, in which alternatives are found and the choice is made.
3. The future, in which decisions will be carried out and evaluated.

Herbert Simon, the well-known decision theorist, described the activities associated with three major stages in the following way:

1. **Intelligence Activity:** Simon describes this initial phase as an attempt to recognise and understand the nature of the problem as well as identification of the possible courses.
2. **Design Activity:** During the second phase, alternative courses of actions are developed and analysed in the light of known constraints.
3. **Choice Activity:** The actual choice among available and assessed alternatives is made at this stage.

Henry Mintzberg has developed the phases of some decisions actually taken in organisations as depicted in the following model:

Phase: I Identification	Phase:2 Development	Phase: 3 Selection
1. Recognition 2. Diagnosis	1. Search 2. Design	1. Judgement 2. Analysis

Identification phase: In this phase, a particular problem is recognised and diagnosis is made. Through diagnosis a recognised problem has been segregated into different small and integrated problems, which helps in the selection of alternatives in the decision making process.

Development phase: In this phase, there may be a search for existing standard procedures, readymade solutions or the design of a new solution. As a result, different alternative solutions are developed and the decision maker is in a position to select a particular alternative.

Selection phase: In this phase, the choice of a solution is made. There are different ways of making this selection. The decision-maker can judge the alternatives on the basis of his experience or by analysis of the alternatives on a logical and systematic basis.

Decisions making is an important step towards reducing the gap between the existing situation and the desired situation, through solving problems and crises and making use of opportunities. Decisions may be major or minor, strategic or operational..It is through making decisions and getting them implemented that managers strive to achieve organisational goals. The one most important task of management is to make decisions as may be called for. Decisions are to be made in several areas-marketing, production, finance, personnel, accounting and so on. Most of the managerial decisions are directed towards making the organisation survive, succeed, grow and prosper. Also, several decisions have to be made within a limited time and managers are hard pressed to make the choice without perhaps considering all the needed aspects. They may not even be able to wait for collection and analyses of information.

7.3 PERVASIVENESS OF DECISION-MAKING

Decision making is one of the most important managerial functions. Managers manage by making decisions and getting them implemented in a systematic manner. The character and competence of managers are reflected in the quality of their decisions. It is the responsibility of the top management to create a decision-making system as an integral part of the organisational system.

Such a decision making system is created through:

(a) Proper delegation of authority.

(b) Installation of suitable information system.

(c) Formulation of organisational policies and procedures.

(d) Training of subordinate managers to improve their decision making and judgmental skills.

(e) Creation of an organisational climate conducive to making sound decisions.

Decision-making is integral to all the managerial processes; setting up goals, formulating strategies and policies, design of organisational structure, motivation and leadership processes, control and communication processes and so on. Thus, it runs through all the managerial functions. Also, there is a close relationship among the decisions made in performing the various managerial functions. For example, planning decisions affect control decisions and vice versa.

Herbert Simon, treats decision making as being the same as management. He regarded the whole spectrum of pre-decisional, decisional and post-decisional activities of managers as synonymous with the functions of manager. Since managers manage by making decisions and getting them implemented, decision making is equated with managing itself.

7.4 TYPES OF MANAGERIAL DECISIONS

There are many types of decisions which would be required to be made by a manager.

1. **Personal and Organisational Decisions:** This way of classifying decisions was suggested by Chester Barnard, nearly fifty years ago in his classic book, 'The Functions of Executive'. In his opinion, the basic difference between the two decisions is that personal decisions cannot ordinarily be delegated to others, whereas oganisational decisions can often, if not always be delegated. Thus the manager makes organisational decisions that attempt to achieve organisational goals and personal decisions that attempt to achieve personal goals. It may be that personal decisions can affect the organisation, as in the case of a senior manager deciding to resign. Also, organisational decisions can affect the person within the organisation, as in the case of declaration of dividend.

2. **Basic and Routine Decisions:** Another common way of classifying types of decisions is according to whether they are basic or routine. Basic decisions are those which are unique, one-time decisions involving long-range commitments of relative permanence or duration or those involving large investments. Examples of basic decisions in a business firm include plant location, organisational structure, wage negotiations, product line, etc. Routine decisions are at the opposite extreme from basic decisions. They are the everyday, highly repetitive management decisions, which by themselves have little impact on the overall organisation. Examples of routine decisions are an accountant's decision on a new entry or a store keeper's decision regarding the quantity to be ordered on a particular day.

3. **Programmed and Non-Programmed Decisions:** Simon distinguishes between programmed and non-programmed decision. While programmed decisions are typically handled through structured techniques, non-programmed decisions must be made by managers using available information and their own judgement.

   On the basis of the above discussion on the classification of decisions, it is seen that there is no single and satisfactory way of classifying decisions. Moreover, the foregoing classifications have ignored two important problem related dimensions:

   i) How complex is the problem in terms of number of factors associated with it.

   ii) How much certainty can be placed with the outcome of a decision.

Based on these two dimensions, four kinds of decision modes can be identified:

1. Judgemental: Marketing, investment and personnel problems.
2. Adaptive: Research and Development & long-term corporate planning.
3. Machanistic: Daily routines and scheduled activities.
4. Analytical: Complex production and engineering problem.

Judgemental Decisions: A judgemental decision involves a problem with a limited number of decision variables, but the outcomes of decision alternatives are unknown. Many marketing, investment and resource allocating problems come under this category.

For example, the marketing manager may have several alternative ways of promoting a product, but he may not be sure of their outcomes. Good judgement is needed to increase the possibility of desired outcomes and minimise the possibility of undesired outcomes.

Adaptive Decisions: An adaptive decision involves a problem with a large number of decision variables, where outcome are not predictable. Because of the complexity and uncertainty of such problem, decision makers are not able to agree on their nature or on decision strategies. In such a case, decision and implementation strategies have to be frequently modified to accommodate new developments in technology and the environment.

Mechanistic Decisions: A mechanistic decision is one that is routine and repetitive in nature. It usually occurs in a situation involving a limited number of decision variables where the outcomes of each alternative are known. Most mechanistic decision problems are solved by standard operating procedures or clerical routines.

For example, the manager of a bicycle shop may know from his experience when and how many bicycles are to be ordered.

Analytical Decisions: An analytical decision involves a problem with a large number of decision variables, where the outcomes of each decision alternative can be computed. They may be complex, but solutions can be found. Management science and operation research provide a variety of techniques that can be used to find optional solutions.

Types of Managerial Decisions		
Decision Variables	Outcomes of Decision Alternatives	
	Known	unknown
Limited	Mechanistic	Judgemental
Unlimited	Analytical	Adaptive

Fig 7.1

7.5 DECISION-MAKING STEPS

Whether a decision is programmed or nonprogrammed and regardless of manager's choice of model of decision making, six steps typically are associated with effective decision process. These are summarised below:

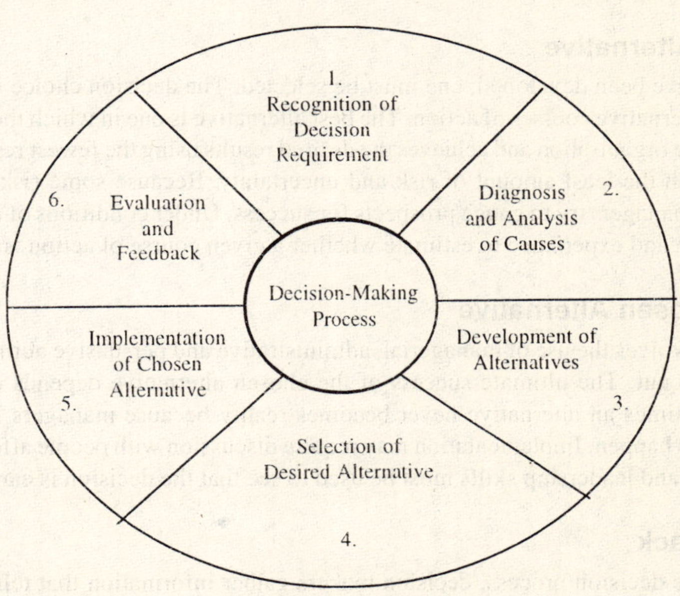

Fig 7.2: Six Steps in the Managerial Decision-Making Process

Recognition of Decision Requirement

Managers confront a decision requirement in the form of either a problem or an opportunity. A problem occurs when organisational accomplishment is less than established goals. An opportunity exists when managers see potential accomplishment that exceeds specified current goals.

Awareness of a problem or opportunity is the first step in the decision sequence and requires surveillance of the internal and external environment for issues that merit executive attention.

Recognizing decision requirements is difficult, because it often means integrating bits and pieces of information in novel ways. Some companies are finding that the World Wide Web can help them translate bits of data into useful information for better decision making.

Diagnosis and Analysis of Causes

Once a problem or opportunity has come to a manager's attention, the understanding of the situation should be refined. Diagnosis is the step in the decision-making process in which managers analyse underlying causal factors associated with the decision situation. Managers make a mistake here if they jump right into generating alternatives without first exploring the cause of the problem more deeply.

Development of Alternatives

Once the problem or opportunity has been recognised and analysed, decision makers begin to consider taking action. The next stage is to generate possible alternative solutions that will respond to the needs of the situation and correct the underlying causes.

For a programmed decision, feasible alternatives are easy to identify and in fact usually are already available within the organisation's rules and procedures. Nonprogrammed decisions, however, require developing new courses of action that will meet the company's needs. For decisions made under conditions of high uncertainty, managers may develop only one or two custom solutions that will satisfice for handling the problem.

Selection of Desired Alternative

Once feasible alternatives have been developed, one must be selected. The decision choice is the selection of the most promising of several alternative courses of action. The best alternative is one in which the solution best fits the overall goals and values of the organisation and achieves the desired results using the fewest resources. The manager tries to select the choice with the least amount of risk and uncertainty. Because some risk is inherent for most nonprogrammed decisions, managers try to gauge prospects for success. Under conditions of uncertainty, they may have to rely on their intuition and experience to estimate whether a given course of action is likely to succeed.

Implementation of Chosen Alternative

The implementation stage involves the use of managerial, administrative and persuasive abilities to ensure that the chosen alternative is carried out. The ultimate success of the chosen alternative depends on whether it can be translated into action. Sometimes an alternative never becomes reality because managers lack the resources or energy needed to make things happen. Implementation may require discussion with people affected by the decision. Communication, motivation and leadership skills must be used to see that the decision is carried out.

Evaluation and Feedback

In the evaluation stage of the decision process, decision makers gather information that tells them how well the decision was implemented and whether it was effective in achieving its goals. Feedback is important because decision making is a continuous, never-ending process. Feedback provides decision makers with information that can precipitate a new decision cycle. The decision may fail, thus generating a new analysis of the problem, evaluation of alternatives and selection of a new alternative.

7.6 THE ENVIRONMENT OF DECISION-MAKING

One primary difference between programmed and non -programmed decisions relates to the degree of certainty or uncertainty managers deal with in making the decision. In a perfect world, managers would have all the information necessary for making decisions. In reality, however, some things are unknowable; thus, some decisions will fail to solve the problem or attain the desired outcome. Managers try to obtain information about decision alternatives that will reduce decision uncertainty. Every decision situation can be organised on a scale according to the availability of information and the possibility of failure. The four positions on the scale are certainty, risk, uncertainty and ambiguity. Whereas programmed decisions can be made in situations involving certainty, many situations that managers deal with every day involve at least some degree of uncertainty and require nonprogrammed decision making.

Certainty. Certainty means that all the information the decision maker needs is fully available. Managers have information on operating conditions, resource costs or constraints and each course of action and possible outcome. For example, if a company considers a Rs.10,000 investment in new equipment that it knows for certain will yield Rs.4,000 in cost savings per year over the next five years, managers can calculate a before-tax rate of return of about 40 percent. If managers compare this investment with one that will yield only Rs.3,000 per year in cost savings, they can confidently select the 40 percent return. However, few decisions are certain in the real world.

Risk. Risk means that a decision has clear-cut goals and that good information is available, but the future outcomes associated with each alternative are subject to chance. However, enough information is available to allow the probability of a successful outcome for each alternative to be estimated. Statistical analysis might be used to calculate the probabilities of success or failure. The measure of risk captures the possibility that future events will render the alternative unsuccessful. Some oil companies use a quantitative simulation approach to estimate hydrocarbon reserves, enabling oil executives to evaluate the variation in risk at each stage of exploration and production and make better decisions.

Uncertainty. Uncertainty means that managers know which goals they wish to achieve, but information about alternatives and future events is incomplete. Managers do not have enough information to be clear about alternatives or to estimate their risk. Factors that may affect a decision, such as price, production costs, volume, or future interest rates, are difficult to analyse and predict. Managers may have to make assumptions from which to forge the decision even though it will be wrong if the assumptions are incorrect. Managers may have to come up with creative approaches to alternatives and use personal judgment to determine which alternative is best.

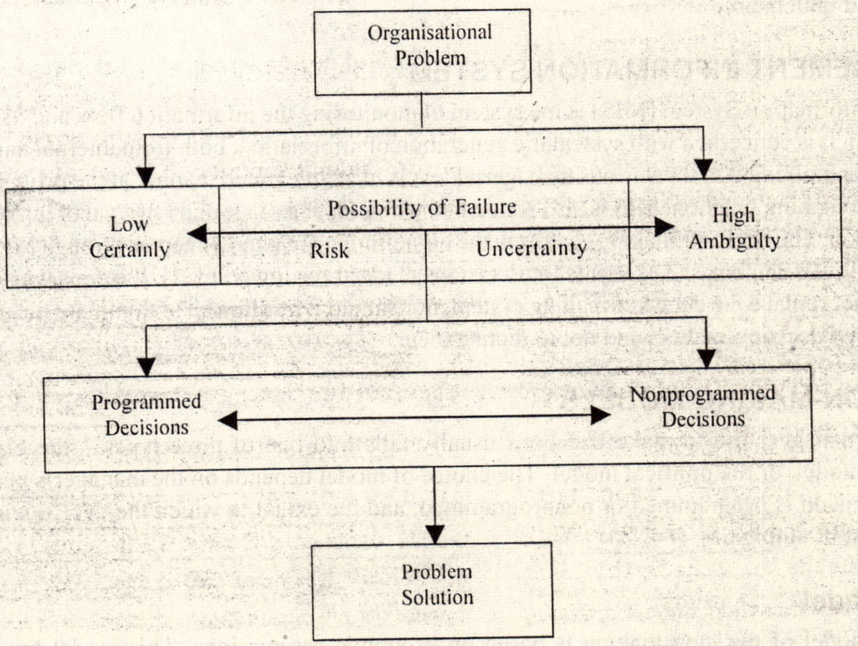

Fig 7.3 : Conditions That Affect the Possibility of Decision Failure

Many decisions made under uncertainty do not produce the desired results, but managers face uncertainty every day. They must find creative ways to cope with uncertainty in order to make effective decisions.

Ambiguity. Ambiguity is by far the most difficult decision situation. Ambiguity means that the goals to be achieved or the problem to be solved is unclear, alternatives are difficult to define and information about outcomes is unavailable. Ambiguity is what students would feel if an instructor created student groups, told each group to complete a project, but gave the groups no topic, direction or guidelines whatsoever. Ambiguity has been called a "wicked" decision problem. Managers have a difficult time coming to grips with the issues. Wicked problems are associated with manager conflicts over goals and decision alternatives, rapidly changing circumstances, fuzzy information and unclear linkages among decision elements. Fortunately, most decisions are not characterised by ambiguity. But when they are, managers must conjure up goals and develop reasonable scenarios for decision alternatives in the absence of information.

7.7 IMPORTANCE OF INFORMATION IN DECISION-MAKING

Information is a primary requirement for decision-making. It significantly determines the effectiveness of not only the final decision but also the process of decision-making itself. That is why, decision-making is sometimes regarded as the processing and conversion of information into action. This is also the reason why timely collection and processing of information is of such great importance – all big concerns now have organised management information system, mostly computer based.

Decision-makers require information to identify and define problem situations, to develop alternative courses of action and to select the best alternative. During the course of decision making new information may become available which is to be considered. Information helps the decision-maker to get a better view of the decision situations and to reduce the complexity and uncertainty. With the availability of information, the problem situation becomes more controllable and understable.

7.8 MANAGEMENT INFORMATION SYSTEM

Management Information System (MIS) is the system of monitoring the information flow and its circulation within the organisation. It is concerned with systematic generation of information, both from internal and external sources, for purposes of supplying it to the various managerial levels in an integrated manner at the proper time to help them in their decision-making function. MIS is also concerned with proper storage and retrieval of information as required by decision-maker. The decision-making centres in the organisation are interconnected through MIS, so that decisions made at higher levels can be used as inputs for decisions made at the lower levels. It is however, to be remembered that MIS does not replace the decision-making system, nor should it be allowed to dominate the managerial system. It is used to assist decision-makers and not to dictate them.

7.9 DECISION-MAKING MODELS

The approach managers use to make decisions usually falls into one of three types – the classical model, the administrative model, or the political model. The choice of model depends on the manager's personal preference, whether the decision is programmed or nonprogrammed, and the extent to which the decision is characterised by risk, uncertainty, or ambiguity.

Classical Model

The classical model of decision making is based on economic assumptions. This model has arisen within the management literature because managers are expected to make decisions that are economically sensible and in the organisation's best economic interests. The assumptions underlying this model are as follows:

1. The decision maker operates to accomplish goals that are known and agreed upon. Problems are precisely formulated and defined.
2. The decision maker strives for conditions of certainty, gathering complete information. All alternatives and the potential results of each are calculated.
3. Criteria for evaluating alternatives are known. The decision maker selects the alternative that will maximise the economic return to the organisation.
4. The decision maker is rational and uses logic to assign values, order preferences, evaluate alternatives and make the decision that will maximise the attainment of organisational goals.

The classical model of decision making is considered to be normative, which means it defines how a decision maker should make decisions. It does not describe how managers actually make decisions so much as it provides guidelines on how to reach an ideal outcome for the organisation. The value of the classical model has been its ability to help decision makers be more rational.

In many respects, the classical model represents an "ideal" model of decision making that is often unattainable by real people in real organisations. It is most valuable when applied to programmed decisions and to decisions characterised by certainty or risk, because relevant information is available and probalilities can be calculated.

Administrative Model

The administrative model of decision making describes how managers actually make decisions in difficult situations, such as those characterised by nonprogrammed decisions, uncertainty and ambiguity. Many management decisions are not sufficiently programmable to lend themselves to any degree of qualification. Managers are unable to make economically rational decisions even if they want to.

Bounded Rationality and Satisficing. The administrative model of decision making is based on the work of Herbert A. Simon. Simon proposed two concepts that were instrumental in shaping the administrative model: bounded rationality and satisficing. Bounded rationality means that people have limits, or boundaries, on how rational they can be. The organisation is incredibly complex and managers have the time and ability to process only a limited amount of information with which to make decisions. Because managers do not have the time or cognitive ability to process complete information about complex decisions, they must satisfice. Satisficing means that decision makers choose the first solution alternative that satisfies minimal decision criteria. Rather than pursuing all alternatives to identify the single solution that will maximise economic returns, managers will opt for the first solution that appears to solve the problem, even if better solutions are presumed to exist. The decision maker cannot justify the time and expense of obtaining complete information.

The administrative model relies on assumptions different from those of the classical model and focuses on organisational factors that influence individual decisions. It is more realistic than the classical model for complex, nonprogrammed decisions. According to the administrative model:

1. Decision goals often are vague, conflicting and lack consensus among managers. Managers often are unaware of problems or opportunities that exist in the organisation.
2. Rational procedures are not always used, and when they are, they are confined to a simplistic view of the problem that does not capture the complexity of real organisational events.
3. Manager's search for alternatives is limited because of human, information and resource constraints.
4. Most managers settle for a satisficing rather than a maximising solution. This is partly because they have limited information and partly because they have only vague criteria for what constitutes a miximising solution.

The administrative model is considered to be descriptive, meaning that it describes how managers actually make decisions in complex situations rather than dictating how they should make decisions according to a theoretical ideal. The administrative model recognizes the human and environmental limitations that affect the degree to which managers can pursue a rational decision-making process.

Political Model

The third model of decision making is useful for making nonprogrammed decision when conditions are uncertain, information is limited, and there is disagreement among managers about what goals to pursue or what course of action to take. Most organisational decisions involve many managers who are pursuing different goals and they have to talk with one another to share information and reach an agreement. Managers often engage in coalition building for making complex organisational decision. A coalition is an informal alliance among managers who support a specific goal. Coalition building is the process of forming alliances among managers. In other words, a manager who supports a specific alternative, such as increasing the corporation's growth by acquiring another company, talks informally to other executives and tries to persuade them to support the decision. When the outcomes are not predictable, managers gain support through discussion, negotiation and bargaining. Without a coalition, a powerful individual or group could derail the decision-making process. Coalition building gives several managers an opportunity to contribute to decision making, enhancing their commitment to the alternative that is ultimately adopted.

The political model closely resembles the real environment in which most managers and decision makers operate. Decisions are complex and involve many people, information is often ambiguous and disagreement and conflict over problems and solutions are normal. The basic assumptions of the political model are:

1. Organisations are made up of groups with diverse interests, goals and values. Managers disagree about problem priorities and may not understand or share the goals and interests of other managers.
2. Information is ambiguous and incomplete. The attempt to be rational is limited by the complexity of many problems as well as personal and organisational constraints.
3. Managers do not have the time, resources, or mental capacity to identify all dimensions of the problem and process all relevant information. Managers talk to each other and exchange viewpoints to gather information and reduce ambiguity.
4. Managers engage in the push and pull of debate to decide goals and discuss alternatives. Decisions are the result of bargaining and discussion among coalition members.

Recent research into decision-making procedures has found rational, classical procedures to be associated with high performance for organisations in stable environments. However, administrative and political decision-making procedures and intuition have been associated with high performance in unstable environments in which decisions must be made rapidly and under more difficult conditions.

7.10 INFLUENCES ON DECISION MAKING

At least three general factors influence decisions. First, there are the characteristics of the decision maker. Such factors as his or her knowledge of the problem, ability to analyse and solve the problem, and motivation to solve it affect the decision. Second, are the characteristics of the problem itself, including the extent to which the problem is familiar to the managers, the ambiguity and complexity of the problem and the extent to which the problem is stable or volatile. Third, the decision is influenced by the environment in which the decision is made. Included in the environment are the degree to which the decision is irreversible, its significance or importance, the person accountable for the decision and its consequences and any time or money constraints involved in the decision process. Taken together, these factors represent the major ingredients involved in the decision.

7.11 Personal Decision Framework

Not all managers go about making decisions in the same way. In fact, there are significant differences in the ways individual mangers may approach problems and make decisions concerning them. These differences can be explained by the concept of personal decision styles. Personal decision style refers to differences among people with respect to how they perceive problems and make decisions. Research has identified four major decision styles: directive, analytical, conceptual and behavioural.

1. The directive style is used by people who prefer simple, clear-cut solutions to problems. Managers who use this style often make decision quickly because they do not like to deal with a lot of information and may consider only one or two alternatives. People who prefer the directive style generally are efficient and rational and prefer to rely on existing rules or procedures for making decisions.
2. Managers with an analytical style, on the other hand, like to consider complex solutions based on as much data as they can gather. These individuals carefully consider alternatives and often base their decisions on objective, rational data from management control system and other sources. They search for the best possible decision based on the information available.
3. People who tend toward a conceptual style also like to consider a broad amount of information. However, they are more socially oriented than those with an analytical style and like to talk to others about the problem and possible alternatives for solving it. Managers using a conceptual style consider many broad alternatives, rely on information from both people and systems and like to solve problems creatively.
4. The behavioural style is often the style adopted by managers having a deep concern for others as individuals. Managers using this style like to talk to people one-on-one and understand their feelings about the problem and the effect of a given decision upon them. People with a behavioural style usually are concerned with the personal development of others and may make decisions that help others achieve their goals.

Although most managers have a dominant decision style, frequently they will use several different styles or a combination of styles in making the varied decisions they confront daily. For example, a manager might use a directive style for deciding on which printing company to use for new business cards, yet shift to a more conceptual style when handling an interdepartmental conflict. The most effective managers are able to shift among styles as needed to meet the situation. Being aware of one's dominant decision style can help a manager avoid making critical mistakes when his or her usual style may be inappropriate to the problem at hand.

7.12 Techniques For Improving Decisions Making

We have focused on the problems and processes involved in decision making and have examined several decision models, we can now consider additional ways of improving the decision-making process. At the beginning of the chapter, we mentioned that decisions can be divided into two phases: problem formulation and problem solution. Strategies to improve decision-making can also be divided into the same two categories.

Improving Problem Formulation

Problem formulation focuses on identifying the causes for unsatisfactory behaviour and finding new opportunities and challenges. This process is often inhibited by the failure of group members to look beyond the familiar. Groupthink and escalating commitment often limit critical analysis or comprehensive searches for information and solutions. As a result, improvement in problem formulation may require the use of structured debate. Structured debate is a process to improve problem formulation through the use of a devil's advocate, multiple advocacy and dialectical inquiry.

Devil's Advocate: A devil's advocate is a group member whose role is to disagree with the group. For example, if you asked a group of American automobile company executives why their sales are down, they might blame Japanese imports. In this case, a devil's advocate would argue that the problem lies not with the Japanese, but with the Americans themselves and their poor product quality. Through this process, the group is forced to justify its position and as a consequence, develop a more precise and accurate picture of the problem and its underlying causes.

Multiple Advocacy: Multiple advocacy is like the devil's advocate approach, except that more than one opposing view is presented. Each group involved in a decision is assigned the responsibility of representing the opinions of its constituents. Thus, if a university is concerned with accommodating racial and cultural diversity on campus, it might establish a commission including Africans, Americans, Asians, women's groups and so forth. The resulting dialogue should lead to the identification of a useful agenda for discussion.

Dialectical Inquiry: Dialectical inquiry occurs when a group or individual is assigned the role of questioning the underlying assumptions of problem formulation. It begins by identifying the prevailing view of the problem and its associated assumptions. Next, an individual is asked to develop an alternative problem that is credible but has different assumptions. By doing so, the accuracy of the original assumption is examined and possibly altered. As a result, group members are forced to "think outside the box" and look at new ways to analyse a problem. These efforts are particularly helpful in overcoming groupthink and escalating commitment, because they question the underlying assumptions of group behavior.

Improving Problem Solution

Problem solution involves development and evaluation of alternative courses of action and selection and implementation of the preferred alternatives. To improve this process, group members must be as thorough and creative as possible. Stimulation of creativity expands the search for and analysis of possible alternatives. Three such mechanisms are useful.

Brainstorming: Brainstorming is a process generating many creative solutions without evaluating their merit. It is a frequently used mechanism to provide the maximum number of ideas in a short period of time. A group comes together is given a specific problem and is told to propose any idea that come to mind to solve the problem. In such sessions – at least at the early stages – criticism is minimised so as not to inhibit expression. Once all the ideas are on the table, the group considers the positive and negative aspects of each proposal. Through a process of continual refinement, the best possible solution under the circumstance should emerge.

Nominal Group Technique: The nominal group technique, typically referred to as NGT, consists of four phases in group decision making. First, individual members meet as a group, but they begin by sitting silently and independently generating their ideas on a problem in writing. This silent period is followed by a round-robin procedure in which each group member presents an idea to the group. No discussion of the idea is allowed at this time. The ideas are summarised and recorded (perhaps on a blackboard). After all individuals have presented their ideas, each idea is discussed to clarify and evaluate it. Finally, group members conclude the meeting by silently and independently ranking the various ideas or solutions to the problem. The final decision is determined by the pooled outcome of the member's votes on the issue.

The NGT allows the group to meet formally, but it does not allow members much discussion; hence, the term nominal group technique. A chief advantage of this procedure is that everyone independently considers the problem without influence from other group members. As we found, this influence represents one of the chief obstacles to open-minded discussion and decision making.

Delphi Technique: In contrast to NGT, the Delphi technique never allows decision participants to meet face to face. Instead, a problem is identified and members are asked through a series of carefully designed questionnaires to provide potential solutions. These questionnaires are completed independently. Results of the first questionnaire are then circulated to all group members (who are still physically separated). After viewing the feedback, members are again asked their opinions (to see if the opinions of others on the first questionnaire caused them to change their own minds). This process may continue through several iterations until group member's opinions begin to show consensus.

The decision-making process includes a variety of problems. Individuals and groups have various biases and personal goals that may lead to suboptimal decisions. Moreover, groups often censor themselves. Even so, techniques such as those discussed here aim to minimise many of these problems by insulating individual participants from the undue influence of others. This allows individuals greater freedom of expression and the group receives far less filtered or slanted information with which to make its decision. Thus, although not perfect, these techniques can give managers mechanisms to improve both the quality and the timeliness of decisions made in organisations.

CONCLUDING COMMENTS

The decision-making process typically has two aspects: problem formation and problem solution. Individually, people often select solutions that meet their minimum objectives rather than spending extra time and energy trying to find the solution that maximises their objectives. However, to appear rational, they often construct objectives and criteria after the fact to justify the decision they have already made. Groups add a social dynamic to the decision-making process that, depending on the dynamics, can result in either better or worse decisions than individuals might make on their own. The decision of how much to involve others is a function of several factors: the potential participants in the decision, the nature of the problem and decision and the environment in which the problem exists and the decision needs to be made. Understanding these basics provides a foundation for awareness of how cultural values can influence decision making and how managers can make effective decisions in an increasingly global and culturally diverse environment.

Chapter 8

The Function of Organising

8.1 INTRODUCTION

The organising function of management follows the planning function and tries to implement the plans and convert them into tasks, to be divided into jobs. The work flow of the organisation is designed around a network of authority-responsibility relations. Thus the objective of organising is to develope structural framework within which managers and other employees perform their functions and play their roles.

8.2.1 Concept of Organising

Organising is the establishing of effective behavioral relationships among persons so that they may work together efficiently and gain personal satisfaction in doing selected tasks under given environmental conditions for the purpose of achieving some goal or objective. As this definition suggests, the organising function of management bring together human and physical resources in an orderly manner and arranges them in a coordinated pattern to accomplish planned objectives.

The word organising stems from the word organism, which is an entity with parts so integrated that their relation to each other is governed by their relation to the whole. When a group of two or more persons work together toward a common goal, the relationship and interaction among them give rise to problems such as who decides what issues, who does what work, and what action should be taken when certain conditions exist. Hence, persons working together effectively, each doing what each can best do, and persons achieving the best possible results are basic in the concept of organising.

8.2.2 Importance of Organising

All of us have been members of organisations, teams, classes, or groups that were very "organised". Likewise, we have been members of groups that could be characterized as being very "disorganised". There are more likely to be good feelings and positive results from our association with the former. Organising promotes collaboration and negotiation among individuals in a group and thus improves the effectiveness and efficiency of communications within the organisation.

The organising function creates clear-cut lines of authority and responsibility in an organisation, thus improving the activation and controlling functions of the manager. For example, hiring and placing a person in the wrong job can result in subsequent motivational difficulties.

8.2.3 Process of Organising

In general terms, organising is a process involving the following three inter-related steps: (1) Determining the activities necessary for the accomplishment of the plan, (2) Grouping these activities into logical categories, i.e. departmentation, and (3) Delegating the authority to others to get the activities performed.

1. **Determination, identification and enumeration of activities -** Once the goals and objective of the organisation have been established, the activities required to achieve these objectives are identified. These activities are broken down into sub-activities as far down the hierarchy as possible so that each individual knows as to what part of the activity he is responsible for. Care must be taken so that all necessary activities

are taken into account and any activity that is unnecessary is taken out. The process applies to both managerial as well as operational activities.

2. **Grouping and assigning of activities -** All similar activities are grouped together and assigned on the basis of divisions or departments. These sets of activities may further be sub-divided into sections or units. These groupings may be done on the basis of primary functions such as production, finance, sales, personnel and so on, or these may be done on derivative basis such as types of customers, geographical areas and so on. These activities are then assigned to personnel as head of the departments, such as production managers, marketing managers, personnel managers and so on. They in turn delegate and distribute jobs to their subordinates down the line. Care should be taken that the personnel and their jobs are well matched.
3. **Delegation of authority –** Since the persons who are assigned particular activities are responsible for performing these duties to the best of their ability; they must be given corresponding authority to discharge their obligations. Responsibility and authority are tied together. Responsibility is really the accountability of authority. Authority without responsibility is a dangerous element. For example, if a marketing manager has the responsibility to increase sales, but does not have the authority to hire and maintain a competent sales force, then the responsibility in itself has little meaning.

8.3 SPAN OF CONTROL PRINCIPLE

The span of control principle states that the number of people reporting directly to any one manager must be limited because one manager can't effectively supervise a large number of subordinates. Span of control is a concept as old as organisations. In fact, it began with Roman military commander's belief that narrow spans of control were effective in combat. The traditional viewpoint of management holds that the ideal number of subordinates reporting to any one manager should be no fewer than four and no more than twelve.

For the most part, successful organisations in the future will have flat structures, that is, few levels of management. Many companies already have flattened their structures by reducing the number of management layers between the CEO and first-line managers. This approach broadens the span of control, with a much larger number of people reporting to each manager. For example, when Lee Byung-Chull founded Samsung in 1938, it had a total of 40 employees. Its business was to produce fertilizer for framers in South Korea. He personally knew each employee and customer. Today, Samsung is led by Lee Kun Hee who oversees Samsung's more than 160,000 employees who are employed in one of Samsung's twenty-eight different companies, ranging from memory chips to autos. He has delegated decision-making authority to the president of each company. The company presidents have clear goals and assignments that can be divided into manageable parts.

There is no "correct" number of subordinates that a manager can supervise effectively. However, four key factors determine the best span of management for any situation.

1. **The competence of both the manager and the employees:** If a manager and/or employees are new to a task, they obviously require more supervision than knowledgeable veteran managers and employees do. The less experienced the manager and/or employees, that narrower the span of control should be.
2. **The similarity or dissimilarity of tasks being supervised:** A process focus means widely varying products and tasks, whereas a product focus means more standardisation. The more numerous and dissimilar the products, the narrower the span of control should be.
3. **The incidence of new problems in the manager's department:** A manager should know enough about the operations of the department to understand precisely the problems that subordinates are likely to face. The more the manager knows about these factors, the broader the span of control can be.
4. **The extent of clear operating standards and rules:** Clear rules and standard operating procedures leave little to chance and lessen the need for adaptive decisions. The greater the reliance on rules, the broader the span of control may be because the rules do much of the controlling.

8.4 AUTHORITY, RESPONSIBILITY AND ACCOUNTABILITY

Authority

Authority, the fourth element of organisational structure, is the right to make a decision and act. Authority is exercised, for instance, when a board of directors authorises a bond issue to raise capital, when an executive approves a new advertising campaign, when a sales manager signs a contract with a client, when a production manager promotes a worker to first-line manager, and when a supervisor fires someone. In short, authority is the glue of organisational structure.

Authority implies both responsibility and accountability. That is, by exercising authority, managers accept the responsibility for acting and are willing to be held accountable for success or failure. Furthermore, when delegating tasks to others, managers should take care to match the responsibility they confer with authority and then insist on accountability for results.

Responsibility

Responsibility is an employee's obligation to perform assigned tasks. The employee acquires this obligation upon accepting a job or a specific assignment. A manager is responsible not only for carrying out certain tasks but also for the actions of subordinates.

Accountability

Accountability is the expectation that employees will accept credit or blame for the results of their work. Employees are expected to report those results, and this feedback enables management to determine whether effective decisions are being made and tasks are being done properly. No supervisor can check everything an employee does. Therefore management establishes guidelines within which responsibilities are to be carried out. Employees are accountable for performance within these limits. Thus, unlike authority, accountability always flows from the bottom up. The news assistant of a newspaper is accountable to the senior reporter, the senior reporter is accountable to the editor, the editor is accountable to the publisher.

Accountability is the point at which authority and responsibility meet and is essential for effective performance. For example, the state grants you the authority to drive an automobile and assigns you the responsibility for obeying traffic laws. You are then held accountable for your behaviour while driving a car. If you drive without mishap, your license is renewed and your insurance coverage is extended; if you continually disobey traffic laws and are caught or cause accidents, your license and insurance may be revoked. When either authority or responsibility are lacking, managers cannot judge a subordinate's accomplishments fairly. And when managers are reluctant to hold subordinates accountable for their tasks, subordinates can easily pass the buck for nonperformance.

Delegation of Authority

Delegation of authority is the process by which mangers assign to subordinates the right to make decisions and act in certain situations. Thus, in addition to assigning a task to a subordinate, the manger also gives the subordinate adequate decision-making power to carry out the task effectively. Delegation starts when the structure of the organisation is being established and tasks are divided. It continues as new tasks are added during day-to-day operations.

Delegation of authority occurs in conjunction with the assignment of responsibilities, as when a company president assigns to an executive assistant the task of preparing a formal statement for presentation to a congressional committee, or when the head of a computer department instructs a programmer to debug a new management reporting system. In each case a manager gives decision-making power to a subordinate. The basic components of the delegation process are determining expected results, assigning tasks and the authority needed to accomplish them and holding those to whom the tasks were assigned accountable for results achieved. These components shouldn't be separated.

Improving Delegation

The following six principles are useful for improving delegation of authority.

1. **Establish goals and standards:** Subordinates should participate in developing the goals that they will be expected to meet. They should also agree to the standards that will be used to measure their performance.
2. **Define authority and responsibility:** Subordinates should clearly understand the work delegated to them, recognise the scope of their authority and accept their accountability for results.
3. **Involve subordinates:** The challenge of the work itself won't always encourage subordinates to accept and perform delegated tasks well. Managers can motivate subordinates by involving them in decision making, by keeping them informed and by helping them improve their skills and abilities.
4. **Require completed work:** Subordinates should be required to carry a task through to completion. The manager's job is to provide guidance, help and information – not to finish the job.
5. **Provide training:** Delegation can be only as effective as the ability of people to perform the work and make the necessary decisions. Managers should continually appraise delegated responsibilities and provide training aimed at building on strengths and overcoming deficiencies.
6. **Establish adequate controls:** Timely, accurate feedback should be provided to subordinates so that they may compare their performance to agreed-upon standards and correct their deficiencies.

Organisations in which decisions are effectively delegated have managers whose communication competencies build string interpersonal relationships across departmental or product line.

Barriers to Delegation: Delegation can only be as effective as the ability of people to delegate. The greatest psychological barrier to delegation is fear. A manager may be afraid that if subordinates don't do the job properly, the manager's own reputation will suffer. Such a manager may rationalise: I can do it better myself or My subordinates aren't capable enough. or It takes too much time to explain what I want done. In addition, some managers also may be reluctant to delegate because they fear that subordinates will do the work their own way, do it too well and outshine the boss!

Failing to delegate can be justified only if subordinates are untrained or poorly motivated. However, it is the manager's responsibility to overcome such deficiencies.

Among the organisational barriers that may block delegation is a failure to define authority and responsibility clearly. If managers themselves don't know what is expected or what to do, they can't properly delegate authority to others.

Overcoming Barriers to Delegation: Table 8.1 lists five factors that can help managers become better delegators. Effective delegation requires that employees be given some freedom to accomplish assigned tasks. Managers must accept that there are several ways to deal with problems and that their own ways of solving them aren't necessarily those their subordinates will choose. Subordinates will make mistakes, but, whenever possible, they should be allowed to develop their own solutions to problems and learn from their mistakes. This approach is very difficult for many managers, but unless they use it, they won't be able to delegate effectively. They'll be so busy with minor tasks or with checking on subordinates that they'll fail to complete their own important assignments. Thus managers must always keep in mind that the advantages of delegation justify giving subordinates freedom of action, even at the risk of letting mistakes occur.

Improved communication between mangers and subordinates also can overcome barriers to delegation. Managers who make it a point to learn the strengths, weaknesses and preferences of their subordinates can more effectively decide which tasks can be delegated to whom. Such knowledge will give them greater confidence in their delegation decisions. In addition, subordinates who are encouraged to use their abilities and who feel that their managers will back them are likely to accept responsibility eagerly.

Table 8.1

The Art of Delegation

- Delegate strategically by measuring employee's successes against jointly set goals.
- Treat delegation as a career-building tool that provides employees with the needed experiences to prepare them for greater responsibility.
- Find the right person for the task.
- Let employees establish their own plan(s) of action.
- Make sure that you stay on top of things and hold employees accountable.

8.5 LINE AND STAFF AUTHORITY

Line authority belongs to managers who have the right to direct and control the activities of subordinates who perform tasks essential to achieving organisational goals. Line authority thus flows down the organisation through the primary chain of command, according to the scalar principle. In contrast, staff authority belongs to those who support line functions through advice, recommendations, research, technical expertise and specialised services.

Line functions are closely tied to organisational goals and processes. These functions differ from one type of organisation to another. For example, Fig 8.2 shows an organisation chart. In this case, line departments perform

Line and Staff Structure

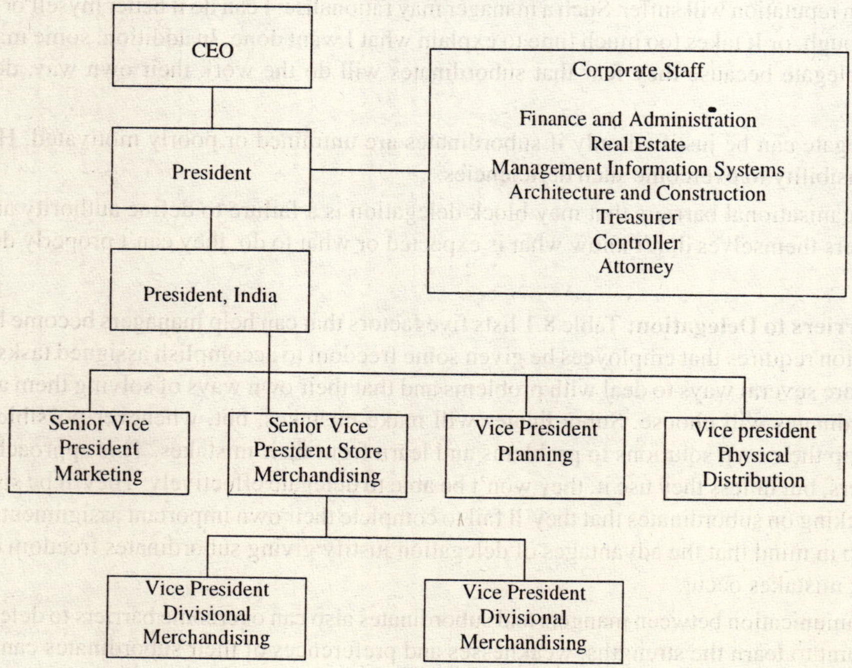

Fig 8.2

tasks such as marketing, store merchandising and physical distribution. Staff departments provide specialised information and services to the line departments, including finance and administration, real estate and management information systems.

The line departments follow the line of authority from the office of CEO to the vice-presidents for divisional merchandising and so on staff departments exist at the corporate level and support the managers in the performance of their tasks.

Location of Staff Departments

Usually, the location of staff departments within an organisation is determined by the differences between generalised and specialised functions. If staff services are used extensively throughout an organisation, staff departments may need to be located relatively high up in the hierarchy. In fact, most large organisations centralise general staff functions at the top. In figure 8.2 for instance, corporate staff handles finance and administration, real estate, management information systems, treasury functions and corporate legal functions. The vice presidents who manage these staff functions usually are in corporate policy-making positions.

If a staff department provides necessary services to a specific line function, it should be located near that function both physically and in terms of management authority. A staff specialist who performs some support functions that a line manager would otherwise have to perform usually reports directly to that line manager.

8.6 DECENTRALISATION OF AUTHORITY

8.6.1 Meaning of Decentralisation

Decentralisation is a word that we frequently hear, talked about by political leaders and business managers. Many of them view decentralisation as a panacea or a magical device that will compensate for poor management, encourage participation, increase efficiency and raise morale. Most people do not have a clear view of what decentralisation is.

Decentralisation is a situation in which ultimate authority to command and ultimate responsibility for results is localised as far down in the organisation as efficient management of the organisation permits. According to Allen, decentralisation refers to the systematic effort to delegate to the lowest levels all authority except that which can only be exercised at central points. Thus, decentralisation means reservation of some authority (to plan, organise, direct and control) at the top level and delegation of authority to make routine decisions at points as near as possible to where action takes place.

8.6.2 Essential Characteristics of Decentralisation

The essential characteristics of decentralisation are:

(i) *Decentralisation is not the same thing as delegation* – It is something more than delegation. Delegation means entrust, meat of responsibility and authority from one individual to another. But decentralisation means scattering of authority throughout the organisation.

(ii) *Decentralisation is distinct from dispersion* – Decentralisation is often confused with the separation of physical facilities which is not correct. Dispersion occurs when plants and offices located at different places with physical distance between them. A company may be highly decentralised even though all physical facilities and employees are located in a single building.

(iii) *Decentralisation is not a type of organisation.* Some people believe that a company can decentralise by changing its organisational structure. This is not true. Decentralisation may be achieved even without changing the organisational structure.

8.6.3 Factors affecting Decentralisation

The important factors that affect decentralisation of authority are as follows:

(i) The nature of company's products or markets may require decentralisation of decision-making to provide special emphasis to product line or a market.

(ii) Decentralisation of authority is facilitated when it is required to take quick and appropriate decisions at a level at which they are really required.

(iii) When the top management wants to reduce communication work, decentralisation of authority is preferred.

(iv) Physical dispersion of activities of the company may require decentralisation of authority for better results.

(v) Growth and diversification of activities of the company may make decentralisation necessary to introduce flexibility in operation.

(vi) The strategy of an organisation influences the types of its markets, its technological environment and its competition with other organisations. These factors, in turn, influence the degree of decentralisation of the organisation.

8.6.4 Advantages of Decentralisation

The merits of decentralisation are listed below:

(i) It leads to a competitive climate in the organisation.

(ii) It relieves the management of much workload.

(iii) It makes jobs at the lower levels of the organisation more attractive and interesting.

(iv) It encourages initiative at lower levels where the employees are allowed to participate in the decision-making process.

(v) Decision made closer to the actual situations is likely to be more realistic.

(vi) It is easier to judge the performance of an executive when he is put in charge of an autonomous unit of administration.

(vii) It ensures development of more capable managers.

(viii) It facilitates diversification of products, activities and markets.

8.6.5 Disadvantages of Decentralisation

Decentralisation of authority suffers from the following limitations or weaknesses:

(i) The executives at lower levels may develop a narrow outlook to the detriment of the over-all interest of the organisation.

(ii) It increases the administrative cost due to duplication of specialised services and the appointment of capable executives at lower level.

(iii) It becomes difficult for top management to exercise control over what people at lower levels are doing or even to know what decisions they are taking.

(iv) Emergency situations cannot be tackled properly in decentralised structure.

(v) It hampers uniformity in decision-making and consistency of procedures.

8.7 CENTRALISATION OF AUTHORITY

8.7.1 Meaning of Centralisation

Centralisation is "the systematic and consistent reservation of authority at central points in an organisation, while decentralisation refers to consistent and systematic delegation to the lowest levels all authority except that which can only be exercised at central points". According to Allen, centralisation denotes that a majority of the decisions having to do with the work being performed are not made by those doing the work but at a point higher in the organisation.

Centralisation represents certain attitudes and approaches which the management follows. The major implication of centralisation is the reservation of decision-making power in regard to planning, organising, directing and control at the top level.

8.7.2 Need of Centralisation

Centralised structure of organisation may be preferred by the top management because of the following factors:

(i) **Utilisation of Personnel** – Centralised structure permits better utilisation of highly qualified personnel, particularly in administrative and technical capacities.

(ii) **Flexibility** – Centralisation permits greater flexibility in the utilisation of existing personnel and facilities and in handling fluctuating volumes of work.

(iii) **Uniformity of Action** – Where a company wishes all its operative units to do the same things in the same way, there must be centralisation of appropriate decision-making.

(iv) **Integration** – Certain degree of centralisation of authority is necessary to unite and integrate the total operations of the enterprise.

(v) **Personal Leadership** – Personal leadership is important for the success of small enterprises.

(vi) **Handling Emergencies** – Centralisation of decision-making is essential when the business conditions are uncertain and there are chances that emergency conditions may develop to endanger the very existence of the company.

8.7.3 Disadvantages of Centralisation

Centralisation of authority has certain demerits also. In case of centralisation, most of the decisions are taken not at a point where work is being done, but at a point higher in the organisation. They may involve considerable cost and delay in making the decision. Centralisation of authority increases the burden on the top managers and hampers the growth of low level managers. Because of these disadvantages, absolute centralisation is not found in practice.

8.7.4 Centralisation vs. Decentralisation

Centralisation and decentralisation are the opposite ends of an organisation continuum. On the one hand, centralisation brings uniformity of policy and action, utilises the skills of centralised and specialised staff and enables closer control over operating units. And on the other hand, decentralisation tends to effect faster decision-making and action on the spot without consulting higher levels. Decentralisation has the effect of motivating the subordinates since they have a greater share in management decision-making.

Factors Affecting Centralisation and Decentralisation

Several factors can affect management's decision to centralise or decentralise decision-making responsibilities. Let's briefly consider six of these factors.

Costliness of Decisions: Cost is perhaps the most important factor in determining the extent of centralisation. As a general rule, the more costly it is to the organisation, the more likely top management will make the decision.

Uniformity of Policy: Managers who value consistency favour centralisation of authority. These managers may want to assure customers that everyone is treated equally in terms of quality, price, credit, delivery and service. Uniform policies have definite advantages for cost accounting, production and financial departments. They also enable managers to compare the relative efficiencies of various departments.

Organisation Culture: A firm's culture will play a large part in determining whether authority will be centralised or decentralised. Organisational culture comprises the norms, values and practices that characterise a particular organisation.

Availability of Managers: Many organisations work hard to ensure an adequate supply of competent managers and employees-an absolute necessity for decentralisation. Such organisations believe that practical experience is the best training for developing managerial potential. They are willing to permit employees to make mistakes involving small costs.

Control Mechanisms: Even the most avid proponents of decentralisation insist on controls and procedures to determine whether actual events are meeting expectations.

Environmental Influences: External factors (e.g., unions and tax policies) affect the degree of centralisation in an organisation. Laws and government regulations regarding hours, wages and the employment of minorities make decentralising hiring authority difficult for an organisation. Unions with long-term contracts also exert a centralising influence on many organisations. When unions bargain on behalf of the employees of an entire organisation, top management can't risk decentralising labour negotiations. But when small local or regional unions represent employees in various departments, top management may delegate the authority to negotiate the terms of labour contracts to departmental managers.

8.8 THE ORGANISATIONAL CHART

One way to visualise the interrelationships of four basic elements of organisational structure is to create an organisation chart. It is a diagram showing the reporting relationships of functions, departments and individual positions within an organisation. Fig 8.3 is the organisation chart of a small-package delivery service industry. The chart could be expanded to show even greater detail by including the titles of departmental managers and identifying work teams within the departments according to the specific tasks they perform. For example, the managers of various

Organisational Structure

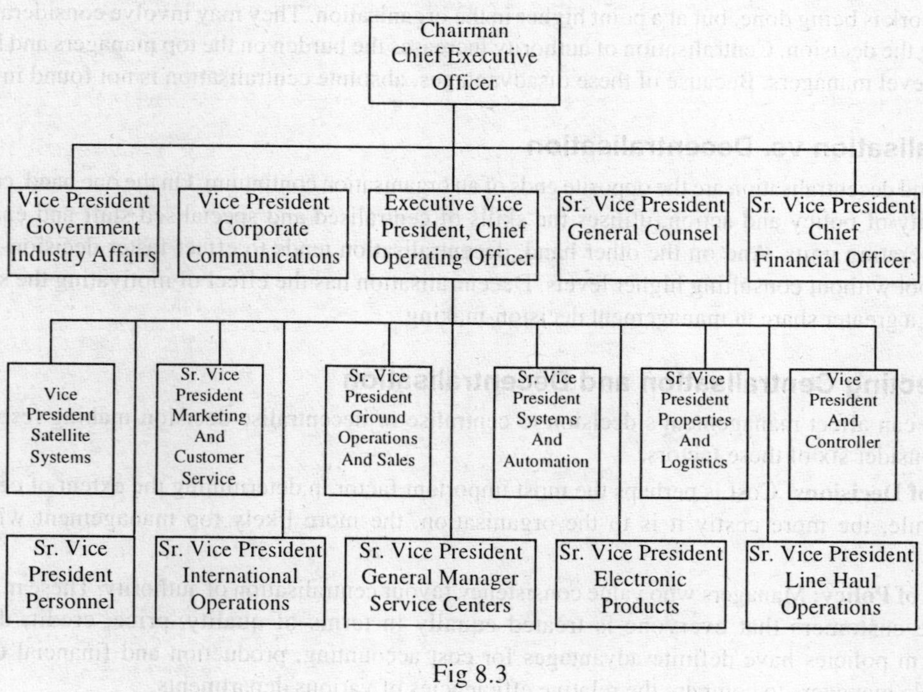

Fig 8.3

departments, such as express products, retail marketing, cooperative marketing and customer service, report to the senior vice-president of marketing and customer service.

In general, an organisation chart provides four important pieces of information about an organisation's structure.

1. **Tasks:** The chart shows the range of different tasks within the organisation. For instance, tasks of this concern range from personnel to properties and logistics to satellite systems to line haul operations.
2. **Subdivisions:** Each box represents a subdivision of the organisation that is responsible for certain tasks. For example, the senior vice-president for line haul operations is responsible for maintenance services, quality programmes, flight operations and support and aircraft acquisition and sales.
3. **Levels of management:** The chart shows the management hierarchy from the chairman of the board to the various divisional managers. All those directly subordinate to the same individual usually appear at the same management level and report to that individual.
4. **Lines of authority:** Vertical line connecting the boxes on the chart show which positions have authority over others. The executive vice-president reports to the president. The senior vice-presidents of marketing and customer service, ground operations and sales, properties and logistics and international operations, among others, report to the executive vice-president.

The advantages and disadvantages of organisation charts have been debated for years. One advantage is that such a chart shows employees how the pieces of the entire organisation fit together. That is, it indicates how their own specialised tasks relate to the whole. Thus everyone knows who reports to whom and where to go with a particular problem. The chart also may help management detect gaps in authority or duplication of tasks.

A major disadvantage of the organisation chart is that it's just a piece of paper sometimes without much validity. It simply can't show everything about an organisation's structure nor much about the way things often really get done. For example, it can't show who has the most political influence or where the vital informal channels of communication operate. In addition, employees may incorrectly read status and power into their jobs, based on the proximity of their boxes to that of the CEO. These disadvantages can be overcome if the chart is used for its intended purpose – to illustrate the basic, formal structure of the entire organisation.

8.9 PRINCIPLES OF GOOD ORGANISATION

Organisation is generally defined as "the analysis and grouping of all the activities necessary to the objectives of any undertaking so as to provide a structure of duties and responsibilities". In order that this structure may ultimately attain the objectives of the organisation, the following principles must be adhered to:

(i) *There must be clear lines of authority running from the top to bottom of the organisation*–In military circles, a line of authority can be traced from the topmost level to the lowest rank. Similarly, in an industrial organisation, it should be possible to trace authority from the president to a worker on the assembly line. In military parlance this is termed "the chain of command".

(ii) *No one in the organisation should report to more than one line supervisor.* Everyone in the organisation should know to whom he reports and who reports to him.This principle is known as "the unity of command". In other words, it implies that every person in an organisation should report to only one boss. This principle is generally the one that is most often violated. Unless every person is clear as to who assigns work to him, some may be overworked while others underworked.

(iii) *The responsibility and authority of each supervisor should be clearly defined in writing.* It enables quick decision-making. It also enables the smooth transfer of responsibilities from one executive to the other.

(iv) *Responsibility should always be accompanied with the corresponding authority*-Once authority is delegated, then the power to make decisions should be with the individual to whom the authority has been delegated. An often quoted weakness on the part of supervisors is to delegate authority but retain the power of decision-making. The dangers of such a situation are manifold.

(v) The responsibility of higher authority for the acts of its subordinates is absolute. Although a supervisor delegates responsibility he still remains responsible for what is done by those to whom he delegates authority. The inefficiency of all subordinates becomes the responsibility of all supervisors.

(vi) *Authority should be delegated as far down the line as possible* – The application of this principle implies decentralisation. All minor duties should be delegated as far down the line as possible so that those in higher authority may devote their time to corporate planning.

(vii) *The number of levels of authority should be kept at a minimum* – In order that decision-making may be fast and efficient the number of levels of authority should be kept at a minimum.

(viii) *The work of every person in the organisation should be confined as far as possible to the performance of a single leading function* – This principle concerns the horizontal dimension of staffing. It implies that the total duties in an organisation are to be divided into various functions and each department must be held responsible for one such function.

(ix) *Separation of line and staff function* – Wherever possible line functions should be separated from staff functions and adequate emphasis should be placed on important staff activities.

(x) *There is a limit to the number of positions that a single executive can coordinate* – This principle is usually known as the span of control. This span of control should not be too wide nor too narrow. If an executive has too wide a span of control then inefficiency may crop in. If on the other hand he has too narrow a span of control then it is quite likely that there may be overlapping of responsibilities.

Chapter 9

Designing Effective Organising

9.1 INTRODUCTION

Organisational structure provides the framework for managers and other staff members of an organisation for performing the various functions expected of them and for facilitating the work flow in the organisation. The structure of an organisation is its main element around which the processes and functions of the organisation are executed.

9.2 ORGANISATIONAL STRUCTURE

All too often managers are too far removed from day-to-day operations to apply their competencies effectively and structure their organisations for greater productivity. Only a dramatic turn of events, such as plunging sales and/or profits, may motivate managers to identify and deal with problems of organisational structure.

9.2.1 Concept

Organisational structure is a formal system of working relationships that both separates and integrates tasks. Separation of tasks makes clear who should do what and integration of tasks indicates how efforts should be meshed. Organisational structure helps employees work together effectively by

1. Assigning human and other resources to tasks.
2. Clarifying employee's responsibilities and how their efforts should mesh through job descriptions, organisation charts and lines of authority.
3. Letting employees know what is expected of them through rules, operating procedures and performance standards.
4. Establishing procedures for collecting and evaluating information to help managers make decisions and solve problems.

9.2.2 Elements of Organisational Structure

Organisational structure includes four basic elements : specialisation, standardisation, coordination and authority.

Specialisation is the process of identifying particular tasks and assigning them to individuals or teams who have been trained to do them. Functional managers usually supervise a particular department, such as marketing, accounting or human resources. First-line managers usually are in charge of a specific area of work, such as printing, medical records or data processing. Thus one person can specialise in any of a number of different management jobs.

Standardisation refers to the uniform and consistent procedures that employees are to follow in doing their jobs. Written procedures, job descriptions, instructions, rules and regulations are used to standardise the routine aspects of jobs. Standards permit managers to measure an employee's performance against established criteria. Job descriptions and application forms standardise the selection of employees. On-the-job training programmes develop standardised skills and reinforce values important to the organisation's success. This approach may seem mechanical, but if jobs weren't standardised, many organisations couldn't achieve their goals.

Coordination comprises the formal and informal procedures that integrate the activities separate individuals, teams and departments in an organisation. In bureaucratic organisations, written rules are enough to link such activities. In less structured organisations, coordination requires managerial sensitivity and willingness to share responsibility and effective interpersonal communication.

Authority is basically the right to decide and act. Various organisations distribute authority differently. In a centralised organisation, top managers make decisions about what merchandise to buy and where to locate a new store and communicate these decisions to lower level managers. In a decentralised organisation, decision-making authority is given to lower level managers and employees working in teams. Firms often combine the two approaches by centralising certain functions (e.g., accounting and purchasing) and decentralising others (e.g., marketing and human resources).

9.2.3 Factors Affecting Organisational Structure

There are number of determinants affecting the organisation structure. Good organisational design is a function of a number of factors like technology, environment and size of the organisation. These three factors would determine the philosophy and strategy of the top management which forms the foundation for the organisational structure. This is illustrated in Fig 9.1.

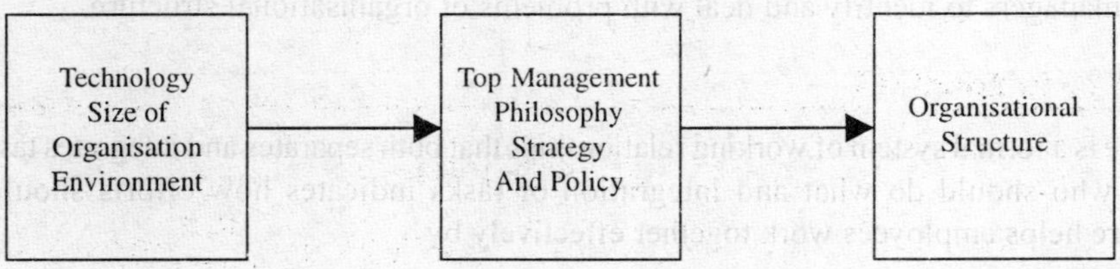

Fig 9.1 Determinants of Organisational Structure

(a) **Socio-cultural Environment** – The specific organisational structure depends upon the social, cultural and environmental forces prevailing at the time the organisation is established. Even though modifications are made over time, organisations seem to retain a strong flavour of their regional form. Many researchers on management have investigated the relationship between socio-cultural environment and organisation structure. Organisations which have purposes that can be efficiently reached with the socially possible organisational forms tend to be founded during the period in which they become possible. Then, both because they can function effectively with those organisational forms and because the forms tend to become institutionalised, the basic structure of the organisation tends to remain relatively stable.

(b) **Technology** – Technology is a combination of tools, technique and know-how and has a major influence on organisational structure, which would depend upon whether the technology is simple and routine requiring few repetitive tasks, in which case a mechanistic structure would be more desirable. However, when the technology is advanced and intensive and complex requiring high interdependence among members of the work force, then the organic structure would be operationally more effective.

(c) **Size and Complexity** – Two important factors influencing structure are size of the organisation and complexity of operations. The research findings relating to structure to organisational size are not conclusive. Some have concluded that size is one of the major determinants of the structure of organisations. Others have argued that size is not a critical factor in determining the structural form. Almost all researchers do agree that large organisations have more complex and elaborate structures. However, there may be other intervening variables such as technology and complexity that are also characteristics of large organisations.

There is a general view that as organisations increase in size, the number of administrative personnel increases more than proportionately. However, research findings suggest that the ratio of administrative personnel to operative personnel decreases. However, there is a relationship between the number of administrative personnel and the complexity of operations. As an organisation increases in specialisation and complexity, the scope of the managerial coordination problems increases. Therefore, it seems logical that the number of people engaged in administrative tasks would also increase.

9.3 DEPARTMENTALISATION

9.3.1 Concept

Departmentalisation addresses two of the four basic elements of organisational structure: specialisation and standardisation. Departmentalization involves subdividing work into tasks and assigning them to specialised groups within an organisation. It also includes devising standards for the performance of tasks.

Management can use any of four basic types of departmentalisation: by function, by place (location), by product (goods and/or services) and by customer. Division of work is the first step in departmentalisation, but how people are grouped depends on the goals of the organisation.

The key to effective departmentalisation lies in organising people and activities in such a way that decisions easily flow throughout the organisation. Large, complex organisations actually use different forms of departmentalisation at various organisational levels to facilitate this flow. Levi Strauss for instance, has eight-product divisions including jeanswear, womenswear and menswear, that reflect a product structure. Each division is then broken into functional departments (e.g., accounting, production and marketing) that support the division's products.

9.3.2 Need and importance

The need of departmentalisation arises once an organisation grows to a size beyond the direct managerial capability of a single individual. As soon as the enterprise picks up growth, the owner-manager has to differentiate the activities more and more, add new activities and arrange them rationally so that they are complementary to each other and cumulatively contribute to the achievement of the enterprise goals. As the enterprise grows further, the size of the individual activity clusters grows, giving rise to the need for appointing a manager over the supervisors and the process goes on. In any organised, goal-oriented group activity, division of labour and specialisation are need to achieve economy and efficiency of effort. Departmentalisation exemplifies these principles, among others things.

The importance of departmentalisation is obvious from the fact that it determines the design of the horizontal dimension of the organisational structure. Activities are one of the means for achieving the goals of an organisation. The key activities needed for goal achievement are to be identified, analysed, divided, grouped and integrated in an optimal manner.

Departmentalisation has important implications for organisational performance and effectiveness. It vitally influences the pattern and pace of workflow in the organisation. It helps the process of determination of the size, composition, skills and capabilities of the personnel required and thus aids man-power planning and control. The degree of delegation of authority to managers at various levels depends on the range, significance and volume of activities for which they are responsible. It is also claimed that appropriate departmentalisation is important form the point of view of employees and managers. Their growth and development, achievement and satisfaction substantially depend on the nature of location and interaction among activity clusters with which they are associated.

9.3.3 Methods or Bases of Departmentation

The basic patterns or methods of departmentation are as under:

(a) Functions, (b) Product, (c) Process, (d) Customers, (e) Geographical area, (f) Time, (g) Project, (h) Combined and (i) Matrix.

A. Functional Departmentalisation

Recall that functions are the groups or sets of tasks that an organisation performs, such as production, marketing and finance. Functional departmentalisation groups employees according to their areas of expertise and the resources they draw on to perform a common set of tasks. Functional grouping is the most widely used and accepted form of departmentalisation.

Functions vary widely, depending on the nature of the organisation. For example, hospitals don't have product development departments, but they do have admitting, emergency room and nursing departments. Churches don't have production departments, but they do have youth, education and choir departments.

Grouping tasks and employees by function can be both efficient and economical. It is particularly efficient for small organisations making a single product because it creates a clear hierarchy of authority and decision-making. Large firms organised by function often assign responsibility and authority for several departments to one senior manager.

Functional departmentalisation has both advantages and disadvantages. Table 9.2 shows several of each.

Table 9.2

Advantages and Disadvantages of Functional Departmentalisation

Advantages

- Promotes skill specialisation.
- Reduces duplication of resources and increases coordination within the functional area.
- Enhances career development and training within the department.
- Allows superiors and subordinates to share common expertise.
- Promotes high-quality technical problem solving.
- Centralised decision making.

Disadvantages

- Emphasizes routine tasks.
- Reduces communication between departments.
- May create conflict over product priorities.
- May make interdepartmental scheduling difficult.
- Focuses on departmental rather than organisational issues and goals.
- Develops managers who are experts in narrow fields.

Functional Departmentalisation

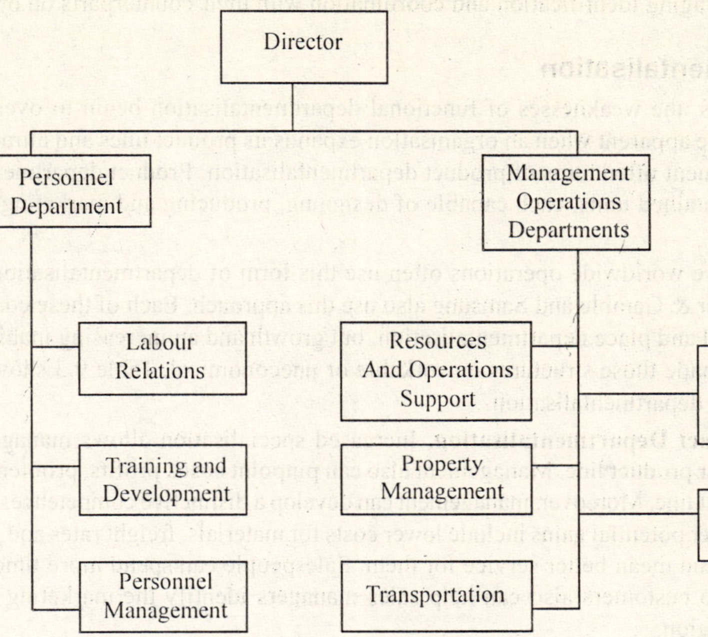

Fig 9.3

Advantages of Functional Departmentalisation. Departmentalisation by functions is economical because it results in a simple structure. It is often the best form for organisations that sell a narrow range of goods and/or services mainly in one market (product and geographic). Management creates one department for each primary task to be performed (e.g., engineering, sales and R&D). This structure keeps administrative expenses low because everyone in a department shares training, experience and resources. Job satisfaction may increases if employees can improve their specialised skills by working with others in the same functional area. Employees can see clearly defined career paths within their own departments. As a result, the organisation can more easily hire and promote personnel who have or develop good problem-solving skills in each area of specialisation.

Disadvantages of Functional Departmentalisation. The disadvantages of functional departmentalisation become obvious when an organisation has diversified products or markets. For instance, General Electric offers a variety products, ranging from light bulbs to refrigerators. Making decisions quickly becomes difficult when employees have to work their way through layers of structure for approvals. For example, a sales representative may lose a good account because he has to wait for the sales manager to get the production manager to make a scheduling decision. In addition, when there's friction between departments, managers have to spend time resolving the issues involved. Pinpointing the accountability and performance levels of employees who are performing separate functions may also be difficult. In other words, a top manager may not be able to determine easily which department-production, sales or credit-is responsible for declining profits.

Another disadvantage is that top management may have a hard time coordinating the activities of employees in different departments. Functional departmentalisation tends to de-emphasize the goals of the entire organisation. Employees may focus on departmental goals, such as meeting their own budgets and schedules and lose sight of the big picture. Moreover, when functional employees begin to worry about their own areas of expertise, they may have trouble seeing other's point of view. Employees develop a loyalty to their own departments, which in turn may erect barriers instead of encouraging identification and coordination with their counterparts on other departments.

B. Product Departmentalisation

As an organisation grows, the weaknesses of functional departmentalisation begin to overshadow its strengths. These weaknesses become apparent when an organisation expands its product lines and attracts diverse customers. In response, top management often turns of product departmentalisation. Product departmentalisation divides the organisation into self-contained units, each capable of designing, producing and marketing its own goods and/or services.

Organisations that have worldwide operations often use this form of departmentalisation. Large multiproduct companies such as Procter & Gamble and Samsung also use this approach. Each of these companies started with a combination of functional and place departmentalisation, but growth and an increasing inability to serve the needs of particular customers made those structures unworkable or uneconomical. Table 9.3 shows the advantages and disadvantages of product departmentalisation.

Advantages of Product Departmentalisation. Increased specialisation allows managers and employees to concentrate on a particular product line. Management also can pinpoint costs, profits, problems and successes more accurately for each product line. Moreover, management can develop a distinctive competence, or strategic advantage, for each product line. Other potential gains include lower costs for materials, freight rates and labour. For marketing, locating near customers can mean better service for them. Salespeople can spend more time selling and less time traveling. Being closer to customers also can help sales managers identify the marketing tactics most likely to succeed in a particular region.

Disadvantages of Product Departmentalisation. Because functions are duplicated for each product line (i.e., each business), resource utilisation is relatively inefficient. Products with seasonal highs and lows in sales volumes may result in high personnel costs. Coordination across product lines usually is difficult. Employees tend to focus on the goals for their particular product, rather than on broader company goals. This situation often creates unhealthy competition within an organisation for scarce resources.

Table 9.4

Advantages and Disadvantages of Product Departmentalisation

Advantages

- Suited to fast changes in a product.
- Allows greater product visibility.
- Fosters a concern for customer demand.
- Clearly defines responsibilities.
- Develops managers who can think across functional lines.

Disadvantages

- May not use skills and resources effectively.
- Doesn't foster coordination of activities across product lines.
- Fosters politics in resource allocation.
- Restricts problem solving to a single product.
- Limits career mobility for personnel outside their product line.

Career mobility is restricted when employees develop skills that are relevant only to a particular product line. Specialisation doesn't allow people to develop the skills needed to move up in the organisation's hierarchy or into its other business. Top management may set common profit standards for all product lines, which may not be realistic for the industries in which some of them have to compete.

Place and Product Departmentalisation

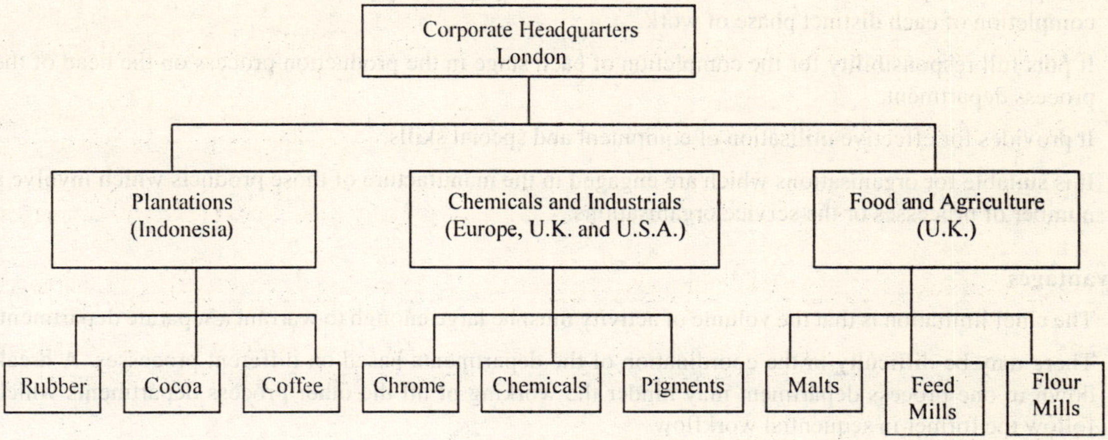

Fig 9.5

C. Departmentation by Equipment or Process

This form of departmentation is more useful for manufacturing organisations. In a textile factory, processes like spinning, weaving, dyeing etc. may be grouped as departments at a secondary level to enjoy benefits of specialised equipment or process. Electronic computer is generally installed in a separate department so that its full utilisation may be made by all other departments of the enterprise. The departmentation by process or equipment is shown in Fig 9.6

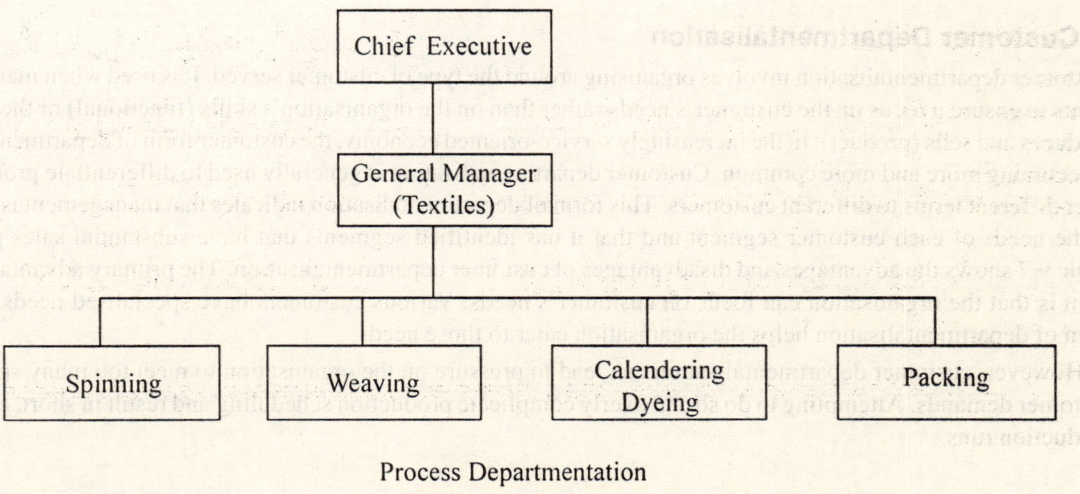

Process Departmentation

Fig 9.6

Departmentation by process may also be followed in engineering and oil industries. The justification of a separate department around equipment is that it is not always possible to install a costly equipment in every department which needs its use. Moreover, skilled personnel are required to operate the equipment.

Advantages

- The process departmentation facilitates coordination by grouping production facilities needed for the completion of each distinct phase of work.
- It puts full responsibility for the completion of each stage in the production process on the head of the process department.
- It provides for effective utilisation of equipment and special skills.
- It is suitable for organisations which are engaged in the manufacture of those products which involve a number of processes or the service organisations.

Disadvantages

- The chief limitation is that the volume of activity must be large enough to warrant a separate department.
- There may be difficulty in the coordination of the departments based on different processes. A break down in one process department may hinder the working of all the other process departments which follow the former in sequential workflow.
- It does not provide good training ground and opportunity for the overall development of managerial talent.
- It is difficult to compare the performance of different process-based departments, except in some notional way by calculating the profits of each department on the basis of transfer pricing.
- When the process is sequential, the dependent departments generally become hostile to other departments and they express their resentment either by complaining directly about other departments or by passing on inferior work to their successive departments.

D. Customer Departmentalisation

Customer departmentalisation involves organising around the type of customer served. It is used when management wants to ensure a focus on the customer's needs rather than on the organisation's skills (functional) or the brands it produces and sells (product). In the increasingly service-oriented economy, the customer form of departmentalisation is becoming more and more common. Customer departmentalisation is generally used to differentiate products and offer different terms to different customers. This form of departmentalisation indicates that management is sensitive to the needs of each customer segment and that it has identified segments that have substantial sales potential. Table 9.7 shows the advantages and disadvantages of customer departmentalisation. The primary advantage of this form is that the organisation can focus on customer's needs. Various customers have specialised needs, and this form of departmentalisation helps the organisation cater to those needs.

However, customer departmentalisation can lead to pressure on the organisation to meet too many specialised customer demands. Attempting to do so can overly complicate production scheduling and result in short, expensive production runs.

Table 9.7

Advantages

- Allows greater customer focus.
- Clearly identifies key customers.
- Suited to understanding customer needs.
- Develops managers who become customer advocates.

Disadvantages

- Doesn't foster coordination between customers.
- Fosters politics in resource allocation.
- Employees feel pressure from customers to give them privileges.
- Restricts problem solving to a single type of customer.

E. Place Departmentalisation

Place departmentalisation groups all functions for a geographic area at one location under one manager, rather than dividing functions among different managers or grouping all tasks in one central office. It is commonly used by organisations with operations in many different locations. Many large companies, including Procter & Gamble, have set up regional and district offices. Multinational firms often use this form of departmentalisation to address cultural and legal differences in various countries, as well as the lack of uniformity among geographic markets. The departmentation on the basis of territory is shown in Fig 9.8.

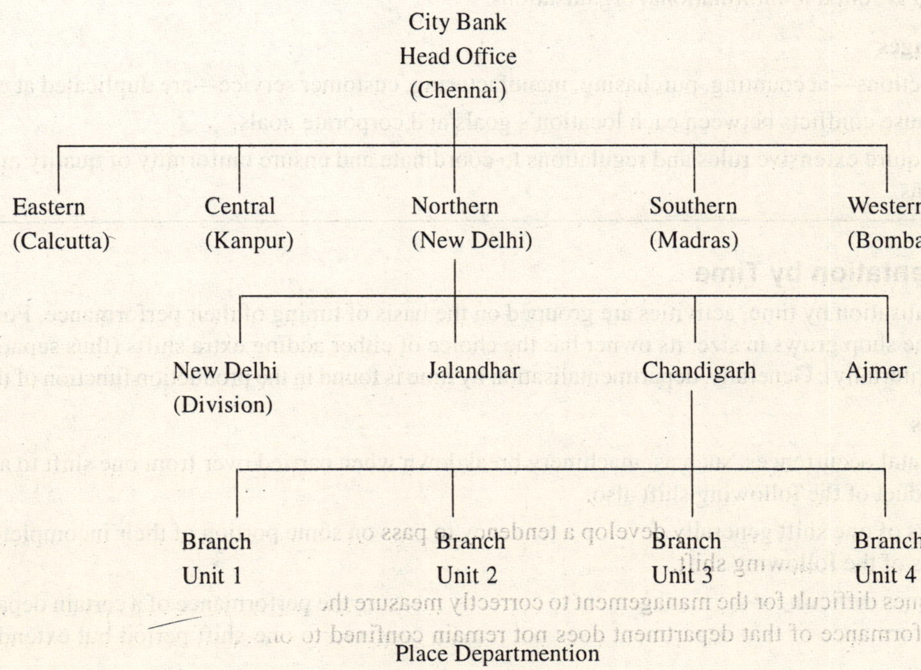

Place Departmention

Fig 9.8

Advantages of Place Departmentalisation. Table 9.9 summarizes the advantages of place departmentalisation, which are primarily those of efficiency. If each unit is relatively small and in direct contact with its customers, it can adapt more readily to market demands. For production, place departmentalisation might mean locating plants near raw materials or suppliers. In addition, because their attention is more focused, managers are likely to use their planning and administration competency to organise subordinate's efforts to meet customer demands.

Disadvantages of Place Departmentalisation. Table 9.9 also shows some disadvantages of place departmentalisation. Organising by location clearly increases problems of control and coordination for top management, which often is far away. To ensure uniformity and coordination, organisations that use place departmentalisation, make extensive use of rules that apply to all locations. One reason for doing so is to guarantee a standard level of quality regardless of location, which would be difficult if units in various locations went their own separate ways. Also, employees may emphasize their own unit's goals or focus only on problems that occur within their own geographic areas without some direction from headquarter. Because most of an organisation's functional departments must be duplicated at each location, costs are higher than for an organisation that adopts a functional form of departmentalisation.

Table 9.9

Advantages and Disadvantages of Place Departmentalisation

Advantages

- Equipment used for products is all in one place, saving time and costs.
- Managers develop expertise in solving problems unique to one location.
- Managers know customer's problems.
- Method is suited to multinational organisations.

Disadvantages

- All functions—accounting, purchasing, manufacturing, customer service—are duplicated at each location.
- May cause conflicts between each location's goals and corporate goals.
- May require extensive rules and regulations to coordinate and ensure uniformity of quality among locations.

F. Departmentation by Time

In departmentalisation by time, activities are grouped on the basis of timing of their performance. For example, as a small machine shop grows in size, its owner has the choice of either adding extra shifts (thus separating the two sub-groups territorially). Generally, departmentalisation by time is found in the production function of the enterprise.

Disadvantages

- Accidental occurrences, such as, machinery breakdown when carried over from one shift to another affect the product of the following shift also.
- Workers of one shift generally develop a tendency to pass on some portion of their incomplete work to the workers of the following shift.
- It becomes difficult for the management to correctly measure the performance of a certain department when the performance of that department does not remain confined to one-shift period but extends to the next shift.

9.4 COORDINATION

Departmentalisation divides the organisation's work and allows for specialisation and standardisation of activities. However, to achieve organisational goals, people, projects and tasks have to be coordinated. Without it, people's efforts are likely to result in delay, frustration and waste. For precisely that reason, coordination is one of the basic elements of organisation design.

Many managers believe that good people can make any organisation design work. Although such managers may be overstating the case, people who work well together are an extremely valuable asset. A good analogy is football, where teamwork is essential. During practice sessions, coaches try to transform the individual players into one smoothly functioning team. Players learn their functions as part of a cooperative effort, see how each task relates to every other task and relate these tasks to the whole. Coordination is required as the players execute their functions, particularly when they are called onto innovate or adjust to the unexpected in a game situation. Similarly, managers have to encourage employees to subordinate their individual interests to the organisation's broader goals and yet be able to innovate when the situation demands.

There are two basic principles of coordination : the unity of command principle and the scalar principle. These principles are directly related to planning and administration competency.

Unity of Command Principle

The unity of command principle states that an employee should have only one boss. Every employee is supposed to know who is giving direction and to whom he or she reports. According to this precept, managers must minimise any confusion over who makes decisions and who implements them because uncertainty in this area can lead to serious productivity and morale problems.

Scalar Principle

The scalar principle states that a clear and unbroken chain of command should link every person in the organisation with someone at a level higher, all the way to the top of the organisation. Tasks should be delegated clearly, with no overlapping or splitting of assignments.

If followed rigidly, the scalar principle would require that all job-related communications between employees in different product departments at the same level be approved by their respective superiors. Obviously, strict adherence to this principle would waste time and money-and be extremely frustrating. In practice, informal relationships across departmental lines spring up to facilitate problem solving and communication within the organisation.

Coordination Versus Departmentalisation

In any organisation tension exists between coordination and departmentalisation. When forces for coordination are stronger than those for departmentalisation, functional departmentalisation works best. In general, when a problem arises, top managers must be able to coordinate the actions of various functional departments quickly to find a solution. Under such conditions, functional departmentalisation helps ensure the necessary degree of coordination.

When forces for coordination and departmentalisation are equal, a customer form of departmentalisation works best. The customer structure addresses the conflict between, say, the product manager's need to satisfy a customer and the functional department's need to provide technical help. Employees move from customer to customer, depending on the customer's needs.

When forces for departmentalisation are stronger than those for coordination, place or product departmentalisation is best. Managers decide what is appropriate for only their market area or product, without having to consider the impact of their decisions on other areas or product lines. Because each market is unique, programming activities between divisions isn't needed. However, some coordination is necessary in the use of the same or similar methods for financial, accounting or environmental reporting so that the corporate level receives comparable data from all three divisions.

For multinational companies the use of several types of departmentalisation and methods of coordination is common. In such organisations there is no single best way to balance the tension between coordination and departmentalisation. The methods of coordination vary for each division, depending on its circumstances. In some of the functional departments, the scalar principle and narrow spans of control are effective. In departments that reflect place departmentalisation, violation of the scalar principles is common and wide spans of control are effective.

Selecting an Organisational Structure

No particular type of departmentalisation – functional, place, product or customer-is best in all circumstances. Managers must select the organisational structure that matches the firm's specific needs. Table 9.10 lists characteristics that can help managers decide which structure is best for their particular situations.

Alphagraphics and many other types of small organisations that have standard products and diverse customers, probably would find functional departmentalisation the best. Procter & Gamble, Johnson & Johnson and other organisations with large and diverse product lines probably would find product departmentalisation most useful.

Table 9.10

Organisational Characteristics and Type of Departmentalisation

Organisational Characteristic	Type of Departmentalisation Favoured
Small size	Functional
Global or national scope	Place
Depends on customer needs	Customer
Essential to use scarce resources appropriately	Customer
Customer base is -	
Diverse	Product
Stable	Functional or customer
Makes use of specialised equipment	Product
Requires skill specialisation	Functional
High transportation costs for raw materials	Place or customer

Organisations in the pharmaceutical industry that utilise numerous complex technologies probably would find product and customer departmentalization most appropriate. Organisations that operate internationally in numerous regions probably would benefit from place departmentalisation.

Clearly, the choice depends on the situation. Some organisations even use all four types of departmentalisation. For example, Novartis, a global biological and chemical company headquartered in Basel, Switzerland, with operations in more than seventy countries. Because of cultural and product line differences, it is organised by country (France, United States, Canada and Australia), product line (health-care, agriculture and chemicals), function (R&D, marketing and finance) and customer (hospitals and other institutions).

9.5 TRADITIONAL ORGANISATIONAL STRUCTURES

Management theorists classify traditional organisational structures into three types: Line Structure, Line and Staff Structure and Functional Structure. These are called traditional structures because historically organisational structures over several centuries are of this type. Most organisation even now has traditional structures which have been time-tested and have proved to generally all right in practice. Let us now discuss these structures:

Line Structure

An organisational structure which is designed around line activities and line authority only is called a line structure. In this structure, line authority flows through all managerial positions created around the basic or core organisational activities which are considered vital for achievement of organisational goals. There are only line managers in a line structure and they are placed in superior-subordinate relationships along the vertical chain of command. In a line structure, there are no separate supportive, facilitative and service activity units. The line managers are required to incorporate these activities in their respective units and assume responsibility for providing such services themselves, as necessary.

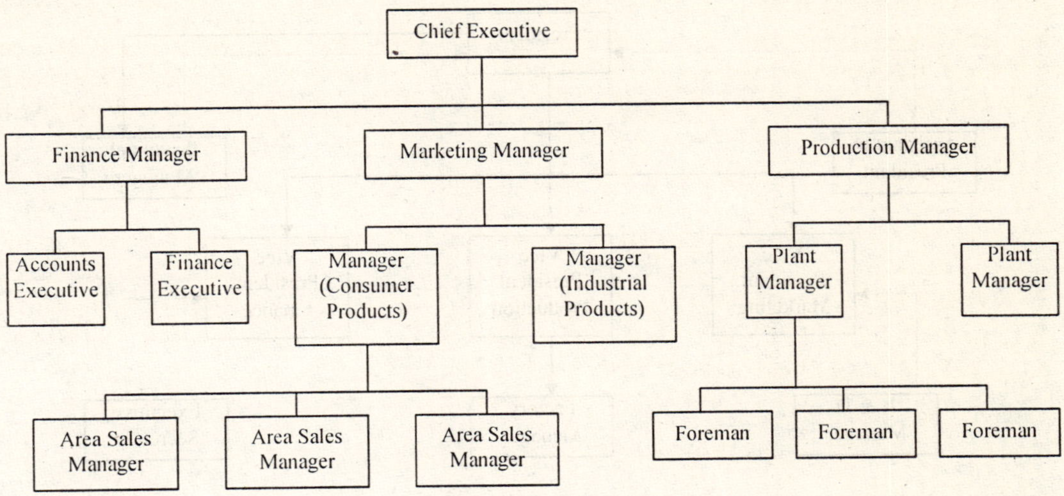

Line Organisational Structure

Fig. 9.11

Advantages & Disadvantages of Line Structure

The line structure is the oldest form of organisational structure. Its chief virtues are simplicity and unitary nature of authority. It is ideal for small organisations which can carry on with a modest division of core activities into homogeneous units. In a line structure, the lines of authority are simple, direct and clear; so are the lines of communication and control. These conditions facilitate quick decision-making and implementation by line managers who need not depend on others for supportive, advisory and other services.

The major limitation of line structure is that it is narrowly designed around only basic organisational activities. As an organisation grows and becomes large, there is need for further differentiation of activities and formation of separate seconday, supportive, service units. A line structure does not make provision for such an arrangement. There is a possibility that line managers in charge of operating units become over-burdened with many secondary auxiliary service activities which may dilute their abilities. Also duplication of service type, specialised and secondary activities in each line department may be quite expensive and uneconomical.

Line and Staff Structure

When both line and staff authorities are included in an organisation, it is known as a line and staff organisation. Fig 9.12 shows an organisation structure indicating what organisational relationships are lines and what are staffs. The solid lines which represent the lines of authority, extend from the president down through the fundamental organisational units, including the production, marketing and finance vice presidents, the personnel manager and the factory manager. Staff is represented by the broken lines, including the assistant to the president, the R&D manager and the executive secretary. Observe that the line authority is the avenue for direct performance of the work, whereas the staff line supports the line. Also, generally speaking, most staff managers do not exercise their staff authority along the channels of line authority but rather to the line of authority. It is helpful to remember that if the authority over the activities is directly related to accomplishment of the major objectives, the units are line. In contrast, if the authority over the activities is indirectly related to accomplishment of the major objectives, the units are staff.

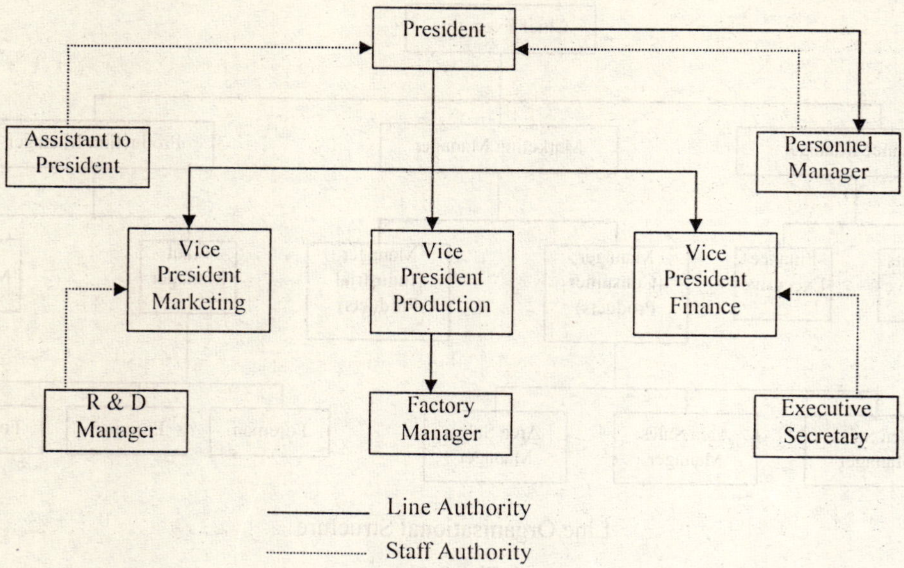

Line and Staff Structure

Fig. 9.12

Line-staff relationships

In actual practice, the harmonious working together of line and staff management members encounters roadblocks; there are honest differences of opinion on who should decide what, which decision is best and who takes what action when a decision is adopted. The difficulty is commonly a combination of failures to (1) identify and utilise staff authority, (2) recognise the true line-staff relationship and (3) cope with a noncooperative behaviour pattern by some management members.

Quite common is the line manager's complaint that staff people tend to grab credit for work that turns out successfully and lay the blame on line when work does not. Staff managers tend to take advantage of the fact that they report and have frequent access to high-line managers. It is easy for them to tell top-line manager why a project is or is not successful. Another complaint is that staff assumes line authority. In their eagerness to push their programmes, they overstep their staff prerogatives and tend to "run the show". At one time most staff authority was advisory only; now a sizable portion of staff authority actually has mandatory power. Furthermore, it is sometimes stated by line managers that staff assistance is impractical, unbalanced and fails into account all the ramifications of the situation. What is offered stresses too much the staff's particular specialty. The big picture is ignored.

In contrast, those with staff authority do not always hold line managers in high esteem. From the staff viewpoint, difficulties in line-staff relationships occur because line managers resist most new ideas and are too cautions and conservative. At times the line manager is accused of ignoring the staff and wanting to run the department independent of staff support. Line has staff to help but doesn't make full use of it or calls it in too late to realise maximum benefits. Another common theme is that staff is not given proper and adequate authority. Staff authority managers are experts; they know more about their specialty than line, but they are not given the right kind and amount of authority to enforce their decisions.

What can be done to improve these relationships? A long list could be given, but these suggestions suffice: (1) acquire a better understanding of the basic authority relationships; (2) develop a clear concept of the interrelationships of those with different types of authority within the organisation; and (3) stress interdependence, not separation, of the various organisation units and their respective managements. Fostering better communication, clarifying the authority differentiation among various management members, emphasizing performance for the maximum benefits of the total enterprise and holding members accountable for results are additional helpful means.

Deficiencies of traditional organisational structures

Some modern management theorists and researchers are very critical of traditional organisational structures and traditional concepts of organising. They regard these structures as mechanistic which are suitable for a stable environment. The traditional structure is characterised by excessive division of labour and specialisation of tasks; jobs, roles and relations are rigidly defined and structured; there is a high degree of differentiation of activities and fragmentation of tasks. The structure is characterised by official, formal one-way top-down communication channels. Such values as loyalty, discipline, conformity, order, stability, continuity and reliability command premium as against creativity, initiative dissent, freedom and so on. Management tends to be authority and control-oriented. Organisational goals are given precedence over the needs, expectations and values of people. Most of the decisions in the organisation are made by reference to established procedures, decision rules and programmed processes.

9.6 MODERN ORGANISATIONAL STRUCTURES

Traditional structures are also regarded as some what out of step with contemporary requirements and realities of rapid change, uncertainty and complexity of environment. Attempts are hence made to modify the traditional structure so as to evolve refined forms of structure. These are variously described as systems structure, project structure, programme structure, matrix structure, task force structure and free form structure. These modern structures are regarded as more organic, adaptive and flexible and are suitable for complex organisations which employ highly sophisticated technology and which encounter a very diverse, volatile environment. We may discuss the major modern structural designs as follows:

A. Horizontal Matrix Approach

The matrix approach combines aspects of both functional and divisional structures simultaneously in the same part of the organisation. The matrix structure evolved as a way to improve horizontal coordination and information sharing. One unique feature of the matrix is that it has dual lines of authority. In Fig 9.13 the functional hierarchy of authority runs vertically and the divisional hierarchy of authority runs horizontally. While the vertical structure provides traditional control within functional departments, the horizontal structure provides coordination across departments. The matrix structure therefore provides a formal chain of command for both functional (vertical) and divisional (horizontal) relationships. As a result of this dual structure, some employees actually report to two supervisors simultaneously.

The matrix structure often is used by global corporations. The problem for global companies is to achieve simultaneous coordination of various products within each country or region and for each product line. An example of a global matrix structure is illustrated in Fig 9.14. The two lines of authority are geographic boss in Germany

Dual-Authority Structure in a Matrix Organisation

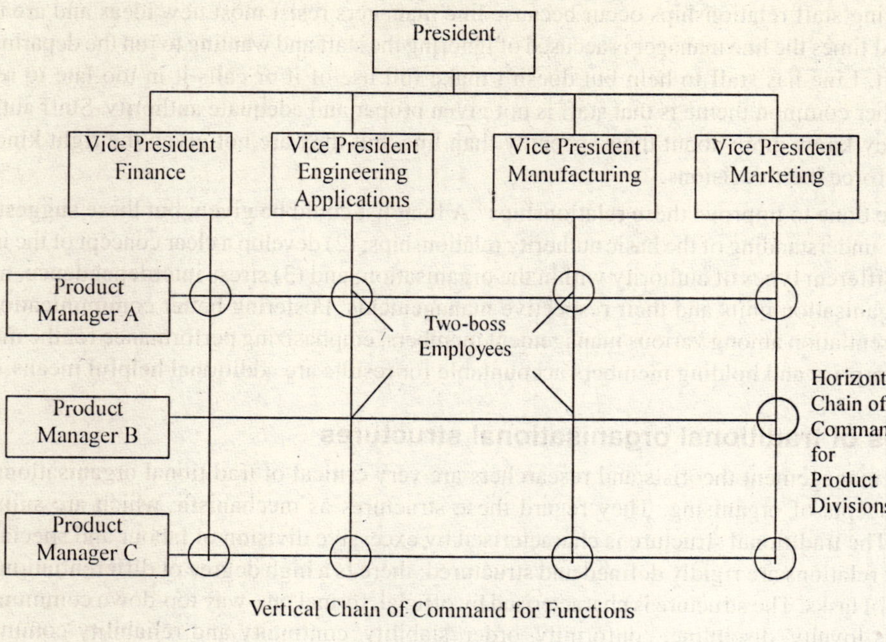

Fig 9.13

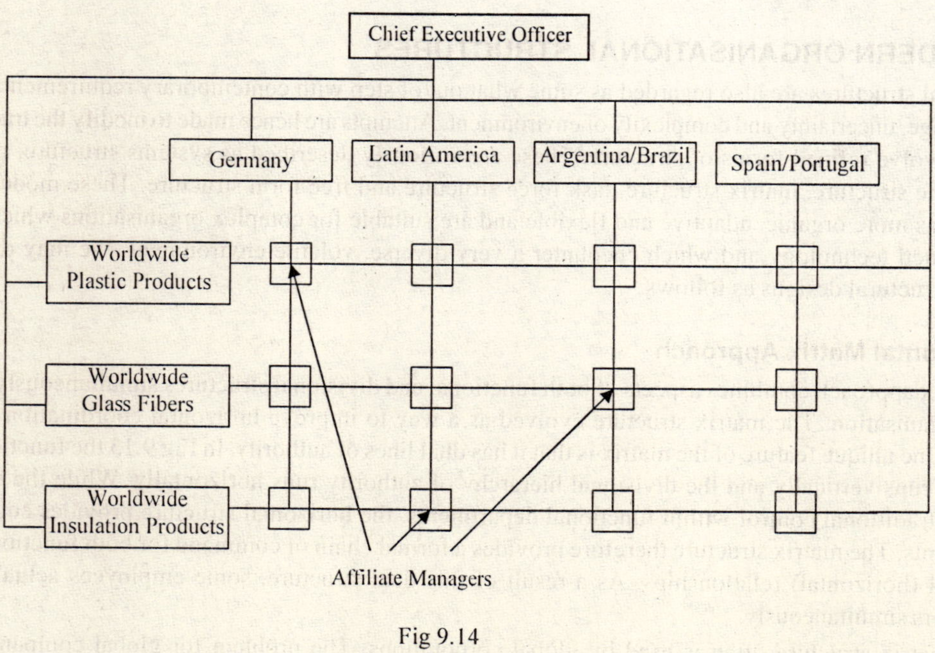

Fig 9.14

coordinates all affiliates in Germany and the plastics products boss coordinates the manufacturing and sale of plastics products around the world. Managers of local affiliate companies in Germany would report to two superiors, both the country boss and the product boss. The dual authority structure violates the unity-of-command concept. Dual lines of authority can be confusing, but after managers learn to use this structure, the matrix provides excellent coordination simultaneously for each geographic region and each product line.

The success of the matrix structure depends on the abilities of people in key matrix roles. Two-boss employees, those who report to two supervisors simultaneously, must resolve conflicting demands from the matrix bosses. They must confront senior mangers and reach joint decisions. They need excellent human relations skills with which to confront managers and resolve conflicts.

The matrix boss is the product or functional boss, who is responsible for one side of the matrix. The top leader is responsible for the entire matrix. The top leader oversees both the product and functional chains of commands. His or her responsibility is to maintain a power balance between the two sides of the matrix. If disputes arise between them, the problem will be kicked upstairs to the top leader.

Advantages and Disadvantages

The matrix structure is controversial because of the dual chain of command. However, it has been used successfully by companies such as IBM and Ford Motor Company, which have fine-tuned the matrix structure to suit their particular goals and cultures. The matrix can be highly effective in a complex, rapidly changing environment in which the organisation needs to be flexible and adaptable. The conflict and frequent meetings generated by the matrix allow new issues to be raised and resolved. The matrix structure makes efficient use of human resources because specialists can be transferred from one division to another. The matrix also provides training for both specialist and general management skills. People within a functional department or within a specific country in a global matrix have access to in-depth training and specialisation. At the same time, they coordinate with other programmes or divisions, which help employees, develop a general management perspective. Finally, the matrix structure engages the participation of employees in team meetings and in the achievement of divisional goals. Thus, it challenges and motivates employees, giving them a larger task than would be possible in a functional structure.

The matrix structure also has several disadvantages, however. The major problem is the confusion and frustration caused by the dual chain of command. Matrix bosses and two-boss employees have difficulty with the dual reporting relationships. The matrix structure also can generate high conflict because it pits divisional against functional goals in a domestic structure, or product line versus country goals in a global structure. This lead to the third disadvantage: time lost to meetings and discussions to resolving this conflict. Often the matrix structure leads to more discussion than action because different goals and points of view are being addressed. To survive and perform well in a matrix, employees need human relation training to learn to deal with two bosses, to get by with only "half" of each employee, and to confront and manage conflict. Finally, many organisations find it difficult to maintain the power balances essential for matrix success. The functional and divisional sides of the matrix must have equal power. If one side acquires greater formal authority, the advantages of the matrix structure are lost. The organisation then operates like a functional structure with informal lateral relationships.

The advantages and disadvantages of the matrix structure are summarized in Table 9.15 as below:

Table 9.15

Advantages	Disadvantages
More efficient use of resources than single hierarchy.	Frustration and confusion from dual chain of command.
Flexibility, adaptability to changing environment.	High conflict between two sides of matrix.
Development of both general and specialist management skills.	Many meetings, more discussion than action.
Interdisciplinary cooperation, expertise available to all divisions .	Human relations training needed.
Enlarged tasks for employees.	Power dominance by one side of matrix.

B. Team Approach

Probably the most widespread trend in departmentalisation has been the effort by companies to implement team concepts. The vertical chain of command is a powerful means of control, but passing all decisions up the hierarchy takes too long and keeps responsibility at the top. Today, companies are trying to find ways to delegate authority, push responsibility to low levels, and create participative teams that engage the commitment of workers. This approach enables organisations to be more flexible and responsive in the competitive global environment.

Cross-functional teams consist of employees from various functional departments who are responsible to meet as a team and resolve mutual problems. Team members typically still report to their functional departments, but they also report to the team, one member of whom may be the leader.

Some organisations have created permanent teams, groups of employees who are brought together as a formal department. The permanent-team approach resembles the divisional approach, except that teams are much smaller. Teams may consist of only 20 to 30 members, each bringing a functional specialty to the team.

Many companies reorganise into permanent teams after going through a process called reengineering. Reengineering is the radical redesign of business processes to achieve dramatic improvements in cost, quality, service and speed. Because the focus is on process rather than function, reengineering often leads to a shift away from a vertical structure to one emphasizing teamwork and empowerment.

Advantages and Disadvantages

Designing team relationships often helps overcome shortcomings in a functional, top-down approach to organising. With cross-functional teams, the organisation is able to retain some advantages of a functional structure, such as economies of scale and in-depth training, while gaining the benefits of team relationships. The team concept breaks down barriers across departments. Team members know one another's problems and compromise rather then blindly pursue their own goals. The team concept also allows the organisation to more quickly adapt to customer requests and environmental changes and speeds decision-making because decisions need not go to the top of the hierarchy for approval. Another big advantage is the moral boost. Employees are enthusiastic about their involvement in bigger projects rather than narrow departmental tasks. Jobs are enriched. The creation of teams also enables responsibility and authority to be pushed down the hierarchy, requiring fewer managers for supervision.

But the team approach has disadvantages as well. Employees may be enthusiastic about team participation, but they may also experience conflicts and dual loyalties. A cross-functional team may make different demands on members than do their department managers and members who participate in more than one team must resolve these conflicts. A large amount of time is devoted to meetings, thus increasing coordination time. Unless the organisation truly needs teams to coordinate complex projects and adapt to the environment, it will lose production efficiency with them. Finally, the team approach may cause too much decentralisation. Senior department managers who traditionally made decisions may feel left out when a team moves ahead on its own. Team members often do not see the big picture of the corporation and may make decisions that are good for their group but bad for the organisation as a whole. Top management can help keep the team in alignment with corporate goals.

The advantages and disadvantages of the team structure are summarised in Table 9.16.

Table 9.16

Advantages	Disadvantages
Some advantages of functional structure.	Dual loyalties and conflict.
Reduced barriers among departments, increased compromise.	Time and resources spent on meetings.
Less response time, quicker decisions.	Unplanned decentralisation.
Better morale, enthusiasm from employee involvement.	
Reduced administrative overhead.	

C. Network Approach

The most recent approach to departmentalisation extends the idea of horizontal coordination and collaboration beyond the boundaries of the organisation. The network structure means that the firm subcontracts many of its major functions to separate companies and coordinates their activities from a small headquarters organisation. The organisation may be viewed as a central hub surrounded by a network of outside specialists, as illustrated in Fig 9.17. Rather than being housed under one roof, services such as accounting, design, manufacturing and distribution are outsourced to separate organisations that are connected electronically to the central office. The

Network Approach to Departmentalisation

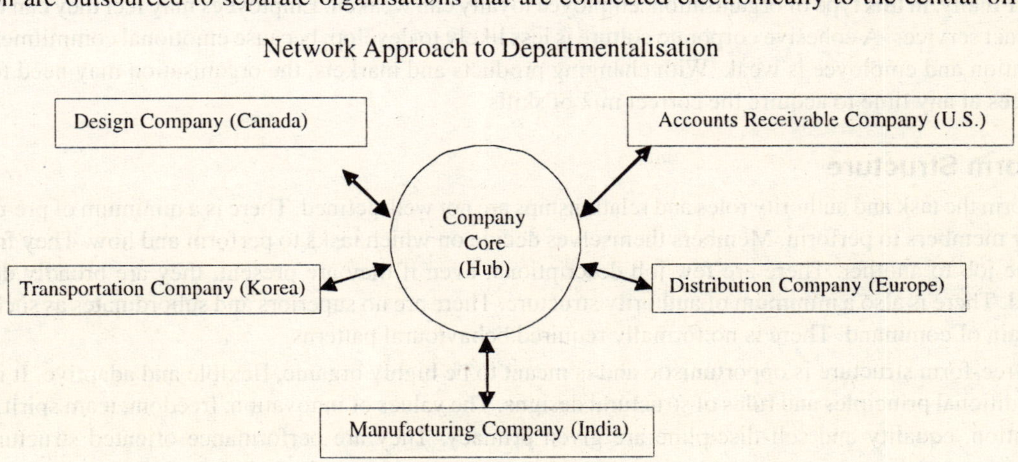

Fig 9.17

nature of the network structure means that subcontractors flow into and out of the system when needed. Much like building blocks parts of the network can be added or taken away to met changing needs. A further development of the network is the virtual network organisation, which is a continually evolving group of companies that unite temporarily to exploit specific opportunities or attain strategic advantages and then disband when objectives are met. Data and information are shared electronically among participating companies. Unlike the network structure, in which the hub organisation maintains control over work done by various subcontractors, in a virtual organisation each independent company gives up some control to temporarily become part of a new, larger organisational system.

The network approach is revolutionary, because it is difficult to answer the question "Where is the organisation?" in traditional terms. For example, a firm may contract for expensive services such as training, transportation, legal and engineering, so these functions are no longer part of the organisation. Or consider a piece of ice hockey equipment that is designed in India, engineered in the United States, manufactured in Korea and distributed in Canada by a Japanese sales organisation. These pieces are drawn together contractually and coordinated electronically, creating a new form of organisation. The network approach allows companies to concentrate on what they do best and to outsource the rest.

Advantages and Disadvantages

The biggest advantage to the network structure seems to be competitiveness on a global scale. Network organisations, even small ones, can be truly global. A network organisation can draw on resources worldwide to achieve the best quality and price and can sell its products and services worldwide. A second advantage is workforce flexibility and challenge. Flexibility comes from the ability to hire whatever services are needed, such as engineering design or maintenance and to change a few months later without constraints from owing plant, equipment and facilities. The organisation can continually redefine itself to fit new product and market opportunities. For those employees who are a permanent part of the organisation, the challenge comes from greater job variety and job satisfaction from working within the lean structure. Finally, this structure is perhaps the leanest of all organisation forms because little supervision is required.

One of the major disadvantages is lack of hands-on control. Managers do not have all operations under one roof and must rely on contracts, coordination, negotiation and electronic messages to hold things together. If a sub-contractor fails to deliver, goes out of business or has a plant burn down, the head quarters organisation can be put out of business. Uncertainty is higher because necessary services are not under one roof and under direct management control. Finally, in this type of organisation, employee loyalty can weaken. Employees may feel they can be replaced by contract services. A cohesive corporate culture is less likely to develop, because emotional commitment between organisation and employee is weak. With changing products and markets, the organisation may need to reshuffle employees at any time to acquire the correct mix of skills.

Free form Structure

In this form the task and authority roles and relationships are not well-defined. There is a minimum of pre-determined tasks for members to perform. Members themselves decide on which tasks to perform and how. They freely move from one job to another. There are few job descriptions; even if they are present, they are broadly defined and designed. There is also a minimum of authority structure. There are no superiors and subordinates as such and there is no chain of command. There is no formally required behavioural patterns.

The free-form structure is opportunistic and is meant to be highly organic, flexible and adaptive. It is liberated from traditional principles and rules of structural designs. The values of innovation, freedom, team spirit, collective contribution, equality and self-discipline are given primacy. They are performance oriented structures. A few organisations in USA are moving towards the free form structure in a gradual manner.

Chapter 10

Individual Perspective

10.1 INTRODUCTION

People differ in many ways. At work, these differences influence how they interpret an assignment, whether they like to be told what to do and how they handle challenges. Manager's personalities and attitudes can also profoundly affect the workplace. People are an organisation's most valuable resource and the source of some of the most difficult problems. People problems can be particularly challenging due to the complex and unique qualities that people bring to the workplace. Three basic leadership skills are at the core of identifying and solving people problems: (1) diagnosing or gaining insight into the situation a manager is trying to influence; (2) adapting individual behaviour and resources to meet the needs of the situation; and (3) communicating in a way that others can understand and accept. Thus, managers need insight about individual differences to understand what a behavioural situation is now and what it may be in the future.

To handle this responsibility, managers need to understand the principles of organisational behaviour, that is, the ways individuals and groups tend to act in organisations. By increasing their knowledge of individual differences in the areas of attitudes, personality, perception, learning and stress management, managers can understand and lead employees and colleagues through many workplace challenges.

10.2 PERSON VARIABLES

So far as the person or organisation variable is concerned, the most important aspects of a person which mould his behaviour are his physiology, personality traits, abilities and motives. Both striking similarities and differences are observable among individuals with respect to these three aspects.

Personality traits, abilities, needs and motives of humans are dynamic in nature. Within an individual, they tend to change in their range, intensity and importance over a period of time. They also tend to be in conflict with each other. In any case, traits, abilities and motives play a very important role in rousing, maintaining or stopping action behaviour of individuals; they also determine the choice and direction of behaviour.

10.3 ATTITUDE

Managers observe that some people show up at work eager to get started, whereas others appear to wish they were elsewhere. Some employees tackle problems with the expectation that they and their coworkers will cooperate to find a solution; others grumble or panic. These different kinds of behaviour partly reflect variations in employee attitudes. Defined formally, an attitude is *an evaluation that predisposes a person to act in a certain way.* A person who has the attitude "I love my work; it's challenging and fun" probably will tackle work-related problems cheerfully, while one who comes to work with the attitude "I hate my job" is not likely to exhibit much enthusiasm or commitment to solving problems.

Components of Attitudes

Behavioural scientists consider attitudes to have three components: cognitions (thoughts), affect (feelings) and behaviour. The cognitive component of an attitude includes the beliefs, opinions and information the person has about the object of the attitude, such as knowledge of what a job entails and opinions about personal abilities. The affective component is the person's emotions or feelings about the object of the attitude, such as enjoying or hating a job. The behavioural component of an attitude is the person's intention to behave toward the object of the attitude in a certain way.

Often, when we think about attitudes, we focus on the cognitive component. However, it is important for managers to remember the other components as well. When people feel strongly about something, the affective component may predispose them to act, no matter what someone does to change their opinions. For example, if an employee is passionate about a new idea, that employee may go to great lengths to implement it. Likewise, an employee who is furious about being asked to work overtime on his birthday may act on that anger-by failing to cooperate, lashing out at coworkers or even quitting-no matter what arguments the employee's manger presents about the need to work. In cases such as these, effective leadership includes addressing the affect (emotions) associated with the attitude.

Recognizing components of attitudes also is useful for managers when they want to change an attitude. As a general rule, changing one component of an attitude-cognitions, affect or behaviour can contribute to an overall change in attitude. Suppose a manager concludes that some employees have the attitude that the manager should make all the decisions affecting the department, but the manager prefers that employees assume more decision-making responsibility. To change the underlying attitude, the manager would consider whether to educate employees about the areas in which they can make good decisions (changing the cognitive component), build enthusiasm with pep talks about the satisfaction of employee empowerment (changing the affective component) or simply insist that employees make their own decisions (behavioural component) with the expectation that, once they experience the advantages of decision-making authority, they will begin to like it.

Work-Related Attitudes

The attitudes of most interest to managers are those related to work, especially attitudes that influence how well employees perform. To lead employees effectively, managers logically seek to cultivate the kinds of attitudes that are associated with high performance. Two attitudes that may relate to high performance are satisfaction with one's job and commitment to the organisation.

Job Satisfaction: A positive attitude toward one's job is called job satisfaction. In general, people experience this attitude when their work matches their needs and interests, when working conditions and rewards (such as pay) are satisfactory and when the employees like their co-workers.

Many managers believe job satisfaction is important because they think satisfied employees will do better work. In fact, research shows that the link between satisfaction and performance is generally small and is affected by other factors. The importance of satisfaction varies according to the amount of control the employee has; an employee doing routine tasks may produce about the same output no matter how he or she feels about the job. But, there are reasons managers should care about job satisfaction. When unemployment rates are low and workers can easily find jobs elsewhere, managers want their productive employees to be happy enough to stay with the organisation. In addition, as human being, managers may simply want employees to feel good about their work and they may prefer to work with people who have a positive outlook.

Organisational Commitment: Another important attitude is organisational commitment, which is loyalty to and heavy involvement in the organisation. An employee with a high degree of organisational commitment is likely to say "we" when talking about the organisation. Such a person tries to contribute to the organisation's success and wishes to remain with the organisation.

Most managers want to enjoy the benefits of loyal, committed employees, including low turnover and willingness to do more than the job's basic requirements. Organisational commitment has become especially important in recent years. Managers can take action to promote organisational commitment by keeping employees informed, giving them a say in decisions, providing the necessary training and other resources that enable them to succeed, treating them fairly and offering rewards they value.

Conflicts among Attitudes

Sometimes a person may discover that his or her attitudes conflict with one another or are not reflected in his or her behaviour. For example, a person's high level of organisational commitment may conflict with the person's commitment to family members. If employees routinely work evenings and week-ends, their long hours and dedication to the job may conflict with their belief that family ties are important. This can create a state of cognitive dissonance, a psychological discomfort that occurs when individuals recognize inconsistencies in their own attitudes and behaviours.

In the case of working overtime, a person who feels in control of her hours might restructure her responsibilities so that she has time for both work and family. In contrast, another individual who is unable to restructure his workload might change his attitude toward his employer, reducing his organisational commitment. He might resolve his dissonance by saying he loves his children but has to work long hours because his unreasonable employer demands it.

10.4 PERSONALITY

In the workplace, we find people whose behaviour is consistently pleasant or aggressive or stubborn in a variety of situations. To explain that behaviour, we may say, "He has a pleasant personality" or "She has an aggressive personality". An individual's personality is the set of characteristics that underlie a relatively stable pattern of behaviour in response to ideas, objects or people in the environment. Understanding an individual's personality can help managers predict how that person will act in a particular situation. Managers who appreciate the ways their employee's personalities differ have insight into what kinds of leadership behaviour will be most influential.

Personality Traits

In common usage, people think of personality in terms of traits or relatively stable characteristics of a person. Researchers have investigated whether any traits stand up to scientific scrutiny. Although investigators have examined thousands of traits over the years, their findings have been distilled into five general dimensions that describe personality. These often are called the "Big Five" personality factors. Each factor may contain a wide range of specific traits. The Big Five personality factors describe an individual's extroversion, agreeableness, conscientiousness, emotional stability and openness to experience. Each of these qualities is defined below:

1. Extroversion – The degree to which a person is sociable, talkative, assertive and comfortable with interpersonal relationships.
2. Agreeableness – The degree to which a person is able to get along with others by being good-natured, cooperative, forgiving, understanding and trusting.
3. Conscientiousness – The degree to which a person is focused on a few goals, thus behaving in ways that are responsible, dependable, persistent and achievement oriented.
4. Emotional stability – The degree to which a person is calm, enthusiastic and secure, rather than tense, nervous, depressed, moody or insecure.
5. Openness to experience – The degree to which a person has a broad range of interests and is imaginative. creative, artistically sensitive and willing to consider new ideas.

These factors represent a continuum. That is, any individual may exhibit a low, moderate or high degree of each quality. A person who has an extremely high degree of agreeableness would likely be described as warm, friendly and good natured, while one at the opposite extreme might be described as cold, rude or hard to get along with. In general, having a moderate-to-high degree of each of the personality factors is considered desirable for a wide range of employees. In addition, certain factors may be particularly important for specific kinds of work. For example, many successful entrepreneurs, display a high degree of creativity (openness to ideas) and conscientiousness.

Despite the logic and even the validity of the Big Five personality factors, they can be difficult to measure precisely. Furthermore, research has been mostly limited to subjects in the United States, so this theory is difficult to apply in an international context.

Attitudes and Behaviours Influenced by Personality

An individual's personality influences a wide variety of work-related attitudes and behaviours. Among those that are of particular interest to managers are locus of control, authoritarianism, Machiavellianism and problem-solving styles.

Locus of Control: People differ in terms of what they tend to attribute as the cause of their success or failure. Their locus of control defines whether they place the primary responsibility within themselves or on outside forces. Some people believe that their actions can strongly influence what happens to them. They feel in control of their own fate. These individuals have a high internal locus of control. Other people believe that events in their lives occur because of chance, luck or outside people and events. They feel more like pawns of their fate. These individuals have a high external locus of control.

Research on locus of control has shown real differences in behaviour across a wide range of settings. People with an internal locus of control are easier to motivate because they believe the rewards are the result of their behaviour. They are better able to handle complex information and problem solving, are more achievement oriented, but are also more independent and therefore more difficult to lead. On the other hand, people with an external locus of control are harder to motivate, less involved in their jobs, more likely to blame others when faced with a poor performance evaluation, but more compliant and conforming and therefore, easier to lead.

Authoritarianism: Authoritarianism is the belief that power and status differences should exist within the organisation. Individuals high in authoritarianism tend to be concerned with power and toughness, obey recognized authority above them, stick to conventional values, critically judge others and oppose the use of subjective feelings. The degree to which managers possess authoritarianism will influence how they wield and share power. The degree to which employees possess authoritarianism will influence how they react to their managers. If a manager and employees differ in their degree of authoritarianism, the manager may have difficulty leading effectively.

Machiavellianism: Another personality dimension that is helpful in understanding work behaviour is Machiavellianism, which is characterized by the acquisition of power and the manipulation of other people for purely personal gain. Machiavellianism is named after Niccolo Machiavelli, a sixteenth-century author who wrote 'The Prince' a book for noblemen of the day on how to acquire and use power. Psychologists have developed instruments to measure a person's Machiavellianism (Mach) orientation. Research shows that high Machs are predisposed to being pragmatic, capable of lying to achieve personal goals, more likely to win in win-lose situations and more likely to persuade than be persuaded.

Different situations may require people who exhibit one or the other type of behaviour. In loosely structured situations, high Machs actively take control, while low Machs accept the direction given by others. Low Machs thrive in highly structured situations, while high Machs perform in a detached, disinterested way. High Machs are particularly good in jobs that require bargaining skills or that involve substantial rewards for winning.

Problem-Solving Styles: Managers also need to understand that individuals differ in the way they go about gathering and evaluating information for problem solving and decision-making. Psychologist Carl Jung has identified four functions related to this process: sensation, intuition, thinking and feeling. According to Jung, gathering information and evaluating information are separate activities. People gather information either by sensation or intuition, but not by both simultaneously. Sensation-type people would rather work with known facts and hard data and prefer routine and order in gathering information. Intuitive-type people would rather look for possibilities than work with facts and prefer solving new problems and using abstract concepts.

Information evaluation involves making judgments about the information a person has gathered. People evaluate information by thinking or feeling. These represent the extremes in orientation. Thinking-type individuals base their judgements on impersonal analysis, using reason and logic rather than personal values or emotional aspects of the situation. Feeling-type individuals base their judgments more on personal feelings such as harmony and tend to make decisions that result in approval from others.

According to Jung, only one of the four functions – sensation, intuition, thinking or feeling-is dominant in an individual. However, the dominant function usually is backed up by one of the functions from the other set of paired opposites.

10.5 PERCEPTION

People often approach an assignment differently because one person "sees" the assignment differently from others. "Seeing" things differently is an inevitable outcome of perception-the process people use to make sense out of the environment by selecting, organising and interpreting information from the environment. Because of individual differences in what people perceive and how they organise and interpret it, perceptions vary among people and differ from objective reality. Recognising the difference between what is perceived and what is real is a key element in diagnosing a situation.

We can think of perception as a step-by-step process, as shown in Fig 10.1. First, we observe information (sensory data) from the environment through our senses: taste, smell, hear, see and touch. Next, our mind screens the data and will select only the items we will process further. Third, we organise the selected data into meaningful patterns for interpretation and response. Most differences in perception among people at work are related to how they select and organise sensory data.

The Perception Process

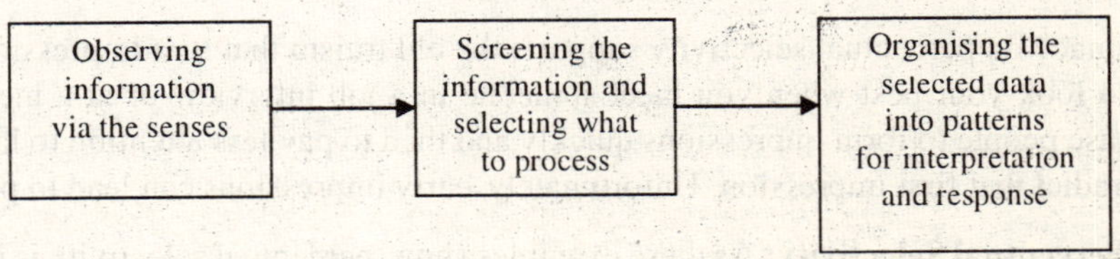

Fig 10.1

Perceptual Selectivity

We all are aware of our environment, but not everything in it is equally important to our perception of it. We tune in to some data and tune out other data. People are bombarded by so much sensory data that it is impossible to process it all. The brain's solution is to run the data through a perceptual filter that retains some parts (selective attention) and eliminates others. Perceptual selectivity is the process by which individuals screen and select the various objects and stimuli that view for their attention. Certain stimuli catch their attention and others do not.

Exactly what a person screens and selects depends on a number of factors. These relate either to the stimuli being perceived or characteristics of the perceiver.

Characteristics of the Stimuli: The following characteristics of the stimuli can enhance the chance it will be selected:

- Contrast – People notice a stimulus more if it stands out from background stimuli. Examples include a loud noise in quiet room or bold type on a white page.
- Novelty – A stimulus that is new or different from stimuli previously perceived may attract more attention.

- Familiarity – People tend to perceive stimuli that are known or familiar.
- Intensity – People are more inclined to notice a stimulus that is intense in some way, for example, by being loud or bright.
- Motion – Objects that move a lot tend to be noticed more.
- Repetition – Repeated stimuli tend to attract more attention.
- Size – A larger object generally receives more attention than a smaller object.

The influence of stimuli characteristics on the perceptual process comes into play in an employment interview. In evaluating a job applicant, interviewers may notice particular characteristics that are either novel or comfortingly familiar. In addition, if a candidate repeatedly refers to some qualification, the interviewer is likely to pay more attention to that piece of information.

Contrast and novelty also influence how people are perceived in many situations. People who differ in some way-by race, sex or disability status, for example-receive more than their share of scrutiny.

Characteristics of the Perceiver: Several characteristics of the perceiver also can influence the selection of sensory data:

- Needs and motivation – People tend to notice stimuli that provide a way to satisfy their needs.
- Values and beliefs – People tend to pay the most attention to stimuli that are consistent with their values and beliefs.
- Personality – People pay the most attention to stimuli that reinforce their personality.
- Learning – Experience with similar stimuli teaches people what it is important for them to pay attention to.
- Primacy – People pay relatively greater attention to stimuli near the beginning of an event.
- Recency – People pay relatively greater attention to stimuli toward the end of an event.

The impact of primacy on perceptual selectivity supports the old truism that first impressions are important. It really is important to look your best when you meet someone in a job interview or at a meeting. The primacy characteristic can cause people to form impressions quickly and then to pay less attention to later behaviour, even though it could contradict that first impression. Unfortunately, early impressions can lead to perceptual errors.

Applications of Perceptual Selectivity: As these examples show, perceptual selectivity is not a simple process of reducing data to an amount that is easy to perceive. It is a complex filtering process that determines which sensory data will receive attention. Managers can use these principles of selective perception to obtain clues about why one person "sees" things differently from others and they can apply the principles to their own communications, especially when they want to attract or focus attention.

An obvious application of selective perception is advertising; organisations want to use the factors that enhance perception to create ads that grab attention.

Perceptual Organisation

Once people have selected the sensory data to be perceived, they begin grouping the data into recognisable patterns. Perceptual organisation is the process by which people organise or categorise stimuli according to their frame of reference. Individuals learn to simplify and make sense out of their perceptions through a gradual process of organising sensory data from their experiences. The process begins early in life with experiences about how to interpret facial expressions and what objects we can safely and pleasurably eat (bread is good, sand is not). This process continues throughout our lives. In the workplace, the process of organising sensory data is affected by our experiences in meetings, performance appraisals, interaction with our bosses and co-workers and so forth.

Several factors in perceptual organisation contribute to individual differences among people in the work setting. These include perceptual grouping, figure-ground and perceptual distortions.

Perceptual Grouping: To make sense of a highly complex world, people engage in perceptual grouping or the organising of sensory data into patterns. This process is beneficial when it leads to conclusions that accurately reflect objective reality. Mechanisms for perceptual grouping include closure, continuity, proximity and similarity.

Closure is the tendency to perceive incomplete data in its whole, complete form. Most people see this series of spots as a dog. Through closure, the brain imagines the missing details.

Continuity is the tendency to perceive sensory data in continuous patterns, even if they are not actually continuous. Because people tend to organise messages in a way that makes sense to them, managers must be extremely careful in how they communicate messages that may be unexpected or difficult to understand.

Proximity is the tendency to perceive sensory data as related because of close physical location. For example, people working on the same floor of a large office building may be perceived as a unit even though they represent portions of several departments of the company.

Similarity is the tendency to group sensory data because they are alike in some way. For example, a manager might use the mental category "scientific research" for research reports he considers valid and reliable. He might tend to assign reports to this group whenever they contain a lot of numerical data or a large number of respondents. However, for perceptions to be accurate, it is important to examine the criteria for assigning a stimulus to a particular group. In this example, not every survey with a lot of data or a large sample will be objectively "scientific". When a report is significant to the manager, he should therefore examine its conclusions carefully before relying on it.

Figure-Ground: Another factor in perceptual organisation is figure-ground – people's tendency to perceive the sensory data they are most attentive to as standing out against the background of sensory data to which they are less attentive. Managers who want to change their own or others, perceptions must be patient and try showing the new interpretation from more than one angle.

Perceptual Distortions: Errors in perceptual judgment, called perceptual distortions, can arise from inaccuracies in any part of the perception process. Some types of errors are so common that managers should become familiar with them. These include stereotyping, the halo effect, projection and perceptual defense. Managers who recognise these perceptual distortions can better adjust their perceptions to more closely match objective reality.

Stereotyping is the tendency to assign an individual to a group or broad category (e.g., female, black, elderly or male, white, disabled) and then to attribute widely held generalisations about the group to the individual. Thus, someone meets a new colleague, sees he is in a wheelchair, assigns him to the category "physically disabled" and attributes to this colleague generalisations she believes about people with disabilities, which may include a belief that he is less able than other co-workers. However, the person's inability to walk should not be seen as indicative of lesser abilities in other areas. Indeed, the assumption of limitations may not only offend him, it also prevents the person making the stereotypical judgment form benefiting from the many ways in which this person can contribute. Because stereotyping clouds individual differences, it prevents people from truly knowing those they classify in this way. In addition, negative stereotypes can prevent talented people from advancing in an organisation and fully contributing their talents to the organisation's success.

The halo effect occurs when the perceiver develops an overall impression of a person or situation based on one attribute, either favourable or unfavourable. In other words, a halo blinds the perceiver to other attributes that should be used in generating a more complete assessment. The halo effect can play a significant role in performance appraisal. For example, a person with an outstanding attendance record may be assessed as responsible, industrious and highly productive; another person with less-than-average attendance may be assessed as a poor performer. Either assessment may be true but it is the manager's job to be sure the assessment is based on complete information about all job-related attributes and not just his or her preferences for good attendance.

Projection is the tendency of perceivers to see their own personal traits in other people; that is, they project their own needs, feelings, values and attitudes into their judgment of others. For example, a manager who is achievement oriented may assume that her subordinates are as well. This may cause her to restructure jobs in her department to be less routine and more challenging, without regard for her employees actual satisfaction. The best guards against errors based on projection are self-awareness and empathy.

Perceptual defense is the tendency of perceivers to protect themselves against ideas, objects or people that are threatening. People perceive things that are satisfying and pleasant but tend to disregard things that are disturbing and unpleasant. In essence, people develop blind spots in the perceptual process so that negative sensory data do not hurt them.

10.6 MOTIVATION

Meaning

The term 'motivation' has its origin in the Latin word "movere" which means to "move". Thus, motivation stands for movement. One can get a donkey to move by using a "carrot or a stick", with people one can use incentives or threats or reprimands. However, these only have a limited effect. These work for a while and then need to be repeated, increased or reinforced to secure further movement. The term motivation may be defined as "the managerial function of ascertaining the motives of subordinates and helping them to realise those motives.

According to Dubin, Motivation can be defined as *"the complex of forces starting and keeping a person at work in an organisation. Motivation is something that moves the person to action and continues him in the course of action already initiated"*.

In the words of Dalton E. McFarland, *"Motivation is the way in which urges, desires, aspirations, striving or needs direct, control or explain the behaviour of human being". According to him, motivation is a form of tension occurring within individuals, with resulting behaviour aimed at reducing, eliminating or diverting the tension.* Understanding the needs and drives and their resulting tensions helps to explain and predict human behaviour ultimately providing a sound basis for managerial decision and action. Thus, motivation is the term which applies to the entire class of urges, drives, desires, needs and similar forces.

A Conceptual Model of Motivation

Motivation refers to the forces either within or external to a person that arouse enthusiasm and persistence to pursue a certain course of action. Employee motivation affects productivity and part of a manager's job is to channel motivation toward the accomplishment of organisational goals. The study of motivation helps managers understand what prompts people to initiate action, what influences their choice of action and why they persist in that action over time.

A simple model of human motivation is illustrated in Fig 10.2. People have basic needs, such as for food, achievement or monetary gain, that translate into an internal tension that motivates specific behaviours with which to fulfill the need. To the extent that the behaviour is successful, the person is rewarded in the sense that the need is satisfied. The reward also informs the person that the behaviour was appropriate and can be used again in the future.

Rewards are of two types: intrinsic and extrinsic.

Intrinsic rewards are the satisfactions a person receives in the process of performing a particular action. The completion of a complex task may bestow a pleasant feeling of accomplishment or solving a problem that benefits others may fulfill a personal mission.

Extrinsic rewards are given by another person, typically a manager and include promotions and pay increases. They originate externally, as a result of pleasing others.

The importance of motivation as illustrated in Fig 10.2 is that it can lead to behaviours that reflect high performance within organisations. One recent study found that high employee motivation goes hand-in-hand with high organisational performance and profits.

A simple Model of Motivation

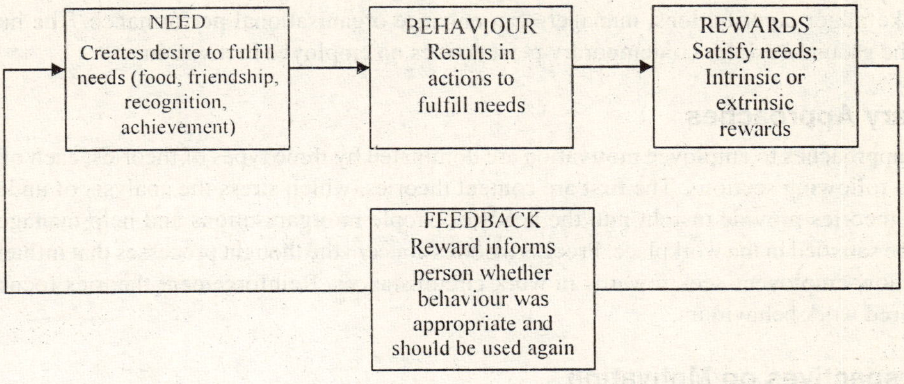

Fig 10.2

Managers can use motivation theory to help satisfy employee's needs and simultaneously encourage high work performance. Particularly in today's era of low unemployment, with many companies scrambling to find and keep qualified workers, managers are searching for the right combination of motivational techniques and rewards to keep workers happy and productive. Workers at many of today's leading companies say they are motivated by factors such as a fun, challenging work environment; flexibility that provides a balance between work and personal life; and the potential to learn, grow and be creative in their jobs.

Foundations of Motivation

A manager's assumptions about employee motivation and use of rewards depend on his or her perspective on motivation. Three distinct perspectives on employee motivation that have evolved are the traditional approach, the human relations approach and the human resources approach. The most recent theories about motivation represent a fourth perspective called contemporary approaches.

Traditional Approach

The study of employee motivation really began with the work of Frederick W. Taylor on scientific management. Scientific management pertains to the systematic analysis of an employee's job for the purpose of increasing efficiency. Economic rewards are provided to employees for high performance. The emphasis on pay evolved into the perception of workers as economic people-who would work harder for higher pay. This approach led to the development of incentive pay systems, in which people were paid strictly on the quantity and quality of their work outputs.

Human Relations Approach

The economic man was gradually replaced by a more sociable employee in managers' minds. Beginning with the landmark Hawthorne studies at a Western Electric plant, non-economic rewards, such as congenial work groups who met social needs, seemed more important than money as a motivator of work behaviour. For the first time, workers were studied as people, and the concept of social man was born.

Human Resource Approach

The human resource approach carries the concepts of economic man and social man farther to introduce the concepts of the whole person. Human resource theory suggests that employees are complex and motivated by many factors. For example, the work by McGregor on Theory X and Theory Y argued that people want to do a good job and that work is as natural and healthy as play. Proponents of the human resource approach believed that earlier approaches had tried to manipulate employees through economic or social rewards. By assuming that employees are competent and able to make major contributions, managers can enhance organisational performance. The human resource approach laid the groundwork for contemporary perspectives on employee motivation.

Contemporary Approaches

Contemporary approaches to employee motivation are dominated by three types of theories, each of which will be discussed in the following sections. The first are content theories, which stress the analysis of underlying human needs. Content theories provide insight into the needs of people in organisations and help managers understand how needs can be satisfied in the workplace. Process theories concern the thought processes that influence behaviour. They focus on how employees seek rewards in work circumstances. Reinforcement theories focus on employee learning of desired work behaviours.

Content Perspectives on Motivation

Content theories emphasize the needs that motivate people. At any point in time, people have basic needs such as those for food, achievement or monetary reward. These needs translate into an internal drive that motivates specific behaviours in an attempt to fulfill the needs. An individual's needs are like a hidden catalog of the things he or she wants and will work to get. To the extent that managers understand worker needs, the organisation's reward systems can be designed to meet them and reinforce employees for directing energies and priorities toward attainment of organisational goals.

Hierarchy of Needs Theory

Probably the most famous content theory was developed by Abraham Maslow. Maslow's hierarchy of needs theory proposes that humans are motivated by multiple needs and that these needs exist in a hierarchical order as illustrated in Fig 10.3. Maslow identified five general type of motivating needs in order of ascendance:

1. ***Physiological needs.*** These are the most basic human physical needs, including food, water and sex. In the organisational setting, these are reflected in the needs for adequate heat, air and base salary to ensure survival.
2. ***Safety needs.*** These are the needs for a safe and secure physical and emotional environment and freedom from threats-that is, for freedom from violence and for an orderly society. In an organisational workplace, safety needs reflect the needs for safe jobs, fringe benefits and job security.
3. ***Belongingness needs.*** These needs reflect the desire to be accepted by one's peers, have friendships, be part of a group and be loved. In the organisation, these needs influence the desire for good relationships with coworkers, participation in a work group and a positive relationship with supervisors.
4. ***Esteem needs.*** These needs relate to the desire for a positive self-image and to receive attention, recognition and appreciation from others. Within organisations, esteem needs reflect a motivation for recognition, an increase in responsibility, high status and credit for contributions to the organisation.
5. ***Self-actualisation needs.*** These represent the need for self-fulfillment, which is the highest need category. They concern developing one's full potential, increasing one's competence and becoming a better person. Self-actualisation needs can be met in the organisation by providing people with opportunities to grow, be creative and acquire training for challenging assignments and advancement.

According to Maslow's theory, low-order needs take priority-they must be satisfied before higher-order needs are activated. The needs are satisfied in sequence: Physiological needs come before safety needs, safety needs before social needs and so on. A person desiring physical safety will devote his or her efforts to securing a safer environment and will not be concerned with esteem needs or self-actualisation needs. Once a need is satisfied, it declines in importance and the next higher need is activated.

Fulfillment off the job	Need Hierarchy	Fulfillment on the job
Education, religion, hobbies, Personal growth	Self-actualisation Needs	Opportunities for training, advancement, growth and creativity
Approval of family, friends, community	Esteem Needs	Recognition, high status, increased responsibility
Family, friends, community, groups	Belongingness Needs	Work groups, clients, coworkers, supervisors
Freedom from war, pollution, violence	Safety Needs	Safe work, fringe benefits, job security
Food, water, sex	Physiological Needs	Heat, air, base salary

Maslow's Hierarchy of Needs

Fig 10.3

Two-Factor Theory

Frederick Herzberg developed another popular theory of motivation called the two factor theory. Herzberg interviewed hundreds of workers about times when they were highly motivated to work and other times when they were dissatisfied and unmotivated at work. His findings suggested that the work characteristics associated with dissatisfaction were quite different from those pertaining to satisfaction, which prompted the notion that two factors influence work motivation.

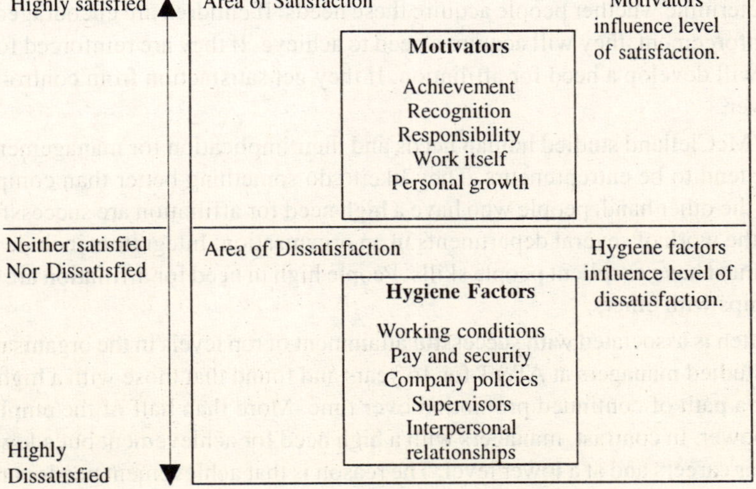

Herberg's Two-Factor Theory

Fig. 10.4

The two-factor theory is illustrated in Fig 10.4. The center of the scale is neutral, meaning that workers are neither satisfied nor dissatisfied. Herzberg believed that two entirely separate dimensions contribute to an employee's behaviour at work. The first, called hygiene factors, involves the presence or absence of job dissatisfiers, such as working conditions, pay, company policies and interpersonal relationships. When hygiene factors are poor, work is dissatisfying. However, good hygiene factors simply remove the dissatisfaction; they do not in themselves cause people to become highly satisfied and motivated in their work.

The second set of factors does influence job satisfaction. Motivators are high-level needs and include achievement, recognition, responsibility and opportunity for growth. Herzberg believed that when motivators are absent, workers are neutral toward work, but when motivators are present, workers are highly motivated and satisfied. Thus, hygiene factors and motivators represent two distinct factors that influence motivation. Hygiene factors work only in the area of dissatisfaction. Unsafe working conditions or a noisy work environment will cause people to be dissatisfied; their correction will not lead to a high level of motivation and satisfaction. Motivators such as challenge, responsibility and recognition must be in place before employees will be highly motivated to excel at their work.

The implication of the two-factor theory for managers is clear. Providing hygiene factors will eliminate employee dissatisfaction but will not motivate workers to high achievement levels. On the other hand, recognition, challenge and opportunities for personal growth are powerful motivators and will promote high satisfaction and performance. The manager's role is to remove dissatisfiers-that is, to provide hygiene factors sufficient to meet basic needs-and then use motivators to meet higher-level needs and propel employees toward greater achievement and satisfaction.

Acquired Needs Theory

The final content theory was developed by David McClelland. The acquired needs theory proposes that certain types of needs are acquired during the individual's lifetime. In other words, people are not born with these needs but may learn them through their life experiences. The three needs most frequently studied are these:

1. Need for achievement: The desire to accomplish something difficult, attain a high standard of success, master complex tasks and surpass others.
2. Need for affiliation: The desire to form close personal relationships, avoid conflict and establish warm friendships.
3. Need for power: The desire to influence or control others, be responsible for others and have authority over others.

Early life experiences determine whether people acquire these needs. If children are encouraged to do things for themselves and receive reinforcement, they will acquire a need to achieve. If they are reinforced for forming warm human relationships, they will develop a need for affiliation. If they get satisfaction from controlling others, they will acquire a need for power.

For more than 20 years, McClelland studied human needs and their implication for management. People with a high need for achievement tend to be entrepreneurs. They like to do something better than competitors and take sensible business risks. On the other hand, people who have a high need for affiliation are successful "integrators," whose job is to coordinate the work of several departments in an organisation. Integrators include brand managers and project managers who must have excellent people skills. People high in need for affiliation are able to establish positive working relationships with others.

A high need for power often is associated with successful attainment of top levels in the organisational hierarchy. For example, McClelland studied managers at AT&T for 16 years and found that those with a high need for power were more likely to follow a path of continued promotion over time. More than half of the employees at the top levels had a high need for power. In contrast, managers with a high need for achievement but a low need for power tended to peak earlier in their careers and at a lower level. The reason is that achievement needs can be met through the task itself, but power needs can be met only by ascending to a level at which a person has power over others.

In summary, content theories focus on people's underlying needs and label those particular needs that motivate people to behave. The hierarchy of needs theory, the two-factor theory and the acquired needs theory all help managers understand what motivates people. In this way, managers can design work to meet needs and hence elicit appropriate and successful work behaviours.

Process Perspectives on Motivation

Process theories explain how workers select behavioural actions to meet their needs and determine whether their choices were successful. There are two basic process theories: equity theory and expectancy theory.

Equity Theory

Equity theory focuses on individuals' perceptions of how fairly they are treated compared with other. Developed by J. Stacy Adams, equity theory proposes that people are motivated to seek social equity in the rewards they expect for performance.

According to equity theory, if people perceive their compensation as equal to what others receive for similar contributions, they will believe that their treatment is fair and equitable. People evaluate equity by a ratio of inputs to outcomes. Inputs to a job include education, experience, effort and ability. Outcomes from a job include pay, recognition, benefits and promotions. The input-to-outcome ratio may be compared to another person in the work group or to a perceived group average. A state of equity exists whenever the ratio of one person's outcomes to inputs equals the ratio of another's outcome to inputs.

Inequity occurs when the input/outcome ratios are out of balance, such as when a person with a high level of education or experience receives the same salary as a new, less educated employee. Perceived inequity also occurs in the other direction. Thus, if an employee discovers she is making more money than other people who contribute the same inputs to the company, she may feel the need to correct the inequity by working harder, getting more education or considering lower pay. Perceived inequity creates tension within individuals that motivate them to bring equity into balance.

The most common methods for reducing a perceived inequity are these:

- ***Change inputs:*** A person may choose to increase or decrease his or her inputs to the organisation. For example, underpaid individuals may reduce their level of effort or increase their absenteeism. Overpaid people may increase effort on the job.
- ***Change outcome:*** A person may change his or her outcomes. An underpaid person may request a salary increase or a bigger office. A union may try to improve wages and working conditions in order to be consistent with a comparable union whose members make more money.
- ***Distort perceptions:*** Research suggests that people may distort perceptions of equity if they are unable to change inputs or outcomes. They may artificially increase the status attached to their jobs or distort others, perceived rewards to bring equity into balance.
- ***Leave the job:*** People who feel inequitably treated may decide to leave their jobs rather than suffer the inequity of being under or overpaid. In their new jobs, they expect to find a more favourable balance of rewards.

The implication of equity theory for managers is that employees indeed evaluate the perceived equity of their rewards compared to others. An increase in salary or a promotion will have no motivational effect if it is perceived as inequitable relative to that of other employees. Some organisations, for example, have created a two-tier wage system to reduce wage rates. New employees make far less than experienced ones, which creates a basis for inequity. Smart managers try to keep feelings of equity in balance in order to keep their workforces motivated.

Expectancy Theory

Expectancy theory suggests that motivation depends on individual's expectations about their ability to perform tasks and receive desired rewards. Expectancy theory is associated with the work of Victor Vroom, although a number of scholars have made contributions in this area. Expectancy theory is concerned not with identifying types of needs but with the thinking process that individuals use to achieve rewards.

Expectancy theory is based on the relationship among the individual's effort, the individual's performance and the desirability of outcomes associated with high performance. These elements and the relationships among them are illustrated in Fig 10.5. The keys to expectancy theory are the expectancies of the relationships among effort, performance and outcomes with the value of the outcomes to the individual.

E → P expectancy involves whether putting effort into a task will lead to high performance. For this expectancy to be high, the individual must have the ability, previous experience and necessary machinery, tools and opportunity to perform.

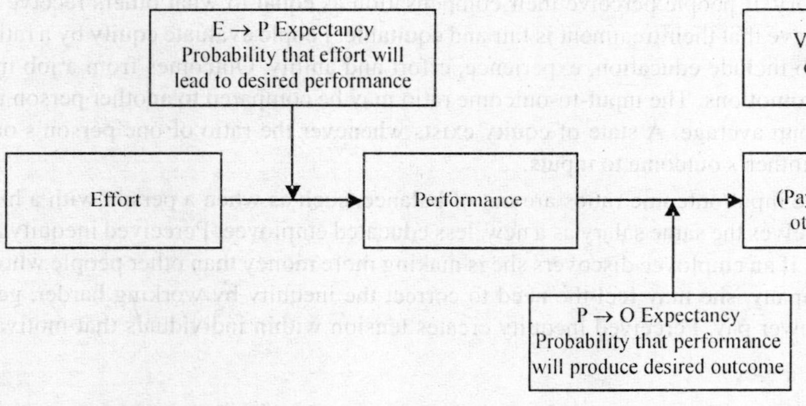

Major Elements of Expectancy Theory

Fig 10.5

P → O expectancy involves whether successful performance will lead to the desired outcome. In the case of a person who is motivated to win a job-related award, this expectancy concerns the belief that high performance will truly lead to the award. If the P → O expectancy is high, the individual will be more highly motivated. If the expectancy is that high performance will not produce the desired outcome, motivation will be lower.

Expectancy theory attempts not to define specific types of needs or rewards but only to establish that they exist and may be different for every individual. One employee may want to be promoted to a position of increased responsibility and another may have high valence for good relationships with peers. Consequently, the first person will be motivated to work hard for a promotion and the second for the opportunity for a team position that will keep him or her associated with a group.

Implications for Managers: The expectancy theory of motivation is similar to the path-goal theory of leadership. Both theories are personalised to subordinate's needs and goals. Managers' responsibility is to help subordinates meet their needs and at the same time attain organisational goals. Managers must try to find a match between a subordinate's skills and abilities and the job demands. To increase motivation, managers can clarify individual's needs, define the outcomes available from the organisation and ensure that each individual has the ability and support (namely, time and equipment) needed to attain outcomes.

Some companies use expectancy theory principles by designing incentive systems that identify desired organisational outcomes and give everyone the same shot at getting the rewards. The trick is to design a system that fits with employee's abilities and needs.

Reinforcement Perspective on Motivation

The reinforcement approach to employee motivation sidesteps the issues of employee needs and thinking processes described in the content and process theories. Reinforcement theory simply looks at the relationship between behaviour and its consequences. It focuses on changing or modifying the employee's on-the-job behaviour through the appropriate use of immediate rewards and punishments.

Reinforcement Tools

Behaviour modification is the name given to the set of techniques by which reinforcement theory is used to modify human behaviour. The basic assumption underlying behaviour modification is the law of effect, which states that behaviour that is positively reinforced tends to be repeated and behaviour that is not reinforced tends not to be repeated. Reinforcement is defined as anything that causes a certain behaviour to be repeated or inhibited. The four reinforcement tools are positive reinforcement, avoidance learning, punishment and extinction. Each type of reinforcement is a consequence of either a pleasant or unpleasant event being applied or withdrawn following a person's behaviour.

Positive Reinforcement: Positive reinforcement is the administration of a pleasant and rewarding consequence following a desired behaviour. A good example of positive reinforcement is immediate praise for an employee who arrives on time or does a little extra in his or her work. The pleasant consequence will increase the likelihood of the excellent work behaviour occurring again. Studies have shown that positive reinforcement does help to improve organisational performance. In addition nonfinancial rewards, such as positive feedback, often are as effective as financial incentives.

Avoidance Learning: Avoidance learning is the removal of an unpleasant consequence following a desired behaviour. Avoidance learning is sometimes called negative reinforcement. Employees learn to do the right thing by avoiding unpleasant situations. Avoidance learning occurs when a supervisor stops criticising or reprimanding an employee once the incorrect behaviour has stopped.

Punishment: Punishment is the imposition of unpleasant outcomes on an employee. Punishment typically occurs following undesirable behaviour. For example, a supervisor may berate an employee for performing a task incorrectly. The supervisor expects that the negative outcome will serve as a punishment and reduce the likelihood of the behaviour recurring. The use of punishment in organisations is controversial and often criticised because it fails to indicate the correct behaviour. However, almost all managers report finding it necessary to occasionally impose forms of punishment ranging from verbal reprimands to employee suspensions or firings.

Extinction: Extinction is the withdrawal of a positive reward, meaning that behaviour is no longer reinforced and hence is less likely to occur in the future. If a perpetually tardy employee fails to receive praise and pay raises, he or she will begin to realise that the behaviour is not producing desired outcomes. The behaviour will gradually disappear if it is continually nonreinforced. Some executive use reinforcement theory very effectively to shape employee's behaviour.

10.7 ESSENTIALS OF A SOUND MOTIVATIONAL SYSTEM

A careful comparison and integration of the above theories of motivation suggest the essentials of a sound motivational system. These essentials are described below:

1. It should adopt a positive, purposeful and progressive view of man – that he is capable of being moulded to offer constructive co-operation to task requirements.

2. It should recognize individual differences in perceptions, values, needs and abilities, as also their dynamic nature.
3. It should relate the goals of the organisation with the individual goals of participants.
4. It should give due weightage to group dynamics.
5. It should incorporate aspects of training and development of people, sound leadership and supervision, wholesome working condition, redesign of jobs to make them more meaningful.
6. There should be an appropriate combination of monetary and non-monetary incentives.
7. The structure of motivating factors should be equitably designed at different levels of the organisation.
8. The system should rule out manipulatory devices to motivate people by such superficial gimmicks of socialisation, paternalism and patronising attitudes and so on towards people.
9. There should be adequate and efficient mechanism for feedback on performance.
10. Efforts should be made to monitor the attitudes and behaviour of people – both as individuals and as members of groups.
11. The linkages between abilities and effort and performance efforts and rewards need to be clarified in unmistakable terms.
12. There should be contingent provisions for persistently unacceptable performance and behaviour in the part of some people.

10.8 JOB DESIGN FOR MOTIVATION

A job in an organisation is a unit of work that a single employee is responsible for performing. A job could include writing tickets for parking violators in New Delhi City or doing long-range planning for ABC television. Jobs are important because performance of their components may provide rewards that meet employee's needs. An assembly line worker may install the same bolt over and over, whereas an emergency room physician may provide each trauma victim with a unique treatment package. Managers need to know what aspects of a job provide motivation as well as how to compensate for routine tasks that have little inherent satisfaction. Job design is the application of motivational theories to the structure of work for improving productivity and satisfaction. Approaches to job design are generally classified as job simplification, job rotation, job enlargement and job enrichment.

Job Simplification

Job simplification pursues task efficiency by reducing the number of tasks one person must do. Job simplification is based on principles drawn from scientific management and industrial engineering. Tasks are designed to be simple, repetitive and standardised. As complexity is stripped from a job, the worker has more time to concentrate on doing more of the same routine task. Workers with low skill requirements can perform the job and the organisation achieves a high level of efficiency. Indeed, workers are interchangeable, because they need little training or skill and exercise little judgment. As a motivational technique, however, job simplification has failed. People dislike routine and boring jobs and react in a number of negative ways including sabotage, absenteeism and unionisation.

Job Rotation

Job rotation systematically move employees from one job to another, thereby increasing the number of different tasks an employee performs without increasing the complexity of any one job. For example, an autoworker may install windshields one week and front bumpers the next. Job rotation still takes advantage of engineering efficiencies, but it provides variety and stimulation for employees. Although employees may find the new job interesting at first, the novelty soon wears off as the repetitive work is mastered.

Job Enlargement

Job enlargement combines a series of tasks into one new, broader job. This is a response to the dissatisfaction of employees with oversimplified jobs. Instead of only one job, an employee may responsible for three or four and will have more time to do them. Job enlargement provides job variety and a greater challenge for employees.

Job Enrichment

Recall the discussion of Maslow's need hierarchy and Herzberg's two-factor theory. Rather than just changing the number and frequency of tasks a worker performs, job enrichment incorporates high-level motivators into the work, including job responsibility, recognition and opportunities for growth, learning and achievement. In an enriched job, employees have control over the resources necessary for performing it, make decisions on how to do the work, experience personal growth and set their own work pace. Many companies, have undertaken job enrichment programmes to increase employee's motivation and job satisfaction.

10.9 MOTIVATION AND OTHER RELATED CONCEPTS

In this Section, we may briefly explain how motivation is related or differs from ability, morale and job satisfaction.

Motivation and Ability: In a very simple sense, motivation may by regarded as the will to work while ability may be referred to as the skill to work. Ability is also a composite to several variables, physical strength, individuals attitude, knowledge and experiences. Efforts and performance of individuals are product of the skill (motivation x ability). Motivation is an inner psychological urge and drive. Ability is a function of physical energy, untellectual knowledge and understanding, combined with applicational skills. Motivation is a matter of attitude and is influenced by perceptions, values, needs, goals, beliefs and expectations. Ability is partly a matter of aptitude and can be acquired by training, learning and practice. Motivation leads to effort while ability partly leads to performance. If an individual is well motivated, he is induced to put in the needed efforts whereas if an individual is able, he performs well. Motivation can be induced by a network of positive and negative incentives, both monetary and non-monetary. Ability can be induced or improved by proper supporting facilities and atmosphere, training opportunities for self-expression and learning, co-operation from the group and the supervisor and so on.

Motivation and Morale: The concept 'morale' is defined as an over-all state of a group's emotional health, arousal and enthusiasm. It is a network of socio-emotional associations and attitudes, which members of a group develop towards each other, towards its goals, roles and tasks. The state of morale in a group or in an organisation is a function of the total job situation and the internal organisational climate, as perceived by the members.

Motivation and morale are conceptually and otherwise different. They could be distinguished along the following lines:

1. Motivation is an individual's state of disposition and decision to do or not to do things, to behave or not to behave in a particular way, in response to stimuli, whether internal or external. But morale, as explained above, is more a group situation.
2. Motivation is only one of the factors that explains the 'why' of individual behaviour and performance. An individual's over-all behaviour and performance is a function not only of motivation but also several other factors. Morale represents the totality of impact of several interacting forces in the atmosphere of a group.
3. A well motivated individual tends to experience a high degree of morale also. As against this, an individual or group characterised by a high state of morale may or may not have a high degree of motivation to perform.
4. It is possible to build up motivation in an individual or group by a combination of rewards and penalties. But morale can be built up only by positive and favourable means, i.e. carrots and not in combination with sticks.

5. Organisations in general, devote more direct attention towards motivational aspects of people's behaviour than to aspects of morale. The field of motivation is more extensively explored than morale by theorists.

Motivation and job satisfaction: Having defined morale and distinguished it from motivation, we may turn our attention to understand the concept of job satisfaction. It refers to a pleasurable or positive emotional attitude of an individual towards his job arising out of the outcomes he gets from his job and job climate. It is the psychological contentment which an individual experiences and derives from the various factors associated with his job. It may also be described as the extent to which an individual's needs and expectations on the job are actually fulfilled in terms of rewards and outcomes, both extrinsic and intrinsic, monetary and non-monetary.

The relationship between motivation and job satisfaction is interesting. They are inner psychological states. They cannot be observed but can be inferred from an individual's behaviour. Motivation is aroused by an individual's expectations how his needs are likely to be met by the outcomes he gets through his performance in his job. Job satisfaction is a measure of the individual's assessment on how his expectations and needs are actually met on the job.

Further there is a circular relationship between motivation and job satisfaction tends to arouse motivation for good performance in future. This means that satisfaction causes performance. It is also true to some extent that motivation which leads to performance also causes satisfaction. This means that performance leads to satisfaction.

10.10 TYPES OF MOTIVATION

Motivation may be classified on various bases. Firstly, motivation may be positive or negative. Positive motivation is the process of attempting to influence the employee's behaviour through the possibility of reward. Negative motivation is based on fear, i.e., demotion, lay off, etc. The second classification relates to extrinsic and intrinsic motivation. Extrinsic motivators arise away from the job. They do not occur on the job. These factors include wages, fringe benefits, medical reimbursement, etc. Thus, they are generally associated with financial incentives. But intrinsic motivators occur on the job and provide satisfaction during the performance of work activity itself. Intrinsic or internal motivators include recognition, status, authority, participation etc.

Lastly, motivators may be financial and non-financial. Financial motivators are those which are associated with money. They include wages and salaries, fringe benefits, bonus, retirement benefits, etc. Non-financial motivators are those which are not associated with monetary rewards. They include intangible incentives like ego-satisfaction, self-actualisation and responsibility.

Carrot and stick approach

Traditionally, management has resorted to be autocratic. This form of motivation in industry emphasize authority and economic rewards. This approach consists of forcing people to work by threatening to punish or dismiss them or to cut their rewards if they do not work. The assumption is that people would work if they are driven by the fear of punishment. To prevent people from going away from the work, there must be close supervision. Management must spell out every rule and give the workers the narrowest range of discretion. This approach paid off fairly well in the early days of industrial revolution. It is because needs for food, clothing and shelter were paramount. This approach is known as 'carrot and stick' approach.

In recent times, this approach has become less effective because people expect more from their jobs rather than mere wages or salaries. Moreover, the growth of worker's unions, the rising standard of living and changing pattern of living have made this approach less effective as a motivational device. The basic assumption of the 'be strong' approach is that if a man does not do what he is told to do, he will be fired, has gone wrong because unions have made it difficult to fire a man.

Financial and Non-Financial Incentives

The term 'incentive' means an inducement which rouses or stimulates one to action in a desired direction. An incentive has a motivational power; it influences the decision of individuals on putting in efforts towards task performance. In modern organisations, a large variety of incentives are used to motivate the people. These incentives may be broadly grouped into: (i) financial or pecuniary incentives and (ii) not-financial incentives. The financial or pecuniary incentives are monetary in nature as they involve flow of money from the organisation to its staff. The examples of pecuniary benefits are wages, salaries, allowances, bonus, fringe benefits, etc. On the other hand, non-pecuniary incentives do not involve much financial commitments on the part of the organisation. They do not add to money income of those who receive them. They take the form of job enrichment, participative management, praise, opportunity for growth, etc.

Role of Money in Motivation

Money plays an important role in motivation. Managements generally make use of financial incentives like wages and salaries, bonus, retirement benefits, health insurance, medical reimbursement, etc. to motivate the workers. However, such incentives may not always prove to be motivating. In many cases management may have to increase the financial incentives to keep the workers with organisation. This can be appreciated from the practice of making wages and salaries competitive between various enterprises so as to attract and maintain good work-force.

Money is a real motivating factor when the physiological and security needs of the workers have not been fully satisfied. Money plays a significant role in satisfying these needs. Therefore, management can use financial incentives for motivation. Money helps in satisfying the social needs of the workers to some extent because money is often recognised as a basis of status, respect and power. Money is also an important means of achieving a 'minimum standard of living' although this 'minimum' has the tendency to go up as people become more affluent. But this should not lead one to conclude that money will always be a motivating factor to all people. To some people, importance of money will be reduced after a certain stage. To them, non-financial rewards are more important. They are motivated by money only upto the stage they are struggling for physiological and security needs.

From the above discussion, it can be said that money is not the only motivator and it is not always a motivator. A good management should devise a motivational system which is capable of satisfying the different kinds of human needs. On-the-job satisfaction can be provided by helping the employees to develop themselves. Job enlargement, participative management, recognition, status symbols and making the job challenging are some of the other non-financial incentives which motivate the employees.

Role of Non-Financial Incentives in Motivation

Financial incentives do not work for ever to motivate the people at work. As a matter of fact, when the physiological and security needs are fulfilled with the help of money, money ceases to be the motivating force; it becomes the maintenance factor as said by Herzberg. Therefore, the employees do not always run after money. They have other needs also. They want status and recognition in the society, they want to satisfy their egoistic needs and they want to achieve something in their lives. In order to motivate the employees having these needs, management can take the help of following non-financial incentives:

1. **Competition** – Competition is a kind of non-financial incentive. If there is a healthy competition among the individual employees or groups of employees, it will lead them to achieve their personal or group goals in a better way.
2. **Group Incentives** – Group incentives are more powerful to motivate the employees than the individual incentives. When the prestige of the group is at stake, its members will work with a team spirit. They will have high morale and their productivity will go up.

3. **Praise** – Praise satisfies one's ego needs. Sometimes, praise is more effective than any other incentive. We have seen that in industry, at home or elsewhere, people respond better to praise. However, this incentive should be used with greater degree of care because praising an incompetent employee would create resentment among competent employees. Of course, occasionally, a part on the back of an incompetent employee may act as an incentive to him for improvement.
4. **Job Enrichment** – Job enrichment means increasing the contents of a job leading to upgradation of responsibility, scope and challenge in its performance. Executives at the higher levels prefer job enrichment because the job becomes more challenging. Job enrichment gives higher satisfaction to the job-holders and increase the level of their motivation.
5. **Opportunity for Growth** – Opportunity for growth is another kind of incentive. If the employees are provided opportunities for their advancement and growth and to develop their personality, they feel very much satisfied and become more committed to the organisational goals.
6. **Knowledge of Results** – Knowledge of the results leads to employee satisfaction. A worker likes to know the result of his performance. He gets satisfaction when his superior appreciates the work he has done.
7. **Worker's Participation in Management** – Employees' participation in management provides an important incentive to the employees. It gives them psychological satisfaction that their voice is being heard because workers' participation in management provides for two-way communication.
8. **Suggestion System** – Suggestion system is an incentive which satisfies many needs of the employees. Many organisations which use the suggestion system make use of cash awards for useful suggestions. They, sometimes, publish the worker's name with his photograph in the company's magazine. This motivates the employees to be in search for something which may be of greater use to the organisation.

Chapter 11

Group and Group Dynamics

11.1 INTRODUCTION

Increasingly, the practice of management takes place in a context of group and teams, rather than of individuals. Of course, there will always be a place for the brilliant employee working alone who produces a remarkable innovation or creative achievement. Also, not all individuals or cultures adapt equally well to a group-oriented organisational environment. Yet, more and more around the globe, organisation depend on highly networked and interconnected relationships. Managing such networks requires strong collaborative skills and the ability to work successfully with and in, groups and teams.

Because so many complex tasks and objectives are beyond the capabilities of a single person, groups, rather than individual employees, will form the fundamental building blocks of 21st-century organisations. Groups develop new products, design automobiles, construct budgets and formulate strategic plans. Even those who are inclined to be independent entrepreneurs will eventually face this reality test: If an organisation is not based on high-performance groups and teams, it cannot compete effectively in tomorrow's world.

11.2 GROUPS AND TEAMS

Concept

Groups and teams are so pervasive in modern industrialised societies they are often taken for granted. However, it is important at the outset to be sure that we undersand something about their basic nature and about the different types that can exist in organistions.

A group is typically defined as a set of people, limited in number who have some degree of interaction and shared objectives. A team, on the other hand, is a type of group that has additional characteristics: a high degree of interdependent, coordinated interaction and a strong sense of member's personal responsibility for achieving group outcomes (see Fig 11.1). Also, groups that become teams typically have created a high level of identity about being

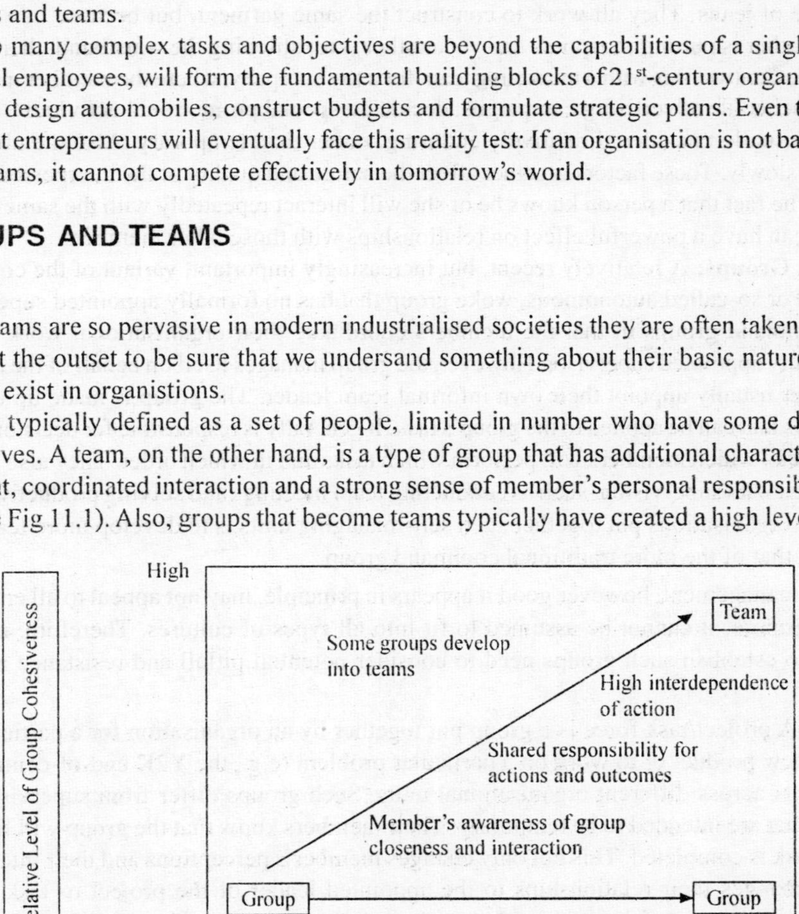

Changes as Groups Become Teams

Fig 11.1

a member of the unit. Put simply, all teams are groups, but not all groups, are or become, teams. A major objective in many of today's organisations is to have work groups behave more like teams, although such results cannot be guaranteed. Regardless of whether groups develop into teams, it is useful first to identify the several different types of groups that can exist in any organisation.

11.3 TYPES OF GROUPS

Most people in organisations are part of at least one group and often of several groups. Groups to which an employee could belong may be of the following types:

Command Groups: A command group consists of a supervisor or manager and all those who report to that person; for example, those who report to a particular production supervisor or to a sales manager in a department. Such groups are usually considered to be the basic work units of an organisation. Depending on nature of the tasks assigned to each person, however, the amount of interaction among members may very considerably from one command group to another. For example, in a clothing manufacturing plant, a group of workers may be assigned to work on a particular style of jeans. They all work to construct the same garment, but because one is sewing the pocket to the leg while another is putting in zippers and yet another is topstitching the waistband, there is very little opportunity for interaction. Contrast this with a marketing team for a toy company, where the member meet frequently to discuss new products, schedule advertising campaigns, decide on special promotional activities.

Command groups are usually considered relatively enduring, rather than temporary. Also membership in this groups changes relatively slowly. These factors together affect the nature and quality of the interpersonal interaction among group members. The fact that a person knows he or she will interact repeatedly with the same people for an indefinite length of time can have a powerful effect on relationships with those other members.

Self-Managing Work Groups: A relatively recent, but increasingly important, variant of the command work group is the self managed or so-called autonomous, woke group that has no formally appointed supervisor. These groups are similar to command groups in that the members coordinate their organisational work as if they all reported to the same formally appointed supervisor. However, the group manages itself on behalf of the organisation's objectives, and its member usually appoint their own informal team leader. The group is made up of member of members with diverse skills that can be applied to the group's task. It generally is responsible for decisions concerning how to accomplish the work –which members will perform which tasks and in which order. They also frequently do jobs traditionally associated with supervision, such as conducting team meetings and solving productivity problems. A major reason that some organisations put together such self-managing units is to develop more team like group behaviour compared with that of the more traditional command group.

The idea of group self-management, however good it appears in principle, may not appeal to all employees who might be affected. Furthermore, it cannot be assumed to fit into all types of cultures. Therefore, managers and organisations who want to establish such groups need to consider potential pitfall and resistance as well as the possible advantages.

Project/Task Forces: A project/task force is a group put together by an organisation for a particular purpose; for example, to design a new product or to work on a particular problem (e.g., the Y2K end-of-century computer software problem) that cuts across different organisational units. Such groups differ from supervisory and self-managing work teams in that are intended to be temporary. Their members know that the group will likely cease to exist once the project or task is completed. This not only changes member's perceptions and their interactions with one another, but it also changes their relationships to the appointed leader of the project or task force group. Because of the nature and importance of the goals and objectives set for them, though, task forces constitute some of the most critical group like activities within and even across, organisations.

Committees: Committees can be permanent or temporary in terms of the length of their existence. Typically, the most important feature of committees in organisations is that their members meet only occasionally and otherwise report to different permanent supervisors in the organisation's structure. Thus, interaction is episodic and for most members this is not the formal organisational group to which they have the highest degree of commitment. For instance, a budget committee may meet several times during a company's fiscal year, with the members likely coming from each of the major departments or divisions. The primary jobs of the budget committee members, however, are in their own organisational work units, not serving together on the budget committee. Nevertheless, such a committee's decisions may have critically important implications not only for its members but also for the larger organisation.

The preceding types of groups are all examples of formal groups; that is, groups that are designated, created and sanctioned by an organisation to carry out its basic work and to fulfill its overall mission. Other types of groups also exist in organisations, however.

Informal Groups: An informal group is one whose members choose to interact voluntarily, not by organisational mandate. A typical example is friendship groups. Although there is no formal joining process, these groups often have fairly obvious boundaries between members and nonmembers. At any given time, people think they know whether they are a member of a certain group or not. Just observing who eats lunch with whom, for instance, is often a clear signal of a friendship group's boundaries. Such informal groups can be fairly temporary, but more typically they last for considerable periods of time. Most important from the organisation's point of view is that friendship and other informal groups can significantly affect the attitudes and performance of their member's in relation to organisational tasks and objectives. A set of employees who were originally strangers, for example, might develop into informal group after carpooling together over a period of time. If the conversations within this group focus on reactions to new organisational polices, then the group may become a significant source of support or opposition to those policies.

11.4 FORMATION AND DEVELOPMENT OF GROUPS AND TEAMS

Groups in organisations form for many reasons and in many ways. Most often, of course, the company or organisation deliberately put groups together to serve stated organisational purposes. Informal groups, however, are another matter. They form more or less spontaneously on the basics of actions by their members and to serve those member's self-interest, which may or may mot coincide those of the organisation.

Factors Influencing the Formation of Groups

The most important factors influencing the formation of groups in organisations are the goals of the organisation, the opportunities for routine interaction and the psychological needs of potential group members.

Organisational Goals: The goals and purposes of the larger organisation directly affect the nature of its formal groups. The organisation creates new groups, whether command, task forces or committees, based on its judgment that needs are not being met adequately by existing groups. New groups may arise because of organisational growth, changes in the products or services the organisation offers or simply perceptions by key managers that greater efficiency and effectiveness can be gained by adding to, altering or combining existing groups.

Organisational Proximity: In the formation of groups and their possible development into teams, proximity or closeness, in working relationships is a key factor. When people have the opportunity to work together, it can facilitate learning about similarities of interests and experiences. These similarities can provide a basis for the development of friendships, which in turn often lead to the formation of informal groups within the formal group. Thus, the firm or company is frequently the indirect and often inadvertent, initiator of informal groups.

Psychological Factors: Although proximity is a great aid in the formation of informal groups and th development of other types of groups into teams, it is not absolutely essential. Other factors also motivate organisational members to form close relationships in groups, especially basic human needs for security, social support, self-esteem status. By belonging to groups, employees are often able to fulfill needs that may not be well satisfied by the work itself. Thus, the feeling of belonging to a group at work can be highly rewarding for many individuals. It can be, in effect, a significant way for individuals to achieve a distinct social identity that is meaningful both for themselves and for others who interact with them.

11.5 STAGES OF GROUP DEVELOPMENT

Whether groups are formed by the organisation or by voluntary actions of individuals, they tend to move through distinct or identifiable development stages as they mature. One popular early statement on this issue utilises an easy-to-remember set of terms for such stages: "forming" (getting acquainted), "storming" (expressing differences of opinion), "norming" (building consensus on basic issues), "performing" (carrying out cooperative group actions).

Stages of Group Development

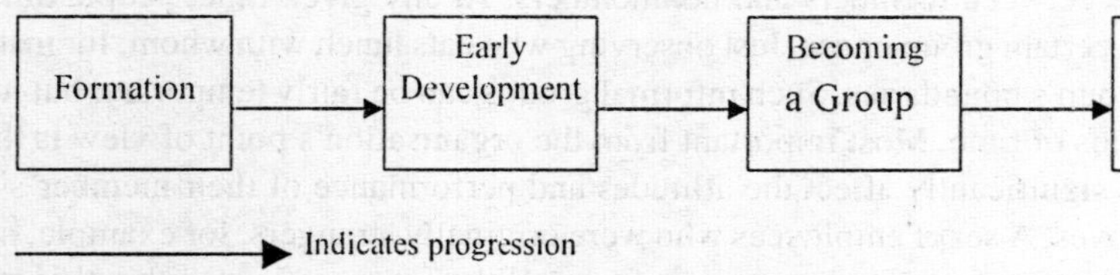

Fig 11.2

Although this model has considerable appeal as a way to think about phases of group development across time, it does not apply universally to all groups. As one set of management scholars has noted, "It seems unlikely that a single sequence can describe the development of all kinds of groups".

Despite this fact, several identifiable stages do show up with some regularity in organisational contexts (Fig 11.2).

Formation: New groups and their leader face some unique challenges. In particular, in the formation or orientation stage, members need to understand who is in the group, who is leading the group and where each person is "coming from" in terms of his or her attitude and viewpoint. Nearly all new groups go through this "getting to know you" stage.

Early Development: Following a group's formation and initial interactions, an early-development stage settles in that may last for some time, depending on the nature of the group and its tasks. In this stage, members learn what is expected of them, what is acceptable behaviour and how well they relate to each other. Typically, members cautiously exchange and sometimes jealously guard information. It is also a time for learning about how opinions within the group overlap or differ on important matters and as a consequence, conflicts over group goals or the means to reach them may emerge.

Becoming a Group: In this stage, at least a minimum amount of consensus about group issues begins to appear as well as a degree of individual identity with the group and its goals. How much consensus and group identity will actually emerge vary widely from group to group at this stage, depending in large part on how well the group is meeting member needs and on how well it is being led. In this stage particularly, organisations and managers can have considerable impact on a groups development and help it to become a true team.

Performing as a Team: In this stage, a group is able to perform like a team and take actions as an entity and not just as individuals. Internally, this means that the group is able to influence members attitudes and behaviour on matters of importance to the group and externally it means that others in the organisation are being affected by its actions.

11.6 GROUP DYNAMICS

It was Kurt Lewin who propounded the concept of Group Dynamics. By Group Dynamics we mean interaction of forces among group members in a social situation. The social process by which people interact face-to-face in small group is called Group Dynamics. Thus, in group dynamics we are concerned with the face-to-face interaction of individuals. It focuses on team work wherein small groups are constantly in contact with each other and share common ideas to accomplish the given tasks. Lewin has developed here leadership styles i.e. Authoritarian, democratic and Laissez-faire for explaining the group dynamics. The other meaning of Group dynamics is that it is a set of techniques. It implies that the members role in a management situation is discussed and team building exercise is carried out to develop each member. This meaning is close to Lewin concept of Group Dynamics.

11.7 REASONS FOR EMERGENCE/FORMATION OF INFORMAL GROUPS IN ORGANISATIONS

In any formal organisation, informal groups emerge for several reasons. The causes of their emergency may be as follows:

Proximity and similarity: Individual sharing the same work space in an organisation may come together and form into a group. Similarly, people who handle same or similar type of work, have same or similar economic, educational, communal and regional background tend to be attached together, because they generally feel attracted to each other.

Need satisfaction: Individuals have a range of needs which they seek fulfillment. Groups cater to the safety needs of individuals, social affiliation needs, ego needs and self-actualisation needs. Groups, especially small informal groups are formed to meet the above and other similar needs of members.

Promotion of interests and pursuit of goals: Many informal groups are formed with an explicit or implicit aim of protecting and promoting the economic and other interests of members. There could also be groups which provide opportunities to promote the professional, literary or artistic tastes, interests and goals of members.

11.8 CHARACTERISTIC FEATURES OF INFORMAL GROUPS

Their basic characteristics as follows:

1. They are small in size and relatively homogeneous in one or more important respects.
2. There are strong elements of social control over the behaviour and performance of members through a network of 'norms' to which members are expected to comply.
3. Co-operation, cohesiveness and conflict co-exist in informal groups.
4. There are strong social rankings among members depending on their power relations, even though there are no superiors and subordinates as such.
5. Membership is over-lapping as an individual may belong to more than one informal group.
6. Though membership is voluntary, it is not automatic. It involves some informal process.
7. Informal groups are loosely structured.
8. The goals of informal group tend to be different from and are often in conflict with the goals of the organisation.

11.9 DYSFUNCTIONAL ASPECTS OF INFORMAL GROUPS

Informal groups create a lot of problems for the organisation due to its dysfunctional aspects. These problems include –

(i) **Conformity** – The informal group very often exerts strong pressure on its members for conformity. The members may become so loyal to their group that following the group norms becomes the part and way of their life. This implies that members become subject to willful control of the group towards selfish ends.

(ii) **Negative Attitude of Informal Leaders** – Sometime the informal leader may turn out to be a troubleshooter for the organisation. In order to increase his influence, he may work against the policies of management and manipulate the behaviour of his followers. Thus, he can be a source of conflict between the management and the workers.

(iii) **Generation of Rumours** – Informal communication may give rise to rumours which is not desirable from organisation point of view. Rumour originates for a number of reasons. One cause is plain maliciousness, but it is probably not the most important. A more frequent cause is employee's anxiety and insecurity because of poor communication in the organisation. Rumour tends to change as it passes from peron to person. The rumour gets twisted and distorted always when it passes from one mouth to another.

(iv) **Resistance to Change** – Informal groups generally have tendency to resist change. Change requires group members to make new adjustments and acquire new skills. But groups want o maintain statusquo. Sometimes, groups react violently to the proposed changes being brought by the management.

(v) **Role Conflict** – Every member of the informal group is also a member of the formal organisation. Sometimes, there may be role conflict because what the informal group requires of a member is just the opposite of what is expected of him by the formal organisation. In such a situation, group members may conform to their social norms. And if an individual member wants to follow the formal instructions of his boss, he may be snubbed by the informal leader and compelled to conform to informal group norms.

11.10 CHARACTERISTICS OF GROUPS AND TEAMS

All groups have certain characteristics that affect the degree and type of influence they have on their members and their level of collective performance. Some of these are structural, while others relate to basic features of groups, such as their norms and the degree of cohesion among their members. For all of these characteristics, it is important for leaders and managers to understand their likely effects.

Structural Characteristics

Just as organisations have structure so do groups, except of course, on a smaller scale. Four of the most essential structural features of groups are size, composition, differentiated roles and differentiated status.

Size: As one review of research on groups stated, "Current literature yields a consistent guideline for determining the best size for a group : use the smallest number of people who can do the task". Similarly, another review of recent studies carried out in the United States found that member satisfaction decreased as groups got larger and leader's behaviour toward members became more task-and less people-oriented.

What is an optimal group size? Of course, there is no single answer to this question, since it would vary based on the types of tasks facing the group. However, research shows that with increasing group size the sense of personal responsibility for a group's output or performance tends to decrease. The phenomenon of reduced effort per person in large-size groups has been labeled social loafing. Individuals in large groups apparently are more likely than those in smaller groups to assume that other members will "carry the load," thus reducing the necessity for their own efforts. In large groups, also, individual members specific contributions are less easily identified and this appears to be a major factor in encouraging such "loafing".

The other major reason why group performance per persons may decrease as group size increases is simply the increasing costs of coordination or process costs. As groups become larger, the number of person-to-person relationships increases significantly and thus coordination becomes more cumbersome. Also, with larger size come additional opportunities for interpersonal conflicts between individuals and among subgroups within the group.

All of the disadvantages of large group size must be weighed, of course, against to potential advantages of having a more extensive pool of talent, skills and expertise to boost performance and take on additional problem-solving tasks. Having too few people in a group, especially when tasks are many and complex, defeats the whole purpose of putting together people in the first place. In determining the best size for formal work groups, managers need to consider the probable losses due to process costs in relation to the likely gains due to larger integrated efforts.

Composition: Groups may be composed of individuals who are very similar or very dissimilar. If the former, we describe the group as homogeneous. If the latter, the composition would be regarded as heterogeneous or diverse. Most groups these days have some degree of diversity and many have a great deal.

The managerial question, of course, is: Does a greater amount of diversity within groups help of hinder such outcomes as turnover of membership and group performance? Research to date shows that there is no simple answer to this question.

Research to date is only suggestive and not conclusive, but it tends to show that increased diversity has –

- Somewhat negative effects on members reactions.
- Somewhat positive effects on increasing the quality of the outputs of members thinking together as a group, presumably because a wider range of opinions and ideas are discussed.
- Decreased frequency of communication within a group but more communication with those outside a group.

In short, the challenge for managers is to maximise the significant benefits that are possible by having group diversity and to try to minimise potential disadvantages by anticipating what some of those might be an directly addressing them. The use of multinational groups is becoming increasingly commonplace, as is the use of increasingly diverse work teams in general. In other words, the diversity challenges for managers are growing, not lessening.

Differentiated Roles: In groups of any size, different members perform different roles; that is, they occupy different positions with sets of expected behaviour attached to those positions. This is most vividly illustrated in certain athletic teams, where players have specialised roles when the team is on offense and different roles on defense. Roles in work groups are not always as clear-cut and can range from being fairly general, such as performing analytical duties, to being highly specialised with specific task assignments, such as monitoring particular pieces of equipment. More and more, however, organisations are attempting to loosen rigid role boundaries in groups and thus generate greater flexibility in meeting unexpected competitive and environmental challenges.

Differentiated Status: Not only do members have different roles in groups, they also often have different levels of status or rank. Status is the standing or prestige that a person has in a group and it can be based on a number of factors such as perceived leadership abilities, seniority or special skills, among others.

Research has shown that status differences can strongly influence interactions within the group. For example, higher-status members tend to receive more communications than do lower-status members and lower-status members tend to defer to higher-status members when groups are making-decision. Such effects might be especially strong, of course, in high-power distance cultures. However, in cultures with low or medium power distance, effective communication and decision-making are likely to be inhibited in groups if status differences and their effects are too extreme. Relevant information would be less likely to be widely shared and thus not be given sufficient attention.

11.11 GROUP NORMS

Group norms are a group's share standards that guide the behaviour of its individual members. For example, when members of a group behave similarly toward supervisors or outsider, such as stopping nontask conversations when they enter the room, they are demonstrating the effect of group norms. It would be very difficult, if not impossible, for groups to function if they did not have norms. Each person's behaviour would be too unpredictable for coordinated action to take place. Norms also help to reduce ambiguity; thus, they provide members with cues and useful guidelines about how to behave. Such normative information is particularly important for new members of a group who need to learn what is going on in the work situation as rapidly as possible.

Characteristics of Group Norms: An understanding of norms and their significance can be gained by reviewing several of their main features:

- Norms are usually established for the more important issues of concern to the group.
- Norms do not necessarily apply to all members of the group; some apply only to certain members, usually based on the status or particular role of those members.
- Norms vary in the degree of their acceptance by group members; some norms are accepted and endorsed by virtually all members, others by only a majority.
- Norms vary in how much deviation members are permitted in following them; in other words, some norms are very loose and permit a great deal of leeway in behavior, while other norms, especially those regarding key group issues, are much more restrictive on members behaviour.

Development of Group Norms: Norms do not suddenly and magically appear in groups. They seldom, if ever, develop in a purely spontaneous way. Rather, they arise out of interaction among group members. An example of a typical norm development process is shown in Fig 11.3. Key factors that often have a major influence on the process include the following:

- ***Early behaviours:*** Typically, initial behaviours, especially in newly formed groups, establish standards for subsequent behaviour. In committees, for example, the first few meetings help establish norms about how candid or how indirect, discussion of sensitive issues is likely to be. Such quickly established norms are often difficult to reshape or change later.

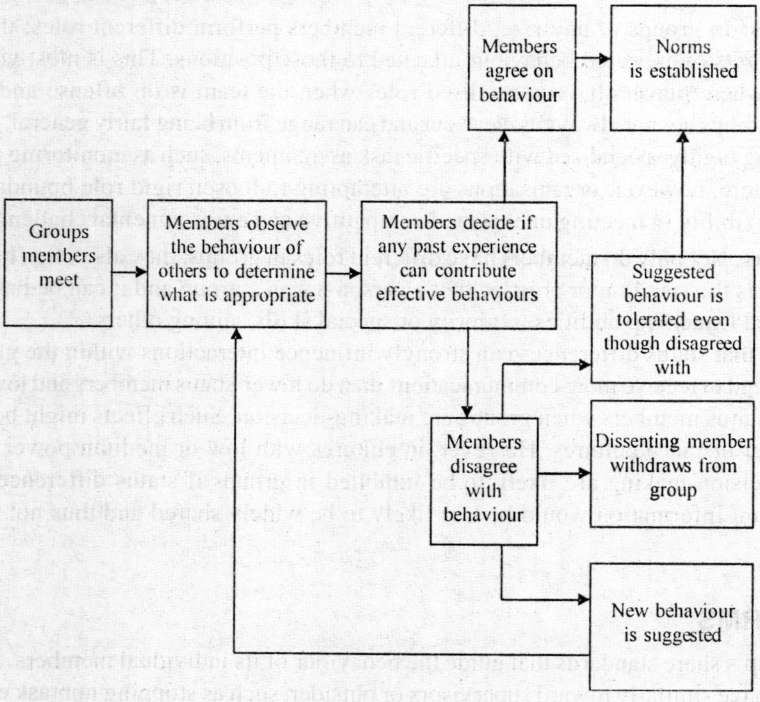

Example of the Development of Group Norms

Fig 11.3

- *Imported behaviours:* Members of a group often bring with them standards of behaviour that were prominent in their former groups. The more similar the type and purpose of the previous group were to the present one, the more likely those norms will serve as guideposts in the new situation. "When in doubt, stay with the familiar" seems to be the (sometimes incorrect) watch-word of many people in organisations. When a high-status member imports a norm, as in the case of those with acknowledged expertise or high power, the prominence of that norm is likely to be string. A new chief executive officer (CEO), for example, may believe in a norm of communication "only through channels" regarding suggestions and input from members of the organisation, even though his may run counter to the previous norm of openness and "the door is open at any time" fostered by the former CEO. However, because the new CEO has high status, few are likely to challenge this imported norm.
- *Critical events* : A sudden challenge to the group, such as criticism from another group, can create specific and vivid responses that form the basis for how members should be expected to respond in the future. A time of crisis makes people particularly alert to cues in their environment and thus tends to reinforce norms that emerge from that period. In a corporation that has announced layoffs, for example, new norms regarding the overt display of diligent work habits may emerge.
- *Explicitly stated standards:* Not to be overlooked is the fact that leaders or high-status members of a group may simply assert that "this is how we will do it around here!" Newly appointed supervisors and athletic coaches, for example, frequently use this approach with their groups or teams. The explicitly stated norms included unity, cohesion, no cliques, discipline concerning the amount of drinking the night before a game and adherence to the highest standards.

11.12 GROUP COHESION

Another major property of groups is their amount of cohesion, "the degree to which members are motivated to remain in a group," to want to stay in it. Group cohesion is usually considered to have many advantages and to be highly desirable if it can be developed. Indeed, when managers and organisations attempt to turn groups into teams, they are, in effect, trying to generate stronger group cohesion.

Development of Group Cohesion: There are no surefire ways for managers to build strong cohesion in the groups for which they are responsible. However, the available research suggests three factors that are potentially important for developing greater group cohesion:

- Strong interpersonal attraction among group members.
- High performance and past success of the group.
- High level of competition with other groups.

The most consistently important of these factors appears to be the first, namely, whether members of the group think they have something in common with other members and tend to like being with them; that is, whether they feel like they belong to a team. The evidence for the other two factors in bringing about cohesion is not as clear-cut, but both past group success and current or anticipated conflict with other groups seem to unite groups and increase their cohesion, especially if string interpersonal attraction among members is already present. Obviously, a group whose members don't especially like being with each other may disintegrate when faced with competition from external groups, rather than develop greater cohesion. This reinforces the point that few clear guidelines exist that guarantee the development of group cohesion.

Effects of Group Cohesion: Increased cohesiveness of groups can have a number of potential advantages. Chief among these is an increase in the quantity and quality of group interaction.

A second potential advantage of greater group cohesion is that the group has stronger influence on each member to conform to the group's standards or norms. Assuming-and this is a critical assumption-that those norms are positive from the manager's perspective, then this is a significant advantage.

A third possible advantage is that cohesive groups appear to be more effective in achieving goals that group members accept.

A final possible advantage of higher group cohesion is that members tend to have greater satisfaction with the group.

As positive as these potential advantages might seem, high group cohesion can be a mixed blessing from a manager's point of view. First, if the group has norms that do not support the organisation's goals, then greater cohesions is definitely a minus. Individuals may be more influenced by the "wrong" direction, as when, for example, a group of workers tolerates sexual harassment, than if here is little cohesion. Another possible disadvantage of strong group cohesion is that deviance from group norms may not be handled effectively. Highly cohesive groups are more likely to reject any deviance, even if it represents creative or discordant ideas that could ultimately be useful to the group. Related to this is the danger that groupthink may be accentuated in highly cohesive groups.

Still another potential disadvantage of high within-group cohesion, but one that is frequently overlooked, is that between-group cooperation may be adversely affected. Most organisations have many work groups; some have hundreds or more. The challenge, from the organisation's perspective, is to have these groups and teams work together and interact smoothly and reliably. So it is a concern if higher within-group cohesion hinders intergroup cooperation. For example, in developing and marketing a new product, problems may develop among the production, marketing and sales departments. If the production group is highly cohesive and has a norm of never allowing outsiders to know they have problems, they may be reluctant to notify other units that a key piece of equipment is not functioning correctly. Without this information, the marketing department might generate unrealistic expectations for the release date and the sales teams then would promise higher numbers of the product to customers than would actually be available.

This example illustrates that the active promotion of strong within-group (team) cohesion by managers actually may decrease overall functioning of the larger organisation because of increased fragmentation. This situation is sometimes encountered in highly decentralised organisations, where employees show extremely strong loyalty to their own unit, for example, marketing but considerably less concern for the welfare of other units, say, production and the need to coordinate with them. Thus, in this case, intra-unit cohesion may gain greater autonomy for the unit, but it can hinder the achievement of integrated organisation wide objectives.

11.13 GROUP CONFLICT

Just as cohesion is a common feature of groups, so is conflict. Group conflict, that is, disagreement or opposition between or among group members, can occur for a number of reasons and have a variety of consequences. Although the effects of group conflict, such as a marked decrease in cohesion within the group, often can be negative, that is not always so. In fact, some types of conflict, particularly substantive conflict in some circumstances can have positive effects. The important point to remember is that conflict among members within groups is fairly common and it is not always something to be avoided.

Types of Group Conflict

Researchers have generally distinguished two basic types of group conflict: substantive conflict and relationship conflict. Substantive conflict is conflict that focuses on differences in ideas and courses of action in addressing the issues facing a group. It is also sometimes called cognitive (thinking) or task conflict. The absence of any conflict can be a sign that the group is not generating a variety of viewpoints and potential approaches for solving problems and making good decisions. Therefore, research indicates that at least some amount of substantive conflict can be beneficial to the group, especially for less routine and more complex tasks.

The other major type of conflict that can occur in groups, relationship conflict, is usually thought to be almost always dysfunctional. Relationship conflict focuses on interpersonal differences and is sometimes called affective or emotional conflict. Research suggests that it is a negative type of conflict for groups, because it distracts focus from tasks and ideas. It discourages rather than encourages consideration of multiple points of view.

Causes of Group Conflict

There are many potential causes of group conflict, but they can usually be linked to one of the two types of conflict.

The causes of substantive conflict, for example, include –

- Ambiguities regarding the task.
- Differences in goals, objectives and perspectives among group members.
- Scarcity of resources to accomplish group goals.

Two possible causes of relationship conflict are –

- Dissimilarities in the composition of the membership of the group, including demographic diversity and status/power differences.
- Differences in interpersonal styles of individual members.

Several of the potential causes of group conflict can occur together; for example, when a very diverse group that includes several people with distinctive interpersonal styles encounters a highly ambiguous task. When there are such multiple causes, finding ways to deal with the conflict becomes even more difficult, of course.

Managing Group Conflict

Probably the most important managerial objective in dealing with group conflict is to attempt to increase the ratio of substantive to relationship conflict. This would particularly include encouraging a culture of openness to express differences of opinion on task methods and objectives, especially novel or creative approaches to the task requirements. In this way, unintended groupthink tendencies can be minimised. In addition, managers can clarify and reduce task ambiguities and try to help the group focus on larger goals beyond individual member interests that emphasize the common interests of all the group members.

Most of what we have been talking about so far applies to conflict within groups. In organisational settings, of course, conflict between or among groups- intergroup conflict can also occur frequently. Therefore, managers should look for opportunities to reduce unnecessary relational conflicts in those intergroup interaction situations and increase the focus on substantive differences. Also, emphasizing larger, common goals can help increase cooperation and thus performance. So, if marketing and production can concentrate on the issue of customer satisfaction-to elevate it to the highest priority-then their differences on how many variations of a product to make and market can be minimised or resolved.

11.14 IMPROVING GROUP EFFECTIVENESS

Teams and groups are not static parts of organisations. They come into existence, go out of existence and change over time. Among the changes that can occur are increases or decreases in effectiveness. Social scientists have focused considerable attention over the years on studying groups and their findings have resulted in some useful guidelines for managers in attempting to improve the performance of their groups in organisational settings.

For a group to perform effectively, it must be able to do three things especially well:

1. Exert enough effort to accomplish its tasks at acceptable levels of quantity and quality.
2. Obtain sufficient knowledge and skills to carry out its work.
3. Use appropriate strategies to apply its effort, knowledge and skills effectively.

These three bases for achieving high levels of group effectiveness sound simple, but they are major challenges for organisations and leaders of groups. To assure that these components are actually in place consistently, managers need to address several issues:

Developing Appropriate Groups Structures: To be effective, groups need clearly defined tasks and objectives that can motivate their members. They also need a group size appropriate to the tasks and a membership with a sufficient mix of skills and expertise.

Developing Appropriate Support from the Organisation: Groups operating within companies and organisations need support from their surrounding environment such as rewards for effective collaboration among members, education and technical training for performing critical group tasks, relief from other duties and access to necessary information.

Developing Appropriate Coaching and Consultation: Most groups need outside help to reduce potential conflicts, increase coordination in dealing with problems within the group and provide strategies for approaching the group's tasks.

Chapter 12

Introduction To Organisational Behaviour

12.1 INTRODUCTION

Organisations are coalitions of individuals and groups who pool that resources, skills and efforts to achieve certain goals. Individuals and groups behave in diverse ways in organisational settings. Such behaviour is influenced by a wide range of factors and in turn influences the functioning and effectiveness of organisations. Human behaviour, whether in organisations or outside, is very complex. It has several dimensions, multiple causes and wide-ranging consequences. The concern for scientific study and analysis of human behaviour in organisations has been shaped into a discipline known as 'Organisational Behaviour'. As a field of scientific study and analysis of human behaviour, organisational behaviour is inter-disciplinary in nature, drawing in the combined talents of psychologists, sociologists and anthropologists.

12.2 CONCEPT OF ORGANISATIONAL BEHAVIOUR

Organisational behaviour is not a discipline in the usual sense of the term, but is rather an elastic field of study involving the integration of the behavioural sciences (e.g., psychology, sociology, anthropology, etc.) into the study of people's behaviour within organisations. It is the integration of relevant knowledge of these areas that has given us a new field of study. Organisational behaviour can be defined as follows:

Organisational behaviour (frequently abbreviated as OB) is the study and application of knowledge about human behaviour related to other elements of the organisation such as structure, technology, and social system.

Thus, OB is primarily concerned with that aspect of human behaviour which is relevant for organisational performance. Therefore, it studies human behaviour at individual level, group level, and organisational level. It applies the knowledge gained about individuals, groups, and the effect of organisational structure on behaviour towards the end of making organisations work more effectively.

12.3 ORGANISATION AS SOCIAL ENTITY

Modern society is essentially organisational in nature, with large and complex organisations increasingly dominating every sphere of human activity. The importance of organisations has attracted the attention of a wide assortment of intellectuals leading to the emergence of an important and distinctive field of organisational study and research referred to variously as 'Organisational Behaviour', 'Behaviour Science', or 'Organisation Theory'. Though they differ in their approaches, they have common orientation, that is, oragnisation as social entity.

12.4 INFORMAL ORGANISATION

The term informal organisation is defined as the patterns of activities, interactions, processes and behaviour in an organisation which spontaneously and naturally emerge in the course of functioning of the organisation. The informal patterns in the organisation represent an unintended and unplanned modification of or departure from the formal patterns and arrangements of activities and relationships.

Distinction between formal and informal organisation

Based on the above definition, we may further explain the distinction between the formal and informal organisation along the following lines:

1. Formal organisation is a 'de jure' organisational structure and processes while informal organisation is 'de facto' organisational structure and processes.
2. Formal organisation is an ideal type, normative organisation to indicate how an organisation should be like, while the informal organisation is the real-life patterns of activities and relations which are free from pretensions and which are difficult to portray in organisational charts.
3. Formal organisation is a network of formal work groups while the informal organisation is a network of informal work and other groups.
4. Formal organisation is a rational, contrived system. Informal organisation is a natural, social human system with a mixture of order and disorder.
5. Formal organisation could also be described as deterministic in its orientation while the informal organisation is less so.
6. Formal organisation is established with the explicit aim of achieving certain goals. The informal organisation pursues a mixture of organisational, personal and group goals of people.
7. Formal organisation gives priority to its own perceptions, perspectives, needs and requirements. Informal organisation gives priority to the needs and values of organisational members and to give expression to the real-life sentiments and attitudes.
8. The structure and processes of the formal organisation are generally established by reference to certain concepts and principles. The informal organisational structure tends to violate and modify some of the principles, in tune with organisational realities, requirements and sentiments of people.
9. Formal organisation has a set of legitimate, socially sanctioned rights expressed in the concept of 'authority'. In the informal organisation, authority is combined, diluted and often reinforced by power – which is a border instrument of influence than authority.
10. In formal organisation, communication channels generally follow authority channels. On the other hand, the communication system in the informal organisation is highly complex, haphazard and spontaneous.
11. Leadership in formal organisation is vested in managers. But in informal organisation, leadership need not always be associated with managership.
12. There is a rigid status hierarchy, based largely on authority, in a formal organisation. In the informal organisation also, there are social rankings among people, but they are less conspicuous and obvious.

Reasons for emergence of informal organisation

The informal organisation emerges due to the following reasons:

1. Formal organisational prescribes certain interactions, activities and sentiments. Informal organisation is a natural outgrowth of formal interactions, activities and sentiments. People do not always relate to each other. It is natural and normal for them to depart from them, to ignore some of them to develop new ones, not envisaged in the formal organisation.
2. Informal organisation emerges to fill up some of the gaps and deficiencies in formal organisation. Informal organisation, is capable of making innovations, with a view to overcome the deficiencies in the formal organisation.
3. Formal organisation gives little or no scope for members to behave in a natural and uninhibited manner. Informal organisation emerges as a reaction to the rigidity, oppressiveness and formality of formal organisation, and to meet the social, psychological and emotional needs and aspirations of members, which are denied by the formal organisation.

Benefits of informal organisation

The informal organisation is beneficial both to the organisation and to its members personally.

1. **To the organisation:** Informal organisation provides a natural setting for managers to get things done through people by exercising not only their authority but also their other bases of power. The formal organisation develops its own ways of coping with organisational activities, based on art of the possible. Informal processes and styles of doing things are found more productive than formal processes and styles.
2. **To the members:** Informal organisation is a forum for socialisation of new members and for helping them to learn the work practices and rules and for integrating themselves into the organisational culture. The informal organisation is a big source of support, solace and stimulation. The formal organisation tends to antagonise many members on accounts of its rigid approaches. People are required to behave and function in a particular manner; many people tend to feel suffocated in such a setting. The informal organisation provides a natural setting to behave in a relaxed manner and to feel at home. Members get a sense of identity, emotional support and freedom.

Problems of informal organisation

There are sufficient grounds to contend that informal organisation undermines and distorts the functioning of formal organisation in several respects.

1. Informal organisation upholds and gives priority to the individual and social goals and values of the organisational members which often run counter to the goals and values of the formal organisation.
2. Members of informal organisation collectively evolve their own norms of behaviour, standards of performance and techniques of doing work.
3. Members are required to conform to group norms and standards to ensure informal group cohesiveness as against organisational cohesiveness.

12.5 ORGANISATIONAL CLIMATE

The concept of organisational climate was formalised by the human relation theorists in the late 1940's. Now, it has become a very useful for thinking about and describing system.

According to Joe Kelly, "Climate may be thought of as the perception and the characteristics of an organisation. It conveys the impressions people have of the organisational internal environment within which they work."

Features of organisational climate

1. Organisational climate is the summary perception which people have about an organisation. It is a global expression of what the organisation is.
2. Organisational climate is a relatively enduring quality of the internal environment that is experienced by its members, influences their behaviour, and can be described in terms of the values of a particular set of characteristic of the organisation.
3. Organisational climate is the set of characteristics that describe an organisation and influence the behaviour of the people in the organisation.
4. The concept of "Organisational Climate" is different from that of "Organisational Culture." According to Stephen P. Robbins: "Organisational culture is a relatively uniform perception held by the organisation, it has common characteristics, it is descriptive, it can distinguish one organisation from another and it integrates individual group and organisation system variables."

Dimensions of Organisational Climate

The organisational climate is a highly discussed topic, and over the last three decades, extensive research has been conducted which has helped us to determine some of the key dimensions of organisational climate as mentioned hereunder:

1. **Individual Autonomy –** It is the degree of freedom for accountability to others. By this we mean employees are free to manage themselves and have considerable decision making power.
2. **Position Structure –** It is the extent of direct supervision and formalisation. It is the degree to which objectives of the job and methods for accomplishing it are established and are communicated to the subordinate by supervisor.
3. **Reward Orientation –** It is the extent of incentives provided for higher effort and performance.
4. **Conflict - It** is the extent of expression of differences and blocking of each other.
5. **Consideration, warmth and support -** It is the extent of socio-emotional support provided by significant others in the organisation.
6. **Progressiveness and Development -** It is the scope of growth of self, other members and organisation as a whole. The organisations with given organisational climate try to foster the development of employees.
7. **Control** – It is the degree of check imposed on behaviour on organisational members. The organisations differ in terms of control imposed on employees.
8. **Risk Taking -** It is the extent of freedom to experiment with new ideas and take risks without fear of reprisal, ridicule or other punitive action.

12.6 STATUS PATTERNS IN ORGANISATION

An important concept of understanding the behaviour in organisations or groups is 'status', which is defined as the relative social ranking of members within a group. In a formal organisation or work group, status ranking are done on the basis of formal designations, wage/salary levels, authority content and nature of tasks performed. Everyone in a group or organisation, has some status; it may be high or low in a creative sense.

Bases of Status

There are criteria or bases of status by reference to which members of a group or organisation get relative social rankings. We may classify them in the following categories:

1. **Ascribed v. achieved status:** Ascribed status refers to status attached to persons on account of their age, sex, ethic origin, family background and inherited wealth. As against it, achieved status refers to status earned by persons by their personal virtues, skills, abilities and achievements.
2. **Scalar status v. functional status:** Scalar status refers to status related to authority of a person in a chain of command. Functional status refers to status associated with the nature of functions performed by a person in a group.
3. **Positional v. personal status:** Positional status is akin to scalar status. The manager in an enterprise has a certain positional status by virtue of the post occupied by him. Manager in the same enterprise is more knowledgeable and articulate and virtually managers the entire production unit, he enjoys a higher personal status than the production manager even though his positional status is lower.

Status systems

The term may be defined as the structure and pattern of social ranking and relationship. They exit in most groups, whether large groups or small groups. Some status distinctions are based on real differences in abilities, attributes, achievements and responsibilities, tasks and roles; in some cases however, status distinctions are based on traditional or conservative perceptions and misconceptions.

Status systems have considerable relevance and functional value in groups and organisations which are outlined as follows:

1. They satisfy one of the important ego needs of people – the need or motive for status. Individuals tend to feel motivated to perform well to enable them to reach the aspired status levels.
2. Status systems facilitate upward social mobility of people, if such systems are based on personal achievements, abilities and skills.
3. Status systems also reflect the differential prestiges associated with different occupations or professions. Each society places particular values to individual occupations depending on their perceived relative importance.
4. Status distinctions reflect real differences in abilities and achievements among people. Status distinction represents recognition of individual differences in abilities and attainments.
5. It reduces uncertainty, complexity and anxiety in social interactions and transactions in the everyday world by communicating meaning and messages about the behaviour expected of one another.

Case against status systems and distinctions

Inspite of the above positive aspects of status systems in groups and organisations, they are often disfavoured for various reasons. The contentions against status systems are:

1. Status systems generate superiority-inferiority complexes among people.
2. Status differentials generate social disaffection and disunity among people in an organisation, they hamper free interaction and communication between people.
3. Status systems are undemocratic to the extent that they institutionalise inequality among people.
4. Status systems foster unhealthy competition among people for grabbing and retaining desired status symbols.

12.7 INFLUENCE

Any leader cannot implement the change or get the work done where one is not able to influence the others. Influence is a dynamic process of affecting the behaviour of others. It denotes any change in behaviour of a person or group due to anticipation of the responses of others. There are two parties in the influence process, namely, influencer and influencee or target of influence. The target may be an individual, a group, an organisation, a crowd or a nation.

According to Oxford Dictionary, influence means "an action invisibly exercised on". The term 'influence' is often used in conjunction with other terms such as power, authority, control and conformity. Some people try to distinguish between influence and other terms.

Building the Influence of Managers

Although it is true that influence is earned by an individual through his personal behaviour, in the final analysis it is the combined result of both his personal behaviour and the behaviour of other senior managers in the organisation. Management can build the influence of an employee in the following ways:

1. By giving him an impressive title, salary, office and privileges.
2. By regularly paying attention to his advice.
3. By channeling all important information through him.
4. By backing-up his decisions.

Ways to Influence Behaviour

Managers may use the following methods to get the desired results from the subordinates:

1. **Inducement (Utilitarian or Reward Power)** – The manager may make use of means to influence the behaviour of subordinates. The subordinates produce the desire behaviour as they are offered rewards.
2. **Domination** – The manager may have a dominating personality. He may be able to get the desired response from others through command as he is in a dominating commanding position.
3. **Manipulation** - This involves a lot of policies often referred as 'psychopolitics' over the subordinates. The manager does not clearly tell what he expects of the subordinates. But he influences their behaviour through rumours, propaganda and sabotaging the activities of his opponents.
4. **Pressure (or Coercive Power)** – This is the power that is based on fear. The fear can take many forms such as punishment, assault, confinement, etc.
5. **Normative Power** – It involves use of symbols of prestige and esteem. Those who want to get these will obey their bosses.

12.8 POWER

The term 'Power' may be defined as the ability to exert influence of a person who has power; it means he is able to change the behaviour or attitudes of other individuals. A manager's power may be measured in terms of the ability to (1) give rewards, (2) promise rewards, (3) threaten to withdraw current rewards, (4) withdraw current rewards, (5) threaten punishment, and (6) punish."

Types of Power

French and Raven have suggested five types of power which may occur at all levels of the organisation. These are:

1. **Legitimate Power** – It is also signified by the term 'authority'. It exists when an influence acknowledges that the influencer is lawfully entitled to exert influence;
2. **Expert Power** – It is dependent on the perception or belief that the influencer has some relevant expertise or specialised knowledge that the influenced does not have.
3. **Referent Power** – It is dependent on the influencee's desire to identify with or imitate the influencer.
4. **Coercive Power** – It is dependent on the influencer's ability to punish the influencee for not carrying out orders or for not meeting requirements;
5. **Reward Power** – It is dependent on the influencer or agent having the ability to reward the influencee or target for carrying out orders;

Interaction among Sources of Power

The five sources of power are not completely independent of one another. The way the agent uses certain powers can affect the extent of use of other powers. For instance, the use of reward power can increase referent power as people like those who reward them. The appropriate use of reward power – specifying desired behaviour and rewarding them may also increase expert power by heightening the agant's perceived credibility and knowledge.

The use of coercive power tends to decrease referent power, in that people tend to avoid those who administer punishments or withhold rewards. The judicious use of coercive power – specifying undesired behaviour and punishing it when it occurs – can increase expert power. The possession of legitimate power can increase referent power. Legitimate power is often a mark of high status and honour. And people are attracted to high-status individuals. Also increase in expert power, in that target often associate positions of authority with expertise in the field.

The expert power directly affects legitimate power. People more readily accept the authority of those who have expertise and are more willing to accept a system in which knowledgeable individuals have authority. Expert power also affects referent power. One who uses expertise judiciously and who accepts the limits of his expertise can increase attractiveness. One who refuses to share expertise, who claims more than he has, or who fláunts it can lose attractiveness.

Faces of Power

There are primarily two faces of power which have been identified by David McClelland, viz., (i) Negative and (ii) positive.

1. **Negative Face –** The negative face is usually expressed in terms of dominance submission: "I win, you lose". To have power implies having power over another person who is less well off or who lacks it. Leadership based in the negative of power regards people as little more than pawns to be used or sacrificed as the need arises.
2. **Positive Face –** The positive face of power is based or characterised by a concern of group goals – for helping to formulate and achieve such goals. It involves detained influence on behalf of rather than over others. Managers who exercise their power positively encourage group members to develop the strength and competence they need to succeed as people and as members of the organisation.

12.9 AUTHORITY

The Oxford Dictionary gives the meaning of 'authority' as 'power, right to enforce obedience'. Authority is derived from the Latin word auctoritatum or auctoritas, which according to Mommsen, is not readily definable, is something more than command, something that combines with reason. "Authority is the right to give orders and power to exact obedience." Authority denotes certain right generated to a position in an institution. It includes right to take decisions and get them executed from the subordinates.

The purpose of using authority is to influence the behaviour of the subordinates in terms of doing right things so as to achieve organisational goals. It may involve punishment for the erring subordinates and rewards for the outstanding ones.

According to Louis A Allen authority could be defined "as the some of the power and *rights* interested to make possible the performance of the work delegated." He has classified authority into three categories namely, (i) Authority of knowledge, (ii) Authority of position, and (iii) Legal authority.

Distinction between Power and Authority

Sometimes, the terms 'power' and 'authority' are used synonymously but they are distinct, though closely related, concept. Henry Fayol defined authority as the right to give order and the power to exact obedience. He distinguished between a managers official authority of position (formal authority) and his personal authority, which derives from knowledge and experience.

Power, on the other hand, is the ability to exert influence by which a manager directs the actions of others. The term 'power' connotes ability or capacity to do something or to get intend result. A person may have influence on the other's behaviour even without any legal sanction. Power also accompanies the use of authority in the control, direction or utilisations of resources.

The relationship between authority and power should be clearly understood. Power re-enforces authority as one of the major sources of power. The other sources of power may not have appropriate authorisation or legitimation. Some forms of power resides in groups. In every organisations, there are power centers. Managers support one another in effort to dominate or to withstand a struggle for power.

Pfiffner and Sherwood have made distinction between power and authority by defining power as the capacity to secure dominance of one's values or goals and authority as the right to command hierarchical sense. "Sometimes, right and capacity are clearly separated and can be identified easily, but at other times, two get intermingled. In fact, there is a continuum. At one end, right and capacity would be one, while at other end, both would be completely separable. Between these two extremes, it is possible to find a number of variations."

The authority is a downward flowing concept whereas power flows in all directions. Authority can be delegated to the lower levels in the organisation. The lower we go down the hierarchy, the lesser is the authority. But it is not so in case of power which has been defined as the ability or capacity to influence behaviour of others. If a worker is able to influence the behaviour of a departmental manager, it is implied that the worker has exercised power over the departmental manager. Similarly, the departmental manager may be able to influence the behaviour of his superior, peers and subordinates. Thus, power flows in all directions.

12.10 ORGANISATIONAL DEVELOPMENT

Definition and Nature

The term 'organisational development' (OD) first appeared around 1957 when it was used by a number of theorists including Blake and Mouton, Shephard and Beckhard.

Blake and Mouton observe that "O.D. is a systematic way of introducing change based on a structural model for thinking; progressing in a programmatic sequence of steps from individual learning to organisation application, focused upon those silent and often negative attributes of culture which dictate action that so frequently contradict business logic, with emphasis on confronting and resolving conflict as a pre-requisite to valid problem-solving, and employing a variety of techniques of organisational study and self-learning to bring about the necessary change."

According to Beckhard, "organisation development is an effort (1) planned (2) organisation-wide and (3) managed from the top (4) increase organisation effectiveness and health through (5) planned interventions in the organisation's 'processes', using behavioural science knowledge."

CHARACTERISTIC OF ORGANISATIONAL DEVELOPMENT

The characteristics of OD implied in its definition and practice discussed below:

Characteristics of Organisation Development

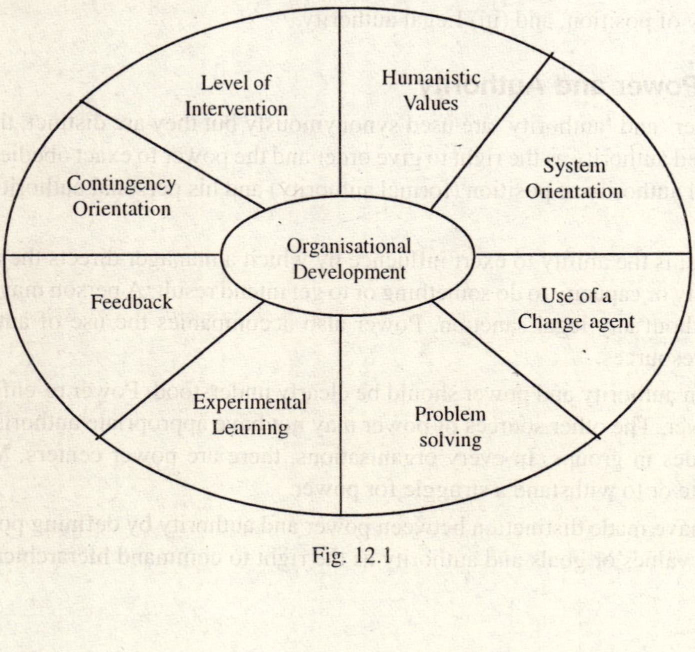

Fig. 12.1

1. **System orientation** – organisation development is system oriented. It is concerned with the interactions of the various parts of the organisation which affects each other. It lays stress on intergroup and interpersonal relationship. It is concerned with structure and as well as attitudes.
2. **Use of Change Agent** – Organisation development is generally implemented with the help one or more change agents, whose role is to stimulate, facilitate, and coordinate change. The change agent usually acts as a catalyst, sparking change within the system while remaining somewhat independent of it.
3. **Problem Solving** – Organisation development is concerned with the problem solving. It seeks to solve the problems through practical experience gained on the work and not merely through theoretical discussions as in a class room. These problems mainly occur at the time when working on the job; hence the organisational members.
4. **Experimental Learning** – Organisation development provides experimental learning to help the participants learn new behaviour patterns through experience. They can discuss and analyse their own immediate experience and learn from it. This approach tends to produce more changed behaviour than the traditional lecture and discussions, in which people talk about abstract ideas. Theory is necessary and desirable, but ultimate test is how it applies in a real situation.
5. **Human Values** – O.D. programmes are often best on humanistic values. The values are positive beliefs about the potential and desire for growth among employees. To be effective and self-renewing, an organisation needs employees who want to increase their skills and contributions.
6. **Contingency Orientation** – Organisation development is situational and contingency oriented. As people learn to develop their behavioural concepts through experience, they can suggest various ways to solve a particular problem and to adapt any of them most suited in the present circumstances. Thus, O.D. is flexible and pragmatic, adapting actions to fit particular needs.
7. **Levels of Intervention** – OD programmes are aimed at solving problems that may occur at the individual, interpersonal group, inter-group and total organisational level. O.D. interventions are designed for each level as for instance career planning at individual level, team building at the group level.
8. **Feedback** – Organisation development supports feedback to participants so that they may be able to collect the data on which decisions are based. For this purpose participants may be divided into several groups according to the functions. Each such group takes its own decisions on the subjects referred to it, and then, groups meet together to thrash out any misunderstanding developed among them. In this way, decisions of each group are checked by other groups and the final decision is reached.

Need of Organisational Development

Organisation Development (O.D) is the discipline directed towards using behavioural science knowledge to assist organisations adjust more rapidly to change. Using a system approach, O.D has grown rapidly in response to a need-the need for organisation to remain viable and to survive in the world of change.

Two important factors have caused the use of O.D as a technique of planned change. Firstly, training for change does not work properly only through reward structure on the job unless there is a proper change in the environment of the organisation in which people work. Secondly, in a dynamic environment, the change is extremely rapid. This requires a highly receptive and effective organisation, so that changes are implemented and absorbed to make organisation survive and grow. O.D helps a lot in this direction. It seeks to build problem-solving capability of communication by improving group dynamics and problem confrontation. In short, it reaches into all aspects of organisation culture in order to make it more humanly responsive.

Benefits of Organisational Development

The following are the benefits of organisation development:

1. It provides opportunities for people to function as human beings rather than mere resources in the productive process.
2. It gives each member of the organisation opportunities to develop to his full potential.
3. It seeks to make the organisation more effective in meeting all its goals.
4. It tries to create an environment in which exciting and challenging work can be found.
5. It gives people in organisations the chance to influence how they relate to work, the organisation, and the work environment.
6. It treats each human being as a person with complex set of needs, all of which are important in his or her work and life.

Limitations of Organisation Development

Organisation development is an important technique of inducting change. It has certain limitations also which are listed below:

1. OD can be no more powerful than the behavioural science concepts on which it is based. Behavioural science has many limitations which are applicable to organisational development also.
2. OD requires use of certain persons who can take initiative to bring about change. Complacent people cannot be helpful in implementing organisation development.
3. OD cannot be applied without giving due consideration to the local circumstances as it may pose a problem in adapting to change.

Chapter 13

Leadership

13.1 INTRODUCTION

Leadership is undoubtedly the most widely discussed, written about and researched topics in the area of general management. We have noted earlier that the process of leading is one of the four management functions. P.F.Drucker has opined that leadership is one of those elusive attributes that separate effective managers from less effective ones. The leadership process is no doubt complex and situationally specific. This is why it often appears that managers know very little about the process which has practical value.

13.2 MEANING & NATURE OF LEADERSHIP

It has to be noted at the outset that leadership derives from power and is similar to – yet distinct from – management. We may first suggest a definition of leadership and discuss various issues connected with this strategic aspect of management.

Definition

It is not that easy to suggest a useful definition of leadership, because it is connected with three related concepts: power, influence, authority.

Power refers to the potential ability of manager to affect the behaviour of others and is generally related to the valued or source resources. The manager is said to be exerting influence when he consciously or unconsciously exercises power to affect the behaviour or attitudes of some else.

Authority refers to the power created and granted by an organisation. If, for instance, the organisation chart specifies that X is the boss, and Y is the subordinate, X is said to have authority over Y. However, what is most important is that subordinates must acknowledge and accept the authority of their superior for it to be really meaningful. Within the context of the organisation, X also has power and influence. Outside the organisation he might not have any power or influence over Y at all.

Like management, leadership has been defined in different ways by different people. In a narrow sense, leadership is defined as the directing of the activities of the immediate subordinates.

In a broad sense, managerial leadership encompasses several additional roles, such as developing the organisation planning and control systems, designing an organisation structure appropriate for the tasks undertaken and acting as a spokesperson for the organisation.

Leadership is usually defined as the skilful use of power. Leaders have power which is often used to influence others. They may or may not have authority. Management and leadership may and often do overlap to a considerable extent. In short, leading is an important part of management, but is not the same as management.

Leadership Traits

There exist some basic traits or set of traits that differentiate from non-leaders. If we can define those traits, we can easily identify potential leader. Leadership traits include such things as intelligence, assertiveness, above- average height, good vocabulary, attractiveness, self-confidence, ability to work to others, creativity, communication skills, and similar attributes. Since such traits vary with situations, it is wrong to identify trait predictor of leadership ability.

As a leader, one works to ensure balance between the goals of the organisation, oneself and one's group. A leader has to work effectively with many people, including superiors, peers and outside groups.

Leadership Roles

In interacting with employees in the work environment the manager has to play four different leadership roles. These are discussed below:

1. **Educator:** Prima facie, as leaders managers have to perform the role of educator by teaching employees not only job skills but also acceptable behaviour and organisational values. Much of such behavioural education is given through the execution of their own daily work. The work habits, attitudes and behaviour of management leaders serve as a role model to the followers.
2. **Counselor:** In his second leadership role of a counselor the manager has to listen, give advice, as also to prevent and solve problems faced by employees. In performing this role managers have to fulfill two expectations of employees: (i) awareness of and concern for the individual employee and (ii) assistance in solving a problem.
3. **Judge:** This role involves a number of functions: (i) appraising or evaluating the performance of subordinates; (ii) enforcing policies, procedures and regulations; (iii) setting disputes and (iv) dispensing justice. The first function necessitates a background knowledge or the standards that are used to measure output. The second function is directly linked to interpersonal communication and to employee training. The performance of the third function demands the exercise of tact and concern for resolution of conflicts. The last function requires giving credit and rewards, as also imposing appropriate discipline.

Ways of Classifying Leaders

The study of leadership often proceeds in terms of the basic approaches used by leaders: autocratic, democratic or laissez faire.

1. **Autocratic or authoritarian leaders:** In general autocratic or authoritarian leaders make most decisions themselves. They do not allow their followers to make them. They are usually thought of a 'Pushers', like military instructors.
2. **Democratic or participative leaders:** Such leaders normally consult their followers heavily in the decision process. They largely rely in the involvement of all members of the group in setting the basic objectives of the group, establishing strategies and determining job assignments.
3. **Laissez faire or free-rein leaders:** Basically such leaders are 'loose' and permissible. They allow followers to do what they want. And there is often drift from one issue to another as they arise and there is hardly any direction or discipline.

   More writers on organisation and management, however, categorise leaders in a different way. This categorisation is based on an examination of their orientation or emphasis in getting the job done. Some leaders emphasize the task; others emphasize followers or subordinates and others still emphasize both.
4. **Task-oriented or production-oriented leaders:** Such leaders mainly focus on the 'work' aspects of getting the job done. The emphasis is on planning, scheduling and processing the work and close control of quality. This approach is also described by the word 'initiating structure'.
5. **People-oriented or employee-oriented leaders:** Such leaders focus on the welfare and fulfill of followers, have enough confidence in themselves and are obviously accepted by their team members (subordinates or followers).

13.3 LEADERSHIP VERSUS MANAGEMENT

Management and leadership are both important to organisations. Because management power comes from organisational structure, it promotes stability, order and problem solving within the structure. Leadership power, on the other hand, comes from personal sources that are not as invested in the organisation, such as personal interests, goals and values. Leadership power promotes vision, creativity and change in the organisation. Fig 13.1 illustrates the different qualities attributed to leaders and managers, although it is important to remember that some people can exhibit a combination of leader/manager qualities.

One of the major differences between the leader and the manager relates to their source of power and the level of compliance it engenders within followers. Power is the potential ability to influence, the behaviour of others. Power represents the resources with which a leader effects changes in employee behaviour. Within organisations, there are typically five sources of power: legitimate, reward, coercive, expert and referent. Sometimes power come from a person' position in the organisation, while other sources of power are based on personal characteristics.

Position Power

The traditional manager's power comes from the organisation. The manager's position gives him or her the power to reward or punish subordinates in order to influence their behaviour. Legitimate power, reward power and coercive power are all forms of position power used by managers to change employee behaviour.

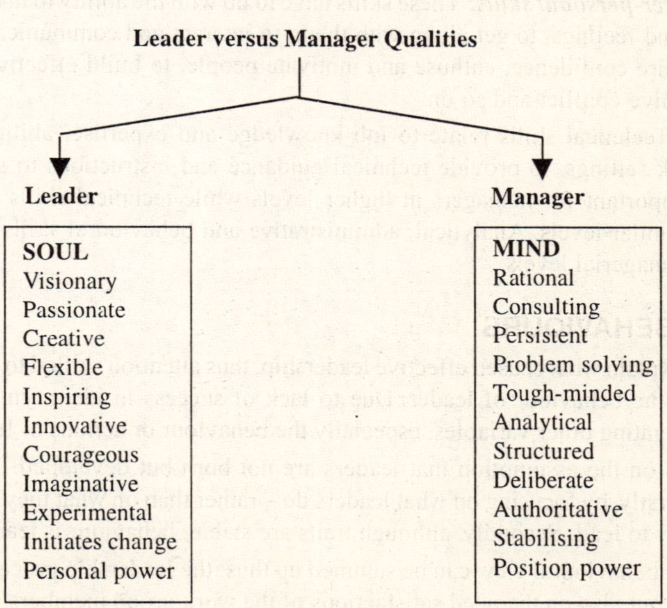

Fig 13.1

Personal Power

In contrast to the external sources of position power, personal power most often comes from internal sources, such as a person's special knowledge or personality characteristics. Personal power is the tool of the leader. Subordinates follow a leader because of the respect, admiration or caring they feel for the individual and his or her ideas. Personal power is becoming increasingly important as more businesses are run by teams of workers who are less tolerant of authoritarian management.

13.4 MANAGERIAL SKILLS

Skills refer to specific abilities to perform certain tasks. They are not inherent abilities in people but are to be acquired or developed through education, training and experience. Managers develop or acquire a range of skills in their jobs. Different types of skills are:

(a) ***Conceptual skills:*** This is the ability to think in abstract terms to form images and ideas to visualise and understand the future and to discern relations and interactions among the elements of a system and changes therein. Conceptual skills are needed to identify and diagnose problems and opportunities, to understand the over-all organisational interests and needs and to relate them to its subsystem, to determine organisational and other derivative objectives and strategies, to plan and implement major changes in an integrated manner and so on.

(b) ***Analytical skills:*** These refer the abilities to proceed in a logical, step-by-step and systematic manner, to examine the various aspects of specific issues and to understand complex characteristics of a phenomenon. Analytical skills are needed for problem solving and decision-making, to evaluate performance and to manage complex situations.

(c) ***Administrative skills:*** They centre around ability to act in a pragmatic manner, to get things done by implementing decisions and plans to mobilise and organise resources and efforts, to co-ordinate diverse activities and to regulate organisational events in a orderly manner.

(d) ***Behavioural or inter-personal skills:*** These skills have to do with the ability to understand people and their problems, needs and feelings, to get along with them, to interact and communicate with them, to provide leadership, to inspire confidence, enthuse and motivate people, to build effective team work, to provide counseling, to resolve conflict and so on.

(e) ***Technical skills:*** Technical skills relate to job knowledge and expertise, ability to apply methods and techniques to work settings, to provide technical guidance and instructions to subordinates. Conceptual skills are more important for managers at higher levels while technical skills are vital for manages at supervisory and similar levels. Analytical, administrative and behavioural skills are more or less equally important at all managerial levels.

13.5 LEADERSHIP BEHAVIOURS

The trait theory failed to explain what caused effective leadership, thus attention shifted to the behavioural approach which involved studying the behaviour of leader. Due to lack of success in identifying useful leadership trait, researchers started investigating other variables, especially the behaviour or actions of leaders.

The approach is based on the assumption that leaders are not born but developed. This assumption has two important implications. Firstly, by focusing on what leaders do – rather than on what they are – it could be assumed that there is one 'best' way to lead. Secondly, although traits are stable, behaviour is learned.

Thus the essence of the behavioural view can be summed up thus: the leadership process must focus not only on the work to be performed but also on the need satisfactions of the work group members.

The most popular behavioural research and theories are (1) Douglas McGregor's theory X and theory Y and (2) Likert's four management systems.

A. Managerial Philosophy

McGregor's Theory X and Theory Y

A manager's approach to leadership is largely, if not entirely, influenced by his philosophy about work and the people performing the work. In this context Douglas McGregor's thesis deserves special mention. His thesis is that leadership strategies are influenced by a leader's assumptions about human nature. As a result of his experience as a business consultant, McGregor has made two contrasting sets of assumptions about managers in industry. The first set is known as Theory X and the second one is Y.

Assumption of Theory X

According to Theory X managers believe the following:

1. The average human being has an inherent dislike for work and will avoid it, if possible.
2. Because of this human characteristic, most people must be coerced, controlled, directed or threatened with punishment to get them to put forth adequate effort to achieve organisational objectives.
3. The average human being prefers to be directed, wishes to avoid responsibility, has relatively little ambition and wants security above all.

Assumptions of Theory Y

According to Theory Y managers believe the following:

1. The expenditure of physical and mental effort in work is as natural as play or rest. The average human being does not inherently dislike work. Depending upon controllable conditions, work may be a source of satisfaction.
2. External control and the threat of punishment are not the only means of bringing about effort towards achieving organisational objectives. People will exercise self-direction and self-control to achieve objectives to which they are committed.
3. Commitment to objectives is a function of the reward associated with their achievement.
4. The average human being, under proper conditions, learns not only to accept but to seek responsibility.
5. The capacity to exercise a relatively high degree of imagination, ingenuity and creativity in the solution of organisational problems is widely not narrowly, distributed in the population.
6. Under the conditions of modern industrial life, the intellectual potentialities of the average human being are only partially utilised.

It is clear that a leader holding Theory X assumptions would prefer an autocratic style, whereas one holding Theory Y assumptions would prefer a more participative style. A manager operating on the basis of Theory X would impose a directive leadership style on the individual or work group he is supervising. The probable actions of the manager would be (1) coercion, (2) negative motivation and (3) refusal to allow employee decision-making. Theory Y will prepare a leader to work with people as individuals, to involve people in the process of decision-making, to openly encourage people to seek responsibility and to work with people to achieve their goals.

B. Behavioural Approaches

The autocratic and democratic styles suggest that it is the "behaviour" of the leader rather than a personality trait that determines leadership effectiveness. Perhaps any leader can adopt the correct behaviour with appropriate training. The focus of recent research has shifted from leader personality traits toward the behaviours successful leaders display. Important research programmes on leadership behaviour were conducted at Ohio State University, the University of Michigan and the University of Texas.

Ohio State Studies

Researchers at Ohio State University surveyed leaders to study hundreds of dimensions of leader behaviour. They identified two major behaviours, called consideration and initiating structure.

Consideration is the extent to which the leader is mindful of subordinates, respects their ideas and feelings and establishes mutual trust. Considerate leaders are friendly, provide open communication, develop teamwork and are oriented toward their subordinate's welfare.

Initiating structure is the extent to which the leader is task oriented and directs subordinate work activities toward goal attainment. Leaders with this style typically give instructions, spend time planning, emphasize deadline and provide explicit schedules of work activities.

Consideration and initiating structure are independent of each other, which means that a leader with a high degree of consideration may be either high or low on initiating structure. A leader may have any of four styles: high initiating structure – low consideration, high initiating structure – high consideration, low initiating structure – low consideration or low initiating structure – high consideration. The Ohio State research found that the high consideration – high initiating structure style achieved better performance and greater satisfaction than the other leader styles. However, new research has found that effective leaders may be high on consideration and low on initiating structure or low on consideration and high on initiating structure, depending on the situation. Thus, the "high-high" style is not always the best.

Michigan Studies

Studies at the University of Michigan at about the same time took a different approach by comparing the behaviour of effective and ineffective supervisor. The most effective supervisors were those who focused on the subordinate's human needs in order to "build effective work groups with high performance goals". The Michigan researchers used the term employee-centered leaders for leaders who established high performance goals and displayed supportive behaviour toward subordinate. The less effective leaders were called job-centered leaders; these tended to be less concerned with goal achievement and human needs in favour of meeting schedules, keeping costs low and achieving production efficiency.

The Michigan Studies carried out by Rensis Likert and his co-workers in the late 1940s identified two basic forms of leader behaviour:

1. **Job-centered leader behaviour:** The leader practices close supervision so as to monitor and control performance closely on the basis of legitimate, reward and coercive power. As griffin put it: " A leader who pays close attention to the work of subordinate, explains what to do and is primarily interested in performance is exhibiting job-centered behaviour".
2. **Employee-centered leader behaviour:** The leader attempts to build effective work groups with high performance goals and pays particular attention the human aspects of subordinate's problems as the way in which to achieve that. The stress is on group formation and development and on employee growth and participation. In the language of Griffin: "A leader who is interested in high performance through the development of a coercive work group and ensuring that employees are basically satisfied with their jobs can be described as employee centered".

This is the early Michigan view of leader behaviour. The two styles of leader behaviour are presumed to be at the ends of a continuum. This suggests that leaders may be job centered, employee centered or any combination of the two. But, Likert studied only the two end styles for contrast and suggested that employee-centered behaviour generally tends to be more effective.

Likert found that "supervisors who practiced general supervision and were employee centered had higher morale and greater productivity than supervisors who practiced close supervision and were more job centered".

The Leadership Grid

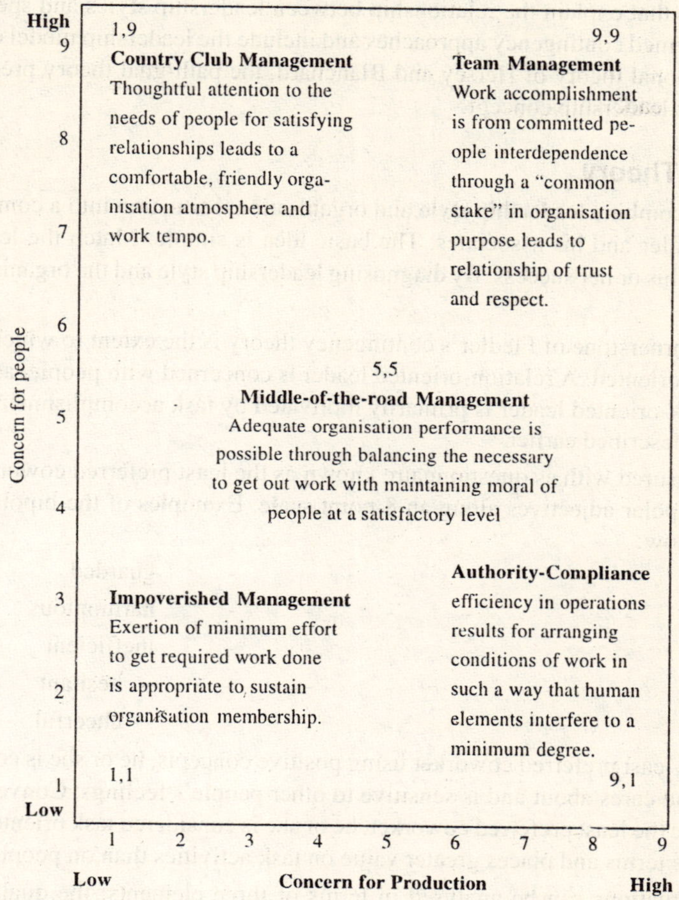

Fig 13.2

The Leadership Grid

Blake and Mouton of the University of Texas proposed a two-dimensional leadership theory called leadership grid that builds on the work of the Ohio State and Michigan studies. The two-dimensional model and five of its seven major management styles are depicted in Fig 13.2. Each axis on the grid is a 9-point scale, with 1 meaning low concern and 9 high concern.

Team management (9,9) often is considered the most effective style and is recommended for managers because organisation members work together to accomplish tasks. Country club management (1,9) occurs when primary emphasis is given to people rather than to work outputs. Authority-compliance management (9,1) occurs when efficiency in operations is the dominant orientation. Middle-of-the-road management (5,5) reflects a moderate amount of concern for both people and production. Impoverished management (1,1) means the absence of a management philosophy; managers exert little effort toward interpersonal relationships or work accomplishment.

C. Contingency Approaches

Several models of leadership that explain the relationship between leadership styles and specific situations have been developed. These are termed contingency approaches and include the leadership model developed by Fiedler and his associates, the situational theory of Hersey and Blanchard, the path-goal theory presented by Evans and House and the substitutes-for-leadership concept.

Fiedler's Contingency Theory

An early, extensive effort to combine leadership style and organisational situation into a comprehensive theory of leadership was made by Fiedler and his associates. The basic idea is simple: Match the leader's style with the situation most favourable for his or her success. By diagnosing leadership style and the organisational situation, the correct fit can be arranged.

Leadership Style: The cornerstone of Fiedler's contingency theory is the extent to which the leader's style is relationship oriented or task oriented. A relation-oriented leader is concerned with people, as in the consideration style described earlier. A task-oriented leader is primarily motivated by task accomplishment, which is similar to the initiating structure style described earlier.

Leadership style was measured with as questionnaire known as the least preferred coworker (LPC) scale. The LPC scale has a set of 16 bipolar adjectives along an 8-point scale. Examples of the bipolar adjectives used by Fiedler on the LPC scale follow:

open - - - - - - - - guarded
quarrelsome - - - - - - - - harmonious
efficient - - - - - - - - inefficient
self-assured - - - - - - - - hesitant
gloomy - - - - - - - - - cheerful

If the leader describes the least preferred coworker using positive concepts, he or she is considered relationship oriented, that is, a leader who cares about and is sensitive to other people's feelings. Conversely, if a leader uses negative concepts to describe the least preferred coworker, he or she is considered task oriented that is a leader who sees other people in negative terms and places greater value on task activities than on people.

Situation: Leadership situations can be analysed in terms of three elements: the quality of leader-member relationships, task structure and position power. Each of these elements can be described as either favourable or unfavourable for the leader.

1. Leader-member relations refer to group atmosphere and member's attitude toward and acceptance of the leader. When subordinates trust, respect and have confidence in the leader, leader-member relations are considered good. When subordinates distrust, do not respect and have little confidence in the leader, leader-member relations are poor.
2. Task structure refers to the extent to which tasks performed by the group are defined, involve specific procedures and have clear, explicit goals. Routine, well-defined tasks, such as those of assembly-line workers, have a high degree of structure. Creative, ill-defined tasks, such as research and development or strategic planning, have a low degree of task structure. When task structure is high, the situation is considered favourable to the leader; when low, the situation is less favourable.
3. Position power is the extent to which the leader had formal authority over subordinates. Position power is high when the leader has the power to plan and direct the work of subordinates, evaluate it and reward or punish them. Position power is low when the leader has little authority over subordinates and cannot evaluate their work or reward them. When position power is high, the situation is considered favourable for the leader; when low, the situation is unfavourable.

Combining the three situational characteristics yields a list of eight leadership situations, Situation I is most favourable to the leader because leader-member relations are good, task structure is high and leader position power is string. Situation VIII is most unfavourable to the leader because leader-member relations are poor, task structure is low and leader position power is weak. All other octants represent intermediate degree of favourableness for the leader.

Contingency Theory: When Fiedler examined the relationship among leadership style, situational favourability and group task performance, he found the pattern shown in Fig 13.3. Task-oriented leaders are more effective when the situation is either highly favourable or highly unfavourable. Relationship-oriented leaders are more effective in situations of moderate favourability.

The task-oriented leader excels in the favourable situation because everyone gets along, the task is clear and the leader has power; all that is needed is for someone to take charge and provide direction. Similarly, if the situation is highly unfavourable to the leader, a great deal of structure and task direction is needed. A strong leader defines task structure and can establish authority over subordinates. Because leader-member relations are poor anyway, a strong task orientation will make no difference in the leader's popularity.

The relationship-oriented leader performs better in situations of intermediate favourability because human relations skills are important in achieving high group performance. In these situations, the leader may be moderately well liked, have some power and supervise jobs that contain some ambiguity. A leader with good interpersonal skills can create a positive group atmosphere that will improve relationships, clarify task structure and establish position power.

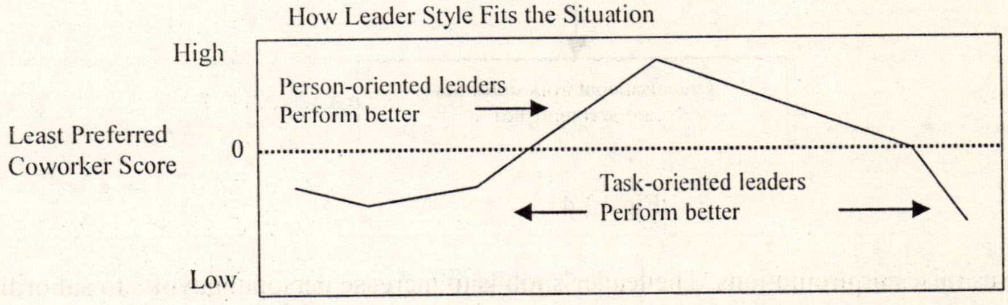

Fig 13.3

A leader, then, needs to know two things in order to use Fiedler's contingency theory. First, the leader should know whether he or she has a relationship-or task-oriented style. Second, the leader should diagnose the situation and determine whether leader-member relations, task structure and position power are favourable or unfavourable.

Fitting leader style to the situation can yield big dividends in profits and efficiency. On the other hand, using an incorrect style for the situation can cause problems.

Path-Goal Theory

Another contingency approach to leadership is called the path-goal theory. According to the path-goal theory, the leader's responsibility is to increase subordinate's motivation to attain personal and organisational goals. As illustrated in Fig 13.4, the leader increases their motivation by either (1) clarifying the subordinate's path to the rewards that are available or (2) increasing the rewards that the subordinates value and desire. Path clarification means that the leader works with subordinates to help them identify and learn the behaviours that will lead to successful task accomplishment and organisational rewards. Increasing rewards means that the leader talks with subordinates to learn which rewards are important to them – that is, whether they desire intrinsic rewards from the work itself or

Leader Roles in the Path-Goal Model

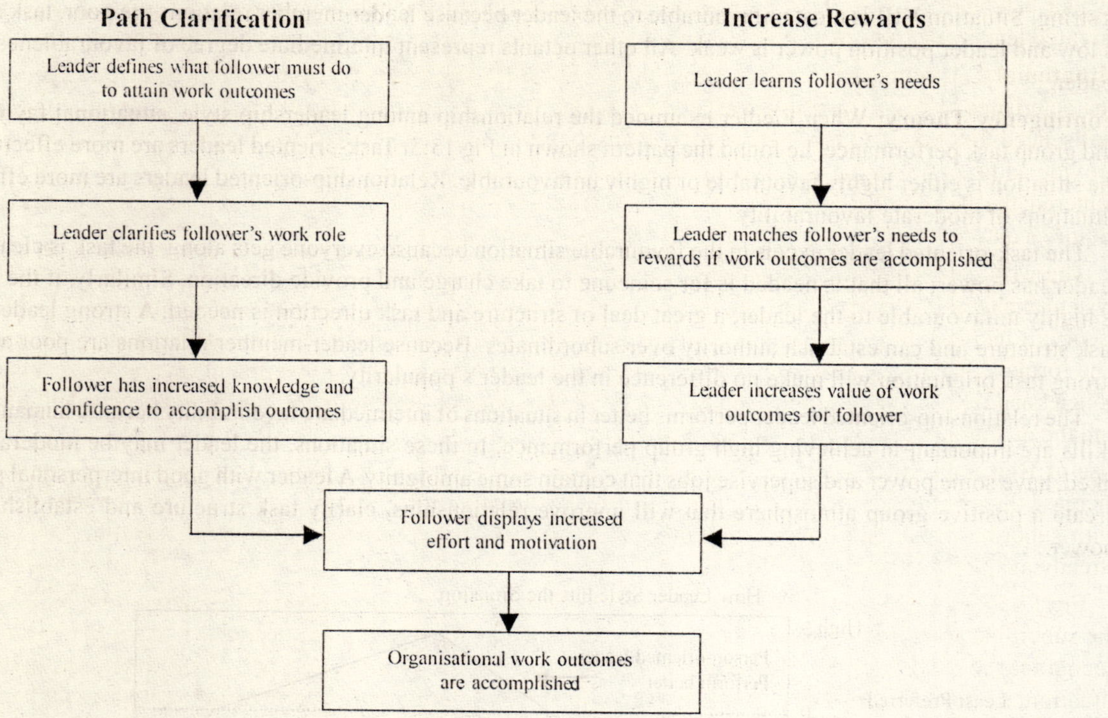

Fig 13.4

extrinsic rewards such as raises or promotions. The leader's job is to increase personal payoffs to subordinates for goal attainment and to make the paths to these payoffs clear and easy to travel.

This model is called a contingency theory because it consists of three sets of contingencies –leader behaviour and style, situational contingences and the use of rewards to meet subordinate's needs. Whereas in the Fiedler theory described earlier the assumption would be to switched leaders as situations change, in the path-goal theory leaders switch their behaviours to match the situation.

Leader Behaviour: The path-goal theory suggests a fourfold classification of leader behaviours. These classifications are the types of leader behaviour the leader can adopt and include supportive directive, achievement-oriented and participative styles.

Supportive leadership involves leader behaviour that shows concern for subordinate's well-being and personal needs. Leadership behaviour is open, friendly and approachable and the leader creates a team climate and treats subordinates as equals.

Directive leadership occurs when the leader tells subordinate exactly what they are supposed to do. Leader behaviour includes planning, making schedules, setting performance goal and behaviour standards and stressing adherence to rules and regulations. Directive leadership behaviour is similar to the initiating-structure leadership style described earlier.

Participative leadership means that the leader consults with his or her subordinates about decisions. Leader behaviour includes asking for opinions and suggestions, encouraging participation in decision making and meeting with subordinates in their workplaces. The participative leader encourages group discussion and written suggestions.

Achievement-oriented leadership occurs when the leader sets clear and challenging goals for subordinates. Leader behaviour stresses high-quality performance and improvement over current performance. Achievement-oriented leaders also show confidence in subordinates and assist them in learning how to achieve high goals.

Situational Contingencies: The two important situational contingencies in the path-goal theory are (1) the personal characteristics of group members and (2) the work environment. Personal characteristics of subordinates are ability, skills, needs and motivations. For example, if an employee has a low level of ability or skill, the leader may need to provide additional training or coaching in order for the worker to improve performance. If a subordinate is self-centered, the leader must use rewards to motivate him or her. Subordinates who want to clear direction and authority require a directive leader who will tell them exactly what to do.

The work environment contingencies include the degree of task structure, the nature of the formal authority system and the work group itself. The task structure is similar to the same concept described in Fiedler's contingency theory; it includes the extent to which tasks are defined and have explicit job descriptions and work procedures. The formal authority system includes the amount of legitimate power used by managers and the extent to which policies and rules constrain employee's behaviour. Work group characteristics are the educational level of subordinates and the quality of relationships among them.

Use of Rewards: Recall that the leader's responsibility is to clarify the path to rewards for subordinates or to increase the amount of rewards to enhance satisfaction and job performance. In some situations, the leader works with subordinates to help them acquire the skills and confidence needed to perform task and achieve rewards already available. In others, that leader may develop new rewards to meet the specific needs of a subordinate.

Fig 13.5 illustrates four examples of how leadership behaviour is tailored to the situation. In the first situation, the subordinate lacks confidence; thus, the supportive leadership style provides the social support with which to encourage the subordinate to undertake the behaviour needed to do the work and receive the rewards. In the second situation, the job is ambiguous, and the employee is not performing effectively. Directive leadership behaviour is used to give instructions and clarify the task so that the follower will know how to accomplish it and receive rewards. In the third situation, the subordinate is unchallenged by the task; thus, an achievement-oriented behaviour is used to set higher goals. This clarifies the path to rewards for the employee. In the fourth situation, an incorrect reward is given to a subordinate and the participative leadership style is used to change this. By discussing the subordinate's needs, the leader is able to identify the correct reward for task accomplishment. In all four cases, the

Path-Goal Situations and Preferred Leader Behaviours

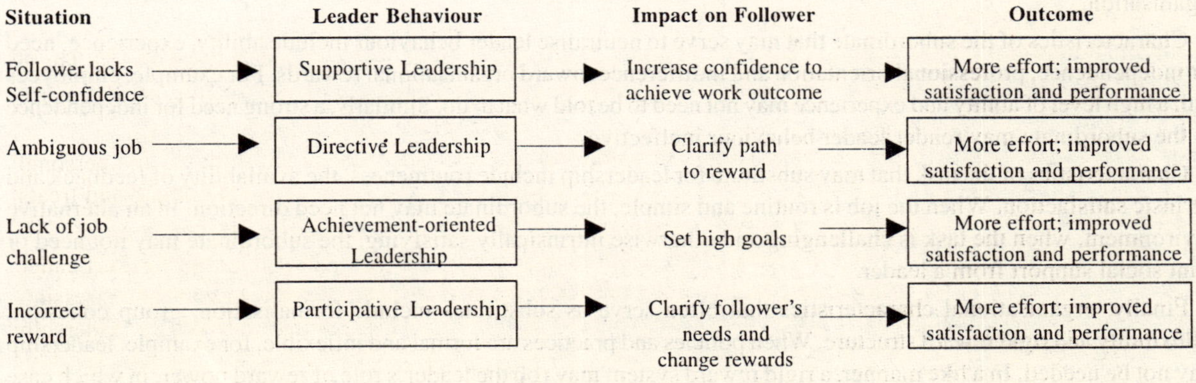

Fig 13.5

outcome of fitting the leadership behaviour to the situation produces greater employee effort by either clarifying how subordinates can receive rewards or changing the rewards to fit their needs.

13.6 IS THERE AN IDEAL LEADERSHIP STYLE?

For quite some time there has been considerable debate about whether there is a normative or ideal leadership style. The centre of the debate is whether the ideal style does exist. This style is considered to be one that actively involves people in goal setting through the use of participative management techniques and focuses on people and task.

Empirical research has given considerable support to there being an ideal leadership style incorporating a participative management approach. Likewise earlier research in motivation theory also supported the participative management approach as the ideal. Leading practitioners of management and management consultants felt that these concepts made enormous good sense. Moreover, there are numerous instances in which both performance and attitudes improved when participative management was introduced.

In recent year, there have been several research studies challenging the view-point that there is one ideal leadership style. Essentially, they say that under various conditions the autocratic approach may get better results.

One research study specially challenges the assumption that leaders who are high in both task and interpersonal behaviour will have more satisfied and productive subordinates than those who are not. In another study, the more desirable style seemed to be 1,9 or a leader's behaviour of low initiating structure and high consideration.

In truth, leadership experience reveals that in some situations an autocratic approach might be the best, in others a participative approach; in some conclusion is that leadership is complex and the most appropriate style depends on several interrelated variables.

The personal behavioural theories have, no doubt, an important role to play in the development of contemporary thinking about leadership. Unfortunately, these theories fell prey to the problem of universalism along the way. So, other approaches to leadership are needed.

13.7 SUBSTITUTES FOR LEADERSHIP

In recent years, a new concept has arisen: the concept of substitutes for leadership in response to the fact that existing leadership models and theories do not account for situations in which leadership is not needed. They simply seek to specify what kind of leader behaviour is appropriate. By contrast, the substitute concepts identify situations in which leader behaviours are neutralised by characteristics of the subordinate, the task and the organisation.

Characteristics of the subordinate that may serve to neutralise leader behaviour include ability, experience, need for independence, professional orientation and indifference toward organisational rewards. For example, employees with a high level of ability and experience may not need to be told what to do. Similarly, a strong need for independence by the subordinate may render leader behaviour ineffective.

Characteristics of the task that may substitute for leadership include routineness, the availability of feedback and intrinsic satisfaction. When the job is routine and simple, the subordinate may not need direction. In an alternative environment, when the task is challenging and otherwise intrinsically satisfying, the subordinate may not need or want social support from a leader.

Finally, organisational characteristics that often serve as substitutes include formalisation, group cohesion, inflexibility and rigid reward structure. When policies and practices are formal and inflexible, for example, leadership may not be needed. In a like manner, a rigid reward system may rob the leader's role of reward power, in which case the importance of the role gradually diminishes.

Factors influencing leadership effectiveness

Leadership has been defined as the ability to persuade others to seek defined objectives enthusiastically. We have also four different approaches to the study of leadership: trait, behaviour, situational or transformational. The trait and behavioural approaches indicate that effective leadership depends on a number of variables such as intelligence, decisiveness and style. The transformational approaches emphasize the notion of charisma, a term coined by the German sociologist Max Weber and how it influences followers. Despite considerable ignorance, ambiguity and disagreement about leadership as a role and as process, organisational theorists have identified a few factors that are likely to influence leadership effectiveness.

1. **Perceptual accuracy:** It was McGregor who indicated how perception plays a role in leadership. In his view, managers who perceive employees may miss the opportunity to achieve optional results. Thus, management perceptual accuracy is extremely important in each of the situational models.
2. **Background, experience and personality of the leader:** The leader's background and experience affect the choice of leadership style. A person who has achieved quite some success in being relationship style. In a like manner, a leader who doesn't trust followers and who has structured the task for years will use an autocratic style.
3. **The background, maturity and personality of the follower:** A leader's choice of style is also influenced by followers in important ways. This is so because leadership is essentially a mutual sharing process. For example, a leader with technically proficient followers is best advised to be more participative and less autocratic. By contrast, inexperienced, newly recruited employees with a minimum of work knowledge may prefer a leader who structures the task and is firm. In such a situation an autocratic or job-oriented leader works the best.

   In this context, Hersey and Blanchard stress the role of the follower's maturity. They define maturity as the ability and willingness of people to assume responsibility for directing their own behaviour. Maturity has two components: job maturity and psychological maturity. While the former is the knowledge, skills and experience to perform without close supervision, the latter is the willingness to do the job.
4. **Superior's expectations and style:** Superiors are comfortable with and prefer a particular leadership style. Research has indicated that a superior who prefers a job-oriented, autocratic approach encourages followers to adopt a similar approach. Initiation of the superior's example is a powerful force in sharing leadership styles.

   Since superiors possess various power bases, their expectations are important. As a genera rule, superiors prefer more task-oriented behaviours instead of relationship-oriented behaviours.
5. **Task understanding:** Leaders must be competent enough to assess correctly the tasks their followers are performing. In an unstructured task situation (where goals are not easily defined) directive or autocratic leadership may be quite inappropriate; the employees need guidelines, freedom to act and the necessary resources to be able to accomplish the task properly. It is absolutely essential for leaders to properly diagnose the task of followers so that proper leadership style choices are made. Due to this requirement, a leader must have some technical knowledge of the job and its requirements.
6. **Peer expectations:** Donnelly has also pointed out that a leader's peers can provide support and encouragement for various leadership behaviours, thus influencing the leader in the future. No doubt, peers are an important source of comparison and information in making leadership style choices and modifications.

13.8 MEASURES FOR DEVELOPING LEADERSHIP ABILITY OF MANAGERS

It is necessary and possible for managers to develop and improve their leadership abilities. It is necessary because managers have to get things done through their subordinates. It is possible because they are several means and techniques of acquiring leadership abilities. Also, leadership abilities are not totally inborn or genetic. They can be acquired and learnt by training and by other means. The measures for developing leadership ability of managers are explained as follows:

1. **Leadership training:** Training programmes are offered to expose managers to several leadership situations and teach them how to tackle them. The trainers create the situations wherein the managers undergoing leadership training are provided opportunities to diagnose problems, think of ways and means of tackling them which partly involve testing of various styles of leadership against realities. The managers under training are to be given immediate feedback on their leadership performance.
2. **Autonomy and accountability:** Managers may be able to sharpen their leadership abilities under conditions of relative freedom. They should be allowed a large amount of freedom to evolve their own methods of tackling situations calling or critical leadership abilities. At the same time they should be provided with the required organisational support in the form of authority, status, top management support and so on. They should bé given adequate discretion dispensing rewards and penalties to their subordinates, within the framework of certain norms and rules.
3. **Setting challenging but realistic goals:** Managers have to be put on their toes most of the time in their career by setting challenging goals to be met within particular time frames. A highly demanding job environment for managers is likely to force them to develop the needed leadership abilities. The goals should be such that they bring out and develop best leadership abilities of managers.
4. **Internal organisational exposure:** Another measure to develop the leadership ability of managers is to expose them within the organisation itself to critical situations calling for application of leadership abilities. Managers may be put in charge of committees assigned with the task of project implementation, co-ordination and control.
5. **Opportunities for interaction:** Managers should also have opportunities to interact with their subordinates in a more intense and continuous manner. Many managers get themselves so extremely busy with their own work that they find little time to talk or listen to their subordinates, to guide them, to understand their viewpoints, to be supportive to them and to develop them.
6. **Job rotation:** Managers may also be helped to develop leadership skills by a process of systematic rotation of their jobs. They should be exposed to a variety of superior subordinate relations and job environments so that they develop the ability of coping with situations, which do not permit them to adopt stereotyped style or approaches.

Chapter 14

Controlling

14.1 INTRODUCTION

Controlling is the last of the five functions of management. It is considered last, not because it is less important than the other four functions: planning, organising, staffing and leading but because it affects and is affected by the other four functions. As Earl Strong and Robert D. Smith have rightly commented: "A combination of well –planned objectives, strong organisation, capable direction and motivation have little probability of success unless there exists an adequate system of control". The control function essentially insures that planned performance is achieved with a minimum of disorder and disruptions. It assures that plans are carried out and objectives are reached. Planning, organising, staffing and directing (leading) must be properly monitored to maintain their effectiveness and efficiency. Hence, there is a real need for competent people to plan, organise and direct a control system that will be effective.

14.2 MEANING OF CONTROL

In truth, organisational life is replete with daily examples of poor control. Poor control may be reflected in project cost over-runs, schedules not being completed on time, poor-quality service or products, botched opportunities and so on. Managerial control consists of the things that management does to ensure that plans are accomplished as intended.

Various names are given to the control function. It is often called evaluating, appraising or correcting. But the term 'control' seems to be appropriate because none of the other terms carries the connotation of (1) setting standards, (2) measuring actual performance and (3) taking corrective action.

Control, the last of the basic functions of management, can be defined as "the regulation of organisational activity in such a way as to facilitate goal attainment". For example, an organisation might find that if desired profits levels are to be maintained, its manufacturing costs must not exceed Rs.40 per unit. A system would then be established to provide ongoing cost information to management. If costs rise above Rs.40, some action would be taken to reduce costs to the desired level. Such actions might be raising productivity, changing suppliers to buy less expensive materials or recycling defective products. In this example, the desired levels of profitability are the goals of the organisation and the regulation of activities required to attain those goals is the management of production costs.

14.3 IMPORTANCE OF CONTROL

Without effective control systems, an organisation could deviate further and further from its derived goals and paths chosen to attain the goals. In this context, we may refer to three reasons for control in modern organisations:

1. ***Changing Circumstances:*** In today's highly complex and turbulent environment, all business organisations must find ways of coping with change. If managers could set goals and achieve them in no time, there would hardly be any need for control. But between the time when a goal is established and the time when it is reached, various things may happen in the organisation and its environment to disrupt movement towards the goal-or even to change the goal itself.

2. ***Compounding of Errors:*** The second important reason underlying managerial control is the process of error compounding. In most cases, the health of an organisation is not damaged by small mistakes and errors. However, if left uncontrolled, small errors may accumulate and become very serious with the passage of time. Control can help managers rectify errors and correct deviations from goals before they compound.
3. ***Organisational Complexity:*** Another reason for control is the complexity of modern organisations. For a firm producing only one product by using only one raw material and having a simple production process and enjoying constant demand for its product, its manager can probably maintain control easily and quickly. But, in a complex organisation that produces a large number of products from various raw materials, has a large market area and a complicated organisation structure and operates in a competitive environment, it is difficult, if not impossible, to maintain adequate control without any elaborate control system.

14.4 LINK BETWEEN PLANNING AND CONTROLLING

There is a very close link between planning and controlling. This is shown in Fig 14.1. This is usually the first part of the management process. In the next stage, the organising and leading functions get the actual work of the organisation done and the controlling function is directly tied back into planning.

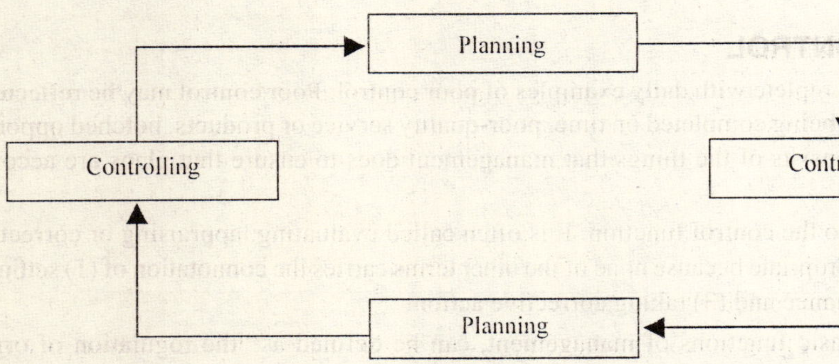

The Link Between Planning and Controlling

Fig 14.1

A modern organisation continuously cycles back and forth between planning and controlling. To start with, the manager makes plans and then uses the control system to monitor progress toword fulfillment of these plans. The control system, in turn, tells the manager that things are in order, i.e., going as they should that things are not going as they should or that the situation has changed.

Controlling and Others Managerial Functions

There is difference between planning and controlling. Controlling establishes performance standards used to measure progress towards organisational goals. The basic objective of controlling is to determine whether people and the various parts of an organisation are on target, achieving the progress towards their objectives that they planned to achieve. Whereas planning chooses goals and maps out the necessary strategy and tactics, controlling attempts to prevent failure by providing the means to monitor the performances of individuals, departments, divisions – and the organisation in it entirety.

In fact, control is related to, is affected by and affects the four other managerial functions. This is especially true for planning.

In truth, controlling complements planning. Managers often layout careful and elaborate plans, but unless these are supported by effective control, plan accomplishment becomes just a matter of luck. Organisation that do not exercise proper control even run tremendous risk. It is even thought that planning is incomplete unless good controls are also established.

Planning and controlling are so closely linked with each other that they have been called: "the Siamese Twins of management". In fact, we shall now observe that the initial step of the control process is actually a planning step – establishing a goal, standard or performance objective. The essence of control lies in comparing actual results with the plan.

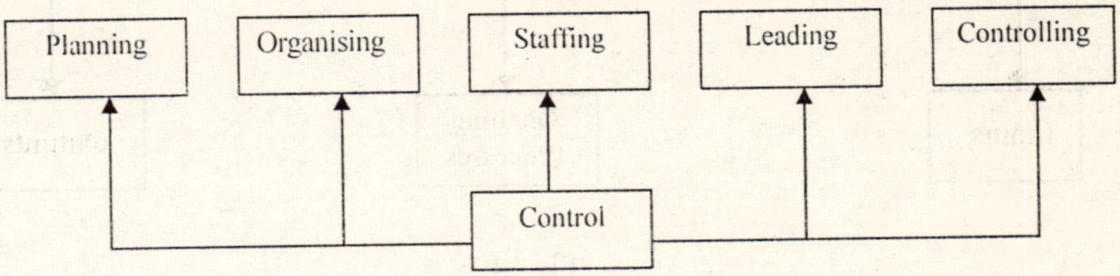

The relationship of control to other management functions

Fig 14.2

The control function of management is also inseparably linked up with the other managerial functions as shown in Fig 14.2. It enables us to assess whether planning, organising, staffing and leading are being performed effectively.

14.5 ORGANISATIONAL CONTROL FOCUS

Control can focus on events before, during or after a process. For example, a local automobile dealer can focus on activities before, during or after sales of news cars. Careful inspection of new cars and cautious selection of sales employees are ways to ensure high quality or profitable sales even before those sales take place. Monitoring how salespeople act with customers would be considered control during the sales task. Counting the number of new cars sold during the month or telephoning buyers about their satisfaction with sales transactions would constitute control after sales have occurred. These three types of control are formally called feedforward, concurrent and feedback and are illustrated in Fig 14.3.

Feedforward Control

Control that attempts to identify and prevent deviations before they occur is called feedforward control. Sometimes called preliminary or preventive control, it focuses on human, material and financial resources that flow into the organisation. Its purpose is to ensure that input quality is high enough to prevent problems when the organisation performs its task.

Feedforward controls are evident in the selection and hiring of new employees. Organisations attempt to improve the likelihood that employees will perform up to standards by identifying the necessary skills and using tests and other screening devices to hire people who have those skills. Many organisations also conduct drug screening to ensure that job candidates or employees do not impair their ability to work safely and effectively. Another example

Organisational Control Focus

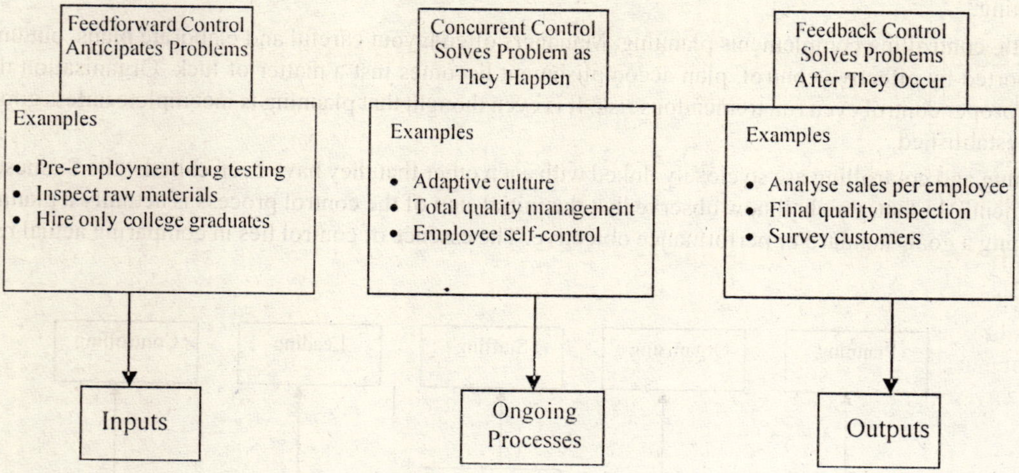

Fig 14.3

is the requirement that professional football, basketball and baseball players pass a physical exam before their contracts are validated. All of these kinds of testing are feedforward controls because they are intended to prevent deviations from acceptable performance.

Another type of feedforward control is to identify and manage risk. The large accounting firms have recognised that they can offer value to their clients by looking for risks the clients have knowingly or unknowingly taken on, rather than merely evaluating their financial performance after the fact.

Concurrent Control

Control that monitors ongoing employee activities to ensure they are consistent with quality standards is called concurrent control. Concurrent control assesses current work activites, relies on performance standards and includes rules and regulations for guiding employee tasks and behaviours. Its intent is to ensure that work activites produce the correct results. It includes self-control, through which individuals impose concurrent controls on their own behaviour.

Many manufacturing operations include devices that measure whether the items being produced meet quality standards. Employees monitor the measurements; if they see that standard are not met in some area, they make a correction themselves of single the appropriate person that a problem is occurring. Technology advancements are adding to the possibilities for concurrent control in services as well.

Other concurrent controls involve the ways in which organisations influence employees. An organisation's cultural norms and values influence employee behaviour, as do the norms of an employee's peers or work group. An organisation that adopts a philosophy of total quality management establishes the norm that employees will seek ways to continuously improve the organisation's activities. Employees who accept that norm will look for ways to improve quality, thus contributing to the standard of continuous improvement.

Feedback Control

Sometimes called post action or output control, feedback control focuses on the organisation's outputs – in particular, the quality of an end product or service. Besides producing high-quality products and services, business needs to earn a profit and even nonprofit organisations need to operate efficiently to carry out their mission. Therefore, many feedback controls focus on financial measurements.

14.6 FEEDBACK CONTROL MODEL/STEPS IN CONTROLLING

All well-designed control systems involve the use of feedback to determine whether performance meets established standards. Managers set up control systems that consist of the four key steps illustrated in Fig 14.4: establish standards, measure performance, compare performance to standards, and take corrections as necessary. The steps are discussed below:

Establish Standards of Performance

Within the organisation's overall strategic plan, managers define goals for organisational departments in specific, operational terms that include a standard of performance against which to compare organisational activities. A standard of performance could include "reducing the reject rate from 15 to 3 percent," "increasing the corporation's return on investment to 7 percent," or "reducing the number of accidents to one per each 100,000 hours of labour".

Feedback Control Model

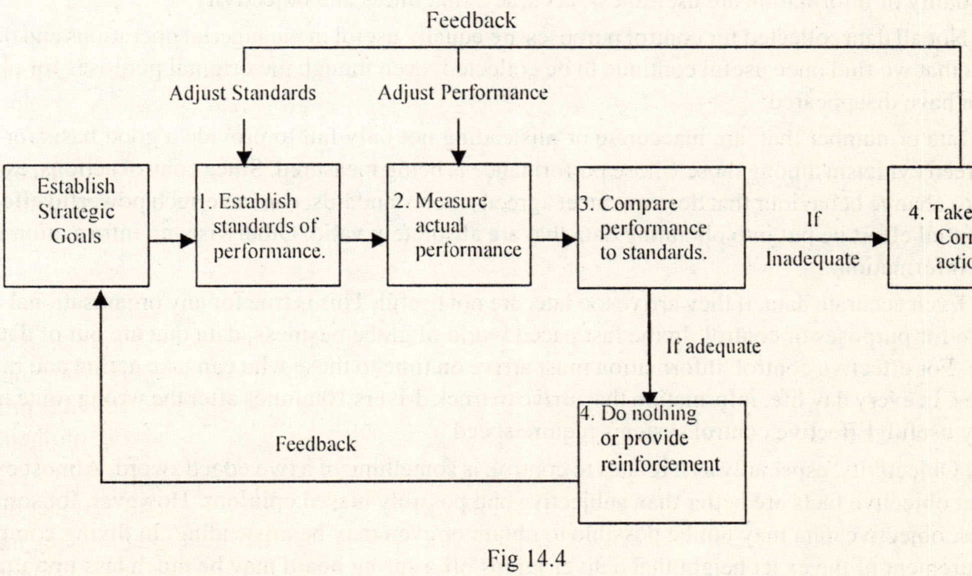

Fig 14.4

Measure Actual Performance: Most organisations prepare formal reports of quantitative performance measurements that manager's review daily, weekly or monthly. These measurements should be related to the standards set in the first step of the control process. For example, if sales growth is a target, the organisation should have a means of gathering and reporting sales data. If the organisation has identified appropriate measurements, regular review of these reports helps managers stay aware of whether the organisation is doing what is should be.

Compare Performance to Standards: The third step in the control process is comparing actual activities to performance standards. When managers read computer reports or walk through the plant, they identify whether actual performance meets, exceeds or falls short of standards. Typically, performance reports simplify such comparisons by placing the performance standards for the reporting period alongside the actual performance for the same period and by computing the variance, that is, the difference between each actual amount and the associated standard.

When performance deviates from a standard, managers must interpret the deviation. They are expected to dig beneath the surface and find the cause of the problem. If the sales goal is to increase the number of sales calls by 10 percent and a salesperson achieved an increase of 8 percent, where did she fail to achieve her goal? Perhaps several businesses on her route closed, additional salespeople were assigned to her area by competitors or she needs training in making cold sales calls more effectively. Managers should take an inquiring approach to deviations in order to gain in broad understanding of factors that influenced performance.

Take Corrective Action: When performance deviates from standards, managers must determine what changes, if any, are necessary. In a traditional top-down approach to control, managers exercise their formal authority to make necessary changes. Managers may encourage employees to work harder, redesign the production process or fire employees. In contrast, managers using a participative control approach collaborate with employees to determine the corrective action necessary.

14.7 ROLE OF QUALITY OF INFORMATION IN CONTROL

Effective control requires knowledge based on data; that is, it requires good information. Four characteristics that determine the quality of information are usefulness, accuracy, timeliness and objectivity.

Usefulness: Not all data collected for control purposes are equally useful in managerial operations and decision. Sometimes data that we find once useful continue to be collected, even though the original purposes for obtaining that information have disappeared.

Accuracy: Data or number that are inaccurate or misleading not only fail to provide a good basis for control steps but also breed cynicism among those whose performance is being measured. Since control actions, especially those designed to change behaviour that dose not meet agreed-upon standards, can have such powerful effects, it is vital that substantial effort be put into obtaining data that are absolutely valid. Otherwise, no information is better than inaccurate information.

Timeliness: Even accurate data, if they arrive too late, are not useful. This is true for any organisational actions, but especially so for purposes of control. In the fast paced world of globe business, data that are out of date are of virtually no use. For effective control, information must arrive on time to those who can take action and make any required changes. In every day life, information that arrive to truck drivers 10minites after the wrong route has been taken it not very useful. Effective control systems require speed.

Objectivity: Objectivity, especially as it relates to control, is something of a two edged sword. Almost everyone would agree that objective facts are better than subjective and possibly biased opinions. However, for some kinds of performances, objective data may not be possible to obtain or even may be misleading. In diving competition, objective measurement of the exact height that a diver jumps off a spring board may be much less important than the subjective opinion of an experienced judge about the form of the dive. Similarly, in organisations, some of the most easily measured activities, and therefore the most easily controlled, may be relatively insignificant for the achievement of major, strategic goals. All other factors being equal, objective information would be preferred, but in many situations, those other factors may not be equal, and thoughtful judgments rather than unimportant "facts" may provide the best basis for action decisions.

14.8 RESISTANCE TO CONTROL

Properly deigned control systems are no doubt very useful and effective. Yet, many people resist control for various reasons.

Why Employee Resist Control

Employees resist control for four main reasons, as summarised in Table 14.5. Each of these reasons may now briefly explained:

Table 14.5 : Resistance to Control

Why employees resist control	Techniques for overcoming resistance to control
1. Over control	Create effective control
2. Inappropriate focus	Encourage participation
3. Rewards for inefficiency	Use MBO
4. Accountability	Provides checks and balances

1. ***Overcontrol:*** Occasionally, organisations go into excessiveness and make the mistake of overcontrol; they try to control too many things. This becomes especially problematic when the controls pertain directly to employee behaviour relating to their daily activities (such as whom to work, when to relax, when to have tea and lunch, when to return). Yet, many organisations find it necessary to impose these rules. If controls are perceived as excessive, employees resist them.
2. ***Inappropriate focus:*** The second main reason for resistance is that the focus of the control system may be inappropriate. The control system may be too narrow, or it may focus too much on quantifiable variables, leaving hardly any room for analysis or interpretation. A sales standard, for instance, that encourages high-pressure tactics to maximise short-run sales may do so at the expense of goodwill from long-term customers. Such a standard is too narrow.
3. ***Rewards for inefficiency:*** People naturally resist control when there is punishment for being efficient and reward for being inefficient, i.e., when there is no suitable reward for appropriate effort. For example, department 1 may have budget cut next year for efficiently utilising the fund in the current year and thus exhausting the budgetary allocation. Department 2 may have budget increase for incurring a deficit in the current year.
4. ***Accountability:*** Another reason why some people resist control is that effective control systems create accountability. Some people, especially those who are doing a good job, do not want to be answerable for their mistakes and deficiencies (such as unsatisfactory performance) and therefore, resist control.

Overcoming Resistance To Control

Various techniques are available to help managers overcome resistance to control. Some of these are listed in Table 14.5.

1. ***Create effective controls:*** Perhaps the best way to overcome resistance to control is to create effective control to begin with. If control systems are properly integrated with an organisation's planning system and if the controls are, subsequently, flexible, accurate, timely and objective, the organisation is likely to fall prey to the problems of overcontrol, incorrect focus or rewarding inefficiency. Furthermore, those employees who fear accountability most will perhaps beheld accountable for their poor performance.
2. ***Encourage participation:*** Moreover, employee participation in management can help overcome resistance to change. In a like manner, when employees are involved with planning and implementing the control systems, they are less likely to resist it.
3. ***Using MBO:*** Management by objectives (or MBO) can also overcome employee resistance to control. As P.F. Drucker, the originator of the concept, suggests: "When MBO is used properly employees help establish their own goals or standards. They also know in advance that their rewards will be based on the extent to

which they achieve and maintain those goals and standards. MBO, then, is a vehicle for facilitating the integration of planning and control.

4. ***Checks and Balances:*** Another way to overcome employee resistance to control is to maintain a system of checks and balances. In truth, multiple standards and information systems provide checks and balances for control. Resistance declines because this system of checks and balances serves to protect employees as well as management.

14.9 FINANCIAL CONTROL TECHNIQUES

In every organisation, managers need to watch how well the organisation is performing financially. Not only do budget and financial controls tell whether the organisation is on sound financial footing, but they can be useful indicators of other kinds of performance problem. For example, a sales decline may signal problems with products, customer service or sales force effectiveness. Likewise, if maintenance expenses routinely exceed the amount budgeted, the organisation might investigate whether equipment is too old or whether employees know how to use it properly.

A. Financial Analysis

Managers need to be able to evaluate financial reports that compare their organisation's performance with earlier data or industry norm. These comparisons enable them to see whether the organisation is improving and whether it is competitive with others in the industry. The most common financial analysis focuses on rations, statistics that express the relationships between performance indicators such as profits and assets, sales and inventory. Ratios are stated as a fraction or proportion. Managers decide which ratios reveal the most important relationships for their business.

Liquidity Ratios: A liquidity ratio indicates an organisation's ability to meet its current debt obligations. For example, the current ratio (current assets divided by current liabilities) tells whether there are sufficient assets to convert into cash to pay of debts, if needed. If a hypothetical company, has current assets of Rs.600,000 and current liabilities of Rs.250,000, the current ratio is 2.4, meaning it has sufficient funds to pay off immediate debts 2.4 times. This is normally considered a satisfactory margin of safety.

Activity Ratios: An activity ratio measures internal performance with respect to key activities defined by management. For example, inventory turnover is calculated by dividing total sales by average inventory. This ratio tells how many times the inventory is used up to meet the total sales figure. If inventory sits too long, money is wasted. Another type of activity ratio, the conversion ratio, is purchases orders divided by customer inquires. This ratio is an indicator of a company's effectiveness in converting inquires into sales.

Profitability Ratios: Managers analyse a company's profits by studying profitability ratios, which state profits relative to a source of profits, such as sales or assets. One important profitability ratio is the profit margin on sales, which is calculated as net income divided by sales. Similarly, gross margin is the gross (before-tax) profit divided by total sales.

Another profitability measure is return on total assets (ROA), which is a percentage representing what a company earned from its assets, computed as net income divided by total assets. ROA is a valuable yardstick for comparing a company's ability to generate earnings with other investment opportunities. In basic terms, the company should be able to earn more by using its assets to operate the business than it could by putting the same investment in the bank.

Leverage Ratios: Leverage refers to funding activities with borrowed money. A company can use leverage to make its assets produce more than they could on their own. However, too much borrowing can put the organisation at risk such that it will be unable to keep up with repayment of its debt. Managers therefore track their debt ratio, or total debt divided by total assets, to make sure it does not exceed a level they consider acceptable. Lenders may consider a company with a debt ratio above 1.0 to be poor credit risk.

B. Budgeting

Budgets are useful tools for planning an organisation's expenditures. When managers use budgets to ensure they are meeting their plans, budgets also are a control technique. As a control device, budgets are reports that list planned and actual expenditures for cash, assets, raw material, salaries and other resources. In addition budget reports usually list the variance between the budgeted and actual amounts for each item.

A budget is created for every division or department within an organisation, no matter how small, so long as it performs a distinct project, programme or function. The fundamental unit of analysis for a budget control system is called a responsibility centre. Top managers use budgets for the company as a whole, and middle managers traditionally focus on the budget performance of their department or division. Examples of types of budgets managers use are expense budgets, revenue budgets, cash budgets and capital budgets.

Expense Budget: An expense budget includes anticipated and actual expenses for each responsibility centre and for the total organisation. An expense budget may show all types of expenses or may focus on a particular category, such as materials or research and development expenses. When actual expenses exceed budgeted amounts, the difference signals the need for managers to identify whether a problem exists. The difference may arise from inefficiency or expenses may be higher because the organisation's sales are growing faster than anticipated. Conversely, expenses below budget may signal exceptional efficiency or failure to meet some other standards, such as a desired level of sales or quality of service.

Revenue Budget: A revenue budget lists forecasted and actual revenues of the organisation. In general, revenues below the budgeted amount signal a need to investigate the problem to see whether the organisation can improve revenues. In contrast, revenues above budget would require determining whether the organisation can obtain the necessary resources to meet the higher-than-expected demand for its products.

Cash Budget: The cash budget estimates receipts and expenditures of money on a daily or weekly basis to ensure that an organisation has sufficient cash to meet its obligations. This cash budget shows the level of funds flowing through the organisation and the nature of cash disbursements. If the cash budget shows that the firm has more cash than necessary to meet short-term needs, the company can arrange to invest the excess to earn interest income. In contrast, if the cash budget shows a payroll expenditure of Rs.20,000 coming at the end of the week but Rs.10,000 in the bank, the organisation must borrow cash to meet the payroll.

Capital Budget: The capital budget lists planed investments in major assets such as buildings, trucks and heavy machinery, often involving expenditures over more than a year. Capital expenditures not only have a large impact on future expenses, they are investments designed to enhance profits. Therefore, a capital budget is necessary to plan the impact of these expenditures on cash flow and profitability. Controlling involves not only monitoring the amount of capital expenditures but evaluating whether the assumptions made about the return on the investments are holding true. Managers should evaluate whether continuing investment in particular projects is advisable, as well as whether their procedures for making capital expenditure decisions are adequate.

14.10 PRINCIPLES OF CONTROL

The following principles of control summarise the substantive parts of the above discussion on the controlling function.

1. ***Principles of assurance of objective:*** The task control is to ensure that plans succeed by detecting deviations from plans and furnishing a basis for taking action to correct potential or actual deviations.

2. ***Principle of future-directed controls:*** The more a control system is based on feedfoward rather than simple feedback of information, the more managers have the opportunity to perceive undesirable deviations from plans before they occur and to take action in time to prevent them.
3. ***Principle of direct control:*** The higher the quality of every manager in a managerial system, the less will be the need for indirect controls. The most direct form of control in an organisation is to ensure a high quality of managerial decision making and action behaviour.
4. ***Principle of control responsibility:*** The primary responsibility for the exercise of control rests in the manager charged with performance of the particular plans involved. There is unity of planning and control in each managerial position.
5. ***Principle of organisational suitability:*** The more that an organisational structure is clear, complete and integrated and the more that controls are designed to reflect the place in the organisation structure were responsibility for action lies, the more they will facilitate correction of deviations from plans.
6. ***Principle of standards:*** Effective controls require objective, accurate and suitable standards. Measurement of performance by reference to standards should be verifiable, specific and simple.
7. ***Principle of flexibility of controls:*** If controls are to remain effective, despite failure or unforeseen changes of plans, flexibility is required in their design.
8. ***Principle of action:*** Control is justified only if indicated or experienced deviations from plans are corrected through appropriate planning, organising, staffing and leading. The principle affirms the essential unity of management.
9. ***The exception principle:*** The more managers concentrate control efforts on exception, the more efficient will be the results of their control. This principle suggests that managers should concentrate on significant deviations, both positive and negative, from plans.
10. ***Principle of efficiency of controls:*** Control techniques and approaches are efficient if they detect and illuminate the nature and causes of deviations from plans with a minimum of costs or other unsought consequences.

14.11 QUALITIES OF EFFECTIVE CONTROL SYSTEMS

Properly used controls help managers respond to unforeseen developments and achieve strategic plans. Improperly designed management control systems can lead a company into bankruptcy. When such problems signal that control systems are not working properly, management must examine them for possible clarification, version or overhaul.

Whether organisational control focuses on feedforward or feedback measurement or emphasizes the bureaucratic decentralised approach, certain characteristics should be present. In general, for organisational controls to be effective, they should be tailored to the organisation's needs and facilitate the accomplishment of its tasks. More specifically, effective controls share the following trains:

1. ***Linkage to strategy:*** The control system should not simply measure what was important in the past or be tailored to current operations. It should reflect where the organisation is going and adapt to new strategies. Moreover, the organisation should focus on activities that are relevant for strategic goals.
2. ***Understandable measures:*** Organisations depend on employees to carry out work according to standards. An effective control system ensures that employees know and understand what is expected. In addition, managers must understand what is being measured – an obvious but important criterion in these days of new and sometimes complex control systems.
3. ***Acceptance by employees:*** The more committed employees are to control standards, the more successful the control system will be. The control system should motivate rather than demotivate. This is most likely

when it includes standards that are understandable and reasonable, when employees understand the reason for the control system and when they do not perceive the measurement process as overly intrusive.

4. ***Balance of objective and subjective data:*** Managers can be misled when control system data are either completely numeric or based solely on subjective opinion. Control should be perceived as objective, but quantitative information tells only part of the story. Managers should balance quantitative of performance.
5. ***Accuracy:*** Upward communication, especially about performance, often is influenced by what employees believe management wants to hear. However, the control system should encourage accurate information in order to detect deviations.
6. ***Flexibility:*** Internal goals and strategies must be responsive to changes in the environment and the control system should be flexible enough to adapt as needed. Managers who rely too heavily on existing controls, especially feedback controls, will find themselves out of synchronisation with changing events.
7. ***Timeliness:*** The control system should provide information soon enough to permit a management response. Corrective action is of no value if performed too late.
8. ***Support of action:*** Control goes beyond monitoring performance to taking corrective action. Managers therefore need a system that helps them focus on performance areas in which change is needed. The control system should highlight variances and managers should focus on these variances, diagnosing the cause of each variance and suing judgment to decide when intervention is required.

14.12 CONCLUDING COMMENTS

Control is a crucial, albeit many times difficult and sometimes even unpleasant, managerial function. As we have emphasized repeatedly throughout this chapter, the challenge for manager is to make wise decisions about how much and where, control needs to be used and then how to apply that control. Control is essential, but many a manager and even many an organisation have run into several difficulties because this managerial function has not been well handled.

Knowing the basic elements of the control process is a helpful start in gaining perspective about how to exercise appropriate control. Understanding some of the pitfalls and obstacles that can interfere at each of these steps provides a basis for avoiding unnecessary mistakes. Not many managers would have the aspiration to be a great "controller", but likewise, most would not like to be known as excessively naïve about the need for control. Keeping in mind the factors that influence control effectiveness–such as the focus, amount and degree of flexibility – is a way to reduce the chances of unintended control blunders and improve the probabilities of success.

Clearly, control is a matter of both science and art. On the one hand, there are a variety of quantitative measures of individual group and organisational performance. Particular areas, such as finance and operations, tend to use many quantitative control measures because they deal with things that are easy to count (e.g., money, products, defects). However, just because something can be easily measured doesn't mean it should be. Likewise, just because something is difficult to measure doesn't mean it should not be. The key to managerial success relative to control is making good judgments and then good measurements. Without good judgment concerning what, how and when to measure something, the measurements are of little value. Control can add real value to an organisation, but that outcome is not guaranteed unless managers with judgment make it happen.

Questions for Review

Chapter 1 : *Nature of Organisation and Management*

1. Define the term 'Organisation' and state it's characteristics.
2. Define the term 'Management'. What are the major functions of management?
3. Distinguish the term management and administration. How far is this distinction justified in your opinion?
4. What do you understand by the universality concept of management? Critically examine the acceptability of this concept.
5. Define Co-ordination. Explain the need and importance of co-ordination. Also state the major features of co-ordination.
6. Distinguish between the following :
   (a) Planning and directing functions.
   (b) Primary and Secondary organisations.
7. Write short notes on the following:
   (a) Management Process.
   (b) Management as a field of study.
8. Comment on the following:
   (a) 'The management is getting things done by the people.'
   (b) 'Organisations need people, but people also need organisations.'
   (c) 'All organisations need management. '
   (d) 'Management is a twentieth century phenomenon.'
   (e) 'Management is an influence- interaction process.'
   (f) 'Management is a dynamic process.'
9. Comment on the true nature of management. Is it a science or an art?
10. What are the attributes of a profession? Is management a profession?
11. Discuss the importance of management in the present complex world.

Chapter 2 : *Evolution of Management Thought*

1. Point out the distinctive contribution of Taylor to the theory of management. Why is he regarded as the 'Father of Scientific Management' ?
2. What do you mean by 'Administrative Management Theory' ? How is it different from Scientific Management ?
3. Mention the different schools of management. What are the contributions of behavioural sciences to management?
4. Briefly describe the general principles of management as laid down by Henry Fayol. Is his list exhaustive?
5. Write short notes on:
   (a) Contribution to management thought by Elton Mayo.
   (b) Hawthorne Experiments.
   (c) System approach to management.

6. Comment on the following:
   (a) 'The principles of scientific management are outdated in this complex business environment.'
   (b) 'Human relations approach weakens the role of management in achieving organisational goals.'
   (c) 'The contingency approach to management is a common sense approach.'
7. Distinguish between:
   (a) Scientific management and Quantitative approach.
   (b) System approach and Contingency approach.
   (c) Human relations movement and behavioural science thinking.
8. What are the major functions of a manager according to the contingency approach? How is this approach an effort to integrate all previous approaches?
9. Explain briefly the evolution of management thought from the early pioneer to modern times.
10. Discuss the role of various approaches to management. Which approach do you think adequately clears the nature of management?

Chapter 3 : *Business Environment*

1. What are some recent changes in the general environment that all employees should be aware of? How have these changes affected the business community?
2. How do cultural values influence a managers thinking about locating a plant in a foreign country?
3. What are some of the political tactics that managers can use to influence the environment.
4. What are the competitive forces in an industry? How have these forces affected competition among different enterprises in an industry?
5. Distinguish between:
   (a) Internal and External environment.
   (b) Micro and Macro environment.
6. Can a single business enterprise gain command over it's environment?
7. What are the different elements of external environment? Should an organisation concern itself with the elements of it's external environment?

Chapter 4 : *Social Responsibility*

1. Explain what do you mean by the concept of social responsibility of business. Why it should develop a sense of social responsibility?
2. Attempt a comprehensive role on the 'Social Obligation of Management' in the present - day business environment.
3. 'Economic goals and social obligations of business are always in conflict with each other and cannot possible to be reconciled'. Explain critically.
4. Give arguments for and against the assumption of social responsibilities by management.
5. Explain the social responsibilities of business towards its shareholders, customers and community at large.
6. "In general, business enterprises in India behave in a socially irresponsible manner" Dou you agree? Describe in detail the social performance of business in India.
7. How can management set it's objectives so as to balance a variety of needs and goals? Discuss.

Chapter 5 : *Planning*

1. What is Planning? Why is planning regarded as a pervasive function of management?
2. Explain the importance of planning. Discuss the advantages and the limitations of planning. What should be done to overcome these limitations?

3. Comment on the following statements:
   (a) "Managerial planning seeks to achieve a coordinated structure of operations".
   (b) " Planning involves choice between alternative courses of actions".
   (c) " Planning and control are two sides of the same coin".
   (d) " Planning is essentially forward looking".
   (e) "Planning has little practical relevance in a rapidly changing environment".
   (f) " Planning is the basis of control, action its essence, delegation its key and information is its guide".
4. Distinguish between:
   (a) Planning and Control
   (b) Policies and Objectives
   (c) Standing Plans and Single-use Plan
   (d) Long range and Short range planning
   (e) Planning and Forecasting
5. Write short notes on:
   (a) Flexible Plans
   (b) Planning Premises
   (c) Principles of Planning
   (d) Philosophies of Planning
6. Explain the various steps of planning. What are the requisites of an effective planning?
7. Why is forecasting important in modern business? Discuss briefly the various techniques of business forecasting.
8. Explain the concept 'Planning Premises'. Discuss the various types of planning premises you, as a manufacturer, would have.

Chapter 6 : *Business Policy and Strategy*

1. What do understand by the term 'Strategic Planning'? Discuss the importance of strategic planning in an organization.
2. What are the various steps in strategic planning and implementation process?
3. What do you understand by the term 'Policy'? Expalin the different types of policies and describe how policies are formulated.
4. What is the difference between a policy and a procedure? Should a policy be permanent or subject to regular changes?
5. Distinguish between policy and strategy. Give your suggestions for making policies effective.
6. Why are strategies important? Can an organization be successful without effective strategies?
7. What do you understand by 'corporate strategy' ? What are its important characteristics? As a manager, how can you evaluate corporate strategy?
8. Describe the importance of SWOT analysis as an element of strategic planning.
9. Define Tactical Planning. Why is it performed and who performs it?
10. What parts make up the format of strategic planning? What part do you feel is probably the most difficult to perform? Why?

Chapter 7 : *Decision Making*

1. Define Decision-making. What are the various types of decisions? Also give the characteristics of a decision.
2. Explain the steps in decision-making. Should the steps be always sequential?
3. What is the role of information system in decision-making?
4. Explain the concept of rationality in decision-making. What are the limits of rationality in decision-making?

5. What is bounded rationality? To what extent does bounded rationality reduce the soundness and quality of decisions?
6. Discuss the 'Economic Man Model' of decision-making. How does it differ from 'Administrative Man Model' of decision-making?
7. Comment on the following:
   (a) 'Whatever a manager does, he does through decision-making'.
   (b) 'Decision-making is the essence of management'.
   (c) 'A decision is as good as the information on which it is based'.
   (d) 'Problem definition is half the job in decision-making'.
8. Distinguish between:
   (e) Programmed decisions and tactical decisions.
   (f) Non-programmed decisions and strategic decisions.
   (g) Risk and uncertainty.

Chapter 8 : *The Function of Organising*

1. Define the concept of 'organising' and distinguish it from 'organisation' and 'organisational structure'.
2. Define 'authority' and state the bases of authority.
3. What is 'delegation of authority'? What are the steps involved in delegation?
4. Define 'Centralisation'. What are the advantages and limitations of a centralised structure? Under what conditions is a centralised structure appropriate?
5. Define 'Decentralisation'. Distinguish it from centralisation. Why should organisations go in for decentralisation?
6. What are the factors required to be considered for centralisation and decentralisation? How do you work out a balance between centralisation and decentralisation?
7. What is ' Organisational Chart'? State the purposes, functions and limitations of organisational chart.
8. Comment on the following statements:
   (a) 'Formal organisations are hierarchical'.
   (b) 'Authority is at the base of all formal organisations'.
   (c) 'Authority can be delegated, but responsibility can not'.
   (d) 'Delegation is the essence of management'.
   (e) 'The act of delegation on the part of a manager results in the reduction of his authority'.
   (f) 'Centralisation and delegation of authority are opposite process'.
   (g) 'Centralisation and decentralisation go together'.
   (h) 'Decentralisation is a mere extension of the principle of delegation'.
   (i) 'Span of management is a basic structural concept'.
   (j) 'Line and staff conflicts are natural and normal'.
9. Write short notes on:
   (a) Barriers to effective delegation of authority
   (b) Human behavioural implications of centralisation and decentralisation
   (c) Line and staff structure
   (d) Factors influencing the determination of span of management
10. What is the exact distinction between the concepts of 'Line and Staff'? What are the various forms, roles and functions of staff units in organisations?

Chapter 9 : *Designing Effective Organizing*

1. Define the term 'Organisational Structure'. What factors would you consider while designing an organisational structure?
2. What is 'departmentalisation' and how is it relevant to organisational structure? What are the various forms of departmentalisation?
3. What is 'Composite form' of departmentalisation? Explain with an example.
4. Distinguish between:
   (a) Differentiation and departmentalisation.
   (b) Activity structure and authority structure.
   (c) Scalar principle and authority level principle.
   (d) Profit decentralisation and product divisionalisation.
5. Comment on the following statements:
   (a) 'Organisational structure provides the framework for undertaking the management functions'.
   (b) 'Decentralisation promotes corporate unity amidst subsystem diversity'.
   (c) 'Decentralisation leads to organisational disintegration'.
   (d) 'Modern organisational structures are not basically different from the traditional structures'.
6. Write short notes on:
   (a) Matrix structure
   (b) Effective delegation of authority
   (c) Role of top management in decentralised structure
   (d) Non-commercial organisations
7. What consideration should be kept in view while choosing a particular form of departmentalisation? Distinguish between functional and product form of departmentalisation.
8. What are the major characteristics of modern structure? Why are most of the modern organisations structured on traditional lines?

Chapter Ten: *Individual Perspective*

1. What is 'Perception'? State the characteristics of the perceiver.
2. Define 'Attitude'. What are the different components of attitude?
3. What is 'Personality'? How attitudes and behaviours are influenced by personality?
4. Define the term 'Motivation'. What are the important elements in the conceptual framework of motivation?
5. Distinguish the concept of motivation from ability, morale and job satisfaction. What is the role of punishment in motivation?
6. Explain what is meant by hierarchical nature of the needs? Is this hierarchy rigid? Discuss with suitable examples.
7. Explain Herzberg's Two factors theory of motivation and differentiate it from Maslow's theory of Need hierarchy.
8. Enumerate the assumptions of Mcgregor's Theory X and Theory Y. Which one is applicable in Indian conditions?
9. Distinguish between:
   (a) Hygiene factors and motivators.
   (b) Intrinsic and extrinsic rewards.
   (c) Motivation and satisfaction.
10. Comment on the following:
    (a) 'Non-financial incentives are as strong motivators as the financial ones'.
    (b) 'Money holds the key to work motivation in modern business'.
    (c) 'There is no need for any other motivational technique if people are well paid'.

11. Write short notes:
    (a) Carrot and stick approach to motivation.
    (b) Equity theory of motivation.
    (c) Expectancy theory of motivation.
    (d) Employee participation in management.
    (e) Management by objective.
    (f) Quality circles as motivators.
12. What is job enrichment? Under what conditions is job enrichment most likely to increase employee performance?
13. Explain the role of supportive supervision in motivation of employees.
14. Describe the essential elements of a sound motivational system.

Chapter Eleven: *Groups and Group Dynamics*

1. Define the concept of group. What are the factors influencing the formation of a group?
2. What are the different types of groups usually seen in organisations? State the different stages of group development.
3. Define formal group. Explain its characteristic features.
4. What is an informal group? Describe its features. Distinguish between formal and informal group.
5. Distinguish between:
    (a) Small group and secondary group.
    (b) Informal group and informal organisation.
    (c) Formal organisation and informal organisation.
6. How do informal group emerge and how they do benefit individual members? What should the attitude of management towards informal groups?
7. Define group cohesiveness and explain the relationship between group cohesiveness and productivity. Explain the factors which promote group cohesiveness.
8. What is meant by Group Dynamics? What problems are created by informal groups for the organisation?
9. What is 'group behaviour' and how does it take shape?
10. Write short notes on:
    (a) Group norms.
    (b) Decision making in groups.

Chapter Twelve: *Introduction to Organisation Behaviour*

1. What is Organisational Behaviour? What are its determinants?
2. Why organisations are considered as 'Social Entity'?
3. Define Informal Organisatiion. Distinguish between formal and informal organisation. State the reasons for the emergence of informal organisation.
4. State the benefits and problems of informal organisation.
5. Explain the concept of organisational climate. What are the features of organisational climate?
6. Explain the concept of Status. What are the bases of status?
7. What do you mean by 'Influence'? What are the different ways to influence behaviour?
8. What is power? How is it different from authority? State different sources of power.
9. What are the different causes of organisational conflict? How do you resolve them?
10. Define Organisational Development and state its characteristics. Also describe the need and benefit of organisational development.

11. Write short notes on:
    (a) Influence relationships.
    (b) Bases of power.
    (c) Charismatic power.
    (d) Status symbol.

Chapter thirteen: *Leadership*

1. Define Leadership. Bring out its importance in management.
2. Define Leadership Styles. Explain the various styles of leadership. What factors should govern the selection of a style of leadership by a manager?
3. What are the functions of a leader? Is leader same as the manager? Discuss.
4. Comment on the following statements:
   a. 'Leadership is situational'.
   b. 'There is no one best approach to leadership'.
   c. 'The behaviour of a leader cannot be fully explained by his qualities'.
   d. A successful leader is not necessarily effective'.
5. What are the elements of an effective leadership? What qualities are necessary for a successful leader?
6. Write short notes on:
   (a) Leadership Continuum.
   (b) Likert's system of leadership.
   (c) Managerial Grid.
   (d) Michigan studies of leadership.
7. Describe the following theories of leadership:
   (a) Great Man Theory.
   (b) Contingency Approach.
   (c) Path Goal Theory.
8. What is the basic argument of the situational leadership theorists? Is it easier to change the situation than the leader's style? Why?

Chapter Fourteen: *The Function of Control*

1. Discuss the concept and process of control. State the requirements of an effective control system.
2. Discuss the elements of control. Also elucidate the relationship between planning and control.
3. What are the two main types of control? How is each type used? Which is more important and why?
4. Comment on the following:
   (a) 'Any planned activity needs to be controlled'.
   (b) 'Planning and control are poles apart'.
   (c) Whereas planning is forward looking, control is backward looking'.
   (d) 'The controlling function of management is similar to the function of a thermostat in a refrigerator'.
5. Write short notes on:
   (a) Feedback Control
   (b) Control by Exception
   (c) Concurrent Control
   (d) Principles of Control
6. Examine the critical role of communication and information in control function.
7. Describe the concept of management control. Explain the importance of control in a business enterprise.

PART B

Business Communication

Chapter 1

Communication: Meaning, Importance and Process

Meaning of Communication

Communication, in the view of Fred Luthans, is the use of symbols to transfer the meaning of information. It is basically a personal process that involves in the exchange of behaviours. For example, a person can influence another person through the behaviours he performs, that is, through "communicative exchanges".

However, communication must include both transference and understanding of meaning. Communication is complete only when the information transmitted by the sender is understood by the receiver.

Communication in organisations is a process that results from the interactions within the members of the organisation and in turn affects the events within the organisation itself. Organisational communication is an evolutionary, culturally dependent process of sharing information and creating relationships in environments designed for manageable, goal-oriented behaviour.

Importance of Communication

Communication is important to organisations for the following reasons :

1. **Control mechanism:** Organisational participants have to follow authority hierarchies and formal guidelines that are communicated to them. They have to follow their job description, abide by company policies and in case of any job-related grievances, report to the concerned authorities. In each of the above cases, communication is performing a control function over member behaviour .

2. **Motivational force:** Communication fosters employee motivation. Employees need to be communicated about organisational goals, how they can contribute towards such goals, and a feedback on how well they are performing. Such communication motivates employees to perform better.

3. **Emotional expression:** Employees often express their satisfaction and frustration to their peers in their work group. Communication in this case provides a way for release of emotional expression of feelings.

4. **Interpersonal role:** Communication helps managers in their interpersonal roles. Managers act as leaders of their organisations interacting with subordinates, customers, suppliers, peers and other interested groups.

5. **Informational role:** In their informational roles, managers seek information from their customers, suppliers, colleagues and subordinates about matters that affect their job responsibilities. Managers also communicate relevant information about the organisation as a unit to various interest groups.

6. **Decisional role:** In their decisional roles, managers allocate resources to certain projects, accept or reject new projects, handle disturbing elements that affect the organisation, etc. The decisions reached at by managers are based on information that has been communicated to the managers. Upon reaching the decisions, managers will have to communicate these to the persons concerned for their implementation.

PROCESS OF COMMUNICATION

Communication can be thought of as a process or flow. Communication difficulties occur when there are distortions or blockages in that flow.

Figure 1.1 illustrates a model for the communication process.

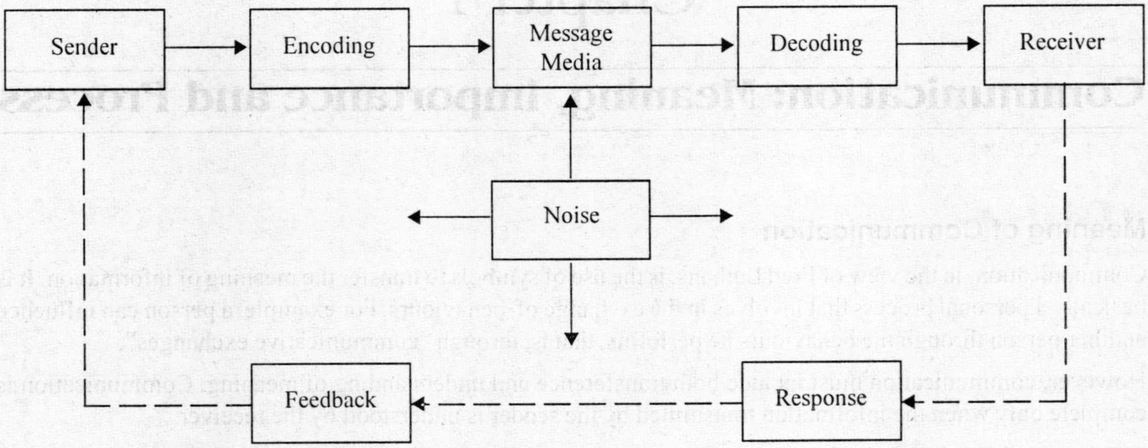

Fig. 1.1 : Elements in Ihe Communication Process

The model consists of the steps that occur between the sender and the receiver for transmission and understanding of meaning.

The elements in the process are discussed in detail as follows:

1. **Sender:** The sender or communication source initiates the communication process by sending a message. There must be a need, desire, reason or purpose for the sender to send a message.

2. **Encoding:** It means converting a communication message into symbolic form—verbal or non-verbal. Encoding is necessary as information can only be transmitted through representations or symbols. The sender's skill, attitudes, knowledge and the socio-cultural system affect the encoding process. The sender's choice of symbols in the form of words and gestures must ensure a "mutuality" of meaning with the receiver.

3. **Message:** It is the physical product from the source coding, which is affected by the code or symbols used for transference of meaning. Speech may be heard, written words may be read, gestures may be seen or felt.

4. **Channel:** A channel is the medium through which a communication message travels. The channel is selected by the sender guided by his personal preferences or habit, but the choice of channel must consider the needs and requirements of the receiver. For example, to communicate the details of a complex engineering diagram, a written manual may be necessary, as a telephonic conversation will not suffice in this case.

5. **Decoding:** It is the process by which the receiver interprets the message and translates it into meaningful information. Decoding is affected by the personal values and beliefs, perception and knowledge of the receiver. The more the receiver's decoding matches the sender's intended message, the more effective is the communication.

6. **Noise:** It is any factor that disturbs or interferes with the process of communication and hence in the understanding of the intended meaning of the message. Noise may be internal (e.g., an inattentive receiver) or external (e.g., conducting a conversation in noise of machines in an assembly line).

7. **Feedback:** It is the process in which a reaction to the sender's communication is expressed. The receiver becomes the sender, feedback follows the same steps as in the original communication process, but in a reverse direction. Organisational feedback usually consists of spoken or written acknowledgement.

Any communication from the sender without feedback from the receiver is a **one-way communication.** A **two-way communication** occurs when the receiver gives feedback to sender.

Chapter 2

Organisational Communication: Dimensions/Directions and Means/Media

The fundamentals of organisational communication are very much the same as interpersonal communication. According to Raymond Lesikar, four factors that affect the effectiveness of organisational communications are :

1. The organisation's authority structure
2. The formal channels of communication
3. Job specialisation
4. Information ownership.

The organisation's authority structure is the major determinant of the direction of communication. Status and power differences in an organisation determines who comfortably communicates with whom. In organisation, communication can flow vertically or laterally. Vertical communication can either be upward or downward.

Downward Communication

Communication that flows from one level of a group or organisation to a lower level is called downward communication. Katz and Kahn have identified five general purposes of downward communication in an organisation:

1. To give specific task directions about job instructions.
2. To give information about organisational procedures and practices.
3. To provide information about the rationale of the job.
4. To tell subordinates about their performance.
5. To provide ideological information to facilitate the indoctrination of goals.

Media Used for Downward Communication

(*i*) Print media e.g., organisational handbooks, manuals, magazines, newspapers, letters distributed on the job, bulletin board items, reports, descriptions of procedures and memos.

(*ii*) Oral media e.g., direct orders or instructions from the managers, lectures, speeches, class room training discourses, meetings and telephones.

(*iii*) Electronic media e.g., electronic mail, video conferencing (allows geographically distant people to be in visual contact), web-sites on the Internet and Intranet.

The main problems in downward communication are :

1. Quality of information is often sacrificed for quantity.
2. People often tend to concentrate on useless rather than useful information.
3. Ignores the importance of the receiver.

According to Fred Luthans, research, the effectiveness of downward communication can be improved in the following ways :

1. ***The communication message should follow the 'path of least resistance" :*** People are more congruent with their existing image and their values. Thus, if messages are so designed that they are incongruent with values, they tend to engender more resistance than messages that are incongruent with rational logic.
2. ***The communication message should fulfil people's needs :*** Most people value need-fulfillment positively. Hence messages that facilitate need-fulfillment are more readily accepted than messages which do not.
3. ***An allowance should be made for the environment of the receiver of the information :*** The total situation affects communication i.e., a message interpreted as congruent in one situation may be interpreted as incongruent in another.

UPWARD COMMUNICATIONS

Communication that flows to a higher level from a lower level in the group or organisation, is called upward communication. The primary purposes for which upward communication are made include —

(*i*) Provide feedback to higher ups. This mainly includes technical information about performance.
(*ii*) Provide personal information about ideas, attitudes and performance.
(*iii*) Relay current problems.

Methods of Improving the Effectiveness of Upward Communication

1. ***The grievance:*** Most collective bargaining agreements provide for this procedure whereby an employee can appeal upward beyond their direct managers, thereby protecting them from arbitrary decisions taken by their immediate superior .
2. ***The open-door policy :*** It literally means that the manager's door is always open for employees, to come and discuss about anything that is bothering them.
3. ***The use of e-mail :*** Any employee may send an e-mail to any higher-up in the organisation. This method preserves the identity of the complainant and is prompt, secure and popular.
4. ***Counselling, attitude questionnaires, and exit interviews :*** The human resource department in an organisation can periodically administer attitude questionnaires, hold confidential counselling sessions, and conduct meaningful exit interviews for those who leave the organisation. Valuable insight about the organisation can be gained by these methods.
5. ***Participative techniques :*** Employees may be involved in the organisational communication process by informal networks or formal participation programmes like union-management committees, junior boards, suggestion boxes and cross functional teams.
6. ***An empowerment strategy :*** Employees can be systematically empowered by giving them access to information and other resources. This creates an atmosphere of openness and trust and facilitates in the attainment of organisational goals.
7. ***The ombudsperson :*** The concept originated in Scandinavia to provide an outlet for persons who have been treated unfairly on in a depersonalised manner by large, bureaucratic government. In an organisational structure it means an official appointed to investigate individuals, complaints against authorities.

LATERAL OR HORIZONTAL COMMUNICATION

When communication occurs between members of the same work group, among members of work groups at the same level, among managers at the same level or among any horizontally equivalent personnel, it is termed as horizontal communication.

The purposes of horizontal communication are :

1. ***Task co-ordination :*** Department heads may meet periodically to co-ordinate among themselves about progress of each department.
2. ***Problem solving :*** The members of a department may meet for a brainstorming session to solve a common problem facing the department.
3. ***Conflict resolution :*** Members of one department meet to discuss a conflict inherent in the department or between departments.
4. ***Information sharing :*** The members of one department may exchange new data or information with another department.

A considerable amount of lateral communication occurs outside the formal chain of command, often with the knowledge and approval of the management.

Horizontal communication can also be seen as communication with peers which provides much needed social support for organisational members that releases them from the job tension.

Chapter 3

Formal vs. Informal Networks of Communication

Communication networks or set of channels by which information flows in an organisation can be formal or informal.

Formal networks are typically vertical (hierarchical), follow the authority chain and are related to task related communications. Informal network is non-directive, skips authority levels and is likely to satisfy group members' social needs. This kind of a network is better known as the grapevine. See Fig. 3.1.

FORMAL CHANNELS

Advantages of Formal Channels of Communication

1. Information sent through formal channels is accurate.
2. As organisations are becoming globalised, with units of the same organisation geographically dispersed, formal channels function as reliable source of information.
3. Formal channels can either be centralised or decentralised. A centralised organisation favours the emergence of a leader who takes the key decisions for his organisation. But in a decentralised organisation there is free flow of information and key decisions are made through group participation and discussion.
4. As only filtered information reaches the top management through formal channels, thus it has to deal with only pertinent information. This prevents the top management from facing an "information overload".

Limitations of Formal Channels of Communication

1. It is integrated, synthesised and condensed as it reaches higher levels of management. Due to this, the objectivity of information often gets lost.
2. Flow of information through different levels in a hierarchical is time consuming and expensive.
3. A highly centralised formal environment is not a conducive training ground for young managers who are deprived of the chance to participate in decision making.

INFORMAL CHANNELS OF COMMUNICATION (GRAPEVINE)

The main characteristics of grapevine are :

1. It is not controlled by management.
2. Members of the organisation consider it as a more reliable and credible source of information.
3. The members of a grapevine exploit the channel to serve their self-interests.

According to Keith Davis, there can be four types of grapevine chains in an organisation, namely,

(*i*) Single strand,

(*ii*) Gossip,

(*iii*) Probability, and

(*iv*) Cluster, as shown in the following diagram.

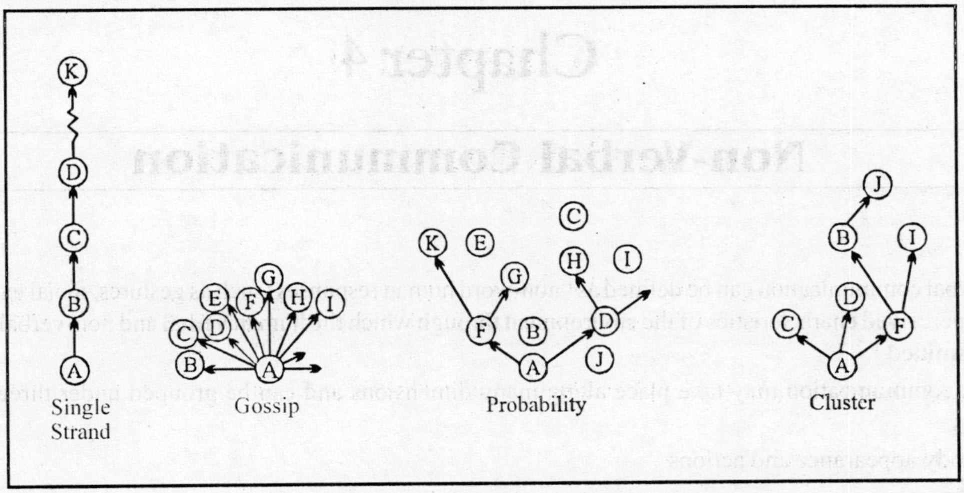

Fig. 3.1 : Types of Grapevine Chains

In the 'single strand' chain, person A tells something to person B, who tells it to person C, and so on down the line. This chain is least accurate at passing on information. In the 'gossip' chain, one person seeks out and tells everyone the information he or she has obtained. This chain is often used when information of an interesting but non-job-related nature is being conveyed. In the 'probability' chain, individuals are different about whom they offer information to; they tell people at random, and those people in turn tell others at random. This chain is likely to be used when the information is mildly interesting but insignificant. In the 'cluster' chain, person A conveys the information to a few selected individuals, some of those individuals then inform a few selected others.

Davis believes that the cluster chain is the dominant grapevine pattern in organisations. Usually, only a few individuals, called "liaison individuals", pass on the information they have obtained, and they are likely to do so only to individuals they trust or from whom they would like favours. They are most likely to pass on information that is interesting to them, job-related, and above all, timely. People do not pass an old information for fear of advertising the face that they are uninformed.

Advantages of Grapevine

1. Managers are often unaware of issues that confuse and provoke employees. These issues that form an active part of the grapevine channel help managers to feel the pulse of the organisation' s members.
2. It picks up information that employees consider relevant, acting both as filter and feedback mechanisms.
3. Around 10% of a grapevine chain actively passes on information to more than one other person. By assuming which liaison individuals will consider a given piece of information to be pertinent, managers can improve their perspective to explain and predict the pattern of information flow in a grapevine.

Demerits of Grapevine

1. Grapevine often leads to rumours.
2. Information through grapevine channels is often inaccurate, incomplete or exaggerated.

Chapter 4

Non-Verbal Communication

Non-verbal communication can be defined as "non-word human responses (such as gestures, facial expressions) and the perceived characteristics of the environment through which the human verbal and non-verbal messages are transmitted."

Such communication may take place along many dimensions and can be grouped under three principal headings:

1. Body appearance and actions
2. The voice
3. The environment

Often non-verbal cues emphasize or negate the impact of verbal messages. Though these dimensions are often separately studied, the reader should keep in mind the cumulative effect principle which implies that no single aspect is meaningful except in the context of others.

Body Language

It is argued that each body movement has a specific meaning and no movement is accidental.

The academic study of body motions is called Kinesics.

The body sends a continuous flow of cues. An introduction to the communicative functions of the body may be gained by recognising the importance of six physical aspects:

1. **Body shape and appearance:** The body conveys meanings even when it is not in motion. Although such meanings vary according to cultural norms, they show that physical attributes can have significant impact on people's attempts at communication. In the UK fat people are considered to be caring but in the US they are generally considered to be negligent and insensitive.

Skin colour and gender can also affect communication. In the US, White Americans are thought to be more trustworthy than African Americans.

Dress is also a form of non-verbal communication. As John Molloy indicates, "The most authoritative pattern is pinstripe, followed in descending order by the solid, the chalk stripe and the plaid".

2. **Posture:** Groups and individuals send messages through their posture. Posture often indicates the kind of interpersonal relationship that exists between people. For example, when two people are positioned face-to-face, a higher rate of interchange in conversation between them is required, while a side-by-side positioning indicates a less intense relationship.

3. **Gestures:** Many gestures have widely understood meanings. Foot shaking and finger tapping signify nervousness, boredom or impatience.

During an on going conversation, head nodding serves two functions: to reinforce the speaker and to control the flow of speech.

4. **Touching:** A touch can also be used as a communication medium. For example, a firm handshake typifies decisiveness while a limp one may signify a lack of interest or vitality. A damp hand may be considered as a sign of anxiety.

Research indicates a person is more likely to touch when giving information, advice or orders, when asking for favour or when trying to persuade.

5. **Face:** Being the most expressive part of the body, the face serves as an important source of non-verbal communication. Paul Ekman has shown that there is a set of facial expressions for six major human emotions.

(*i*) Happiness is conveyed by the lower face and eye area;

(*ii*) Sadness is revealed most by the eyes;

(*iii*) The eye area and lower face convey surprise;

(*iv*) Anger is revealed by the lower face, eye brows and forehead ;

(*v*) Disgust is most revealed by the lower face; and

(*vi*) Fear is conveyed most by the eye area.

Although the face can communicate a great deal, people can often control facial expressions. Hence people lie best with their faces and so facial expressions should be interpreted in context.

6. **Eye contact and gaze:** Eye contact tends to occur when people are seeking feedback about another's reactions or when they wish to convey that communication channel is open. One may use prolonged or intense eye contact to put another under stress.

The Voice: Paralanguage

Paralanguage or voice quality often transmits more meaning than the actual words spoken. Paralinguistics refers to something in speech beyond language itself.

Paralanguage can be divided into four parts:

1. Voice qualities refer to factors such as pitch, range, resonance, rhythm and speaking rate.
2. Voice characterisers include laughing, crying, whispering, groaning, yawning, coughing, whining and clearing the throat.
3. Vocal qualifiers are momentary variations in volume (ranging from overloud to oversoft) or pitch (ranging from very high to very low).
4. Vocal segregates are non-fluencies like "ah", "um", silent pauses and other intruding sounds.

A great deal may be conveyed by any of the following ingredients:

(*i*) A high pitched voice can indicate excitement, while a low pitched voice can show seriousness, sadness or affection.

(*ii*) Loudness may emphasise a point or it might also indicate anger.

(*iii*) Non-fluencies may reveal the speaker's hesitation and many times may a speaker's presentation.

In a group, leadership and influence can be plotted by ranking people according to the number of successful interruptions they achieve, minus the number of times they are interrupted.

Much research on paralanguage has focused on whether the voice can accurately convey a speaker's personal characteristics like a speaker's age, gender, social class. Most of the times, these personal characteristics are correctly interpreted by voice quality. But a speaker's occupation, body type or personality traits are not that well revealed by this means.

While social and organisational norms often constrain people's verbal expression, feelings are expressed frequently, perhaps unconsciously by non-verbal means.

Environment

A major category of unspoken messages is transmitted through environment. For people in organisations, environment includes (i) territory and space; (ii) building, rooms and seating arrangements; (iii) artifacts and objects; and (iv) time.

(A) **Territory and space :** Territoriality may be defined as the tendency of organisms to lay claim to and defend space. Like animals, people tend to mark off boundaries that others recognise without having to be told.

An experienced union negotiating team would not be willing to hold major negotiations in the management's offices and since the management's team would feel the same way about the union's offices, the talks are usually held on a neutral site.

Three principles are associated with the concept of territory to organisational status :

1. *Persons of higher status will have more and better territory:* In corporations, executive personnel often occupy spacious, well-furnished offices located on the top floors of the building.
2. *The territory of higher status people is better protected than that of lower-status people:* Chief executives, are described as " controlling the area which is least accessible, sealed away from intruders by several doors and a handful of minions." Having an office with a door and a secretary who directs phone calls protect managers and staff personnel.
3. *The higher a person's status, the easier it is for him to invade the territory of lower status people:* A superior typically feels free to walk in on subordinates, while the latter have to ask permission or make an appointment before visiting the superior.

An important kind of space in interpersonal relations is termed as Informal Space which is the space that people place between each other when they interact.

Four major patterns of informal space have been identified:

(*i*) *Intimate distance;* from direct contact to eighteen inches, is shared by people who have intimate relations like lovers, parents or close relatives, or close friends, who have maximum emotional involvement.

(*ii*) *Personal distance;* from eighteen inches to four feet, is the range for most conversation, the relation between the parties and the topic of conversation influence the exact distance.

(*iii*) *Social distance;* from four to twelve feet is the distance for most work related interactions. The exact distance is influenced by the nature of the interaction: a formal discussion involves a greater distance between parties than an informal discussion.

(*iv*) *Public distance;* from twelve to twenty-five feet and is used for one-way communication between a speaker and an audience.

(B) **Buildings, rooms and seating arrangements :** Most organisational tasks are centered around human interaction and so physical facilities that discourage needed personal contact can hamper an organisation's performance. It is beneficial for managers to be aware of the advantages of frequent contact with subordinates and have an office layout that facilitates warm human interaction. An organisation' s aspect of settings can be of two types.

1. *Sociopetal:* the tendency of arrangements to bring people close together.
2. *Sociofugal:* the tendency of arrangements to push people apart.

Seating arrangement affect both the amount and the kinds of interactions, that take place between people. An office occupant may arrange his furniture in a fashion that reflects the degree of power and formality that he wants to communicate.

Where group members are seated around a table, people seated across from each other tend to converse with one another more frequently than those seated side by side, given a minimum direction by a designated leader. But under a strong directive leadership, the opposite occurs; with more conversation being directed to neighbours than to those sitting opposite.

(C) **Artifacts and objects:** The objects in an office often convey clear signals about the occupant's status. For example, a wooden desk and area rugs may enhance the power and authority of the office occupant. Object like a chair with arms (that allows one to rest elbows on chair arms and clasp hands together) or a spare chair or couch (to suggest that one is important enough to have visitors) often play a role to exude "power" of the occupant of the office room.

(D) **Time:** The time of the day often conveys the importance of a message. A plant manager can emphasize the importance of a message by timing the announcement during the day in such a manner so that it calls the workers away from work.

Often conceptions of time vary widely with different cultures. While a North American highly values promptness, in Latin America, the manana (it can wait until tomorrow) concept governs.

Implications and Suggestions for Non-verbal Communication

Managers and other organisational members can benefit from improving their awareness and skill in non-verbal communication. Three general recommendations made for this purpose are :

1. **Become a better non-verbal observer :** Understanding of non-verbal signs, helps in prediction of one another's actions. Such understanding may be improved by increasing one's sensitivity to all the different dimensions of non-verbal communication. If one is open to all available channels of information, including non-verbal dimensions, one's quality of decision making improves.

2. **Make improved use of non-verbal dimensions in communicating :** Managers can improve the effectiveness of their actions, like their attempt to motivate others by focusing on and structuring non-verbal dimension they use in their own communication. The impact of a project proposal may be increased manifold through the effective use of non-verbal dimensions like clothing, vocal quality, seating arrangement, time of the day and the decor of the room where the presentation is to be made.

3. **Non-verbal cues should not be oversimplified:** Non-verbal cues must always be interpreted in respect of their context. A man might fold his arms across his chest to signal resistance or due to nervousness. Moreover, the same signal may mean different things to people of different cultures. Thus one must not focus on single cues in isolation, but to understand the full context in which they appear.

Chapter 5

Effective Communication Tools: Active Listening and Feedback

Communication can be greatly enhanced by good communication skills. Active listening and providing feedback are two such critical skills.

Active Listening

Active Listening is listening to a speaker with intensity, empathy, acceptance and a willingness to take responsibility for completeness of the speaker's intended meaning. The ingredients of active listening are discussed below:

(*i*) **Intensity** – It means listening to the speaker's message with total concentration, without turning out during the communication.

(*ii*) **Empathy** – It is the desire and effort required on the listener's part to get inside the speaker's thoughts and feelings. Empathy can be expressed verbally or non-verbally through messages like "I understand" or "I am with you". The speaker, if convinced that the listener is empathetic, will be willing to explore his/her problems and speak more deeply. In this way, the listener tends to interpret the message being communicated more correctly.

(*iii*) **Acceptance** – An active listener can demonstrate acceptance by listening objectively without being judgemental of the content. This can be possible if the listener respects the speaker for his/her individuality and worth as a person.

(*iv*) **Responsibility** – The listener must be willing to take responsibility to get the complete intended meaning from the speaker's communication. This can be achieved by—

(*a*) Listening for feeling and content, and

(*b*) Asking questions to ensure understanding.

Obstacles to Active Listening

1. **Environmental distractions** like loud noises or other physical movements. Such distractions should be eliminated for effective communication.

2. **Physiological limitations** — The human brain is capable of handling a speaking rate of about four times the speed of the average speaker. Thus, during the idle time, the brain tends to tune out and let the mind wander to several miscellaneous thoughts.

3. **Self consciousness** — A listener may be distracted due to personal problems or may be too concerned about the impression he makes on others, and in the process gets a distorted meaning of the message.

4. **Urge to debate** — People have an inherent urge to evaluate others and may form a judgement even before the speaker has finished and thus miss the main point.

Tips for Effective Active Listening

1. Make eye contact.
2. Exhibit affirmative head nods and appropriate facial expressions.

3. Avoid distracting actions or gestures.
4. Ask questions.
5. Paraphrase.
6. Avoid interrupting the speaker.
7. Don't overtalk.
8. Make smooth transitions between the roles of speaker and listener.

Feedback

Providing feedback, or response, completes the communication process. Feedback is of two types—Positive and Negative.

Positive vs. Negative Feedback

Managers like giving the feedback and recipients like accepting it. But in case of negative feedback, the managers are often hesitant about being the bearer of bad news and the recipients are often offended by it. The simple logic behind it is that people always wish to hear good news that fits with what they already believe about themselves, and similarly want to resist hearing bad news.

Negative feedback is likely to be accepted if —

(*i*) It is substantiated by hand data such as statistics and examples.

(*ii*) It is objective and impersonal.

(*iii*) It comes from a credible source.

(*iv*) It concerns with something that the recipient has control over and the recipient can act to improve the situation.

Chapter 6

Barriers to Effective Communication

Any factor that hinders the receiver's understanding of the intended meaning of the sender's message, is a barrier to communication.

The following are the most common barriers to effective communication :

1. **Differing perceptions :** The receivers in the communication process see and hear differently based on their needs, motivations, experiences, background and other personal characteristics. To illustrate, a supervisor, impressed by an employee's work and also to encourage fellow workers, compliments an employee. The other workers may perceive that the particular employee had been "buttering up the boss."

2. **Language differences :** The same word may mean different things to different people, often due to differences in individual perceptions. Age, education and cultural background influences the language a person speaks and understands. Further, barriers may result from use of jargon or technical language.

3. **Emotions :** The emotional conditions like anger, fear, jealousy influences how a receiver interprets a communication message at the time of receiving it. Extreme emotions may hinder in communication by making the receiver prove to disregard his rational and objective thinking process and substitute emotional judgements.

4. **Inconsistent verbal and non-verbal communication :** Non-verbal communications as body movement gestures, clothes, facial expression, eye-contact, etc. send out different messages. To illustrate, a "good morning" wished with a smile and with a cold stare may mean different things to the receiver.

5. **Distrust :** The credibility of a message to a large extent depends upon the perceived credibility of the sender in the receiver's mind.

6. **Filtering :** Filtering is a process in which the sender manipulates information in such a way that he feels will be more favourably received by the receiver. The subordinates condense and synthesise information while sending it to senior executives so that the latter don't get overloaded with information. In the process, personal interests and perceptions of subordinates get mixed in such synthesis, depriving senior managers of an objective insight. The major determinant of filtering is the number of levels in the organisation's structure.

Chapter 7

Tips for Effective Communication

Effective communication is a two step process. First, one must learn to recognise the various types of barriers that can occur. Second, one must act to overcome the barriers. The following factors help to create an effective communication process :

Overcoming differing perceptions

(*i*) The message should be clearly explained so that it is understood by people having various views and experiences.

(*ii*) Whenever possible, one should learn about the background of the person with whom one will be communicating.

(*iii*) Empathising and trying to see the situation from the other person's point of view.

(*iv*) When a subject is unclear, asking for clarifications is critical.

Overcoming differences in languages

(*i*) Meanings of unconventional and/or technical terms must be explained.

(*ii*) Message should be in clear, simple and unambiguous language.

(*iii*) Asking the receiver to confirm or restate main points of the message ensures correct interpretation of important concepts.

(*iv*) If a new terminology is introduced in an organisation, members must be made acquainted with the new topic through training and discourses.

Overcoming emotionality

(*i*) Accepting that human emotions are a part of the communication process.

(*ii*) Trying to analyse as to why the receiver is behaving in a particular way.

(*iii*) Trying to get the receiver talk about his concerns and being attentive to what he says.

(*iv*) A manager should try to understand the emotional reactions of his subordinate while dealing with a crisis situation.

Overcoming inconsistent verbal and non-verbal communication

Being aware of the inconsistencies in communication and trying not to send false messages. This can be facilitated by analysing non-verbal communication of other people and applying one's learning to one self and in how he deals with others,

Overcoming distrust

In general, a manager's credibility will be high if he is perceived as knowledgeable, trustworthy, fair minded and sincerely concerned about the welfare of others in the organisation. Credibility has to be earned through long years of practice.

Overcoming noise

(*i*) If possible, try to eliminate noise. For example, turning off a noisy machine while communicating.

(*ii*) If the receiver is inattentive, then try to regain his attention.

(*iii*) If distracting environment cannot be altogether avoided, then clarity and strength of the message should be increased.

Redundancy

Repeating the message or restating it in a different form counteracts noise by reducing the uncertainty in the transmission of the message.

Tips for effective communication includes overcoming barriers to communication, listening skills and providing feedback.

Chapter 8

Group Importance

A group is defined as two or more people who interact with and influence each other toward a common purpose. Since a group generally consists of a small number of people, the members of the group communicate face-to-face and perceive each other as part of the group.

In the words of Fred Luthans, "if a group exists in an organisation, its members:

1. Are motivated to join
2. Perceive the group as a unified unit of interacting people
3. Contribute in various amounts to the group process (that is, some people contribute more time or energy to the group than do others)
4. Reach agreements and have disagreements through various forms of interaction."

The study concerned with the interactions and forces among members of a group, that is, the way in which a group is organised and conducted, is called as "Group Dynamics". The term was first popularised by Lewin in the 1930s. Group Dynamics is a study of the internal nature of groups, their formation (i.e. the structure and processes) as well as the way such groups function and affect group members, other groups and the organisation itself.

Importance of Groups

The primary importance of a group lies in the fact that a group possesses properties that its individual members do not; so that goals that a group can achieve cannot be accomplished by individual members separately. The importance of groups in an organisation can be listed as follows -

1. ***Affiliation :*** The primary importance of a group is that it satisfies the affiliation motive of the members of the organisation. Employees have a very intense need to belong to, and be accepted by the group. The social need of "belongingness" of the employees can only be satisfied by forming groups within the organisation.

2. ***Employee Satisfaction and Performance :*** Groups contribute to employee satisfaction and performance in the following ways -

(*a*) A group is a well defined unit around which the work is organised.

(*b*) The group decides about selection, training and even rewarding its members.

(*c*) Groups enforce strong norms of behaviour for group members which enhances group performance.

(*d*) A group is a more equitable basis for sharing rewards and resources as compared to the individual basis.

(*e*) A group enhances performance through building within-group solidarity.

3. ***Functional Responsibilities :*** Formally designated work groups, such as departmental committees (finance, marketing, operations and human resource) and cross-functional teams, strive to achieve the organisational objectives by performing specific functional responsibilities. For example, a marketing committee may evaluate the potentiality of an unexplored market. Such functional responsibilities cannot be performed by members all by themselves, but only through specific workgroups.

4. ***Economic and Security Reasons :*** For greater economic benefits, workers may form a group to work on projects which are paid on group-incentive plans, or may form a union to extract a higher wage rate.

For security of jobs, workers may form a group to protest as a united front against the unilateral actions of management.

Characteristics of Groups

A group is characterised by the following factors—

1. ***Structure :*** The structure of a group decides its effectiveness. Group structure is determined by:

(*a*) *Communication networks*- These refer to the patterns of who talks to whom in a group. The networks indicate whether channels help the flow of messages and also the degree of effective communication within the group.

(*b*) *Patterns of status and power*- Even though groups are generally founded on the basis of equality, one or more members emerge as key decision makers due to their abilities to influence others. Thus, a group typically develops power structures that determine its effectiveness.

(*c*) *Subgrouping*- In a group, some members form subgroups for various reasons. Such subgroups may have either favourable or unfavourable effects on the group functioning.

2. ***Cohesiveness :*** Cohesiveness is the average resultant force acting on members in a group. It represents the sum of all the factors that induce members to remain in the group. The more cohesive a group is, members are more likely to cooperate and participate in common efforts. Agreement on group goals, frequency of interaction, intergroup competition etc. enhance group cohesiveness, while large group size, domination by one or more members decrease group cohesiveness.

3. ***Norms :*** Norms are guidelines or prescriptions for acceptable behaviour determined by a group. Group members are expected to conform to such group norms. Norms such as "Do not do too much; do not do too little" will be strongly enforced by work groups if they help in achieving the group objectives.

4. ***Polarisation*** **:** Groups are characterised by the "risky shift" or "polarisation phenomenon", which suggests that while some groups shift towards riskiness, other groups shift towards conservatism. A group's tendency to adopt risky decisions becomes more prominent when the group is highly cohesive and conforming, thereby pressurising the minority viewpoints within the group to conform to the majority viewpoint.

Chapter 9

Group Discussions

The word "discuss" means 'examine by arguments'. Thus, a group discussion is a technique used to critically examine a particular point of interest through arguments. The point of interest is the object of the discussion and the group members arrive at a decision based on such discussion. Thus, group discussion is a fundamental technique of adopting decisions in groups.

In a group discussion, group members are encouraged to pool in all available information on the topic of discussion. Such an information base is then used by the group to make a decision after careful evaluation of all the aspects of the discussion topic. It is to be noted that the individual members of the group must be technically qualified to ensure that high-quality decisions are arrived at. For example, in a situation of rising costs of production, group meeting may be convened to discuss ways to control production costs. Here, the point of interest is how to cut costs. Members pool in the causes of rising costs, the technique of production employed, employee attitude, etc. and suggest viable solutions to control rising costs. The solutions are evaluated and the best alternative is adopted as a decision. Hence, group discussions are critical to the process of generating effective decisions.

Factors that enhance the quality of a group discussion are as follows—

1. **Clearly defined purpose**– The objective or point(s) of interest of a discussion must be clearly articulated. Group members must have a clear perception of the discussion topic to be able to contribute potential ideas as solution.

2. **Preparation and planning**– The group members require adequate preparation and planning before meeting as a group to discuss the problem. This gives the members the scope to research on the point(s) of interest and prepare the potential solutions in advance. Resultantly, the quality of the decision adopted gets greatly enriched.

3. **Involvement and participation**– All group members must be encouraged to join the discussion. Sometimes, a useful solution may not be implemented because at an earlier stage, some members did not actively participate who had the power to kill the idea or those whom the decision will affect. Thus, active participation (even through active listening) evolves a consensus decision, which then becomes easy to implement.

4. **Effective leadership**– The group must unanimously elect a leader to conduct the discussion. This helps to maintain order in the group and provides a scope for disciplined thinking. In the case, where arguments are debated, the opinion of the leader (e.g., putting the debate to vote, consensus opinion or passing a ruling) provides an amicable settlement and the discussion proceeds further.

Certain factors that diminish a group discussion's quality are listed below:

1. **Pressure towards conformity**– The group pressurises the minority members to conform to the majority decision, thereby silencing dissent.

2. **Tendency to adopt the first strongly argued solution**– This limits the number of potential solutions and affects adversely to the decision quality.

3. **Personal bias**– Sometimes establishing one's own argument becomes more important than finding the best solution.

4. **Large group size**– In a large group, communication becomes difficult, issues may become polarised by conflicting opinions and a consensus decision may not be reached. Too large a group defeats the objective of group discussion.

Role of group discussion in team work

In recent times, teams and not committees, have emerged as the most important formal groups in modern organisations. To ensure that teams become more effective, the team members must work together as a team, listen and communicate effectively, deal with conflicts and recognise each other's unique contributions and provide honest feedback.

Group discussion proves to be an effective tool for a team to freely communicate, discuss the conflicts, which it faces and arrive at solutions. It also acts as a means for members to report on their progress and also appreciate individual unique contributions of ideas. Thus, the technique of group discussion is central to effective team functioning.

Chapter 10

Advantages and Disadvantages of Groups

It is a common perception that group decisions are qualitatively superior to individual decisions. However, group decision-making has its own inherent drawbacks and in specific situations (like an emergency), group decisions are not suitable. In this context, it would be worthwhile to analyse the strengths and weaknesses of groups and their resultant influence on the quality of decision-making.

Advantages of Groups

1. **Collective and synergistic effect**– The inherent nature of groups to work collectively produces a synergistic effect (i.e. the whole is greater than the sum of its parts effect). This is the root cause why a well managed group is much more efficient than individual efforts put together.

2. **Participative decision-making**– Participation of group members in decision-making, either formally or informally, results in a consensus. It means members become committed to a decision and will accept it and carry out their parts. Participation ensures that members bring their full resources into play and freely express their opinions.

3. **Quality decisions**– The rich pool of information available to a group can never be available to a single individual. Thus, the number of alternatives available to a group is much larger, and resultantly a high-quality decision becomes easier to evolve.

4. **Democracy**– A group is characterised by democratic ideology. This ensures that the best alternative is chosen by a majority vote. Even though there may be a dissenting minority view, a democratically evolved decision is more acceptable than an autocratic decision of a single individual.

5. **Heterogeneity**– Members in a group have diverse opinions and perceptions about a given problem. This results in accumulation of a variety of expert viewpoints. This heterogeneous character of a group enables each member to build on better ideas using each other's viewpoints. This heterogeneity is the major cause of success for cross-functional teams in organisations.

6. **Solidarity**– Working as groups increases the solidarity and team spirit of employees. They empathise with each other's purposes and problems. This helps reduce conflicts and promote coordination among members. The increased motivation as a result of cooperation raises member's morale and efficiency.

7. **Effective communication**– Groups foster horizontal communication. This form of communication among group members is critical to make a coordinated, cross-functional effort in achieving organisational goals. Group members freely express their ideas and evolve an alternative through discussion. Thus through groups, a high degree of communication can take place which is otherwise not possible.

Disadvantages of Groups

1. **Time and cost**– An inherent disadvantage with groups is that group meetings are time-consuming and costly. The nature of every group meeting is such that every member get a chance to speak out, which involves a considerable time. Since time costs money, group meetings are also costly. Moreover, such meetings may entail transportation, lodging and other overhead costs.

2. **Responsibility fixing**– In a group, there is no individual responsibility or accountability. Hence, managers may escape personal liability for bad or poor decisions by holding the group collectively responsible. Afraid to take responsibility for a decision, such a manager may convene a meeting to make the decision and subsequently blame the group if the decision proves bad.

3. **Domination by few**– Often group decisions are made by a few members who are a small minority in the group. The influence of such persons may so dominate the group that other members may become reluctant to disagree or suggest alternatives. Even silence is interpreted as tacit support to the people exerting the influence. As a result, the decision quality suffers due to lack of participation.

4. **Pressure to conform**– Groups often exert pressure toward members who argue against the majority viewpoint of the group. This intolerance towards a deviant viewpoint forces those individual members to conform and reach consensus. Thus, all viewpoints do not get a fair consideration while the decision is taken.

5. **Group think**– A highly cohesive and conforming group may evolve decisions based on an "agreement-at- any-cost" mentality by avoiding a rational analysis of the ideas contributed by members. There is no proper appraisal of alternative courses of action and members feel they are inherently right. Decisions are adopted prematurely and silence is interpreted as consent. These attributes of a group have been called as "group think" by Irving Janis.

6. **Conflicts**– Groups may give rise to conflicts, both within and without the groups. These arise due to differing perceptions of a problem within a group and incompatible goals between groups. Conflicts cause stress, reduce task motivation of groups, decrease the level of communication and can shatter cooperation.

7. **Compromise in decision making**– Group decisions are often excessively compromised to reach consensus. The urge to consider each and every view of members, may in certain situations prove counter-productive and reduce the efficiency and quality of the decisions adopted.

Chapter 11

Techniques of Group Decision Making

The various techniques designed to obtain effective decisions in groups are discussed below:

Committee Meetings

A committee is a formally designated workgroup in an organisation. This workgroup consists of members drawn from the management hierarchy who are technically competent to analyse and decide solutions for one or more types of specialised problems. For example, a committee may consider only finance-related problems, another may consider only marketing and sales issues, and so on.

Functions: A committee may meet to perform various functions such as service, advisory , co-ordinating, informational and final decision-making. A committee that adopts final decisions on problems usually contain more than one executive head rather than one single leader/executive head, and are called "plural-executive committee". For example, a committee consisting of the president and executive vice-presidents of the company, that acts as the central decision-making authority.

Types: Committee types include standing committees, executive committees, departmental committees, ad-hoc committees, etc.

A standing committee is a permanent body whose members often change periodically by rotation. This committee is responsible for taking routine organisational decisions.

Executive committees are often a company's power-centres responsible for vital organisational decisions.

Departmental committees (marketing, finance, operations and human resource) take specific departmental decisions.

Ad-hoc committees are dissolved on attaining the purpose for which they were formed.

Attributes: Committee meetings can be very effective for conflict control and better coordination between departments. They increase motivation and commitment through participation.

However, committee meetings are costly and time consuming. Committees have no individual responsibility or accountability and the decisions reached are often compromised to suit committees' members.

Command Meetings

A command meeting is a group meeting in which the eventual decisions may be completely determined by a single individual within the group, who may be a formally designated leader (such as the president or executive officer of the company), an informal leader , an expert or an adviser. The other group members can at best express their opinions regarding a point of discussion, but have no role at all in decision-making.

The objective of a command meeting is that the leader issues directions to the group members (who are generally subordinates in the management hierarchy). The leader shares the information, takes note of members' opinions, takes a decision and passes it down as a direction or order.

Command meetings are appropriate when only the leader is competent to take a decision or where in an emergency there is no sufficient time for discussion.

Teams

In recent years, teams have emerged as the most important group decision-making body in organisations. A "team" is a collection of highly motivated individuals that has a specific purpose and the results of teamwork produce not only individual results, but also "collective work-products". A collective work-product is something that two or more members must work together to make:

A team differs from a traditional work group (such as a committee) in that the team members have shared-leadership roles and the team has individual and mutual accountability.

Teams are mainly of two types–

1. Self-managed teams, and
2. Cross-functional teams.

Self managed team members are experienced and empowered to implement decisions and can cohesively act as a team without the involvement of a trainer or supervisor.

Cross-functional team members have different abilities and skills and contribute different inputs to the team, thereby increasing the productivity of the team.

Brainstorming

This is a specialised technique that helps to generate innovative ideas in decision-making. Brainstorming places high regard to group creativity through the following three rules-

1. Members freely express their ideas as and when they occur without regard to quality.
2. Members can not criticise each other or debate unless all ideas have been pooled together.
3. Members help each other to build on previously expressed ideas.

Once all ideas are pooled, members carefully analyse and discuss the ideas to evolve a quality-decision. Apart from enriching the quality of decision-making, brainstorming helps group members to think creatively, encourages active listening and to tolerate others' ideas and promotes effective communication within the group.

Nominal Group Technique

The nominal group technique is a well-known technique available to groups to develop alternatives or make judgements. A nominal group is simply a "paper group", i.e., a group of individuals listed on a paper but who do not interact verbally amongst themselves. Research has shown that nominal groups are superior to real groups in terms of quality, uniqueness and number of ideas.

When a pure nominal group approach is used as a technique for decision-making, it is called as the nominal group technique and involves a four-stage procedure as follows—

1. Group members silently and independently list their ideas in writing about a particular problem.
2. Each person reads one idea to the group and the ideas are then listed on a flip chart or black board.
3. The group clarifies and evaluates the ideas through face-to-face communication.
4. Members secretly vote on priority ideas. The group decision is mathematically derived through rank ordering or rating.

Nominal group technique reduces the adverse real group features such as pressures toward conformity and hasty decision.

The Delphi Technique

This is a group decision-making technique used for long-range forecasting. Here, a group is formed usually of experts but they do not meet face-to-face. The expenses of bringing a group together are thus eliminated. This technique works as follows:

1. Members are presented with a questionnaire designed to collect their opinions or predictions about a specified problem.
2. Members' responses are tabulated, summarised and returned to them, along with a revised questionnaire based on the responses.
3. The process is repeated until the responses clarify the problem and a consensus is reached.

This technique is criticised for its time consuming nature, costs involved and that it has no scientific basis or support.

However, the effectiveness of this technique lies in that group members need not assemble, and its anonymity. Keeping Delphi group members anonymous, encourages the members to be more flexible and thus to benefit from other members' estimates.

Delphi technique can be applied to programme planning and decision problems in any type of organisation.

Chapter 12

Solving Problems in Groups

The purpose of a group is to provide effective solutions to problems. The efficiency of a group in providing such effective solutions depends on how the group perceives the problem, analyses it and adopts the best possible option. In general, the steps that a group undergoes in attempting to solve a problem involves the following:

1. A difficulty is felt and expressed

The first step is to perceive the problem; that is, the group members need to agree that the problem exists and ought to be solved.

2. The problem is identified and defined

The problem is articulated in clear and concise terms, like "shortage of funds" or "actual production is below the budgeted mark". The more clearly a problem is identified, the better the chance of finding an effective solution. The group must, however, guard itself against mistaking a symptom for the problem. For example, a poorly designed product may result in a decreased sales level. Here, the problem is poor product design and the symptom is reduced sales. The group must aim to develop the product better and not attempt to rectify the company's sales efforts.

3. The nature of the problem is analysed

In this stage, the group analyses the factors that have caused and sustained the problem. These causes are recognised and on close scrutiny, the group understands the extent to which the solution can be achieved.

Sometimes, some of the causes resulting in the problem are such that it is beyond the competence of the group to attempt to find a solution. In such cases, the group may relate such causes to another group that has a better potential for solving it. Most often, a group decomposes a given problem into several sub-problems to effectively deal with them and develop a solution.

4. Alternative solutions are generated

Once a problem is understood by the group, the members creatively communicate with each other and propose as many solutions to the problem as possible. This exercise is known as "brainstorming". Members are open to each other's ideas and avoid debating on such ideas until they discuss the possible solutions.

5. A solution is selected

From the pool of possible solutions, which the members have contributed, each potential solution is critically examined in terms of its advantages and shortcomings. Here, it is important that the members give due weights to the possible consequences of each alternative and not merely focus only on the benefits that a particular alternative might offer. For example, a new method of production may offer a host of benefits but may face resistance from workers if it is not user-friendly.

Once a set of viable solutions is selected, the group members bargain and select the solution that best fits the given problem. The objective of the group is to make the best trade-off between the benefits and consequences of all alternatives and come up with a single solution.

6. Action is implemented

The chosen solution is presented to the body responsible for decision implementation. For example, the finance committee presents a solution to the Board of Directors.

Where the group itself has the authority to implement the decision adopted by it, the decision is effectively implemented by making a procedure for evaluating the success of the solution and a scope for making adjustments when the results of implementation are analysed. Thus, the procedure for implementation should be flexible and adapt to new approaches as and when required.

Chapter 13

The Format of a Business Letter

Business letters are an indispensable part of business communication. The practice of "putting it in writing" remains one of the best ways to ensure that the message is accurately received, especially if the message is technical or highly detailed information. Besides, the letter acts as the medium that creates an impression about the firm to the world outside it and helps build goodwill between the firm and its clients, creditors and other people. Herein lies the importance of the appearance of a business letter. Format styles often used in business letters include: (i) Full Block Format; (ii) Block Format; (iii) Semi Block Format; and (iv) Simplified Format. Of these, the Full Block and Semi Block Formats are most common and are illustrated below:

Full Block Format

- All lines start from the left margin of the paper.
- No lines or paragraphs are indented.

(Letterhead of the company)	
NC/0033/04	Reference number
July 15, 2004	Date
Mr. Saurabh Agarwal Vice President, Marketing Bright Industries Ltd., Kolkata	Inside address
Dear Mr. Agarwal:	Salutation
Sub:	Subject line (optional)
Body of the letter (Paragraph 1)	
Body of the letter (Paragraph 2)	
Yours Sincerely (Handwritten signature)	
Vishal Gupta Manager, Materials Unix Ltd.	Complimentary close
Encl.:	Enclosure (if any)
P .S.	Post Script (if any)

SEMI BLOCK FORMAT

- Date is written on the right hand side.
- Inside address and salutation start from the left margin.
- Paragraphs are indented.
- Complimentary Close and Signature are set to the right hand side.

Gupta Publishing House
16, Anna Road, Chennai
(Company Letter Head)

MC/023 — Ref. No. — July 15, 2004 (Date)

Mr. Soumya Mukherjee
30/1, Park Street
Kolkata
— Inside Address

Dear Mr. Mukherjee, — Salutation

Sub: — Subject line (optional)

Body of the Letter (First line of each paragraph is indented)

Body of the Letter

Body of the Letter

Complimentary Close —
Yours Sincerely,
(Handwritten signature)
Philip John
Production Editor

Encl.: — Enclosure (if any)

P.S. — Post script (if any)

Parts of a Business Letter

Most business letters have the following basic parts:

1. Heading or Letterhead

The heading is simply the printed letterhead on the company stationery containing the company name, address, phone number(s), etc. If the letterhead is not printed, it is usually typed at the upper right hand corner of the paper.

2. Reference Number

Business letters contain reference numbers to refer to the sequence of past letters, or to identify a particular officer, or as a reference for all future correspondence.

3. Dateline

The date serves as an important reference to determine when the letter was written. The position of the dateline depends upon the letter-format used.

4. Inside Address

The inside address contains the name of the receiver, designation, company name and division (if any), mailing address and pin code. It is written below the dateline (in full block format) and below the reference number line (in semi block format).

5. Salutation

Salutation refers to the expression of greeting or respect shown to the addressee. It is written below the inside address. The commonly used salutations are given below:

Dear Ms. (or Miss or Mrs.) Joseph

Dear Mr. Sharma

If you do not know the name of the recipient but do know that you are addressing a gentleman or a lady, your salutation would be:

Dear Sir

Dear Madam

Sometimes, general greetings are also used depending on the occasion:

Dear Members

To all Sales Staff

Dear Friends

6. Body of the Letter

The body of the business letter starts below the salutation. The body can be typed in full block style with no paragraph indentations or semiblock style in which the paragraphs are indented.

It is advisable to divide the body into at least two or three paragraphs. The first paragraph begins directly with the purpose of the letter. The second paragraph gradually builds up the purpose. The second paragraph is often developed upon in the successive paragraph (s). The concluding paragraph usually contains a goodwill message specially adapted to the purpose.

7. Complimentary Close

(1) Highly formal closings are used when writing to dignitaries:

Respectfully yours,

Respectfully,

(2) Less formal closings are used in general correspondence:

Yours faithfully,

Yours truly,

Yours sincerely,

If the salutation names the recipient (Dear Mr. Sen, Dear Ms. Jain, etc.), use: Yours sincerely/Yours truly. When the recipient is not named, use:

Yours faithfully,

8. Enclosure Line

The enclosure line serves as a check to both the recipient and sender to ensure line that everything included with the letter was actually sent. The abbreviated form "Encl." is written one line below the complimentary close as follows:

(*i*) Encl.

(*ii*) Encl.: (3)

(*iii*) Encl.: Price list,
Catalogue

9. Postscript

In typical business letters, postscripts are not used as the writer includes all relevant matter in the body of the letter. However, because they do catch attention, postscripts are an effective technique used in sales letter. The abbreviated form "P.S." is used to denote a postscript, and it is written on the left-hand margin two lines below the complimentary close.

10. Copies Line

If you wish the reader to know the other recipients of a copy of the letter, type "Copy to" or "Copies to" or "CC" at the bottom of the letter and add the name or names of the other recipients.

Chapter 14

Tips for Effective Writing

Given below are some tips for writing effective business letters.

(1) Use commonly used and short words/phrases

Examples:

	Long words/phrases	Short words/Phrases
(*a*)	They acceded to the proposition to initiate a business.	They agreed to start a business.
(*b*)	Definitive action was effected subsequent to the reporting date.	Final action was taken after the reporting date.
(*c*)	Prior to accelerating productive operation, ...	Before speeding up production, ...

(2) Adopt the "you" attitude instead of the "we" attitude in writing letters.

Examples:

	We attitude	You attitude
(*a*)	We have received your report of July 1.	Thank you for your report of July 1.
(*b*)	We have despatched the three equipment sets you ordered.	Your three equipment sets should reach you soon.
(*c*)	"I am happy to report ..."	"You will be happy to know..."

(3) Prefer active voice to passive voice in constructing sentences. Active voice is stronger and concise.

Examples:

	Passive Voice	Active Voice
(*a*)	The books were inspected by the auditor.	The auditor inspected the books.
(*b*)	The policy was ratified by the Committee.	The Committee ratified the policy.
(*c*)	The results were reported in our July 18 letter.	We reported the results in our July 18 letter.

(4) The following list is intended to serve as a check list to cut down surplus word

	Wordy	Concise
(*i*)	At the present time	Now
(*ii*)	For the purpose of	For
(*iii*)	During the course of	During
(*iv*)	Refer back to	Refer to
(*v*)	In the near future	Soon

(*vi*)	In very few cases	Seldom
(*vii*)	Due to the fact that	Because
(*viii*)	In spite of the fact that	Although
(*ix*)	In the vast majority of cases	In most cases
(*x*)	Until such time as	Until
(*xi*)	Along the lines of	Like
(*xii*)	In accordance with	By
(*xiii*)	On a weekly basis	Weekly
(*xiv*)	Meet together	Meet
(*xv*)	On the basis of	By

Chapter 15

Memo Writing

A memorandum is one of the most efficient ways to communicate within an organisation. Memos are primarily written messages which are sent to one person or several people within the same organisation.

Memos differ from letters in three ways:

(1) Unlike letters, a memo is more direct in its approach. Since memos involve communicating work-related information, they are typically clear and straightforward;

(2) Memos avoid elaborate explanation, persuasive techniques, etc.; and,

(3) A memo differs from a letter in its format.

The memo format is shown below –

MEMORANDUM	
To:	(Name and designation of recipient)
From:	(Name and designation of sender)
Date:	(Date when the memo is sent)
Reference:	(Optional. Refers readers to other memos/letter or file nos., etc.)
Attachments :	(Optional. Enclosed photographs, diagrams, charts, etc.)
Subject:	(Concisely indicates the topic of the memo).
	(Body of the memo)
TK: spj	[Initials of sender (in capital) followed by initials (in small letters) of the person who prepared the memo]
CC:	("carbon copies"–persons to whom copies of the memo are being sent)

Steps in Preparing a Memo

(1) **Preparation:** Simply jot down a list of items relating to the memo's subject that randomly come to mind. Then use numbers to sort into main points and sub-points.

(2) **Writing:** The Layout of a memo follows the "inverted pyramid structure", as shown below. The memo starts with the main point, supported by further information and the least important details are given last. See Fig. 3. Finally, the memo concludes on a courteous tone.

(3) **Review:** Check for errors in spelling grammar. Edit revise the draft to make the message clear and accurate.

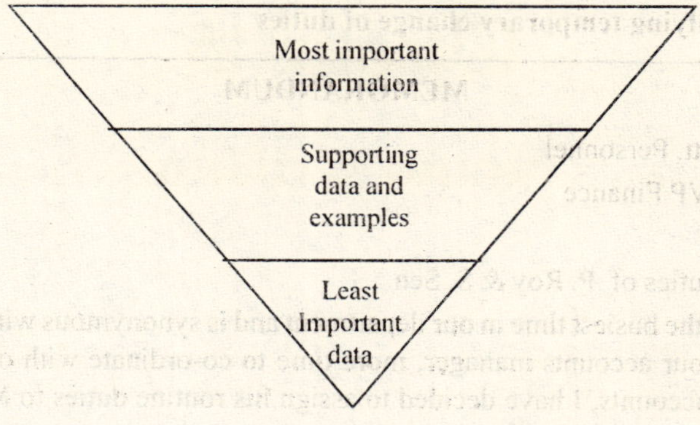

Fig. 15.1 : The inverted pyramid structure

Example 1 : A memo requesting cost information of a meeting.

MEMORANDUM

To: Michael Peter,
Company Secretary,

From: Vikram Bhatt,

Managing Director

Date: July 6, 2002

Subject: Request for cost information concerning 23rd Annual General Meeting.

As per our discussion today, please get the necessary cost information for conducting our 23rd AGM at Hotel Taj Bengal, Kolkata. Our meeting is scheduled at 10.30 a.m. on August 4,2002. We will arrive in the evening of the 3rd and leave the next afternoon.

Specifically, I need to know:

(1) Travel costs of all 12 directors, 5 officers and 9 staff members including air travel to Kolkata and ground travel between airport to the hotel.

(2) Boarding costs for the period, including lunch and dinner.

(3) Costs for the meeting hall and equipment rentals (microphones, etc.)

I'd like to have the information by July 20. If you need further details, please contact me at extension 373.

VB:ps.

Example 2 : A memo announcing a new incentive scheme for employees.

MEMORANDUM

To: All sales staff

From: Sanjeev Shroff, Manager

Date: April 15, 2002

Attachment: Scheme Details

Subject: New Incentive Scheme

It is my pleasure to announce a new scheme of incentive payments that will enable you to earn upto 20 per cent more commission. This is to appreciate the dedication and hard work of the entire sales staff, who have maintained a steady growth in sales, despite a difficult year.

Let's continue this good work and beat last year's records.

SS: mp

Example 3 : Memo specifying temporary change of duties

MEMORANDUM

To: All Accounts Deptt. Personnel

From: S Ramanujan, VP Finance

Date: April 6, 2002

Subject: Changes in duties of P. Roy & S. Sen

The month of April is the busiest time in our department and is synonymous with finalisation of accounts.

To give Pritish Roy, our accounts manager, more time to co-ordinate with other departments and our branches to prepare the accounts, I have decided to assign his routine duties to Mr. S. Sen, Asst. accounts manager.

From tomorrow until April 30, Mr. S. Sen will—

(1) authorise cheques for payment,

(2) receive departmental and branch correspondence,

(3) review regular work of the department.

For matters regarding accounts finalisation, please directly contact Mr. Roy. Your cooperation will help streamline the work for both of them.

SR: tn

Example 4 : Memo advocating safety measures at work.

MEMORANDUM

To: All departments heads

From: Arunava Roy, Managing Director

Date: 17th March, 2002

Attachment: Safety Regulations manual

Subject: Safety precautions for employees

Following the accident in our assembly section last week, safety regulations across all departments have been made more stringent. Please ensure that these regulations are effectively followed in your department.

It would be worthwhile if surprise checks are conducted to ensure compliance with these regulations. I understand that despite these measures, accidents may happen. Thus, creating awareness among employees against possible work-hazards would be a prudent move.

Please let me know, if you have any suggestions to improve safety measures. Your cooperation will help make our company a safer place to work.

AR:tm

Example 5 : Memo requesting the purchase of a new accounting software.

MEMORANDUM

To: Vishal Gupta, VP Finance

From: Srinivasan Jain, Manager (Accounts)

Date: 23rd August, 2002

Subject: New accounting software

I have found an accounting software that is just ideal for our company. It's called "SIMPLEX" and can do the following for us —

Contd...

(1) It can auto generate the annual revenue statements;

(2) Merge the details received from our branches and prepare consolidated accounts;

(3) Calculate year-end foreign debts / receivables;

(4) Provide a breakdown of sales by region, of our branches; and

(5) Contains debugging programmes for errors.

"SIMPLEX" will cost Rs. 25,000 (subject to negotiations), but is justified on the grounds of precise-results and faster processing.

To ensure better maintenance and preparation of accounts, I would like to request you to buy "SIMPLEX" and fund a training programme for the accounting staff ranging between Rs. 3500 to Rs. 4500. So could we really get ourselves a "SIMPLEX"?

SJ: mk

Chapter 16

Proposal Writing

A business proposal is a persuasive offer submitted for soliciting business. For example, an advertising agency's proposal to promote a product, proposals of professional consultants, independent contractors and agents to potential clients offering to provide services, or even one company's proposal to merge with another company.

Proposals may even be used internally within a company. For example, the production manager's proposal to management describing the need to adopt an alternative cost-saving production technique. A proposal sent to prospective customers may be either invited (i.e. in response to a request) or prospecting (i.e. more like a sales letter).

Thus, while writing a proposal to potential customers, you must:

(*i*) Concisely show what you have to offer,

(*ii*) Clearly specify how they will benefit,

(*iii*) Your ability to deliver the service,

(*iv*) Specify time schedules, costs, performance standards, personnel requirements, etc. and

(*v*) Conclude by urging the reader to act on your proposal.

A business proposal consists of —

(1) Letter of transmittal (or cover letter or prefatory note); and

(2) The proposal proper (i.e. the body of the proposal).

Transmittal letters accompany the proposal and identify what is being sent, references for sender and receiver and the reason for sending the proposal .

The format of a proposal is given below:

Company Name
with address

Name

Address
(to whom the
proposal is sent)

(Body of the Proposal)

Signature of the proposer

Example 1 : An advertising agency's proposal to launch a new product .

"SILVERSTONE COMMUNICATIONS LTD."

30, C.R. Avenue
Kolkata- 700 012

Mr. S. Srivastava
Managing Director
Freeman Automobiles Ltd.
Middleton Mansion
Kolkata

Dear Mr. Srivastava,

Last week you shared with Mr. Irani, our executive director, some of your concerns about launching your new brand of motor cycles -"Blazer". We understand your need for creating the 'right impact' for a successful launch. Simultaneously, we appreciate your right move to ask us to present a proposal outlining our approach to the advertisement campaign for Blazer's introduction.

The enclosed pages will show you how we intend to kick-start the campaign, the forms of publicity intended, our planning strategies, the expected timing of the launch, estimated costs and the resumes of our proposed project team members.

We are very optimistic about the project. Our sound strategies will help "Blazer" have a very strong and definite presence before the end of the year. For us it is not just a promotion, but a mission to ignite a craze for "Blazer".

We highly appreciate the opportunity of working with you and would justify your faith in us with concrete success.

With warm regards,

Yours sincerely,
Anirban Bose
President and CEO
Silverstone Communications Ltd.

Enclosures: (9)

PROPOSAL

To

Mr. S. Srivastava
Managing Director
Freeman Automobiles Ltd.

For: Promotion of "Blaze" motor cycles

Promotional Strategies

Your company has established a goodwill that is synonymous with 'quality' and 'value for money'. We intend to capitalise on this perception and project 'Blaze' as the unquestionable leader of competitive brands. We would also propose to highlight —

Contd...

(1) Distinctly better mileage and negligible maintenance costs.

(2) The unique features and accessories available only with 'Blaze'.

(3) The sleek look, steel blue colour finish.

Our biggest promotional plan intends to rope in the leading icon of the Indian Cricket Team to patronise 'Blaze'. This in turn would reinforce the concept of 'solid quality'.

Publicity Vehicles

(*i*) **Print media:** The top 3 widely circulated English dailies and 10 select magazines. (Fully coloured publication).

(*ii*) **Visual media:** Top 12 channels with a 3 minute breath-taking advertisement.

(*iii*) Hoardings and neon signs in select city regions.

Timing and estimated costs

The promotion will kick start 10 days before the proposed launch and will intensively continue for the next 25 days, after which it will routinely continue at par with existing brands for the next few months as may be decided by you.

The entire project is estimated to involve an investment ranging from Rs. 65 lakhs, to Rs. 80 lakhs, details of which are enclosed.

Project Team

The team will be headed by Mr. Irani, our executive director and seven other senior consultants. They all have very successful promotions to their credit. Their detailed resumes are enclosed.

Example 2 : A management consultancy's proposal to restructure the organisational set-up.

Mr. Bhasker Sen July 3, 2002

Chairman and Managing Director

'Times Watches Ltd.

Ansari Rd, Daryaganj,

New Delhi -110002

Dear Mr. Sen,

Monday last, you had discussed with me about some of the organisational problems your company is experiencing. From your apt descriptions of the problems and my subsequent studies regarding your organisational set-up, we have no doubt that these are transitional problems relating to the expansion of your company's operations.

In the enclosed pages please find our firm's proposal as you had requested. The proposal outlines our approach to solve these problems along with an estimate of time and expenses. In our opinion, the right strategy adopted at the right time will help your organisation achieve its goals.

Your company has an excellent team record down the years. We would highly appreciate the opportunity to work with you and assist your company to achieve greater heights.

With warm regards,

Yours sincerely,

R. Mitra

GUPTA AND MITRA ASSOCIATES

Management Consultants

Enclosures: (3)

PROPOSAL

Evaluation of the Current Situation

The company has been subject to organisational problems due to the following reasons:

(1) Goals and objectives are not properly understood throughout the company ranks.

(2) Communications among management levels and subordinate staff are poor. This causes lack of coordination among the various divisions and departments.

(3) Revision of performance standards were effected in 2002-03 but the scheme was not properly administered.

(4) Standards of Quality Control are not strictly adhered to.

(5) Deficiencies in after-sales services have affected company reputation.

(6) Motivation and morale are low, resulting in low productivity.

Our Approach to the Problem

Times Watches Ltd. is finding difficulty in maintaining the same standard after it has expanded its operations into other segments of the market.

Our consulting services will help you reorganise the management structure without hindering the normal flow of business.

This will help you to make a smooth transition from a medium sized company to a large manufacturing company. Our services will include among other things, ways and measures on how to —

(1) Effectively reshuffle key managerial positions,

(2) Set up new office procedures,

(3) Modify accounting procedures to cope up with huge masses of detail,

(4) Reorganise distribution networks, and

(5) Develop communication at all management levels.

We will help you devise sound planning strategies and develop working plans to achieve your company objectives. Our training systems will equip your managers to effectively carry out the required changes.

Estimated Time and Expenses

The entire restructuring exercise will take about four months to complete, after which you will have an organisational structure with clearly defined functional areas, motivated employees, effective communications and office systems.

We will depute Mr. P. Ratan, our senior consultant, as the project-in-charge. He will be assisted by a team of five specialised consultants from amongst our corporate staff. The resumes of our proposed team members are enclosed.

In our estimate, the entire project will involve an investment ranging between Rs. 45,000 to Rs. 60,000. This includes two follow-up visits two months and six months after completion of project.

Chapter 17

Office Orders, Circulars and Notes

OFFICE ORDERS

Example 1 : A Transfer Order

POPULAR TEA LTD.
KOLKATA

Ref: 23/69/Per Date 12.5.2002

Order

Mr. P. Rakshit stands transferred to our Guwahati branch and shall report at Guwahati to Mr. D. Hazarika (Branch Manager), latest by May 20, 2002. He shall hand over his current duties to Mr. Palit by May 13,2002,

Sd/-

J. Narayan – Manager (HRD)
cc: Administrative Officer,
Accounts Officer

Example 2 : Order terminating service

SUNRISE MOTORS LTD.
CHENNAI

Ref: 02/43/Per Date: 15.6.2002

Order

In view of — (a) intermittent absenteeism for prolonged periods without adequate explanation,
(b) failure to complete work orders in time, and
(c) disregard shown towards previously issued warnings, the service of Mr. S Nagpal is terminated with immediate effect. He shall hand over charge of his duties to the Assistant Manager (Accounts) by 16. 6. 2002.

Sd/-

P. Chandra, – Manager (HRD)

Example 3 : Order filling up vacancy due to retirement

ENKAY ENGINEERING CO. LTD.
LUCKNOW

Ref: Per / B 286 Date: 18.6.2002

Order

Shri Vijay Goel has been posted to the Accounts Department as Asst. Manager (Accounts) w.e.f. 1.7.2002. He shall assume charge in place of Shri Bharat Mehta who retires on 28. 6. 2002.

Sd/-

Vikram Patil, -Manager (HRD)
cc: Manager (Accounts)

Example 4: Promotion Order

UNITED STEEL CO. LTD.
KOLKATA

Ref: Per/819 Date: 24.7.2002

Order

Mr. Sumedh Jaiswal, senior marketing executive is promoted as Zonal Manager (Marketing), Eastern Zone, w.e.f. 1.8.2002. He will draw a basic pay of Rs. 12,000 p.m. apart from such perquisites that are available to Grade-I employees.

Sd/-
R. Bose
Manager(HRD)
cc: Manager (Accounts)
Regional Manager (Marketing)

Example 5 : Order granting special increments

INDIAN CHEMICALS LTD.

Ref: PP/06/97 Date: 24.7.2002

Order

The management is pleased to grant Shri Summit Wadia a special incentive bonus Rs. 2,500 p.m. w.e.f. 01.08.2002 in appreciation of his outstanding performance.

Sd/-
M.C. Johnson
Manager (HRD)
cc: Chief Accounts Officer

OFFICE CIRCULARS

Example 6 : Circular insisting economising on use of electricity

GENERAL ENGINEERING CORPORATION
MUMBAI-400 007

Circular. No. 242/002 Dated: 06.06.2002

Employees are requested to strictly follow the following measures, to economise on the use of electricity.

(*a*) Turn off lights which are not required in performing work.

(*b*) Keep windows closed while the air-conditioners are in operation.

(*c*) All air-conditioners will be shut off at 5 p.m. on all working days.

(*d*) Turn off all computer terminals and printer when not in use.

Sd/-
J. Dalmiya
General Manager

Example 7 : Circular declaring a holiday

PRIME ELECTRICALS LTD.
KANPUR

Circular No: 23/002 Date: 23.07.2002

It is hereby declared that the office shall remain closed on Friday, July 26, 2002, on account of repair works. The office premises will reopen on Monday, July 29, 2002.

Sd/-
Manager

Example 8 : Circular insisting punctuality

SILVERLINE PVT. LTD.

Circular No: 22/02 Date: 26.07.2002

Employees are requested to follow the office timings strictly. The attendance register shall remain open till 9.30 a.m. after which it shall remain with the Asst. Manager, Personnel. Employees leaving office before 5:30 p.m. are expected to initial the register, briefly stating the reason for early departure.

Cooperation is solicited from each employee to uphold office discipline.

Sd/-
Manager

OFFICE NOTES

Example 9 : Office note requesting replenishment of stationery

VINAY TEXTILES LTD.

Ref: 45/02 Date: 18.07.2002
From: Accounts Deptt. To: Stores Dept.
Subject: Replenishment of Stationery

Please send us the office supplies listed below.

5 boxes	Letter size bond paper; 8.5" × 11"
4 dozen	No. 234 printer cartridges
10 boxes	Printed letter-heads

Since our stocks of these items are nearly depleted, we would appreciate any extra promptness that you can give this order.

Sd/-
P. Singh
Accounts Dept.

Example 10 : Office note requesting additional workers

KANPUR METAL WORKS LTD.

Ref: F/02/396 Date: 15.07.2002

From: Factory Manager
To: Personnel Manager
Subject: Additional workmen

Three separate work orders have been accepted by the production department during the last week. The deadlines for these work orders almost coincide with those that are currently being processed.

Contd...

In these circumstances, additional workmen are urgently required who are willing to work in multiple shifts. It is therefore suggested that contract workers be hired for work in this department for a period of two months.

Sd/-
R.K. Tiwari
Factory Manager

Example 11 : Office note requesting more funds for advertisement campaign

METRO CHEMICALS LTD.

Ref: CM/23/002 Date: 16.07.2002

From: Marketing Deptt. To: Executive Director, Finance

Subject: Additional funds for advertisement campaign.

The consumer goods market is increasingly experiencing a stiff competition among different brands across product lines. In certain cases, relatively inferior quality products have been able to push through their sales volume on the strength of robust advertisements.

In a situation like this, our product superiority needs to be re-asserted in customers' minds. I, therefore, request you to allocate more funds for a phased advertisement campaign, as compared to last year.

Sd/-
P. Prahlad
Manager (Marketing)

Chapter 18

Report Writing

Defining Report

A business report is an orderly and objective communication of factual information that serves a business purpose.

The key words in this definition. . ., Factual information. . . and the like. To be classified as a business report, a report must serve a business purpose.

Following steps are required to be followed to write a report effectively:

STEP 1: Pre-writing

1. Determine the exact objective of the report—understand clearly the particular business need for which the report is sought.
2. Plan and conduct background research and data gathering.
3. Document all reference materials collected.
4. Organise all gathered information into a logical sequence as a working plan.

STEP 2: Writing the first draft

1. State the subject and purpose of the report.
2. Provide an executive summary—a synopsis of the recommendations and conclusions. (It is a way of practising etiquette—of giving the readers the most important information right away).
3. Body of the report—showing the factual information in detail. Provide charts, graphs etc., where necessary.
4. Write the conclusion and provide recommendations as a logical sequence of the findings.

STEP 3: Revising and preparing the final draft

1. Read through the first draft and see whether information presented is complete.
2. Ensure that opinions are separated from facts.
3. Check whether presentation of information is concise.
4. Proof read your report for errors in spelling and grammar, and check style, layout, etc.
5. Finally, seek suggestions for improving your final draft report. Good writing is often a joint project.

Business Reports are of two kinds —

(1) Shorter Reports, and

(2) Long, Analytical Reports.

For the preparation of examination purpose, we shall focus on two types of the shorter report forms, namely,

(*i*) The Schematic Report, and

(*ii*) The Letter Style Report.

Example 1: A schematic report.

TECHNOSUPER COMPANY LTD.

Salt Lake, Kolkata

Report on Employee Involvement in Management

To: Mr. Gautam Mukherjee, CEO

From: Mr. K. Raman, Manager, HRD.

Executive Summary

A. Employee involvement can be used to improve labour-management relations, achieve increased productivity and efficiency.

B. Employee involvement needs to be done in phases. Adequate training in employee involvement procedures must be given. Commitment and education are necessary for the success of this method.

Terms of Reference

To determine if employee involvement is suitable for our company.

Action Taken

1. Reviewed case histories of four leading Indian companies in our field relating to employee participation in management.
2. Interviewed top level managers, labour leaders and employees of such companies.
3. Reviewed the employee incentive systems and studied in detail the significant labour management problems in our company pertaining to the last 3 years.
4. Analysed the current structure and organisation of our company and evaluated ways in which employee participation would impact our company.

Findings

1. Case studies of the four selected companies reveal that if properly administered, the employee participation programme has been a success.
2. Interviews of executive managers of such companies have revealed that employee participation resulted in an increase in productivity morale, fail in absenteeism and labour-management conflicts. The transcripts of interviews are shown in Appendix I.
3. Job satisfaction has significantly increased in such companies, resulting in low resignations and employee turnover. Questionnaires and the responses are in Appendix II.
4. In our company in four out of five instances of significant labour unrest during the past 3 years, it is observed that the standards set by middle level management were found difficult to be compiled with. Workers' grievances were not properly addressed.
5. There is considerable lack of motivation among employees in our company. They are also apprehensive about their future growth prospects.

Conclusion

Analysing our organisational set-up and interacting with a cross-section of our employees, it can be seen that a comprehensive scope for increasing employee productivity and efficiency exists.

Recommendations

1. In my opinion, employee participation in management needs to be instituted in our company.
2. Production standards and schemes of incentives should be set up after consultations with employee representatives at the production level.

3. Workers should be given adequate chance to influence the decision-making process. This can be done by eliciting suggestions from employees to solve work-related problems. Such suggestions will also help our company to cut costs in production.
4. Representation of employees in the Board of Directors will help the executive management to remain conversant with employee concerns.
5. The procedure of employee participation needs to be instituted in phases, gradually from the middle and line managers down to the workers.
6. Proper training and education programmes need to be undertaken to educate managers for administering this programme.
7. A sound follow-up and monitoring needs to be done by the top executive management.
8. Commitment from both the management and the employee representatives are required to make this programme successful.

K. Raman
12th June, 2002

Example 2 : A letter style report.

TRUSTWORTHY AUTO SPARES LTD.
JAIPUR

Date: August 9, 2002

To : R. Sharma, Production Manager

Subject: Report on safety conditions at factory premises.

As per your request to examine the safety conditions at our factory premises, a complete examination has been made with findings as follows:

The manual on safety norms and guidelines issued from time to time are properly understood and observed by the workers. The emergency exit mechanism was drilled by the workers last week and is found to be in satisfactory condition. Fire extinguishers are in place and in good shape. However, a more in-depth examination has revealed a few shortcomings, which are detailed below.

Our production processes require steam — which is generated by the boiler-tubes. On inspection, these tubes revealed deposits of thick scales, formed due to the use of hard-water. The de-scaling processes are not very frequent since production generally gets delayed. It is therefore suggested that descaling be done at least twice a month on a fixed schedule and in a phased manner to avoid all possibilities of accidents resulting from bursting boilers.

Given that the number of employees have increased in the work area, a short training programme may be conducted to acquaint them with the use of hazardous operations such as metal-cutting.

The need is felt that the ventilation system in the work area be further improved to allow free passage to the acid fumes which sometimes tend to accumulate causing respiratory troubles for the workmen.

Finally, it is recommended that the process of employee-feedback on the safety measures and suggestions for improvements, be strengthened for instant remedial measures.

M. Shukla
Factory Manager

Chapter 19

Meeting, Agenda and Minutes

Meetings

Under the companies Act, a company is required to periodically hold various types of meetings of its shareholders (or members) and the directors to review its functioning and also to validate the future plans of the company. All such meetings must be properly convened and constituted.

For the purpose of Examination, we need to focus on two types of meetings —

(*a*) Annual General Meeting of the Shareholders, and;

(*b*) Board Meeting of Directors of the Company.

Notice

To ensure that a meeting is valid, every member of the Company must be properly notified. Normally, a General Meeting of a company is called by serving notice to members at least 21 days before the date of the meeting. To convene a Board Meeting, the Company Secretary issues notices to each individual director on behalf of the Board. However, the stipulation of 21 days, as applicable for General Meetings, is not mandatory for Board Meetings.

Agenda

The word agenda means, "List of items of business to be considered at meeting." It is the programme or arrangement in order of importance of the items to be discussed at a meeting. It is a common practice to send to directors or members an agenda or a list of items of business proposed to be transacted at a meeting.

The format of a notification of a meeting is given below:

Name of the Company
Address Date Addressee
Body
Signature

The *examples* below illustrate the notification of meetings.

Example 1: Notice convening a Board Meeting.

BISCUIT – KING INDUSTRIES LIMITED

Hungerford Street,
Kolkata
Dated: June 12, 2002

To
Ms./Mr. ABC
Mumbai – 900 001

Dear Madam / Sir ,

Notice is hereby given that a meeting of the Board of Directors which will be held at the registered office of the company at Hungerford Street, Kolkata, on June 24, 2002 at 1 p.m.

You are requested to make it convenient to attend the meeting.

A copy of the agenda of the businesses which are likely to be transacted at the meeting is enclosed for your perusal.

Yours faithfully
For Biscuit-King Industries Ltd.,
S. Smart
Secretary

Encl: Agenda

Agenda

1. The Chairman to announce that the quorum for the meeting is present.
2. To consider the minutes of the previous meeting.
3. The Chairman to make a statement commenting upon the working of the Company.
4. Discussion of the Report of the Audit Committee.
5. To consider setting up of the Investors' Grievance Committee.
6. To consider the applications for share transfer.
7. Any other business with the permission of the chair.
8. Fixing the date of the next Board Meeting.

(Note: Notice should be sent to each individual director with a copy of agenda of the meeting.)

Example 2: Notice and Agenda of an Annual General Meeting

SUNSHINE INDUSTRIES LIMITED

Registered Office: 15, Juhu Road, Mumbai

NOTICE

Notice is hereby given that the eighty-third Annual General Meeting of the members of Sunshine Industries Limited will be held on Tuesday, 6th August, 2002 at 10.30 a.m. at the company's registered office at 15, Juhu Road, Mumbai, to transact the following business:

Contd...

1. To receive, consider and adopt the Audited Profit and Loss Account for the year ended 31 st March, 2002, the Balance Sheet as on that date and the Reports of the Directors and the Auditors thereon.
2. To declare Dividend on the issued Equity Share Capital of the company for the year ended 31 st March, 2002.
3. To appoint a Director in place of Mr. P. Kelkar, who retires by rotation and being eligible, offers himself for reappointment.
4. To appoint M/s. Honest Brothers, Chartered Accountants, as auditors of the company for the financial year 2002-2003 and authorise the Board of Directors to fix their remuneration.

By order of the Board of Directors
Ravi Mennon
Company Secretary

Conduct of Meetings and Procedures

A properly convened meeting is conducted by the Chairperson who exercises authority in controlling the course of the meeting. The Chairperson is entrusted to maintain order and decorum, decide priority of speakers, adjourn the meeting (if required) or may even give a casting vote, i.e., to vote in case of a tie).

However, while the meeting is in progress, it is the responsibility of the company secretary to record all the relevant points raised by members (in AGM) or directors (in Board Meeting). The official record of the proceedings of a meeting, including the decisions adopted, is known as the "minutes".

After the agenda has been discussed, the Chairperson puts to vote certain matters listed in the agenda and on obtaining a majority vote, validates them. Such a process is known as adopting "resolutions".

Minutes

The "minutes" of a meeting refers to the official record of the matters considered in the meeting and the resolutions adopted. It is prepared after the meeting by briefly recording the relevant matters transacted at the meeting. The minutes of any meeting must be prepared within 30 days from the conclusion of such meeting. Though the minutes are prepared by the Secretary, the Chairperson must sign it within 30 days of the meeting. The minutes of each meeting must contain a fair and correct summary of the proceedings.

Example 3: Minutes of a Board Meeting

Minutes of the monthly meeting of the Board of Directors of ABC Ltd., Jaipur, held on August 2, 2002 at 1 p.m. in the Board Room of the Company's registered office.

Present :

1. Mr. Soumya Mukherjee, Chairman
2. Mr. Avishek Chandra, Director
3. Ms. Seema Arora, Director
4. Mr. Asif Gulzar, Director

In attendance: Mr. K. Kumar, Secretary

Leave of absence granted to:

1. *Ms. Preety Singh, Director*

Decisions :

1. The minutes of the meeting of the Board held on June 18, 2002, were confirmed.
2. The Board noted the appointment of Mr. Sunil Dev, director of the company as a Whole Time Director of the Company.
3. The Board was informed that a plot of land measuring 1500 sq. mt. near Gurgaon was suitable for setting up a branch for sale of the company's products.
4. The company secretary was authorised to issue notices to all members, calling the 5th AGM of the company to be held on August 30, 2002, along with a copy of the company's annual report.
5. The next meeting of the Board will be held on September 21, 2002, at the registered office of the Company.

The meeting ended with a vote of thanks to the chair.

Jaipur

Dated: August 16, 2002 Signature: K. Kumar Signature: S. Mukherjee

Secretary Chairman

Resolutions

The dictionary meaning of the word "resolution", is "a formal proposal put before a public assembly or the formal determination of such proposal on any matter". Thus, a resolution is the formal expression of opinion of a meeting. It reflects the will of the company or the extent to which the executive of the company intends to act. The resolution of a meeting are officially recorded in the "minutes" of that meeting.

Resolutions are of two kinds:

(*a*) Ordinary Resolutions, and;

(*b*) Special Resolutions.

Some specimen of ***Ordinary Resolutions*** are given below:

Example 4: Appointment of Whole Time Director in General Meeting.

"Resolved that pursuant to the provisions of section 257 of the Companies Act, 1956, Shri Soumik Paul be and is hereby appointed a Whole Time Director of the Company effective from September 1, 2002, and that he may be paid remuneration by way of salary, commission and perquisites in accordance with the provisions of the Act."

Example 5: Re-appointment of Director in General Meeting.

"Resolved that Shri Saurabh Agarwal, Director of the company, who retires by rotation and being eligible, offers himself for reappointment, be and is hereby reappointed as a Director of the company for a period of five years effective from September 1, 2002."

Example 6: Rectification of name of Company in General Meeting.

"Resolved that as per directions of the Central Government pursuant to the provisions of section 22 of the Companies Act, 1956, the name of the Company be changed from 'Imperial Company Ltd.' To 'Modern Company Ltd."

Some specimen of ***Special Resolutions*** are also given below:

Example 7: Conversion from private company to public company.

"Resolved that the company be converted into a public company.

Resolved further that the articles of association of the company be altered by deleting article. .., that is, the article which contains the restricting, limiting and prohibiting provisions.

Resolved further that the name of the Company be changed from ABC (private) Ltd. to XYZ Ltd."

Example 8: Resolution to buy-back a company's own shares, in General Meeting.

"Resolved that the consent of the Company be and is hereby accorded to the Board to purchase or buy-back its fully paid-up equity shares of the face value of Rs. 10 each upto a maximum of 25,00,000 equity shares and outflow not exceeding Rs. 650 per equity share."

Working Notes

Working notes refer to the summarised, personal notes carried by a member relating to the debate on the draft resolution(s) in a meeting. Such working notes usually contain the arguments on the pros and cons of resolutions, which are proposed to be adopted.

Action Plan and Action Taken Report

To translate the resolutions adopted in the meeting into concrete actions, detailed plans are formulated to methodically execute such actions. These plans are generally called "Action Plans". For example, when the Board of Directors formally adopts the annual sales budget, the Director of Marketing charts out a series of programmes with the Directors of Finance, Productions and Operations and a host of other groups to translate the sales budget into actual sales during the year. Such proposed programmes are the Action Plans.

The Action Taken Report highlights the targets set by the Action Plans, their successes and failures, and the details of how such Action Plans were implemented.

Chapter 20

Summarising or Precis Writing

A summary or a precis is one of the most effective and disciplined form of communication. Since a precis is intended to be both "brief' and "to the point", repeated exercises of writing precis cultivates a sense of judgement to select the essentials of a given passage and strictly exclude the non-essentials.

However, a summary and a precis differ slightly. In a summary , the writer has a certain amount of freedom in the arrangement of the summary , while a precis follows a set of definite rules. To illustrate, a precis is written in a single paragraph, but a summary may be arranged in paragraphs, if required.

Steps to write a good precis

(1) Read the given passage thoroughly to understand the central idea.

(2) Recognise key words, phrases and sentences and underline them.

(3) Note down briefly the essential facts and ideas.

(4) Do not alter the sequence of facts/ideas as given in the passage.

(5) Write a draft precis in your own words.

(6) Check up the length of the precis and then write the final draft.

(7) Add a title to the precis (even if the question is silent about it) so that it reflects the topic of your precis.

Length of the precis

The length of a precis works out at one-third of the original, unless otherwise instructed into the question. The best way to prepare the draft precis is by making a squared sheet (like a grid) with six to eight squares in a line. This helps to keep a count on the number of words used. Here are some specimens worked out.

Example 1: Make a precis of the following passage:

"Although the world is, so far as the buying and selling and exchanging of goods are concerned, a single whole, there are still barriers between nation and nation, barriers erected by the governments. For four years, from 1914 to 1918, the most destructive war that the world has known took place between the great nations of Western Europe. The causes of that war were very many, but chief among them were fear and pride. Each nation was afraid of the power of the other nations and each nation was too proud to admit it.

And because of this fear the nations spent great quantities of money in making rifles and cannons, in building battleships and in training soldiers, until Europe was like a big armed camp. A single match will set a hayrick ablaze, and, with all this war material lying about, Europe was like a hayrack waiting for its match. Almost any match would do; presently somebody struck one, and Europe blew up." [No. of Words: 164]

Solution: Main points-

(*a*) The world, in terms of market economies, is unified.

(*b*) Governments create obstacles and disunite countries.

(*c*) From 1914 to 1918, Western Europe was engaged in war.

(*d*) Arrogance and mutual fear caused such nations to stockpile armaments.

(*e*) A single instigation erupted a great war.

Rough draft—

Even	though	the	world,	in	terms	of
market	economies,	is	unified,	governments	of	different
nations	create	obstacles	and	disunite	countries.	From
1914	to	1918,	countries	of	Western	Europe
were	engaged	in	a	terrible	war.	Arrogance
and	mutual	fear	caused	such	nations	to
stockpile	armaments.	Only	a	single	instigation	was
enough	to	erupt	a	destructive	war.	

Final draft

DISUNITY LEADS TO WAR

Even though the world, in terms of market economies, is unified, governments of different nations create obstacles and disunite countries. From 1914 to 1918, countries of Western Europe were engaged in a terrible war. Arrogance and mutual fear caused such nations to stockpile armaments. Only a single instigation was enough to erupt a destructive war. (55 words).

Example 2: Draft a precis—

"First and foremost there are order and safety. If today I have a quarrel with another man, I do not get-beaten merely because I am physically weaker and he can knock me down. I go to law, and the law will decide as fairly as it can between the two of us. Thus in disputes between man and man right has taken the place of might. Moreover, the law protects me from robbery and violence. Nobody may come and break into my house, steal my goods or run off with my children. Of course there are burglars, but they are very rare, and the law punishes them whenever it catches them.

It is difficult for us to realise how much this safety means. Without safety those higher activities of mankind which make up civilisation could not go on. The inventor could not invent, the scientists find out or the artists make beautiful things. Hence order and safety, although they are not themselves civilisation, are things without which civilisation would be impossible. They are as necessary to our civilisation as the air we breathe is to us: and we have grown so used to them that we do not notice them any more than we notice the air." (206 words)

Solution: Main points—

(*a*) To start with, obedience to law and a sense of security is present.

(*b*) Law and justice have replaced the rule of force.

(*c*) The legal system shields individuals from robbery and violence acts.

(*d*) Though exceptions rarely occur, the law is punitive in such cases.

(*e*) Evaluating the worth of safety is difficult.

(*f*) Law and order propel civilisation.

(*g*) They help in—
1 invention 1 discovery 1 creation of art.

(*h*) Order and safety are preconditions to civilization.

(*i*) Though their pervasiveness is imperceptible, they are really indispensable.

Rough draft—

To	start	with,	obedience	to	law	and	a
sense	of	security	is	present.	Law	and	justice
have	replaced	the	rule	of	force.	The	legal
system	shields	individuals	from	robbery	and	violent	acts;
for	exceptions,	the	law	is	punitive.	Evaluation	of
worth	of	safety	is	difficult.	Safety	propels	civilisation
It	helps	in	invention,	discovery	and	creation	of
art.	Order	and	safety	are	pre-conditions	to	civilisation
Though	overlooked,	they	are	indispensable			

Final Draft

ORDER AND SAFETY: GUARDIANS OF CIVILISATION

To start with, obedience to law and a sense of security is present. Law and justice have replaced the rule of force. The legal system shields individuals from robbery and violent acts; for exceptions, the law is punitive. Evaluation of worth of safety is difficult. Safety propels civilisation. It helps in invention, discovery and creation of art. Order and safety are preconditions to civilisation. Though overlooked, they are indispensable. (69 words).

Chapter 21

Letters of Enquiry / Requests for Quotations and Replies

In a trading transaction, the buyer needs to gather information regarding possible sources of supply, inquire from suppliers about their prices and terms of sale, evaluate the best terms he can get from such sellers and finally place his order .

Letters of enquiry are requests made by prospective buyers to sellers, asking the latter to send details regarding their usual terms of sale in respect of the nature and quality of goods required by such buyers.

A letter of quotation is a seller's reply to a buyer's enquiry , providing the information briefly states the terms of supply, the prices, mode of delivery, etc. Sometimes a quotation contains a clause that due to changing market conditions, the stated terms and prices would remain valid for a specified period only. The letter of quotation is accompanied by an illustrated catalogue and price list, and if possible, samples of the goods sought for.

Some ***examples*** of letters of enquiry and replies are given below.

Example 1: Letter inviting a quotation

KIDS CORNER

Lindsay Street, Kolkata

Popular Garments Ltd.,
Chennai

Date: July 15, 2002

Dear Sirs,

We are a reputed house of retailers dealing in all sorts of kidswear . We are interested in placing bulk orders with you relating to all assortments of kids-apparel, for the age group of 2 to 12 years.

Kindly send us your catalogue and price list at the earliest possible.

Yours faithfully,
T. Basu
General Manager

Example 2: Reply to the above

POPULAR GARMENTS LTD.
Chennai

The General Manager
Kids Corner
Lindsay Street, Kolkata

Date: July 23, 2002

Dear Sir,

We appreciate your prudence in enquiring of our range of kidswear .We are confident that our variety of kids-apparel will match your quest for quality and price.

We are pleased to enclose our latest price list along with the catalogue as requested by you, and a supplementary brochure. We provide a trade discount of 12% for wholesale orders, plus an incentive discount of upto 8% depending upon order size.

Please do let us know of any other details that you may require of us.

Thanking you,
Yours faithfully,
R. Ramesh
Manager (Marketing)

Encl.: Two

Example 3: Enquiry made by a small firm regarding a suitable accounting software

SUPREME RETAILERS
Dhanbad

The Sales Manager
Simplysoft Computek Ltd.
Kolkata

Date: July 17, 2002

Dear Sir,

We are much interested to know about the various accounting softwares that you have in offer for small firms engaged in retail business.

Our business accounting involves, inter alia, the following:

(1) Daily computation of sales and commission for travelling salesmen;

(2) Ascertainment of regular stock positions;

(3) Weekly computation of dues to suppliers;

(4) Preparation of monthly and annual revenue statements.

In view of the large masses of detail, we would like to install a software that would help us maintain our regular accounts better .

Please let us know at the earliest, the softwares that would suit our business needs, their costs (including installation) and the after-sales services that we may expect.

Yours faithfully,
M.K. Sinha
Proprietor

Example 4: Reply to the above

SIMPLYSOFT COMPUTEK LTD.
C.R. Avenue, Kolkata

The Proprietor
Supreme Retailers,
Dhanbad

Dated: July 27, 2002

Dear Sir,

We have immense pleasure in informing you that we have a tailor-made solution to your accounting needs.

We have carefully studied your business profile and sincerely believe that our specially built accounting software "LIVEWIRE" is just ideal for you.

Designed specially for small businesses, LIVEWIRE is Windows based and adaptable to specific needs.

The entire package is available for Rs. 12,000 only. However, for orders placed before August 10, 2002, we will provide a flat discount of 10% and installation will be free of cost. We provide a warranty of one year and an optional annual maintenance contract for a nominal price of Rs. 400.

We are confident of providing you value for your investment, and assure you of our best services at all times.

Yours faithfully,
C.K. Pandey
Sales Manager

Encl.: Brochure of LIVEWIRE

Example 5: Negotiations for better credit terms

RELIABLE ELECTRONIC STORES
Bhubaneshwar

The Manager (Marketing)
Unique Electronics Co Ltd.,
Kolkata

Date: July 12,2002

Dear Sir,

Re: Your Quotation of June 27

Thank you for your letter of 27th June, outlining your terms and conditions along with your price list and catalogue.

However, we must point out that your quoted trade discount of 9% fails to justify the substantial orders we proposed to place with you. In view of competitive offers received from similar wholesale-dealers of repute, we place the following proposal for your consideration:

(1) An additional trade discount of 2%, and

(2) A cash discount of 3% for 30 days for orders exceeding Rs. 20,000.

We hope it would be possible for you to arrange us these concessions in view of our current bulk order and subsequent large orders that we intend to place with you.

Yours faithfully,
R. Mohapatra
Proprietor

Example 6: Reply to the above.

UNIQUE ELECTRONICS CO. LTD.
Kolkata

Mr. R. Mohapatra
Proprietor
Reliable Electronic Stores,
Bhubaneshwar

Dated: July 20, 2002

Re: Your Letter of July 12

Dear Sir,

We thank you for your letter of 12th July. We appreciate your concerns. But at the same time we recognise that in view of the quality of goods offered by us, the trade discount of 9% is the best you can avail from the market.

The additional 2% trade discount coupled with the cash discount asked by you, is bound to compromise the quality of goods. Moreover, our quoted prices are inclusive of freight and packaging costs.

However, in view of your request, we shall be pleased to adjust 10% of the amount exceeding Rs. 80,000 worth of orders in any single calendar year .

We assure you of excellence in quality and service and await confirmation of your orders.

Yours faithfully,
P. Nath
Manager (Marketing)

Chapter 22

Invitation to Tender and Bid

A tender is a formal offer to execute work or supply goods at a fixed price. Organisations invite tenders and bids for particular construction activities (like engineering or architectural works), or for supply of specified goods and/or services (like maintenance services, etc.). They issue tender notices by publishing them in newspapers.

In response to such notices, interested parties collect the tender/bidding forms that contain the detailed requirements of the work or service to be executed. On the basis of these forms, such interested parties submit quotations (tenders) specifying their estimates of price for which they are willing to undertake the work, time schedule for completion of work, their previous experience, etc.

The tender forms are accepted till a specified day. After this, on a specified day and a specified time, all such documents are opened in the presence of the tenderers or their representatives, and the forms are scrutinised. The tender whose terms are the most favourable to the company/organisation inviting such tender, is finally awarded the contract.

A few specimen tender notices are shown below.

Example 1: A tender notice for providing maintenance services

EASTERN RAILWAY

Overhauling of CNC Machines
(JAMALPUR WORKSHOP)

Tender Notice No.: 411/WMP. Sealed tenders are invited from reputed firms having the capabilities for undertaking the maintenance of CNC Machines for overhauling of One No. CNC Chucker (Plant No.10294)

The Estimated Cost for the above work will be Rs. 9,64,000/- approximately. The firm should have adequate credentials of having carried out similar works with Railways/PSUs. Tender form can be obtained from the office of Dy. CME (Prod.)/Eastern Railway workshop Jamalpur on payment of Rs. 1000/- to the Workshop Cashier on any working day in between 11:00 hrs. to 16:00 hrs. from 10.07.2002 and up to 14:00 hrs. on 14.08.2002. Sealed Tenders should reach the Chief Works Manager/E.Rly./JMP Works latest by 14:30 hrs. on 14.08.2002. Tenders will be opened at 15:00 hrs. on the last day of submission i.e. on 14.08.2002.

Example 2: A tender notice for providing transport services

THE KOLKATA MUNICIPAL CORPORATION – TENDER

Sealed offers in duplicate from reliable Transport Agencies / Contractors for supply of hired Lorries (Small) to carry Men and Materials for 2002-03 throughout the Jurisdiction of Kolkata Mpl. Corporation under the supervision of the Asstt. Engineer, Outdoor Shop under Entally Workshop. The firm should have a good number of Lorries (small) with experience of supply of Lorries. He should have S.T. & I.T. clearance Certificate and Trade Licence. Offer will be received in the office of the Manager, E.W.S. on 12-07-2002 upto 2:00 p.m. Tender will be opened at 3:00 p.m. on the same date. The successful offerer will have to execute necessary clause of agreement before taking up the work. Necessary papers relating specification of the Tender will be available at the Manager's Office at 3, Convent Road, Kolkata -700014 on any working hours upto 11.07.2002.

Example 3: A tender notice for specified works

DIRECTOR OF FISHERIES,
ANDAMAN AND NICOBAR ISLANDS

On behalf of the President of India, the Director of Fisheries, A&N Islands, Port Blair, invites sealed tenders from reputed firms / manufacturers, contractors for following works:

(1) Design, supply, installation, testing and commissioning of 15f ton Fish storage capacity Cold Storage Plant to maintain -30°C ±2°C. Ambient room temperature and one 10 ton per day clear ice production capacity plant to be installed based on Ammonia Refrigeration system in the Cold Storage & Ice Plant Building constructed at Rangat (Middle Andaman)

TERMS AND CONDITIONS

(1) The tenderer shall obtain tender application form for the above referred purpose on payment of Rs. 250 (Rupees Two hundred & fifty only) in cash or by Demand Draft in favour of the Accounts Officer (Fy), Directorate of Fisheries, Port Blair.

Other terms and conditions are detailed in the tender documents, which may be obtained from the Accounts Officer (Fy), Directorate of Fisheries, Port Blair-744104.

The last date of receipt of application for tender documents will be 19-08-2002

The tender must reach the undermentioned on or before 3-00 p.m. on 28-08-2002 and they will be opened on the next day at 10-00 hrs. in the presence of the tenderers and their representatives in the Conference Hall of Directorate of Fisheries. The tenders received after 3-00 p.m. on 28-08-2002 shall be summarily rejected due to late receipt.

Director of Fisheries
A & N Islands

Example 4: A notice for sale of worn-out equipments.

THE KALYANI SPINNING MILLS LIMITED

Kolkata-700 013 Dated : 1-07-2002

WORN OUT TEXTILE MACHINERIES FOR SALE AS IS WHERE IS BASIS

Sealed Tenders are invited for the following machineries. MMC Card, Texmaco Ring Frame, Bundle press, Hank Drier, Rejected willow M/c, Blender parts, Beater parts of Blow Room.

Respective Machineries may be inspected at Kalyani Unit, Dist. Nadia and Habra Unit, Dist. North 24 Parganas during office hours. Earnest money @ 5% of the quoted tender value must accompany the tender form by Account Payee Demand Draft/Pay Order drawn in favour of .'The Kalyani Spinning Mills Ltd." payable at Kolkata.

Tender papers may be obtained during office hours on payment of Rs.100/- per set by demand draft payable at Kolkata in favour of Company within 15 days of the publication.

Last date of submission of Tender is 25th July 2002 up to 3.00 P.M. The authority reserves the right to reject any or all tenders in part or full and not to issue the tender papers to any party without assigning any reason thereof.

Sr. Sales Executive

Example 5: Tender notice inviting technical bid and price bid.

GREY IRON FOUNDRY

JABALPUR

The General Manger, Grey Iron Foundry, Jabalpur, invites separate sealed Tenders for TECHNICAL BID & PRICE BID pertaining to supply of the following items from original and established manufacturers with date of opening as shown against each item below.

Sl. No.	Reference	Description/ Nomenclature	Qty.	Date of Opening of Tender
1.	MOULDING MACHINE/EO	Jolt Squeeze type Moulding M/c.	One No.	27-08-2002
2.	FURNACE-3 TON/EO	Medium Frequency Induction Furnace with 3 Crucibles and 2 electricals	One No.	05-09-2002

Descriptions/Nomenclature shown above is only indicative. Detail specification for the items shown above shall be issued with tender documents Bidder can submit Tender for one or more item but separate Tender form to be used for each item.

BIDDER EXPERIENCE

1. The Bidder should be a reputed one and should have sufficient experience of manufacturing and supply of similar Equipment.
2. Bidders should have requisite facilities for manufacturing/testing and shop inspection as per National/ International standards.

The tender form can be obtained from the General Manager, Grey Iron Foundry , Jabalpur on payment of Tender Fee of Rs. 200 (Rupees Two Hundred only) for each items mentioned above by crossed Demand Draft drawn in favour of the GENERAL MANAGER, GREY IRON FOUNDRY, JABALPUR up to 12 noon on the date of opening of the respective Tenders as shown above.

The General Manager, Grey Iron Foundry, Jabalpur, reserves the right to accept or reject any application or tender without assigning any reason. In case of any dispute, decision of the General Manager, Grey Iron Foundry, Jabalpur will be final and binding.

Chapter 23

Placing and Fulfilling Orders

Subsequent to making enquiries, receipt of quotations and further negotiations of any, the buyer evaluates that seller' offer which is most favourable to him in terms of prices, quality, reliability, etc. and places the order. An order letter should be in exact terms in which the seller's offer was made. Otherwise, it becomes a counter offer and the seller has every right of not accepting the order.

The following points are to be taken care of while drafting an order letter:

1. Details regarding quantity, quality, size, packaging, mode of delivery, method of payment, insurance, etc. should be clearly mentioned;
2. In stating the price, total amount should be given both in figures and words;
3. When the order follows a quotation, the number be mentioned.

Some ***examples*** of orders and their replies are shown below.

Example 1: An order for paints.

PAINT HOUSE
Park Street, Kolkata

Ref:PN/02 Dated: July 15,2002

Unique Paints Co. Ltd.
Okhla Industrial Area,
Mumbai

Re: Order for paints

Dear Sir,

We thank you for your letter of July 7 and accept your enclosed quotation for paints. We have pleasure in placing the following order with you:

1. 12 doz. "Luxor" distemper tins, colour: lilac blue — @ Rs. 480 per doz.
2. 5 doz. "Royal" emulsion of 1 lit. each, colour: emerald green — @ Rs. 960 per doz.
3. 10 doz. Cement primer of 2 lts. each — @ Rs. 600 per doz.

We would appreciate a prompt delivery. Payment is subject to 9% trade discount and cash-on-delivery as per your catalogue. We request you to confirm despatch of goods by post.

Yours faithfully,
S. Roy
Manager

Example 2: Reply to the above

UNIQUE PAINTS Co. LTD.
Okhla Industrial Area, Mumbai

The Manager
Paint House
Park Street, Kolkata

Date: July 25, 2002

Sub: Confirmation of despatch of your order no. PN/02 dated 15.7.02

Dear Sir,

We have received your order and confirm having sent the order of paints through Express Road Carriers on 24.7.02, L.R. No.283. The invoice for Rs. 15, 070 after allowing a discount of 9% for cash-on-delivery (C.O.D) along with carriage charges for Rs. 1,500 is enclosed. We are confident that our products will meet your expectations, and await your future orders.

Yours faithfully,
P. Dave
Marketing Manager

Encl.: Invoice

Example 3: Order for electric fans

MASCOT AGENCIES
Chandigarh

Popular Electricals Ltd.
Chandni Chowk
New Delhi

Dated: July 17, 2002

Re: Order for fans

Dear Sirs,

We thank you for your letter of 10th July and the enclosed illustrated catalogue. We shall be glad if you will kindly send us by road, the following items listed in your catalogue, latest by August 5, 2002.

No.33	"Cooler" ceiling fan, 10 pcs.	@ Rs. 625 per pc.
No.42	"Chetak" table fan, 15 pcs.	@ Rs. 495 per pc.
No.53	"Delux" pedestal fan, 20 pcs.	@ Rs. 810 per pc.

Kindly ensure that the fans are packaged carefully. On receiving your consignment, we shall immediately remit the amount of the invoice. We shall be glad to receive confirmation of goods despatched by you.

Yours faithfully,
S. Tripathy
General Manager

Example 4: Letter from supplier requesting extension of delivery period to the above order.

POPULAR ELECTRICALS LTD.
Chandni Chowk, New Delhi

The General Manager
Mascot Agencies
Chandigarh

Dated: July 22, 2002

Dear Sir,

We acknowledge receiving your letter of July 17 and thank you for your order of fans.

However, we regret to inform you that due to some technical difficulties, production was suspended in our factory for three days. As a result, some previous commitments are also pending.

In the given circumstances, we will be able to fulfill your order latest by the 12th of August. If you will be kind enough to wait for this little period, we shall be glad to serve you with our usual promptness.

Yours faithfully,
M. Mittal
Sales Manager

Chapter 24

Sales Letters / Offers

The basic idea in writing sales messages to prospective customers involves selling something—either a product, a service or both. The *first* step in sales writing is knowing your products and services thoroughly. This will help you in making your potential customer understand, how your product works and what it will do.

Secondly, try to learn about your customers—identify their interests, needs and motivations. Knowledge about their economic status, age, professional standing, etc. will help you to adapt your sales messages so that your product or service fits their needs.

While writing a sales letter try to follow these steps —

(1) Gain positive attention in the opening of your sales message;

(2) Create desire in the reader's mind by introducing the right appeal, emphasising the supporting facts and stressing the "you" viewpoint;

(3) Provide complete information in all respects by including brochures, leaflets, etc.

(4) Attempt to secure a sale by urging your reader to act now; and

(5) Possibly, add a postscript.

These steps are similar to the AIDA strategy (attention, interest, desire, action), which was developed almost a century ago.

The layout of sales letters somewhat differs from that of ordinary business letters. For example, sales letters may use impersonal salutations such as —

"Dear Students",

"Dear Sir",

"Dear Customer", and the like.

A good sales letter kindles a strong interest in the reader's mind about your product or service and effectively drives the person for action.

Remember, imagination in writing sales messages will increase the possibilities of an actual sale — since you make your product or service too tempting to resist.

A few ***sample*** sales messages are given below.

Example 1 : A sales letter offering specialised financial services

Dear Mr. Roy: June 12, 2002

- Would an extra Rs. 80,000 a year make you better off?
- Has the tax-man walked off with the bulk of your earnings?
- Worried with financial problems?

Then just relax and tell us! We at "Arrows" will take complete care about your money matters, tax planning and consultancy needs all the year round. Our expertise is a product of 32 years of intensive research, study and experience that is both time -proven and hailed as among the best.

To make this extra income and save on your taxes, you will need to send us your corporate profile-investment details, income details for the last 3 years and a few other things which we will tell you later. After we process your information, you will get an eye-opening report. It will tell you how much money your investments should make, and how to make it. This will be followed by monthly reports telling you the best places to invest and save taxes.

Even your pattern of office management will receive thorough treatment. You will know how to cut costs and add to revenue. Also, we will effectively plan your taxes so that your tax-liability is reduced.

Trust us now and you will always. So won't you let your worries be ours and enjoy your profits in peace? All these and more will be yours for a modest investment of Rs. 15,000. So just fill out the enclosed form and mail it back in the addressed and stamped envelope provided for your convenience.

The extra income will justify your faith in us.

Yours Sincerely,

For "Arrows"

Money Managers and Consultants

K.Swamy

Partner

Encl.: Brochure

Example 2: An offer for a new variety of sunglasses.

Dear Customer: July 18, 2002

Your quest to wear the trendiest look ends here!

Introducing the "Nu Age" assortment of sunglasses from Montz. These ultra-lightweight, smart sunglasses are set to revolutionise the way you look. You can choose from over 500 assortments of various shades now available at all our city showrooms. With a starting range of Rs. 350 and extending upto Rs. 29 ,000, you can be sure to make the best-buy money can get.

Montz is the preferred choice of celebrities across continents and is set to become your favourite too. Adaptable for a variety of occasions, the Montz assortment protects your eyes from the harmful solar radiations.

So its time to check out at your nearest showroom and give yourself a truly international look.

Yours sincerely,
Montz International
Park Street, Kolkata

PS: Bring this letter before 31st July and avail an introductory 5% discount on all items.

Chapter 25

Circular Letters

A circular letter is a medium through which a business concern notifies all its customers about some fundamental change which has occurred or which it intends to bring about in the nature of its business activities. Generally, circular letters convey the following information:

(*a*) Opening of a new branch or outlet;

(*b*) Change of address;

(*c*) Launch of new products;

(*d*) Announcing seasonal discounts;

(*e*) Announcing the appointment of authorised distributors / selling agents;

(*f*) Announcing special installment schemes, etc.

Like sales letters, circular letters are also persuasive and often attractive. Even though they are direct in covering the information, they solicit custom and patronage.

Some *example* circular letters are illustrated below.

Example 1: A circular informing inauguration of a new branch

THE WONDER WORLD
C.R. Avenue, Kolkata

Date: July 12,2002

Dear Patron,

We have immense pleasure in announcing the inauguration of our new showroom at 10, M.G. Road, which is catering to all our valued clients from the tenth of this month.

This fully air-conditioned showroom houses all assortments of cards and gift items of all ranges for your convenience. Be it any occasion, or a special event you are sure to find the right card or gift to express your feelings. Our showroom is the ultimate one-stop shop for availing all the gift items you want.

We have always valued your continued support. As a token of appreciation we are offering all our existing customers a special 5% discount on all items purchased from our new showroom till the end of July.

Looking forward to your inspiration and patronage.

Yours faithfully,
R.K. Mathur
Partner

Example 2: Circular informing change of address.

FORTUNE RETAILERS LTD.
Mumbai

Dear Madam/Sir, Date: July 16,2002

We thank you for your immense support for all these years. With a view to serve you better, we have moved our retail store to the undermentioned premises.

"Skylark Apartments"
73, Dr. Baba Saheb Ambedkar Marg, (Ground Floor)
Our contact numbers are as follows:
2829562,2826293,2836751.

We trust that you will patronise this new venue just like the earlier one. With warm regards,

Yours faithfully,
S.Rao
Proprietor

Example 3: Circular announcing launch of a new product

HOMECARE INDIA PVT. LTD.
New Delhi

Date: July 24, 2002

Dear Madam/Sir,

You will appreciate that we have launched the extra-special oil-balance shampoo, as a part of our Bodycare Series.

This shampoo is herbal-based and is the result of our constant research and development. A single trial will help you realise its qualitative difference from any other brand. Its unique treatment will give your hair that ultra special health you have been wanting so long.

We are confident that as an user of our products you do not have the slightest of doubt regarding our excellent product quality. Since our products are only distributed through authorised distributors, we request you to order your pack soon.

With warm regards,

Yours faithfully,
A. Sareen
Marketing Manager

Example 4: Circular announcing seasonal discounts

THE SUNDAY CLUBS & RESORTS LTD.
Chanakya Puri, New Delhi

Dear Member, Date: July 15, 2002

We are privileged to present you with our special summer-retreat package of a round tour of Europe through 12 wonderful cities.

To make this summer really memorable, we are offering you free air-travel and a special discount of 15% for yourself and your family on the entire tour. For detailed information do call us at 2348954/2349823/2104896.

The trip is scheduled for August 5, and we would be obliged to receive your confirmation by July 25.
With best compliments,

Yours faithfully,
Y .C. Banerjee
Hony. Secy.

Example 5: Another circular announcing seasonal discounts

THE REGENCY
Middleton Row, Kolkata

Date: July 19,2002

Dear Patrons,

Being one of our esteemed customers, it gives us great pleasure to invite you to our store once again.

The end-of-season sale is being held at "The Regency" and select outlets. Get the finest menswear in India for 25% less, from 5th to 18th July, 2002.

You'll agree, this is a great opportunity for you to add more class to your wardrobe.

We look forward to seeing you soon.

Yours Sincerely,
Management and Staff
The Regency, Middleton Row
Kolkata

Chapter 26

Complaints and Replies to Complaints

Occasionally, when something goes wrong with the supplier's goods and services, the buyer writes to the supplier requesting that the problem be settled.

The causes for complaints may relate to -

(1) Receiving damaged or defective goods;

(2) Receiving only a part of the order;

(3) Delay in fulfilling order;

(4) Variations in the conditions of payment;

(5) Poor sales-support; or other problems. -

While handling complaints by writing, the following steps should be kept in mind-

(1) Identify the order (invoice number and date, nature of the product, etc.)

(2) Make a direct statement of the problem.

(3) Include all essential facts to support your claim, so that the supplier offers a fair adjustment.

(4) Explain what you expect from the supplier.

(5) Make a courteous close stating your confidence that the supplier will respond favourably to your claim.

On receiving a customer's complaint the supplier writes back — either offering adjustment to the problem, or refusing adjustment. An adjustment letter follows these steps —

Letter offering adjustments

(*a*) Begin directly offering an adjustment.

(*b*) Explain why the problem occurred and convince that it will not happen again.

(*c*) Try to gradually rebuild your customer's confidence and end courteously.

Letter refusing adjustments

(*a*) Assure the customer that you have understood the problem.

(*b*) Explain how you handled the claim — state clearly the results of your findings.

(*c*) State the refusal politely, based on your findings.

(*d*) Offer an alternative solution or substitute and end courteously.

Given below are a set of ***alternative replies*** to a problem.

Example 1: A complaint regarding defective items.

SUNSHINE CHEMICALS PVT. LTD.
Noida, Uttar Pradesh

August 5, 2002

Mr. C. Verma,
Sales Manager
Prakash Plastic Ltd.
Lucknow

Sub: Leakage of your "Tuff Plastik" containers. Your invoice C/95 dated Aug. 1, 2002

Dear Mr. Verma,

The condition, in which we received the 25 special containers, has made them unsuitable for the purpose for which we had ordered them.

On close inspection in our warehouse, we were shocked to see that at least 11 of such containers had thin cracks along the edges. Tests carried out confirmed that these containers would leak once liquid chemical is stored in them.

Since we urgently require these containers for fulfilling a customer's order, please replace this consignment by Friday, August 9.

Since these defects are not apparently visible, we understand this has happened despite your precautions. We would appreciate your promptness in replacing the containers.

Yours sincerely,
T .K. Pandey
Materials Manager

Example 2: Reply to the above offering adjustment.

PRAKASH PLASTICS LTD.
Lucknow

Mr. T.K.Pandey August 7, 2002
Materials Manager,
Sunshine Chemicals Pvt. Ltd.
Noida, U.P.

Dear Mr. Pandey,

Twenty-five new and thoroughly tested "Tuff Plastik" containers will reach you by August 9 in time for your sale. We have despatched them through our own carriage.

Since we value your satisfaction with our service, we have initiated steps to upgrade the Quality Control of our containers in the factory .We are confident of providing you with the best quality one can avail of. When the new containers reach you, please hand over the original lot to our carriers.

The durability of our "Tuff Plastik" products has already made them a preferred choice among customers. We are sure that they will help you win over your customers.

Yours sincerely,
C.Verma, Sales Manager

Example 3: An alternative reply from the supplier refusing adjustment

PRAKASH PLASTICS LTD.
Lucknow

Mr. T. K. Pandey
Materials Manager,
Sunshine Chemicals Pvt. Ltd.
Noida, U.P.

August 7, 2002

Dear Mr. Pandey,

We received your report of August 5, and had forthwith instructed our senior sales staff to inspect the "Tuff Plastik" containers at your warehouse and fix the problem.

From his report we learnt that after the delivery had been made, unintentional mishandling at your warehouse had put undue pressure on the containers causing them to slightly crack at the edges.

Since our containers are thoroughly checked before delivery and are built to withstand normal wear and tear, we regret that we cannot replace the containers.

However, we understand your concerns in meeting your customer's order. So, if you would like to urgently have a fresh batch of containers, we are ready to supply the same on time and without additional transit—charges.

With regards,

Yours sincerely,
C. Verma, Sales Manager

Chapter 27

Corresponding with Customers for Payment

Companies often use a series of letters urging their customers to pay their overdue debts. The nature of these letters (commonly known as Collection Letters) varies with the nature of the customers. Normally, such customers are of 3 kinds—

(*a*) customers willing to pay but require a mild reminder.

(*b*) customers who delay in clearing the overdue amount and require persuasive reminders.

(*c*) customers who are habitual delinquents wanting to evade payments. After all previous attempts fail, letters to these customers assume a tough tone, warning of actions. Such letters are called "letters of last resort" or "final collection letters".

Mild Reminders

The first collection letter is polite and reminds the customer about the unpaid bill. It suggests that perhaps the delay is due to oversight. It also indicates whether the customer is expected to remit a cheque in full, or make partial payments, etc.

Consider the ***examples*** below.

Example 1: A polite reminder

Mr. S. Ramesh
22, Vasant Kunj
New Delhi

August 6, 2002

Dear Mr. Ramesh,

We realise that it is probably just an oversight on your part, but our records show that a balance of Rs. 560 in your account is due just a little over two months.

We understand that this small amount could have easily escaped your notice. Please find a copy of the invoice enclosed for your convenience.

We would appreciate if you could remit the amount due by a cheque in the enclosed return-envelope. We look forward to your continued business.

Yours sincerely,
For Rehman & Sons
T. Rehman
Partner

Encl.: One envelope

Example 2: Another mild reminder

Mr. G. Verma
57, Regent Park,
Kolkata

Date: August 6, 2002

Dear Mr. Verma,

Your payment of Rs. 3520 now two months past due on your account has not yet reached us. We are sure that you would like to settle your account by sending us a cheque right away. Please find a return – addressed and stamped envelope enclosed for your convenience.

We genuinely appreciate your business. It would be our privilege to serve you again.

Yours sincerely,
For Crescent Traders Ltd.
M. Mehra

PS: If you have already sent the payment, please accept our thanks.

Persuasive Reminders

If a mild reminder proves ineffective, a stronger collection letter is sent to the customer. It is more direct than a mild reminder. But the tone of the letter is polite and the manner persuasive, expecting that the customer will still pay up. The letter ends urging immediate action from the customer.

Example 3: A persuasive reminder

Mr. Richard Mathew
8, College Road, Chennai

August 7, 2002

Dear Mr. Mathew,

We have always valued you as our customer and have appreciated doing business with you. Our records say that you have an impeccable "prompt pay" credit standing — and why not! Your record means so much to you in the trade.

This is exactly why we are amazed to find that your payment of Rs. 3560 is now 83 days overdue. We know, it is very painful for a man of your reputation to have such an account. So why don't you write a cheque for Rs. 3560 today and mail it to us right away? Then we are eager to forget the matter as a temporary lapse and keep your credit record in the preferred accounts where it belongs.

Yours sincerely,
For Genesis Distributors
R.K. Nath

Example 4: A more direct persuasive reminder.

Mr. B.K. Khaitan
47, Mysore Road
Bangalore

August 7, 2002

Dear Mr, Khaitan,

We hope the pair of generator sets, which you bought from us last April, is serving you well. You were indeed foresightful to acquire them early, because those sets are much dearer now. Surely, it was a good deal for you.

What is bothering us is that you have not let it to be a good deal for us too. You have permitted your account to remain overdue for over three months. Won't you please save your reputation by sending us a cheque for Rs. 6,950 now? We have enclosed an addressed envelope for your convenience.

We value our customers and always try to accommodate their needs. Your prompt action will help us restore your account in the preferred list.

Yours sincerely,
For Orient Machineries
D.Jain

Last Resort Letters

When delinquent customers have been given every reasonable chance to pay and still no reply or payment is forthcoming, the collection effort must end with a final letter. This letter is called a last resort or final collection letter. It is concise and forceful, and it tells the customers of the consequences if payment is not made. Before ending, the letter gives a final chance — a deadline for payment before action is taken.

Example 5: A last resort letter.

Mr. S Jadeja
49, C.R. Avenue
Kolkata

August 8, 2002

Dear Mr. Jadeja,

Your repeated failure to respond to our requests for payment of Rs. 7815, now 8 months past due, has forced our hands to take you to Court for collection. You have left us no other option. It means apart from the embarrassment of Court action, you would be forced to pay lawyer's costs, procedural costs plus the amount you owe us. It would also permanently damage your credit worthiness and goodwill.

You could still avoid these unsavoury consequences by remitting us the amount due within ten days from the date of this letter. It's all upto you to save your reputation and costs.

Yours sincerely,
For National Electronics,
Suraj Jalan

Chapter 28

Import and Export Correspondence

Import and export correspondences between an importer and an exporter pass through many intermediary stages, like agents, bankers, etc. Generally, the following steps are followed in importing goods:

(1) Placing of an Indent with the foreign supplier. (an indent is a formal order sent to the foreign exporter detailing quantity, quality, price, etc. of goods requisitioned);

(2) Arranging for a letter of credit (L/C) from the local banker favouring the exporter;

(3) Receiving information from exporter that goods have been shipped;

(4) Accepting or paying the Documentary Bill (A Documentary Bill is a Bill of Exchange drawn by the exporter on the importer. It is sent through an agent or banker. Unless this bill is either accepted or paid, the shipping documents are not handed over to the importer. An importer obtains delivery of goods only after presenting the shipping documents).

(5) Arranging for clearance of goods once the ship reaches the port.

The export procedure is typically reverse of an import procedure (such as receiving indent, L/C, sending Documentary Bill, etc.) with a few additional steps such as arranging shipment, paying freight and insurance, etc.

The following ***sample*** letters illustrate the import and export correspondences.

Example 1: Letter placing an indent with a foreign exporter.

UNIQUE TRADING CO. LTD.
Importers and Exporter
Kolkata

The Benson Foods, Inc.
Avenue of the Americas,
New York, USA

August 16, 2002

Dear Sir,

We are sending our Indent (No. MC/52) for the following:

1. 15,000 cans of "cooked trout" of 1 lb. each @ $ 1 — $ 15,000
2. 5,000 tins of 2 lb. each of "salmon" @ $ 1.55 — $. 7,750

Total $ 22. 750

Please negotiate documents as usual through our bankers, The National Bank of India, NY Branch. We will appreciate your usual promptness in handling this order.

Yours faithfully,
B.K. Roy, General Manager

Example 2: Letter requesting bank to arrange an irrevocable letter of credit favouring foreign exporter.

August 12, 2002

The Manager,
National Bank of India
New Delhi

Dear Sir,

Sub: Request for opening a letter of credit

We are an established business house engaged in the manufacture of precision scientific equipments. Related to our manufacture of the same, three sophisticated machineries are sought to be imported from Newton Equipments Inc. of Florida, USA.

Since the import entails furnishing of an irrevocable letter of credit in favour of Newton Equipments, Inc. we request you to provide the same in their favour for a value not exceeding $ 2 million and valid till September 30, 2002. We are willing to accept your usual terms as to furnishing security for the purpose.

Thanking you,

Yours faithfully,
For Scientific Research Emporium,
R.K. Sen (Partner)

Example 3: Importer informs exporter of arrangements to open a letter of credit

SCIENTIFIC RESEARCH EMPORIUM
New Delhi

August 16, 2002

Newton Equipments, Inc.
Florida, USA

Dear Sirs,

We have pleasure in informing you that we have asked our bankers, National Bank of India to open an irrevocable letter of credit worth $ 2 million in your favour, and valid till September 30,2002.

The credit will be confirmed and made available to you through the Florida branch of our bankers. Please forward your Documentary Bill through them and surrender the following documents upon our acceptance to the Bill.

- Bill of Lading (2 copies)
- Certificate of origin (1 copy)
- Consular Invoice (1 copy)
- Commercial Invoice (3 copies)
- Insurance Policy (1 copy)

Please confirm date of shipment through express mail.

Yours faithfully,
R.K. Sen (partner)

Example 4: Intimation of shipment from exporter

NEWTON EQUIPMENTS, INC.
State of Florida, USA

Mr. R.K. Sen, Partner
Scientific Research Emporium
New Delhi

August 30, 2002

Dear Mr. Sen,

Re: Shipment of your order no. 5/99 dated Aug .5, 2002

The three sensitive "Electronica" machines you ordered, were shipped to your care on August 29, 2002, on board SS Black Arrow. The machines have been specially packaged to prevent any in-transit injury. As per terms of payment, we have drawn on you at sight for the full amount of invoice through the National Bank of India, Florida Branch. The documents which you asked will be handed over to you on accepting the 'Documents against Acceptance' (D/A) Bill.

We sincerely appreciate your order and are confident of serving you in the years ahead.

Yours sincerely,
Neil Matson
Manager (Marketing)

Example 5: Requesting a Clearing Agent to receive imported goods from the ship

SCIENTIFIC RESEARCH EMPORIUM
New Delhi

Messrs. Roy and Roy
Shipping and Clearing Agents,
Strand Road, Kolkata

September 18,2002

Dear Sirs,

We request you to clear the undermentioned consignment on our behalf from the Calcutta Port, shipped to us by Newton Equipments, Incorporated, of Florida, USA.

The consignment details are:

Name of vessel: SS Black Arrow

Nature of goods: Machineries

Packages : Three fibre - board crates measuring $16' \times 15' \times 12'$ each bearing the mark "NEINC".

The ship is due at the Calcutta Port on Sep. 24, 2002. The necessary documents for clearance are enclosed. which are to be returned with the delivery of the consignment.

Your bills along with customs charges will be promptly paid after receipt of the goods.

Yours faithfully,
R.K. Sen (Partner)

Chapter 29

Correspondence with Banks

The majority of transactions between a bank and its customers are routine in nature. The correspondence with customers are generally carried out through printed forms. However, for business of specialised nature, correspondence needs to be carefully drafted to serve the purpose. Requests made to bank for overdrafts, loans, cash credits, etc. call for tactful drafting.

A few ***examples*** of correspondence with banks are shown below.

Example 1: Letter to bank for opening a current account

The Manager, July 9, 2002
Associate Bank of India,
Kolkata

Dear Sir,

Sub: Opening of a Current Account

We request you to open a Current Account in our company's name, effective from August 1, 2002. Please find the following documents enclosed:

(1) Copy of the Certificate of Incorporation of our company;

(2) Copies of the memorandum and articles of association;

(3) A Certified copy of the Resolution adopted by the Board of Directors of our company, dated July 6, 2002, authorising the opening of a current account with your branch;

(4) The specimen signatures of Mr. P. Sen, Managing Director, and Mr. N. Chaturvedi, Whole Time Director, who are authorised to operate the account;

(5) A crossed cheque for Rs. 35,000 drawn on National Bank of India; and,

(6) The application form and the pay-in-slip duly filled in.

We would greatly appreciate if you would kindly take the necessary steps to open the account. Please also send us a cheque book, a pay-in-book and the receipted counterfoil of the pay-in-slip sent by us.

We look forward to your active co-operation.

Yours faithfully,
For Bright Industries Ltd.
P. Sen
Managing Director

Example 2: Letter to bank for cash credit facilities

The Manager, July 2, 2002
Bank of Hyderabad,
Hyderabad

Dear Sir,

We request you to kindly grant us cash credit facilities to the extent of Rs. 1 lakh, for three months starting July, 2002.

The imminent need to increase production keeping in view the ensuing festive season, is constrained by a shortage of funds. Your help in this regard would enable us to tide over this problem.

We are willing to offer 1200, 5% IDBI bonds of Rs. 100 each as security. The audited copies of our financial statements are also enclosed for your reference.

We sincerely hope that it would be possible for you to grant us this accommodation. Your early response is eagerly awaited by us.

Yours faithful)y,
For Rahul Industries Ltd.
Ravi Gupta
Managing Director

Example 3: Letter to bank asking for higher credit limit.

The Manager, July 4, 2002
People's Bank of India,
Chennai

Dear Sir,

We highly appreciate your promptness in arranging us a cash credit facility to the tune of Rs. 7 lakhs. However, a revised sales plan has forced us to increase production by almost 15%. Due to this sudden increase in production, our funds requirement has also gone up. Under these circumstances, we would like to request you to kindly raise the maximum credit limit to Rs. 10 lakhs, till the end of August 2002.

For this purpose, we are willing to provide an additional security deposit of 3500 Central Government Stock of Rs. 100 each. We hope that this would prove adequate for the purpose.

Please let us know if we can provide you with any further details. We look forward to your cooperation and understanding.

Yours faithfully,
For Prakash Textiles Ltd.
Priyadarshi Chatterjee
Director Finance.

Example 4: Letter to bank requesting current account statement

The Manager,
National Bank of India
Kolkata

August 2, 2002

Dear Sir,

Re: Current Account No. CB/23

We request you to kindly send us our current account Statement (AC No. CB/23) for the month of July, 2002. This could enable us to reconcile our accounts.

Yours faithfully,
For Oriental Traders
S. Surana
Manager (Accounts)

Example 5: Request to bank for overdraft facility.

The Manager,
Oriental Bank
Trivandrum

July 10,2002

Dear Sir,

We approach you with a request to grant us an overdraft facility to the extent of Rs. 5 lakhs during the months of August and September, 2002.

Our expenses on a particular construction project have exceeded the budgeted estimates, leaving us short of funds for our current needs. The situation is expected to recover as large sums due to us by some of our customers will be realised by the middle or end of September, 2002.

In the absence of any collateral security, we are enclosing an indemnity bond signed by Mr. R. Saxena who has consented to be our guarantor. Mr. Saxena is a long-standing customer of your branch and a distinguished professional in his field.

Sincerely hoping that you would favourably consider our request, we await your early response.

Yours faithfully,
For Sky high Builders,
P. Desai
General Manager

Chapter 30

Insurance Correspondence

Insurance is a contract made by a person with an insurance company whereby the latter agrees to compensate the person against any loss, damage or destruction to property and life. Insurance other than on life, is known as General Insurance. This includes: (a) Fire Insurance, (b) Marine Insurance, and (c) Miscellaneous Insurance.

Mediclaim Insurance, Burglary Insurance, Workers' Compensation Insurance, etc. all fall under Miscellaneous Insurance business. Apart from General Insurance, we have Life Insurance that covers risks on one's life.

The insurance company undertakes any contract of insurance on the payment of a certain sum of money annually — called "premium". A policy of insurance is issued only after the insured pays this premium to the insurance company (i.e. the insurer).

A commercial concern corresponds with insurance companies to insure against loss and damage to property, loss of profit and also to insure the health of the management and staff.

Given below are some ***examples*** of insurance correspondence.

Example 1 : Letter intimating fire and requesting loss assessment.

The Divisional Manager,
Citizen's Insurance Co. Ltd.,
Kolkata

June 14, 2002

Dear Sir,

Re: Fire Policy No. F/32/02

We regret to inform you that a devastating fire broke out in our warehouse at 15, Strand Road on the night of June 12, 2002. The inflammable nature of the stock caused total damage before fire could be extinguished. Preliminary investigations by us suggest that a short circuit may have caused the fire.

Copies of stock records at our office reveal that the estimated loss of stock is about Rs. 1,20,000 in addition to our fire fighting expenses of Rs. 2000. We have not been able to salvage any stock.

Please arrange for your surveyor to call on us at once for an on-the-spot damage assessment. We look forward to your co-operation and an early settlement.

Yours faithfully,
For Universal Paper Co.,
S. Sinha, Manager

Example 2: Reply of Insurance Company to the above.

The Manager,
Universal Paper Co.,
Kolkata

June 18, 2002

Dear Sir,

We have received your letter dated June 14, 2002 and are sorry to know about the loss caused by fire in your warehouse.

Our fire surveyor will get in touch with you very soon and complete his spot survey of the damage. Your claim will be processed immediately after the surveyor's report is received.

Meanwhile, kindly fill in the necessary information and return the enclosed Claim Forms for our prompt action. Please also instruct your staff to fully cooperate with our surveyor for speedy collection of relevant details at your warehouse and office.

We assure you of prompt service and quality support.

Yours faithfully,
For Citizen's Insurance Co. Ltd.,
Sandip Dutta
Divisional Manager

Example 3: Letter from insurance company informing settlement of claim.

The Manager,
Universal Paper Co.,
Kolkata

July 3, 2002

Dear Sir,

Re: Settlement of claim. your fire policy no. F/32/02

You would be pleased to know that your claim for loss of stock has been duly processed by us. Examination of your Claim Forms in light of our Surveyor's report is found satisfactory.

Accordingly, we are enclosing a cheque for Rs. 1,22,000 drawn on National Bank in full settlement of your claim.

Kindly send us a receipt of the said amount as soon as possible. We assure you of our best services at all times.

Yours faithfully,
Sandip Dutta
Divisional Manager
Citizen's Insurance Co. Ltd.

Example 4: Letter to insurance company requesting renewal of policy and seeking an increased insurance cover.

The Manager, Marine Insurance
Delta Insurance Co. Ltd.
Chennai

July 16, 2002

Dear Sir,

Re: Policy No. M/33/02

Please find an enclosed cheque of Rs. 38,000 towards renewal of our Marine Insurance Policy (No. M/33/02) for the financial year 2002-03.

We would also like to request you to kindly raise the insurance cover from the existing Rs. 15 lakhs to Rs. 20 lakhs. Premium payable on a sum insured of Rs. 20 lakhs as per your existing premium schedule is included in our enclosed cheque of Rs. 38,000.

Should there be any difficulty with our proposal, let our old policy remain valid for renewal and excess premium paid may please be refunded.

Yours faithfully,
For Cargo Shippers Ltd.
Saket Shroff
Manager

QUESTIONS FOR REVIEW

Chapter 1

1. Explain the importance of communication in an organisation/business.
2. Why is feedback important in communication process?
3. Comment on the following :
   (a) Communication does not simply involve sending of message by a person.
   (b) Encoding the matter is an element of communication.

Chapter 2

1. Distinguish between :
   Upward communication and downward communication
2. "Horizontal communication facilitates coordination of interdependent activities" – Comment.

Chapter 3 & 4

1. State the major limitations of paralanguage.
2. Comment on the following :
   (a) Sign language cannot be complete substitute for a verbal communication in all cases.
   (b) Body language always speaks the truth while speaker may play with words to hide the truth.
   (c) No one can be held responsible for Informal Communication.

Chapter 5

1. What is active listening? What are the ingredients of active listening?
2. State the major obstacles to active listening?
3. Distinguish between positive and negative feedback.

Chapter 6

1. What are the barriers to communication?
2. How would you ensure good communication in a business?

Chapter 7

1. What are the factors that help to create effective communication?

Chapter 8

1. What is Group? Why group is important in an organisation?
2. State the important characteristics of a group.

Chapter 9

1. Explain briefly the ingredients of discussion.
2. State the factors that diminish the quality of group discussion.
3. Describe the factors that enhance the quality of a group.
4. Explain the role of group discussion in team work.

Chapter 10

1. State the advantages of formation of a group.
2. What problems the group members face when they form a group?

Chapter 11

1. "Brain storming sessions encourage alternative approaches of ideas" – Comment.
2. Distinguish between committee meetings and command meetings.
3. What is 'Delphi Technique', in group decision making process? What are the benefits and shortcomings of this technique?

Chapter 12

1. Discuss the steps a group undergoes in attempting to solve a problem.

Chapter 13 to 30

1. What are the requisites of a good business letter?
2. "The formal close of the letter must match the salutation in the letter" – Comment.
3. Give/Suggest some tips for effective writing of business letters.
4. Write a letter to a manufacturer asking for the price list for the products manufactured by him.
5. Write a letter of complaint to an electrical company that has supplied defective fans in response to your order for the same.
6. Draft a reply to your supplier who has sent a threatening letter to take legal action for non-payment of his bill amount.
7. Write a letter to your supplier of raw materials drawing attention to the inordinate delay in the monthly supply.
8. State the major guidelines which may be followed for drafting letters of complaints and for drafting their replies.
9. "A status enquiry letter is sent by a customer seeking information about price, quantity of goods etc.to be purchased" – Comment.
10. Write a reply to dealer who is interested in dealing in your "Knitting Machines" and asks for trade prices, earliest delivery date and catalogue.
11. Write a letter to your dealers giving reasons as to why you have decided to reduce their commissions on your goods.
12. Write a letter to one of your regular customers drawing his attention to the fact that you have not received any orders from him for the last six months.
13. What is a proposal? What guidelines may be kept in mind while drafting a proposal?
14. Draft a circular letter informing your client about the opening of a new branch at Chandney Chowk of Delhi.
15. Comment of the following :
    (*a*) "Circular letters are unsolicited letters".
    (*b*) "Chasing payments is a problem that has to be tackled with utmost care and cordiality".
    (*c*) "A memo is different from a letter".
    (*d*) "Office orders can be issued only by superiors".
    (*e*) "Office circulars and office notes mean the same thing".

16. Distinguish between :

    (*a*) Minutes and Reports, (*b*) Minutes writing and Report writing.

17. Write a circular letter to your dealers informing them about your efforts to improve the quality of the company's products and asking for their suggestions to push up the sales.
18. Write a letter to a dealer interested in dealing in your new brand of scooter, expressing your ability to execute an order.
19. Write a letter to your dealers communicating the off-season discount scheme.
20. As a wholesale dealer, write a letter to your supplier drawing his attention to the common complaint of your customers against the poor after-sales service.
21. Write a letter to your dealers offering attractive incentive schemes for achieving higher sales.
22. Write a letter to your delears informing them about the delay that is likely to be caused in executing their orders.
23. Write a letter to the consumers of your company's products about a revision in the prices, giving reasons.
24. As an Area Manager of a region, write a letter to the Sales Manager of your company giving reasons for the decline in sales during the past six months and also suggestions to reverse the trend.
25. Write a letter to one of your dealers who has despite reminders, not paid the outstanding bills, threatening legal action after a deadline for the final payment.
26. Write a letter to the Sales Manager of the company complaining against the irregular and delayed supplies which have badly affected your sales.
27. Write a letter to a dealer in gift items giving your requirements of various items of distribution among your clients for the New Year, and requesting him to quote his terms.
28. Write (*i*) a letter to the Area Sales Manager bringing to his notice non-fulfillment of sales target; and (*ii*) reply of the Area Sales Manager thereto.
29. Write a letter to one of your regular customers expressing your anxiety not having received any orders from him for almost four months.
30. Draft a tactful reply to a dealer who has requested for a further discount of 5% over and above 12.5% you already offered on a bulk order, showing your inability to accept to his demand.
31. Write a circular letter to your dealers announcing special off-seasonal discount on coolers, fans and refrigerators.
32. Write a letter in response to an enquiry from a customer desireous of purchasing some electronic items setting out the prices, terms of payments, delivery and assuring him of prompt services and full satisfaction.
33. A sudden strike has been called by the transport operators. As a result, there is a likelihood of delay in despatch of goods to the dealers. Draft a suitable circular letter addressed to them.
34. Write a circular letter to your dealers about launching of a new consumer product.
35. Draft the following:

    (*i*) An office circular to employees emphasising the need for proper use to telephone in the office.

    (*ii*) An office order banning smoking in the office premises, except the canteen.

36. Draft the following:

    (*i*) A circular inviting employees to the silver jubilee function of the company.

    (*ii*) An office order banning smoking in the office premises.

37. Draft the following :

    (*i*) An office circular warning employees proposing to go on a day's token strike..

    (*ii*) An office order informing employees that late arrival by more than ten minutes would be henceforth be treated as half-day leave.

38. As a Personnel Officer of the company, draft the following:
    (*i*) An office order asking employees to strictly adhere to the office timings.
    (*ii*) A circular informing employees about the Board's decision to introduce productivity-linked bonus scheme in the company.
    (*iii*) A note to the Chairman of the company to revise the rates of conveyance allowance allowed to the employees.
39. Draft the following:
    (*i*) An office circular to employees not to remove newspapers and magazines from the staff lounge.
    (*ii*) An office order requiring employees to sign the attendance register at the specified time in both sessions.
    (*iii*) An office note annoucing suspension of transactions for two days due to annual stock-taking.
40. Draft the following :
    (*i*) An office order prohibiting smoking in the office in view of the ban imposed by the Government on smoking in public places.
    (*ii*) A circular informing employees about the new medical reimbursement scheme with ceilings for each category of employees.
41. Draft of following:
    (*i*) An office circular announcing the retirement of an employee of your organisation.
    (*ii*) An office order intimating transferring an employee to another department.
42. Draft the following:
    (*i*) An office order informing employees about the change in working hours of the office and also the reasons for effecting the change.
    (*ii*) A circular informing employees about re-starting the office canteen and advising them to use it only during a break.
43. Draft the following:
    (*i*) An office order banning employees from leaving the office during office-hours except with the exit-card to be issued by the departmental-in-charge for a specific purpose.
    (*ii*) A circular informing employees about the decisions of the management to provide free tea/coffee twice a day.
44. Draft the following:
    (*i*) An office order instituting and enquiry against an employee charged with misappropriation of cash.
    (*ii*) An office circular informing about certain vacancies to be filled in from amongst the employees and inviting applications therefore.
    (*iii*) An office note to the Personnel Manager of your company for revision of the rates of conveyance allowance.
45. Draft the following:
    (*i*) A circular to the employees informing them of the management's decisions to grant them housing loans.
    (*ii*) An office order insisting on strict compliance with the dress code on the part of the employees.
46. Draft the following:
    (*i*) An office order to prohibit smoking in the office premises, except in the canteen.
    (*ii*) A circular announcing a new incentive scheme for the employees to secure higher productivity.
47. Draft the following:
    (*i*) An address by the Chairman of a company announcing the commencement of a new business.
48. Draft the following:
    (*i*) An office order instructing the employees to keep the office clean, smoke-free and dust-free.
    (*ii*) An office circular informing the employees of the sale of furniture and equipment.

UNIVERSITY QUESTION PAPERS

PE-I Exam. 2002

ORGANISATION AND MANAGEMENT

Nature of Organisation and Management

Write short notes on the following:

Contingency Approach to Management. (4 marks)

State with reasons, which of the following statements are Correct and which are Incorrect:

Unity of Command means accountability of a subordinate only to one Superior. (2 marks)

Process of Management is common to every Organisation. (2 marks)

Business Environment

Write short notes on the following:

Elements of External Environment (4 marks)

Planning

Discuss briefly the obstacles to Effective Planning. (8 marks)

State with reasons, which of the following statements are Correct and which are Incorrect:

Tactical planning is carried out under more risky conditions than Strategic planning. (2 marks)

Decision-making

Distinguish between the following:

Programmed decisions and Non-programmed decisions. (4 marks)

The Function of Organisation

State with reasons, which of the following statements are Correct and which are Incorrect:

Both formal and informal relationships are depicted in the Organisational chart. (2 marks)

Individual Perspective

Distinguish between the following:

Motivation and Morale (4 marks)

Write short notes on the following:

Quality Circles (4 marks)

State with reasons, which of the following statements are Correct and which are Incorrect:

Intrinsic motivation includes such factors as wages, fringe benefits medical reimbursements, etc. (2 marks)

Groups and Group Dynamics

What is meant by Group Cohesiveness? Explain briefly the factors which influence group cohesiveness. (8 marks)

Introduction to Organisational Behaviour

Bhashi Television Company is a medium sized manufacturing organisation located in Faridabad, Haryana.

Ravi, earlier an operator in the Assembly Department of the company was promoted to the rank of a Foreman in the same department about six months back. He reports to Mr. Chawla, the Manager of Assembly Department.

Ravi feels disgusted, confused and powerless and meets Angela Bedi—the General Manager of the company and explains his situation to her as follows:

"My problem is that I am responsible for what results come out of my section. Yet I have so little authority to get these results. I am as foreman only as effective as my manager allows me to be. Unfortunately, my manager Mr. Chawla, likes to do everything himself. For example, he recruits workmen for my section without consulting me. I only get to know these people, when they report to me. The people I train and supervise are not always the people I would have hired. I have no idea what wages they are paid and I have no access to their personnel files. Mr. Chawla keeps everything confidential. Besides Mr. Chawla encourages the workers to contact him directly with their complaints against me. He scolds me in their presence justifying their complaints. He does not allow me to explain my viewpoint. I feel humiliated and helpless not knowing what exactly my job is about. I feel it is no use working under Mr. Chawla. I am seriously thinking of either quitting the job or going back to an operator's job."

Mr. Chawla is the departmental manager for the last three years during which time there has been a heavy turnover in foremen.

Angela Bedi has assured Ravi of some action in the matter.

Read the above case and answer the following questions:

(*i*) Why does Mr. Chawla behave the way he does? (3 marks)

(*ii*) Is it possible to get. Mr. Chawla change his approach towards Ravi? (3 marks)

(*iii*) If you were Ravi, what would you do? (3 marks)

(*iv*) What in your opinion could be the reasons for heavy turnover in fareman (3 mark)

(*v*) Would you recommend management to replace Mr. Chawla? (3 marks)

(*vi*) Do you think that it would be more appropriate for the management to shift Ravi to some other section? (3 marks)

Leadership

Discuss briefly the various measures for developing the leadership ability of Managers. (8 marks)

The Function of Control

Distinguish between the following:

Operational control and Management control (4 marks)

Objective

State with reasons, which of the following statements are Correct and which are Incorrect. (Attempt any four statements):

(*i*) Tactical planning is carried out under more risky conditions than Strategic planning.

(*ii*) Unity of Command means accountability of a subordinate only to one Superior.

(*iii*) Intrinsic motivation includes such factors as wages, fringe benefits medical reimbursements, etc.

(*iv*) Both formal and informal relationships are depicted in the Organisational chart.

(*v*) Process of Management is common to every Organisation. (4×2= 8 marks)

BUSINESS COMMUNICATION
PE-I Exam. 2002

Communication : Meaning, Importance & Process

Comment on the following statements in about 30 words each:

Communication does not simply involve sending of a message by a person. (1 marks)

Encoding the matter is an important element of Communication. (1 marks)

Dimensions/Directions of Communication

Comment on the following statements in about 30 words each:

Horizontal communication facilitates coordination of interdependent activities. (1 marks)

The Layout of Business Letter

Comment on the following statements in about 30 words each:

The formal close of the letter must match the salutation in the letter. (1 marks)

Letter of Enquiry/Requests for Quotations and Replies

Comment on the following statements in about 30 words each:

A status enquiry letter is sent by a customer seeking information about price, quantity of goods, etc. to be purchased. (1 marks)

Complaints and Replies to Complaints

State the major guidelines which may be followed for drafting letters of complaints and for drafting their replies-*(Answer to be given in about 200 words)* (10 marks)

Sales Letters/Offers

What is a Proposal? What guidelines may be kept in mind while drafting a proposal?- *(Answer to be given in about 200 words)* (10 marks)

Circular Letters

Comment on the following statements in about 30 words each:

Circular letters are unsolicited letters. (1 mark)

Insurance Correspondence

Draft a letter to an Insurance Company requesting to assess the loss by fire in the godown of your Company. (10 marks)

Memoranda

Comment on the following statements in about 30 words each:

A Memo is different from a Letter. (1 mark)

Office Orders, Circulars and Notes

Comment on the following statements in about 30 words each:

Office orders can be issued only by superiors. (1 mark)

Office Circulars and Office Notes mean the same thing. (1 mark)

Meeting, Agenda and Minutes

Comment on the following statements in about 30 words each:

The official recording of the proceedings of a meeting is called an Agenda. (1 mark)

Summarising or Precis Writing

Write a precis of the following passage reducing it to about one-third of its length:

Child labour is not a recent phenomenon. It prevailed in India as far back as three Centuries B.C., almost in the form of bonded labour. Kautilya's Arthashastra speaks in no uncertain terms of poor children kept as slaves in the houses of rich people. Despite efforts to control the evil of child labour, it still flourishes mostly in economically backward areas in our country.

The reasons for child labour in India are not far to seek. The prime reason for prevalence of child labour is poverty. Poverty stricken parents in order to supplement the meagre family income do not feel reluctant in sending their small children for work. The children get the job involving manual work with comparative ease because they can be hired with low wages. Also, child labour is more prone to exploitation, because he cannot raise any protest against employer on account of his weaker bodily strength. Besides, child labour cannot form a union and hence the absence of union is likely to be exploited. In certain cases, employees also force female workers to bring along with them their young children to be employed therein. Another important reason for the problem of child labour is lack of educational and cultural facilities for young children. In many far-flung areas in our country, schooling facilities are scarce and inaccessible. In many places schools not fully equipped with proper library, playing field and other educational infrastructure hold little attraction for children. In many cases children are forced to stay back at homes, because heir parents cannot afford educational expenses.

Children are mainly employed in the unorganised sectors like Agriculture, Small Restaurants, Construction work, Carpet manufacturing, in houses as domestic servants, etc. The number of child workers in the organised sector is comparatively quite low except in match factories etc. Reasons for employment of large number of children in match factories is that their small fingers are easy with match sticks and hence they work with good efficiency.

The available evidence shows that child labour in India is being exploited too much. He works for longer hours, in unhealthy conditions and for low wages. Agreed that physical work may not harm the health of child workers in all cases, but what is harmful is long and total irrevocable subordination to their masters. What kind of men they will grow up to be as there is no place for sensitivity and love in their lives. The exploitation and ceaseless hatred for the society make these children unhappy and pessimistic about the society they live in.

(10 marks)

Written Communication

Comment on the following statements in about 30 words each:

Sign language cannot be complete substitute for a Verbal Communication in all cases. (1 mark)

Body Language

Comment on the following statements in about 30 words each:

Body language always speaks the truth while speaker may play with words to hide the truth. (1 mark)

Para Language

State the major limitations of Paralanguage. (3 marks)

Formal Vs. Informal Channels of Communication

Comment on the following statements in about 30 words each:

No one can be held responsible for Informal Communication. (1 mark)

Techniques of Group Decision-Making

Comment on the following statements in about 30 words each:

Brainstorming sessions encourage alternative approaches of Ideas. (1 mark)

Corresponding with customers for payment

Comment on the following statements in about 30 words each:

Chasing payments is a problem that has to be tackled with utmost care and cordiality. (1 mark)

What is Discussion

Explain briefly the ingredients of Discussion. (7 marks)

Correspondence with Branch Office

Draft a letter from the Regional Sales Manager to the Area Sales Manager asking him to explain the drop in sales. (10 marks)

May, 2003

Total No. of Questions–12]

Time Allowed–3 Hours
Maximum Marks–100

Answer Questions **1** to **6** and any **four** questions out of Questions **7** to **12.**

Marks

1. *Comment on any* ***ten*** *of the following statements in about 30 words each:* 1 × 10 = 10

   (*i*) The basic purpose of communication is to issue orders to subordinates.

   (*ii*) Replies to letter of complaints should only be aggressive in tone.

   (*iii*) Communication need not be made in words alone.

   (*iv*) Confirmation of minutes of a previous meeting has always to be the last item on an Agenda of meeting.

   (*v*) Compilation of minutes of a meeting is a job of Chairman only.

   (*vi*) Command meeting is different from Committee meeting.

   (*vii*) Delphi technique of decision-making is different from Brainstorming technique.

   (*viii*) Circular letters differ from letters of quotation.

   (*ix*) Resolution and Action plans are directly related.

   (*x*) The space around us is also used as a source of communication.

   (*xi*) Office orders indicate downward communication.

   (*xii*) Communication is a social activity.

   (*xiii*) Sales letters are persuasive in nature.

   (*xiv*) A letter's appearance is a part of its message.

   (xv) Decisions taken by groups are always superior to those taken by individuals.

2. (a) "Communication in an organization is a multidirectional". Discuss the statement by explaining briefly the different types channels of communication based on directions of communication. 7

   (b) Explain briefly the various characteristics of Group Personality. 3

3. What do you understand by the term 'Report'? Explain briefly the points which are considered while writing a Report. (*Answer to be given in about 200 words*) 10

Or

Draft minutes with proper resolutions of an Annual General Meeting of shareholders of a Public Limited Company at which the following business was transacted : 10

   (*i*) Adoption of audited accounts of the company alongwith the reports of Auditors and Directors.

(*ii*) Declaration of Dividend.

(*iii*) Election of Directors.

(*iv*) Appointment of Auditors.

4. What are Circular letters ? How are they different from Office circulars ? Explain briefly the main objectives of writing circular letters. (*Answer to be given in about 200 words*) 10

Or

A bank has received a request from an old customer for enhancing his overdraft facility on his personal guarantee. Draft a suitable reply. 10

5. Write a precis of the following passage reducing it to about one-third of its length : 10

The rash of strikes, gheraos, and alarming rates of absenteeism in our country is a symptom of despair of various classes of workers and employees in the face of extreme insensitivity on the part of management and employers in both private and public sectors. Unfortunately, management, barring a few cases, has a peculiar tendency to sleepover even the genuine demands of workers. Only when the normal life in the factories or in the organizations is completely or substantially disrupted by worker's strikes with consequent colossal loss of production that management wakes up from its deep slumber to take necessary remedial measures. In the wake of a spate of strikes by workers almost everywhere in the country, managers and researchers have been attempting an anatomy of the problem.

It is a pity that absenteeism–a major problem in the workforce today–continues to elude the attention of the Government, management, trade unions, and researchers. And this despite the fact that the cost of absenteeism is quite high for the society, the affected organisations and individual employees. A high rate of absenteeism adversely affects the industrial growth. For a country like India which is on its way to rapid industrialisation, the cost of absenteeism is quite high. Absenteeism is also harmful for an organization because of its costs and operating problems. It not only leads to decline in production and profits, but also in reduced productivity. In the case of frequent absenteeism, either casual or temporary workers, who are comparatively inexperienced are appointed. Where the existing staff is asked to do extra work on overtime basis, it often results in accidents and other mishaps in factories.

The problem of absenteeism should be taken more seriously by all concerned-management, trade unions and the Government. Management should take specific steps to reduce absenteeism only after identifying the factors responsible for it. Complete elimination of absenteeism appears to be rather difficult, but it can be reduced substantially through some suitable measures. Before taking any action on the problem of absenteeism, a systematic study should be carried out in organizations/departments affected by absenteeism to find out its various aspects, such as the number of absentees in a particular period, the rate of absenteeism, the number and names of chronic absentees and part of the year in which most of absenteeism takes place. Such a study would facilitate a proper diagnosis of the problem and that in turn would further help management in taking specific remedial measures.

6. Rahul, the General Manager in a large pharmaceutical company, is a profound proponent of 'Management by Objectives' (MBO). He has always viewed himself a very democratic manager, with a strong belief in employee participation. He does this by involving employees in decision making and goal setting, etc. Though he leaves them alone to achieve their goals but is ever-willing to help them, if needed. He has been very successful in his endeavours in this respect. Recently he hired Puneet, a young MBA from a top Business School of India. Puneet was good at academics as well as at extra-curricular activities. After orientation programme, Puneet was posted in the Production Department. Rahul motivated Puneet to work independently, maintaining his faith in the philosophy of participative management. He discussed the

project assigned to him, set a production target to be achieved within a stipulated period. Puneet, however, failed to complete the project in time. Revised target, after consultation with Puneet, was set. Unfortunately, results were not encouraging. Rahul confronted Puneet and chided him for his non-performance. He was warned to perform or face termination. Puneet was stunned for a while but finally gathered courage and said, "Sir, though I like you, but I feel diffident working with you. I sometimes do not know what to do next. It takes me longer. If I could benefit from your experience by having you tell me each day what steps to take next, I am sure things would work well." He further told Rahul that in his previous job also, his superiors used to help him like that. On hearing this, Rahul became speechless and wondered what to do with Puneet.

Read the above case and answer the following questions :

(*i*) What would you suggest to improve Puneet's work performance ? 4

(*ii*) Do you think Rahul's decision to confront Puneet to express his displeasure at his dismal performance was the right way to handle situation ? 4

(*iii*) Do you think Rahul should abandon his belief in MBO ? 6

(*iv*) Do you think Rahul and Puneet can still work together or should Puneet's services be terminated ? 4

7. What is an Organisational Structure ? Explain the major factors determining an Organisational Structure. 8

8. Explain the concept of Organisational Development. What are its objects ? 8

9. Explain briefly four different approaches to Planning. 8

10. *Distinguish between two of the following :* $2 \times 4 = 8$

(*a*) Job Enlargement and Job Enrichment.

(*b*) Power and Authority.

(*c*) Human Relations Approach and Behavioural Science Approach.

11. *Write short notes on any **two** of the following :* $2 \times 4 = 8$

(*a*) Elements of Internal Environment.

(*b*) Break-Even Analysis.

(*c*) Non-Programmed decisions.

12. *State with reasons which of the following statements are correct and which are incorrect. Attempt any **four** statements :* $4 \times 2 = 8$

(*a*) Coordination permeates all other functions of management.

(*b*) Opportunity for growth is a financial incentive.

(*c*) Leading and Managing do not mean the same thing.

(*d*) There is no difference between Control by Exception and Critical Point control.

(e) The Greatman theory of leadership suggests that leadership qualities are carried in genes.

November, 2003.

Total No. of Questions–12]

Time Allowed–3 Hours

Answer Question Nos. Maximum Marks–100

Marks

1. *Comment on any **ten** of the following statements in about **30** words each:* 1×10=10

(*i*) Communication is a social activity.

(*ii*) Written communication has a longer life than oral communication.

(*iii*) Grapevine communication has its own utility in disseminating information.

(*iv*) Information overload is as bad as information gap.

(*v*) Feedback enhances effectiveness of communication.

(*vi*) Paralanguage is not very reliable.

(*vii*) Group decisions are not always good.

(*viii*) Good business correspondence promotes Company's public relations.

(*ix*) The agenda facilitates smooth conduct of a meeting.

(*x*) AIDA is a guide for drafting effective sales letter.

(*xi*) Letter of enquiry is initiates by the buyer.

(*xii*) Brainstorming is a good technique of new idea generation.

(*xiii*) While communicating with the subordinates, a manager should maintain distance.

(*xiv*) A leader is indispensable for group discussion.

(*xv*) Face to face communication is somethimes better than written communication.

2. (*a*) Explain briefly the process of Communication. 7

(*b*) Outline the role of leadership in the conduct of a group discussion. 3

3. Bring out the difference between an Agenda, Notification and Minutes of a Meeting. Suitably illustrate your answer. (*Answer in about **200** words*) 10

Or

Draft a circular for employees insisting on the following : 10

(*i*) Punctuality.

(*ii*) Hygiene and Cleanliness.

4. "Corresponding with customers should be done with utmost care and cordiality." Comment. How can this be ensured in case of reminders and collection letters ? (*Answer in about **200** words*) 10

Or

As an Exporter of Handicrafts Planning to enter the U.S. market, write a letter to your bank seeking details of services they can offer you. 10

5. Write a precis of the following passage reducing it to about one-third of its length : 10

Career development relates to the readiness for progression through a series of positions during an individual's working life. Career issues emerge as a result of increasing stress of the organisation on developing its human resources and growing expectations of the individuals about what they need to do to facilitate career growth as they become more educated.

Career development as a responsibility of the organisation necessitates collection and analysis of data, decision-making and their implementation. It must be realised that organisational objectives can be accomplished effectively by integrating individual needs and organisational goals. Usually, line supervisors and human resource managers are responsible for implementation of Career Development Programmes. The line supervisors are responsible for the assessment and development of their subordinates and for assisting them in attaining desired positions with the help of varied measures especially counselling. Indeed, their day-to-day involvement in carrer development of subordinates stems largely from counselling. Although they need not be professional counsellors to accomplish effectiveness in career development, they must realise that it forms an integral part of managing, and varied skills and techniques are required to perform this role.

The human resource executive play a significant role in promoting the development of career paths to satisfy the needs of people. They provide career planning assistance to employees, arrange training for supervisors in career development techniques and coordinate career development programmes. Indeed, a human resource department initiates varied career development programmes in the organisation.

6. B is a draftsman for a large industrial equipment manufacturer. He has been with the company for more than ten years and is well respected for his abilities. In a recent conversation with one of his friends, B revealed the following thoughts about his work :

I really shouldn't complain about my job, I guess. The money is good. The working conditions are excellent. I have good friends who work with me, and that's important. Although retirement is a long way off, I'm putting aside funds to help me live comfortably than. I'm also setting aside money to put our children through college when the time comes.

My problem is this : I just don't see anything different in the future. I have already reached the top of the pay scale for draftsmen. Except for cost of living adjustments, my income will never be much greater than it is now. More important, I've reached the top level for promotions that a draftsman can achieve. To get into a higher level design or engineering job, the company requires you to be a college graduate. Since I don't have a college degree, I have no real hope of advancing. Even if I could go back to college to get a degree, it would take years for me to get one. I must support my family; so I can spare neither the time nor the money that would be necessary to get a degree.

As I view the alternative available, I just don't see many within the company itself. Perhaps what I should do is get involved in something off the job that would be stimulating. One of the boy's clubs in town needs someone to teach the kids how to do carpentry and wood work, and I'm pretty good at those things; so I may volunteer to work in the program.

Read the above case and answer the following questions :

(*i*) Which of B's needs are being fulfilled by his organisation. ? 4

(*ii*) Which of B's needs are not being met by his employer ? Why is this particularly discouraging to B ? 5

(*iii*) What steps B is Planning to take to solve his problem ? 4

(*iv*) What steps could B's employer take to change the attitudes of B and improve his inspiration to perform ? 5

7. "Management is an artistic science and a scientific art." Comment. Highlight the distinguishing features of Management. 8

8. What is 'Managerial grid' ? Discuss Likert's four systems of management. $4+4=8$

9. Define Organisational conflict. Briefly describe the common causes behind it. Give a few suggestions for their effective resolution. $2+3+3=8$

10. *Distinguish between any* ***two*** *of the following :* $2 \times 4=8$

   (*i*) Formal and Informal Organisation.

   (*ii*) Delegation and Decentralisation.

   (*iii*) Strategy and Policy.

11. *Write short notes on any* ***two*** *of the following :* $2 \times 4=8$

   (*i*) Social responsibility of Business.

   (*ii*) Swot analysis.

   (*iii*) Systems view of Organisation and Management.

12. *State with reasons, whether the following statements are True or False. (Answer any* ***four****) :* $4 \times 2=8$

   (*i*) All organisations do not need management.

   (*ii*) Planning and controlling are complementary to each other.

   (*iii*) Theory × takes a lenient view of workers.

   (*iv*) Controlling everything implies controlling nothing.

   (*v*) Money alone can motivate employees to put in best performance.